D0189750

The Woman's Guide to Starting a Business

THIRD EDITION

THE
Woman's Guide
TO STARTING A BUSINESS

•THIRD EDITION•

Claudia Jessup
and Genie Chipps

AN OWL BOOK
Henry Holt and Company • New York

Copyright © 1976, 1979, 1991 by Claudia Jessup and Genie Chipps
All rights reserved, including the right to reproduce
this book or portions thereof in any form.
Published by Henry Holt and Company, Inc.,
115 West 18th Street, New York, New York 10011.
Published in Canada by Fitzhenry & Whiteside Limited,
195 Allstate Parkway, Markham, Ontario L3R 4T8.

Library of Congress Cataloging-in-Publication Data
Jessup, Claudia.
The woman's guide to starting a business / by Claudia Jessup and
Genie Chipps.—3rd ed.
    p. cm.
Includes bibliographical references and index.
ISBN 0-8050-1140-4
1. New business enterprises—United States. 2. Women in business—
United States. I. Chipps, Genie. II. Title.
HD69.N3J47 1991
658.1'1024042—dc20   90-4726
                                                          CIP

Henry Holt books are available at special discounts
for bulk purchases for sales promotions, premiums,
fund-raising, or educational use. Special editions
or book excerpts can also be created to specification.
For details contact:
Special Sales Director, Henry Holt and Company, Inc.,
115 West 18th Street, New York, New York 10011.

Third Edition

Printed in the United States of America
Recognizing the importance of preserving the written word,
Henry Holt and Company, Inc., by policy, prints all of its
first editions on acid-free paper. ∞

10 9 8 7 6 5 4 3 2 1

To the memory of my father, Claude A. Jessup,
and my grandfather, Samuel Ambrose Jessup,
both great and inspirational entrepreneurs.

C.J.

To my enterprising sister, who started out, a dozen
or so ventures ago, in the circus business.

G.C.

Contents

Acknowledgments

We thank the women business owners interviewed for this book, who generously shared their thoughts, insights, and experiences in business. And we are grateful to women entrepreneurs everywhere, for their vision and inspiration. Thanks also to Elizabeth Howard for her enthusiasm, resources, and interviewing skills, and to A. David Silver for the additional information he provided on female entrepreneurs. Special thanks to our friends who offered support and put us in touch with so many interesting women: Lorraine Dusky, Karen Erickson, Tom Parrish, Debbie Perry, Maria Robbins, Marcia Shortt, Melissa Stephenson, and Beverly Walker.

Foreword

This to me is the most invigorating, energizing time in history for women starting and running their own businesses. The entrepreneurial spirit is alive in the United States like no place else in the world. Women here are saying, "I think I can," and then going out and doing it. Understand that there is a vast difference between being an entrepreneur and just being a business owner. An entrepreneur is open to things and can see possibilities where others only see closed doors. An entrepreneur is not afraid to change directions wherever opportunities lead.

The entrepreneurial spirit in women is thriving, not only at home but abroad—in Japan, in Eastern Europe, and in the Soviet Union. This fact, I believe, will be the dynamic for women business owners in the 1990s and beyond. The global marketplace is a potential gold mine for women in small- and medium-sized businesses.

As the President of the National Association of Women Business Owners, an affiliate of Les Femmes Chefs d'Entreprises Mondiales (Women Business Owners of the World), I have led a delegation of entrepreneurs to the Soviet Union to help start an association of Soviet women who would like to start businesses. They have little idea of how to go about it. They have little concept of profit, of incentives for employees, of quality control, and how to get quality production out of a work force. They need information, books, education, workshops, and mentors. They don't want corporate know-how or MBAs from Harvard. They are, as I was once, individuals with ideas and dreams. But they don't know how to go about turning them into enterprise. Still, they are bursting at the seams with desire to do so. It is a phenomenal time for them. And for me.

Being President of NAWBO has taken me to Japan and other foreign countries where women are anxious to begin, to learn, to organize themselves. At home, it has taken me into twenty-five cities around the country and to advisory positions with the Small Business Administration and the Secretary of Commerce. It has taken me eight times to the White House to meet with President Bush and once into the Oval office where I was able to tell him of the international trade networks we are trying to set up.

It is difficult to relate all the exciting things that have happened to me since assuming the office of president of NAWBO, but I can tell you that thirteen years ago I set out only to run a business and to do it well.

My business is international languages. It is based in Raleigh, North Carolina. We do translations, send out both consecutive and simultaneous interpreters worldwide, and instruct in over fifty languages. Our primary clients are school systems and companies in international trade.

I started the business because I was frustrated with traditional academic methods of teaching languages. As a teacher, I saw a need for a practical option in language arts—conversational rather than literary, useful rather than academic. The university where I taught was not interested, so I decided to hang out my shingle to see if anyone wanted to learn a foreign language in a practical way.

I did not know anything about running a business. I knew nothing about finance, or choosing an accountant, or even what form my business should take. I only had a burning desire to teach languages well and knew I could do it.

Beyond that, I was very unsure of myself and needed information. For me the answer came in joining a business support group—the local chapter of the National Association of Women Business Owners. As a scared young woman I saw other scared young women who were, in fact, making it. They shared their success stories, which was energizing—and they shared their failures, which taught me what to look out for. Finding resources that work for you, such as the book you are now reading, is a key step in making your idea work.

I went from being a member of my local chapter to being its president to being a representative on the national board. Then, in 1985, I was selected to be one of thirteen women on the first all-female trade mission ever to go out from the United States. We discovered there were markets out there that we hadn't imagined for small businesses. We formed more trade missions and, in league with Les Femmes Chefs d'Entreprises Mondiales, began to expand the international network of women in business.

The potential power of today's small business owner is in international trade. Our counterparts are worldwide. We have the flexibility and the individuality to move and maneuver, tapping into entrepreneurial opportunities the big corporations can't possibly address.

More important, I found that women are phenomenally good international traders. For years we've swept under the rug some of the more nurturing aspects of our nature as we set about competing with men. It's time to take those attributes out and dust them off and say, "Hey, this is marketable." The traditional American way of doing things is to go in, close the deal, and come home with bankable money. We've looked at business as a contract, not a relationship. Internationals, on the other hand, build relationships first. That's very, very feminine. Some call it nurturing—I call it business savvy. Women want to know about the people they do business with. We can take the other person's point of view and be genuinely concerned with the needs of our clients. That natural quality makes us very good international traders.

Working to open up new channels of trade—women to women—will give us a powerful economic base in the future. If women are truly to have an influence then we have to develop ourselves as leaders. Not just leaders of women, but leaders, period. Women have a great deal of idealism and should never apologize for it. It has served us very well. But we're realistic too. We are blazing new trails. The international network is one way, I believe, we can expand and lead.

Ultimately, though, the objective is to do business. Our concerns are not about the differences between men and women.

This is no longer a fight for women's rights. Organizations such as mine are taking a hard look at the economy and trying to positively influence the economic climate in which we all, male and female alike, work.

The women entrepreneurs I meet here and abroad are uniquely creative. We don't think in the same tired old business terms. We don't have historical baggage weighing us down. Women look with fresh eyes and that means a humanizing of the workplace. I believe women in the United States are approaching the old European standards of integrating our business lives with our family and community lives. We are not compartmentalized. It's a new, invigorating way of looking at things.

We now know we can't do it all, have it all, be it all. We tried as women entrepreneurs of the eighties to take advantage of all the options open to us: wife, mother, cook, housekeeper, business owner. We tried to fulfill each of these roles with one hundred percent of our time and energy. In the nineties, the realization that we have a choice, that we can combine roles and simply do our best in each, seems likely to lead us to a more balanced existence.

We choose to work smarter rather than harder. We can still see that everything gets done. We just don't have to do it ourselves. This simple realization will be a key factor in the way we organize our businesses and our lives in the future. The little big word "no" will allow us more time to enjoy the fruits of our success.

Working smarter rather than harder is one of the important results you will achieve by following the information in *The Woman's Guide to Starting a Business*. There is, of course, information here that all business owners must have, male or female. You will learn activities that all must engage in, certain standards of behavior that all must adhere to, but in addition to practicalities, the book provides support and resources unique to women, whether those resources are political, financial, or emotional. This guide encourages you to put your own individual stamp on your business, which is important. Pioneers must not be afraid to do things differently.

As you prepare to open your own business, read all that you can to prepare yourself, join business associations that can assist you, talk to others who have been where you are going, network with both men's and women's groups, but remember that all of these simply give you the ingredients. It will be your head that combines them, your hand that stirs them, and your creativity that blends them into your own recipe for success.

—Carey I. Stacy
June 1990
President of the National
Association of Women Business
Owners (1989–90) and Special
Advisor to the U.S. and Foreign
Commercial Service

· Part I ·

Starting a Business

·1·

The Business of Women

The first step is believing in ourselves, understanding that we are indeed smart, even if we aren't rich. And the second is giving up the myths of power.
—Gloria Steinem

First of all, this book is *not* for women only. The hard-core advice laid down in these pages applies across the board to *all* small businesses, regardless of male or female ownership. But the focus here is on women because women face special hurdles, real and psychological, when they decide to become entrepreneurs. For anyone, education, experience, and preparation are the keys to business success. For a woman, they are absolutely essential.

Back in the days of the Garden of Eden, it was Eve who bit the apple first. But that wasn't where she went wrong. Her big mistake was in giving Adam a taste of that forbidden fruit from the tree of knowledge and power. Adam liked it so much that he wouldn't give it back, and men have been chomping away on it ever since.

The myths of power have grown up out of a world where men hold the reins. They serve the purpose of maintaining power in the hands that hold it. (According to an article in the *New York Times* in August 1989, women earn only seventy cents for every dollar a man earns.) There is no more substance to the myth that business *ownership* is a man's prerogative than there was to the bogeyman scares that kept you in line as a kid. When you got old enough, you realized there was no bogeyman to be scared of. The same goes for the myths of power.

Denise Cavanaugh, the first president of the National Association of Women Business Owners (NAWBO, established in 1974), reported in the first edition of this book: "Owning your own business means being willing to take responsibility and not feeling that it's an extraordinary step to take."

Anyone starting a business runs into problems. A woman starting her own business runs into more problems. But the biggest obstacle of all to overcome is driving away that bogeyman, sweeping aside those power myths that have collected around you all your life.

When this book was first published, there were comparatively few women running their own businesses. They were desperate for a network of information and to talk shop with other female entrepreneurs. Now, years later, an enormous amount has happened on the scene of women's business ownership. Women are coming into their own power in business and as entrepreneurs.

A lot of statistics have been compiled in recent years about women's enterprise, but the most interesting is this: the Small Business Administration (SBA) estimates that by the year 2000, *50 percent* of all small businesses will be owned by women.

Nevertheless, women still face serious problems, especially in the areas of establishing credit, and securing loans and financing. Raising money is difficult for anyone who dreams up a business, regardless of sex or race. But because many women don't have track records as business owners, they lack the network of business connections that most men enjoy.

There is also the special starting handicap of too little business training: many women come to business ownership through indirect routes. That's changing, of course. Today, nearly half of all business degrees awarded in this country are being earned by women, and over two hundred colleges and universities are offering courses in entrepreneurship.*

The bottom line, however, is that *all* businesses have a high failure rate. This is due to improper planning, undercapitalization, and failure to analyze the big picture before jumping in.

The real purpose of this book is to stack the odds in your favor. If you want to start your own business, if you've got the confidence, the determination, and the patience to go about setting it up thoroughly and properly, nothing is going to stop you.

This is the most favorable time in the history of this country

---

*In 1974, Drs. Margaret Hennig and Anne Jardim launched the country's only MBA program designed specifically for women. For information, contact Simmons College Graduate School of Management in Boston, Massachusetts.

to become an entrepreneur. Congress has passed legislation designed to address some of the problems that confront women specifically, and women have pressured Congress by getting behind organizations such as NAWBO, the American Woman's Economic Development Corporation (AWED), and the SBA's Office of Women's Business Ownership. The Women's Business Ownership Act of 1988, Public Law 100–533, includes provisions that will aid and encourage women entrepreneurs enormously as they stride toward the next century. Some of its provisions are:

Establishment of a three-year $10 million program to finance joint public and private sector educational projects that will provide technical assistance and management training.

Amendment of the Equal Credit Opportunity Act of 1974 as it concerns business loans. This will require financial institutions: (1) to notify applicants in writing of their right to receive a written explanation for denial of loan applications; (2) to retain loan application records for a period of at least one year; and (3) to refrain from inquiring into the marital status of applicants.

Creation of a special SBA-guaranteed miniloan program for amounts up to $50,000. This new law permits banks to use a simplified loan application form and halves the fee normally charged by the SBA. This should encourage banks to make more loans available to small business start-ups.

Establishment of a National Women's Business Council made up of high-level private sector representatives and government policy makers, to propose a multiyear plan of action to support women entrepreneurs and overcome discriminatory barriers against women.

In addition, new congressional action is underway to increase government contracting to women-owned businesses.

Congresswoman Patricia Schroeder (D-CO), cochair of the Congressional Caucus for Women's Issues, writes (in *Entrepreneurial Woman,* Summer 1989), "While Congress can help knock down some of the barriers women face in business, you who are in the trenches are crashing through those barriers every day as you prove that women can do it and the United States can't do it without us."

The essence of successful business is good ideas, and women

who start businesses tend to be strong on ideas and nonstop enthusiasm. The ideas themselves need not be groundbreaking; filling a community need is the basis for most successes.

Entrepreneurs are highly motivated people. The very act of starting a business is a creative innovation, but a woman is more likely to carry that creativity into the way she runs things. Women, however, tend to think smaller than men when they start their businesses, partially because most women lack two of the crucial ingredients for large-scale success: capital and role models. That's changing too, but as of this writing the majority of women's businesses remain small and undercapitalized.

Some women want it that way because they are trying to balance work and family, two full-time jobs. Choice, not lack of ambition, is what keeps their scope narrower. The factors that drive all entrepreneurs—the desire for autonomy and freedom—can be fulfilled regardless of whether a business puts your kids through college or puts you into the *Fortune* 500. Building a business is an overtime job, and many women make conscious decisions to live well-balanced lives rather than make the sacrifices necessary to build a billion-dollar enterprise.

The divorce rate is high among entrepreneurs; a business can easily become the "other person" that threatens to break up a marriage.

Much has been written on the differences between male and female entrepreneurs, and each sex has its inherent strengths and weaknesses. One thing that's agreed is that entrepreneurs must be everything to everybody. Women are, by nature, nurturing. They are relationship builders. But although they nurture others, women are often hard on themselves. If they have families, they tend to feel guilty when the business keeps them from fulfilling family responsibilities. But that can happen just as easily when they are working for somebody else. Many women are attracted to business ownership because it affords them a greater flexibility in their working lives.

Women are less apt to let their egos get in the way. They come to business with real enthusiasm, and they are not afraid to ask questions. Women have more to prove and tend to work harder, go the extra five miles. On the other hand, women don't set priorities as well as men. They are not as oriented to problem solving. They are not as comfortable with negotiating, or with conflict. They may fear both failure and success.

6

Women are less confident in the marketplace than men; often they can keep their business going but are afraid to take it as far as it will go.

All the psychological dissimilarities between male and female entrepreneurs fall into generalities that make no difference when you get right down to it. A woman with a sound business idea and a willingness to work hard can be successful. And she has the freedom to decide whether to keep her enterprise small or grow it big.

Few businesses make money right away. If you are your own sole source of income, you'll have to be willing to modify your lifestyle. Until you can take a steady draw, you'll be living off the fraction of your savings you haven't invested in the business.

If you don't have to worry about supporting yourself with your own income, so much the better. There are enough factors working against the aspiring female entrepreneur; don't feel embarrassed if a few work in your favor. If you have a nest egg, or a spouse who brings home a paycheck large enough to pay the rent and keep life running smoothly, use that peace of mind to build confidence for getting things off the ground.

To start a business you'll need confidence, and you'll need a lot more than that. As mentioned before, the failure rate of small businesses is discouragingly high: over 50 percent fail.* There are no statistics available as to whether women-owned businesses fall above or below that mark. In fact, until the seventies there were no statistics on women-owned businesses at all.†

Jeanne Wertz, testifying before the Joint Economic Committee of the Ninety-third Congress, said it as well as anyone: "In my survey I found that the business of women going into business is booming. Women are . . . entering business ownership in significant numbers; at all ages; in all types of business;‡ in every geographic area. . . .

*But, according to a study by the American Express Small Business Services and the National Federation of Independent Business (NFIB), the survival rate for entrepreneurs who truly believe in their dream is higher. Also, 84 percent of entrepreneurs who had an initial investment of $50,000, and 74 percent of those who had less than $20,000 to start, were still going strong in their third year. Also, having six or more employees at the outset was another mark of success.
†In 1976, the first nationwide statistical portrait of women-owned businesses was published by the U.S. Department of Commerce, Bureau of the Census, Office of Minority Business Enterprise: *Women-Owned Businesses in 1972.*
‡According to the SBA, the number of women going into mining, construction, and manufacturing increased 166 percent between 1980 and 1986.

"The factors that determine the difference between success
. . . and failure are in this order: money, motivation, determination, expertise in a particular field, access to expert advice, and
time—which brings one back to money. It takes money to buy
that time."

And it takes meticulous planning and management to make
effective use of what money and time you manage to put together. You have to learn everything about business, and about
the kind of business you're interested in owning. After all, there's
a whole lot more to it than just selling the product, providing the
service, or flipping the switch to activate the machinery.

But there's no mumbo jumbo involved. Running a business
requires, above all else, common sense. There is logic to it, and
creativity as well. You can put on your own show, call your own
shots, make money, and provide jobs for others. Entrepreneurship is part of the American dream. And it's available to anyone
willing to do the work and take the risks.*

The first two parts of this book provide a blueprint for planning and managing, a general guide to starting and succeeding
in your own business—retail, service, manufacturing, or whatever. They map out procedures that are basic for anyone, female
or male, who is serious about starting a business, or buying a
business or franchise, and making it work. Some sections will
naturally apply more to one type of business than another, but
most of the information is valid across the board.

The third part of this book presents the experiences of a number of women entrepreneurs who have businesses of varying
sizes. In their own words they demonstrate their ability to think
on their feet and the flexibility to cope with all kinds of situations
as they arise.

These women have not been deterred by the risks because they
are involved in an ongoing learning, growing experience. They
are propelled by their own self-esteem, not by the expectations
of others. They believe that the experience they have gained is
priceless, and they find what they do exhilarating. They are finding dignity and fulfillment beyond home and family, which in
turn enrich their personal relationships and their own sense of
worth. They are going far beyond where they might have gone
had they continued working for someone else.

*See "Risky Business" by Bob Weinstein, *Entrepreneurial Woman,* May/June 1990,
for in-depth insights on entrepreneurial risk-taking.

Perhaps their example will give you the impetus you need to forge ahead if you've been turning a business idea over in your mind. Do it! That way, at least you won't be left with years of wondering what might have been. And if you do it right (as you should after reading this book), there's no reason why a viable idea shouldn't work, providing you have a potential market. No matter what the outcome, you'll wind up gaining more than you lose.

The last section of the book provides sources for gathering even more expertise and information: books to read on specific kinds of business, videotapes to watch, organizations to join, classes to sign up for. Any woman who wants to start her own business must remember that she cannot be overprepared.

Of course, women can still be discriminated against in the workplace. (In 1980, the Equal Employment Opportunity Commission published its historic guideline on sexual harassment in the halls of business, and since then nearly forty thousand cases have been filed with the federal government.) Discrimination is indeed what motivates some women to start businesses of their own. However, nothing is more self-destructive than crying "male chauvinism!" over a failure that was caused by your own ineffective preparation, presentation, or management.

The legislation and the information and the women's entrepreneurial network now exist. The road has been paved for you, so take advantage of it. That's what it's there for, and what this book is here for: to provide inspiration, sound advice, and a compendium of the resources you will need to succeed.

Business writer Nancy Borman has noted: "We must break through the male fortress if we are to succeed in business. Overcome fears of larger sums. Study banking. Share this lore with one another. Learn about bankruptcy. Find out what would really happen if you could not meet a payment on a loan." In other words, get rid of the fear and the myths.

Back in the sixth century B.C., Lao-tzu wrote, "The journey of a thousand miles must begin with a single step." That first step, as Gloria Steinem said, "is believing in ourselves."

This book will try to help you the rest of the way along the thousand miles. Go for it!

·2·

Capitalization:
A Loan at the Top

Business? It's quite simple. It's other people's money.
— Alexandre Dumas, fils

No business can exist without money. And getting money is the major stumbling block for all entrepreneurs: money to start, money to keep going, and money to expand. All the other specifics—coming up with a business idea, analyzing your potential market, formalizing your business plan, dealing with the legalities, etc.—will be covered in subsequent chapters.

It costs money to create a business. The best place to begin when you're contemplating starting a business of your own is to consider where that start-up cash will be coming from. Business is all about money—making it, spending it, making more. Thinking about money, and where to get it, will force you to look at yourself and your potential business in the professional way that moneylenders will look at it.

In the theater, financial backers are called "angels," and for anyone starting a business, no word could be closer to the truth.

If a man and a woman both graduate (B.A., *summa cum laude*) from the same college in the same year, and both go to work at the same company, we all know which one will get into a higher tax bracket faster. And if they both decide to go into business for themselves, we also know who stands a better chance of raising the money to get it off the ground.

Women *do* run businesses, so it's not impossible for them to raise money. But, the statistics tell us,* the majority of the busi-

*According to the most recent studies by the Small Business Administration (SBA), women now own 28 percent of the small businesses in the United States,

10

nesses women start tend to begin small and stay small. That's because women are inherently more afraid of dealing with money, of using money to their own advantage, of playing the game of money. Men, because of their centuries of business experience, aren't afraid of going into debt. If women are serious about becoming successful entrepreneurs, their fear of debt will change, as it has already started to do. Some women have founded companies that have grown very large indeed.*

One of the major reasons for any business failure is undercapitalization. Bankers state that many women defeat themselves by not having a clear-cut plan for how the money will be used. If a potential lender suspects that the money will be frittered away or discovers that the woman does not have the professional background to prove her stick-to-itiveness, then loans are seldom forthcoming.

You need money, but to get it, you have to prove that you don't need it. Contradictory? Not really. When anyone borrows money, she is granted its use for a specific period of time, at which point it must be returned along with a fee for the privilege of using it (interest, dividends). Whether the source is a lender or an investor, you don't get something for nothing. If you borrow money, the debt must be repaid. If someone invests in your idea, then you will have to give up part of your company to the investor.

So, in embarking upon an entrepreneurial scheme, you must look at yourself and your business through the potential lender's/investor's eyes. Confidence and enthusiasm score points, but you must have a professional presentation to convince people to back your idea. You must know exactly how much money you will need, exactly how you will spend it, and exactly how you will pay it back.

Also, the type of business that you envision and its potential for growth influence the amount of money that's available. The risk involved determines the interest rate you have to pay for a loan,

---

and the percentage grows every year. But the $75 billion in annual gross revenues that 3.7 million women's sole proprietorships generate accounts for only 12 percent of the small business total.

A Touche Ross survey of 3,500 women business owners in Michigan showed that only 19.6 percent of the women had turned to banks or outside investors for initial start-up funds. Just over 50 percent of the women-owned businesses operated without loans of any kind.

*Liz Claiborne, Inc., the fashion design company, is, as of this writing, the only company founded by a woman to be listed in *Fortune*'s 500.

or the amount of your company's stock that you must give to an outside investor.

The end of this chapter spells out the specific information you will need to put together for a loan application or an equity financing proposal. First, however, examine all the types of financing that are available for businesses, both for start-up *and* expansion purposes, because often these go together when you're doing your initial business planning.

TYPES OF FINANCING: DEBT AND EQUITY

What is your ideal method of raising start-up capital (also called seed money, risk capital, or venture capital)? There are two kinds of financing: debt and equity.

If you are going for *debt financing* (a loan), you have to outline explicitly how you intend to repay the money and what collateral will be used to assure repayment. Although interest is paid on a loan, it is tax deductible as a valid business expense. And with debt financing, an owner can retain control over her business.

For *equity financing* you must be able to predict for the potential investor whether the purchased stock will increase in value, and to what extent. There is no legal obligation, however, to return the investment or pay interest to the investor. By giving up equity, though, you are also releasing part of your control of the company. Never give up more than 49 percent (though many investors will try to get at least 51 percent), or you'll end up back where you started . . . working for somebody else.

MONEY: WHAT KIND DO YOU NEED?

When you set out to borrow money, regardless of the source, it's important to know what kind you need: short-term credit, long-term credit, or equity financing. According to the Small Business Administration,* there is an important distinction be-

*The SBA has a library of over a hundred business publications selling for a nominal fee (most under $2). For a free copy of SBA's Directory of Business Development Publications, write to SBA Publications, P.O. Box 15434, Fort Worth, Texas 76119, or contact your local SBA office. Several that explain the ins and outs of financing a business are: *Sound Cash Management and Borrowing*, by John F. Murphy (Management Aids, no. 1,016); *The ABCs of Borrowing* (Business Development Publication, no. FM 1); and *A Venture Capital Primer for Small Business*, by LaRue Tone Hosmer (Financial Management Publication no. FM 5).

tween the types of money and the source of repayment. In general, short-term loans are repaid from the liquidation of current assets (receiving money that's owed you, or selling off your inventory). Long-term loans are generally repaid out of your company's earnings.

Short-term Credit

This is money to keep the cash flowing into your business once it's underway. These types of loans are expected to be repaid in less than one year, or as soon as the purpose of the loan has been served. Often these loans are issued in the form of a *line of credit* that will make funds available to you as you need them. Interest is paid only on the money used.

Banks will give you this kind of money for several purposes:

To get through seasonal slow periods
To finance accounts receivable for roughly thirty to sixty days
To build seasonal inventory during a period up to six months

Banks issue either unsecured or secured short-term loans. An *unsecured loan* does not require you to put up collateral, because of your proven good credit reputation. A *secured loan* requires a pledge of some or all of your assets, to cover the risks involved.

Long-term Credit

These are loans—to provide money for expansion or modernization—that you repay over a longer period of time. Long-term loans are generally those extended for more than five years. Most likely this money will be paid back in periodic installments from your company's profits. The collateral required on long-term loans is generally a mortgage or a promissory note with all the terms negotiated and spelled out.

Equity Capital

This is money obtained from selling an interest in your business to one or more investors. You never have to repay this money per se, but you will have to give over part of your profits to the investors, and they may insist on having a voice in the way your business is run. Make sure you consider the business reputations and personalities of all potential outside investors. Depending on your agreement, you may have to work closely with them. Potential pitfalls are dishonest investors, or those who may eventually fight for greater control or try to take over your company.

MONEY: WHERE TO FIND IT

If a business has a track record—clients, accounts receivable, and encouraging balance sheets—it is easier to borrow money (for working capital or expansion). For newcomers the old adage, "You have to have money to get it," holds true. Raising money is a chunky stumbling block for novice entrepreneurs and, these days, even for seasoned ones. *Everyone* wants money for something.

And, unfortunately, women still have to field such real or implied questions as: "What if you get married/pregnant?" "What if your husband gets transferred?" You might as well be prepared for the inevitable and think positively.*

The major places to look for money are your own savings; your relatives, friends, and close contacts; private investors; banks; venture capitalists; suppliers; small business investment companies; the Small Business Administration (SBA); and, if you're incorporated, a private stock offering. Some newer, offbeat-sources for capital are mentioned later in this chapter as well. Keep in mind, however, that 75 percent of this nation's companies are very small. Only an estimated 5 percent of these have the potential for growth to any significant size. Therefore, small businesses must usually rely on self-financing, at least in the beginning.

The type of business you start, however, will dictate the amount of money you'll need to begin, and where you will come up with the financing. A high-technology plant based on your marketable invention will cost much more to launch than an executive headhunting firm. Outlay of money for inventory and rent in an upscale location for a retail kitchenware store will be far higher than a catering business that's run out of your home.

*In the Women's Business Ownership Act of 1988, an amendment to the Equal Credit Opportunity Act of 1974 requires financial institutions loaning less than one million dollars to refrain from inquiring into the marital status of applicants. Financial institutions are required to tell applicants in writing of their right to receive a written explanation if their loan is denied.

Your Savings

Most potential moneylenders will expect you to put more than your talent on the line. They want to see your own money invested in your idea, figuring that the more you risk, the harder you'll work. This means you must invest every coin you can spare.

You may have more assets than you think. Consider borrowing against the cash value of your life insurance policy, cashing in your investments, or taking a second mortgage on your house. While you're getting the business off the ground, you could live off your spouse's salary or tighten your belt and scale down your standard of living.

If you can raise at least 50 percent of the seed money from direct sources (yourself, plus family and/or friends), then you are in reasonably good shape for going to the professional money-lenders.

Money from Relatives and Friends

People who are close to you, who believe in you and your ideas and energy, are often willing to invest money in your success. These people can (or not, depending on mutual agreement) become partners, limited partners, or shareholders in your business. For many female entrepreneurs, this is the only path open, especially if they lack the background and experience to impress professional investors. The advantage of these loans is that they usually don't have to be repaid by a specific date.

Don't, however, take friends to the cleaners. Borrow only from people who will be able to absorb the loss should your business fail. There must also be a thorough understanding of how long you'll need the money and how it will be used. For everyone's protection, put the financial arrangements in writing. There's no such thing as a friendly loan, especially if you want to keep your friends.

Private Investors

Your accountant, lawyer, banker, business school professor, friends, and relatives may know local businesspeople who are enthusiastic about investing in new businesses. Be imaginative in your search for these angels (who often rush in where banks fear to tread). These potential investors (doctors, dentists, attorneys, executives, and, increasingly, other entrepreneurs who have a soft spot in their hearts for people who want to be like them) are in high income tax brackets and can afford to take risks and absorb losses.

If you don't know any prospects personally, check the classified ads in local newspapers (usually listed under "business opportunities") for people with money to invest. Or run an ad yourself, including phrases like "ground floor opportunity" and "innovative new business." Besides local papers and business publications, other good places to advertise would be alumnae magazines and trade magazines in the field that you are entering.

Often, private investors are the best sources because they are interested in your success. They will talk up your business to their friends and associates. They can also act as advisors, if you wish.

Though you may not want to seem overly suspicious, do check out all potential private investors. Make sure they have the money they claim to have (ask around, and run a credit check through Dun & Bradstreet or Equifax, Inc.). If they have invested in other companies, talk to the owners and find out if the investor stuck by them and aided their success.

Bank Loans

Unless you are a well-established businessperson, with a lint-free credit rating and a chubby checking/savings/money market account, a bank will not lend you money to start a business. Banks seldom lend anyone start-up capital. If they do, they usually expect you to have already put up or raised at least 50 percent of the money you need.

As your business proves itself, you may want to take out a loan for working or expansion capital. If you've been keeping in close contact with your banker, then you stand a better chance of getting the loan. Banks rely considerably on past/present account relationships. They will generally turn down a loan request if (1) you have been slow to repay past personal loans or have overdrawn your account with any regularity; or (2) you do not have an account with the bank and none is likely to evolve from the loan. Banks want interest from loans, but they also want your continuing business.

To grant a loan, bankers must be impressed with your character, integrity, and business credentials. They must be satisfied that you have marketable collateral even though they are *not* looking to liquidate that collateral. They want the loan repaid with interest and must be confident in your ability to do so. Be sure to keep the loan officer informed of your progress, or lack of it, after the loan is issued. If you have already established a good relationship with your banker, even if she cannot grant you a loan she may be able to steer you toward local private investors.

If your application for a loan is refused, ask why. Banks are required by law to tell you, and you have a right to know. That knowledge can help you when you apply for another loan.*

Women's Banks

Women's banks, which have opened in some areas of the country, are basically no different from other commercial banks. Loans are granted on the basis of creditworthiness, without favoritism for women or discrimination against them. In other words, women's banks are not giving women an extra shake; they are giving them a fair shake. If you want a loan, you must be superprepared to show why you need it and how you intend to pay it back.

In *Working Woman* magazine,† Deborah S. McGuire, president and CEO of the First Women's Bank of Maryland, tells women that the bank may require a cosigner, a lot of personal collateral, or an extra point or two of interest depending on the kind of enterprise, not the gender of the person, applying for the loan.

*Banks differ in their policies regarding loans. If one bank turns you down, another may be more sympathetic. Keep trying. If you are turned down by two banks, you are then eligible to apply for a Small Business Administration (SBA) loan. Also, the National Association of Women Business Owners (NAWBO) *Newsletter* reports: "In arriving at the decision to grant or deny credit, the commercial credit lender relies on commercial reporting services, such as Dun & Bradstreet or Equifax, Inc., in the collection and evaluation of information concerning creditworthiness. Please notify the Senate Small Business Committee if you feel you have been unreasonably denied credit, or the business of suppliers, as a result of what you consider to be an unfair credit report. Write the Senate Small Business Committee, Minority Staff, 424 Russell Building, Washington, D.C. 20510."

†"Are Women Starving Their Businesses?" by Roxane Farmanfarmaian, *Working Woman,* October 1988.

"We have to be 99 percent sure that we will get our money back . . . since we are lending depositors' money," she explains. "Start-ups in particular have no track record, are higher risk, and usually have thin income streams, so it's a judgment call. We have to look for a personal guarantee and often charge a little more for a loan in such cases. If the personal assets are jointly owned, the spouse has to sign—whether it's the wife or the husband. Women have been co-signing on their husbands' loans for years. Now it's the men's turn to co-sign on their wives' loans."

Collateral

You are at the core of your banker's assessment of your company. The success of your business (and the repayment of the loan) depends on you. If your business lacks adequate tangible assets (accounts receivable, equipment, inventory, real estate), then you as owner must guarantee the loan by putting up personal property.

In assessing your collateral, you must appraise your assets the way a banker would. Collateral must be readily marketable and assignable, belonging to you outright with no hazy legal titles.* Real estate, life insurance, savings accounts, etc. must be in your name.

Then, there must be a sufficient margin between the appraised value of your assets and the actual cash value (which can vary enormously, depending on the circumstances of the sale). Keep in mind the depreciation.†

Types of business and personal collateral include business accounts receivable, inventory, savings accounts, certificates of deposit, real estate, stocks and bonds, life insurance policies, equipment, machinery, or any other tangible property with real value.

If you lack heavy-duty credit credentials you may be asked to find an endorser, cosigner, or guarantor for your loan.

*Series E Savings Bonds, issued in your name, may not be transferred to anyone else. If assets and property are co-owned with someone else, then s/he will be required to cosign the loan.
†Margin guidelines vary, but a (high) general guide to figuring appraised/actual value for collateral: 75 percent of the value of stocks with the New York or American stock exchanges, and 50 percent of the value of over-the-counter stocks; 80 percent for corporate and municipal bonds, 90 percent for Treasury bonds and notes, and 95 percent of the value of cash items. Real estate must be appraised by the lender in terms of location, condition, etc.

An *endorser* is a person whom you get to sign a note for you to bolster your credit. This person is liable for the note she or he signs. If you don't repay the loan, the bank will go to the endorser.

A *cosigner* or *comaker* agrees to go into the loan obligation with you. This person can be your parent, friend, sister, husband—any person closely connected with you who is willing to back you up by jointly putting up the needed collateral that you and your business lack. The bank can collect from either you or the cosigner. If you wish, the cosigner can be designated as a silent, or limited, partner in the business.

A *guarantor* is a person or lending institution who guarantees the payment of the note (or an agreed-upon percentage of the note) by signing a guaranty commitment. Both private and government lenders often require guarantees from officers of corporations, to assure management continuity in the company. Sometimes a manufacturer will act as a guarantor for customers.

The most important thing to remember is that if you are turned down for a bank loan, it's not the end of the world. Find out *why,* and use that knowledge to bolster your presentation to the next bank you contact. There are approximately thirteen thousand commercial banks around the country. The majority of them have officers who are both sympathetic and accustomed to the challenges that face small businesses.

Interest

When a loan is granted, you must agree to pay a certain percentage of interest. Interest rates bob up and down like bubbles in the economy, and banks adjust their rates to compete. If money is in short supply, the rates go up; when things ease up, the percentage goes down. However, if your interest rate is, say, 10 percent and your bank's rate goes above or below that percentage, you still pay the loan off at the agreed-upon 10 percent.

Loan Limitations and Repayment

When you are granted a loan the bank will impose limitations that will depend, to a large degree, on the type of business you have. The poorer the risk, the greater the restrictions on the loan. These restrictions are called covenants and are tailored to your particular loan.

The points that the loan agreement will itemize are: terms of repayment, the use of security, and periodic reports you will have to make. It will also stipulate things that you may or may not do without the approval of the lender (for example, you may not be allowed to go into further debt, or pledge your assets to another lender). In addition, there will be things that you must do (i.e., maintain a minimum net working capital, carry adequate insurance, repay the loan according to the terms of the agreement, supply financial statements and reports).

Know, however, that you have a right to negotiate the lending terms before you sign the agreement. And you should negotiate no matter how desperately you need the money. Often the lender will give in to some of your terms. In figuring out what terms you and your business can live with, consult associates and outside advisors. Ask to see the loan papers in advance of the signing so you can go over them with your accountant or lawyer. Once the terms have been agreed upon and the loan is issued, you must abide by them, although occasionally loan agreements may be amended. The important thing is to keep the lender informed on what's happening with your business.

No banker on earth will approve a loan if she thinks the repayment will require too long a time or will come from collecting your collateral. If the projected cash flow of your business does not look healthy enough to guarantee repayment, then your loan will be turned down. A loan is never feasible if, in repaying it, your daily operating account runs bone dry.

Venture Capitalists

Banks are creditors. Venture capital firms (VCs) look for businesses in which they can become part owners. They invest only in companies that they feel will grow quickly, and are looking for a good return on their investment. Although very little VC money goes to small business or start-ups, there are some groups that gamble short-term venture capital on start-ups that they feel will net a big profit. This money is usually advanced for up to five years, after which time refinancing is necessary to buy back the VC's share. This is never available, however, unless the entrepreneur has a solid gold track record in her industry and an infallible business plan.

A bit more venture capital money goes to early-stage businesses with enormous growth potential. Over 50 percent of VC funds goes to expansion financing, and another chunk goes to leveraged buyouts and acquisitions.

Most VCs view businesses requiring less than $250,000 warily, figuring they will require too much investigation and administration. VCs turn down about 90 percent of the proposals they receive each year, usually because the company doesn't fit into their established market, technical, or geographic area policies, or the proposal has not been well prepared. The remaining 10 percent of the businesses are investigated up, down, and sideways, including the owners and managers.

What you will be expected to give up to a VC firm will depend on the state of your business. It can be as little as 10 percent if the business is established and profitable, or as much as 80 or 90 percent for new or financially troubled companies. Most VCs, however, aren't interested in acquiring more than 40 percent, because they want the owner to keep her incentive for building the business.

As for managerial control, most VCs are not interested in taking over the running of your company. They will, however, want a say in major decisions that might affect your business or the character of your company.

It's extremely difficult to get venture capital, especially for small start-ups. Your only hope is to have formidable financial plans and pro forma statements drawn up by your accountant that will project earnings for up to three years ahead.*

Corporate Investors and Informal Venture Capital

New companies that require a large outlay of capital are increasingly finding financial aid from *successful businesses in related industries.* Look for an established company with whom your business would be synergistic. You want to find a company that needs what you would be supplying, or from whom you would be buying services or supplies. For example, if you have come up with a new lightweight disc drive, a large computer company might well be interested in investing in your start-up, to complement its own research and development. If they want to use your disc drive in their new portable computers, then you'll obviously receive more than capital; you'll get a major customer and also

*Sky Venture Capital Fund in Des Moines, Iowa, is the first fund designed to finance women-run businesses.

benefit from their marketing knowledge and technical expertise.

This can work no matter what your business does. Sit down and brainstorm about all the kinds of businesses that would need your product/service, and you're sure to come up with some viable possibilities.

Besides large corporations, there is often help available from small businesspeople: *distributors, manufacturers' reps, or suppliers of materials*—wholesalers, retailers, or manufacturers—who might be interested in considering your business as a mini-subsidiary. The idea is to find a company that will *benefit from your success.* In return, it will have a real incentive to help your company grow.

A new and growing source of equity capital is informal venture capitalists.* These are either individuals or informal groups of angels—usually successful entrepreneurs themselves—who are willing to invest in start-ups. They like to build businesses and create new jobs. However, these individuals or groups give not only their money (in exchange for common stock or a percentage of the company) but also their time and expertise to help a new company get on its feet. These people have a stake in your success and can be, according to the agreement you work out, very hands-on in the day-to-day running of the business.

Equity Financing for Corporations

A small business corporation, even if it's still in the idea stage, has a good chance of raising capital if you have already established close contacts in the business community and have a concrete background in the area of your proposed business. For equity financing, you should consult a lawyer, but a *private offering* of shares of stock (no more than twenty-five people may be approached to invest) need not be registered with the Securities and Exchange Commission (SEC).†

Your only hope of attracting this sort of investment is if you

*Venture Capital Networks, Inc., P.O. Box 882, Durham, New Hampshire 03824-9964, tries to match investors with companies looking for money. NASBIC (National Association of Small Business Investment Companies), 1156 Fifteenth Street NW, Suite 1101, Washington, D.C. 20005, publishes a booklet, *Venture Capital—Where To Find It* ($5, including postage) as well as a number of other helpful publications on small business financing.

†Dealing with the SEC is time-consuming and expensive in terms of legal and accounting fees. A *public offering* (not generally considered for small businesses), involving the offer of stock to more than twenty-five people, is required by law to be registered with the SEC.

have a big business idea that may ultimately grow into a multimillion-dollar company. You should continue to maintain controlling interest of your company if you take on shareholders. If you don't, you will have given up your most important asset, the freedom to run your business as you see fit.

Small Business Administration Loans

The SBA has more information (including management consulting services) and increasingly more money to offer women than ever before. In 1989, President Bush and the Senate Small Business Committee appointed Susan Engeleiter as the new head of the SBA. (She is the first woman in the job since the federal agency was established in 1953.) Because the SBA recognizes that woman-owned businesses are the fastest growing segment of the small business community, every SBA district office around the country has a women's business ownership representative. She is responsible for making women aware of SBA's programs and for assisting women clients of the SBA.

This new government help for women is a step in the right direction, although the SBA loan program, as of this writing, still favors one-man (yes, *man*) proprietorships and/or minority groups (a category in which it does not include women).

To qualify for an SBA loan, your business must prove its eligibility, since the agency carries a number of restrictions. (Consult your local SBA representative for the list of no-nos—businesses such as liquor stores, newspapers, radio and TV stations—as well as restrictions on how you will be allowed to use the loan money.) The SBA can't lend you money if you can get a loan on reasonable terms from a bank, or can sell assets that your company does not need in order to grow. Therefore, you must approach the SBA armed with information showing that you can't obtain other financing. You must be prepared to fill out an extremely detailed loan application. Be aware that a lot of delay, red tape, and back-and-forthing are involved. SBA loans take time to come through (from six months to a year).

The SBA seldom provides venture capital. The majority of its loans take the form of guaranteed loans. This means that if your business is approved you can borrow up to $150,000 from a bank and the SBA will guarantee up to 90 percent of the loan, or up to 85 percent for loans between $150,000 and $750,000. These are long-term loans that often run from seven to ten years. (The loan will be approved faster if your bank has been certified by the SBA.) Those denied SBA loans generally lack collateral, reassuring repayment prospects, or sufficient capital of their own (usually 15 to 40 percent of the total financing).

Small Business Investment Companies

SBA-licensed (and partially funded) small business investment companies (SBICs) and the Minority Enterprise Small Business Investment Companies (MESBICs) are *privately* organized and managed. (MESBICs invest only in businesses owned by minorities and women.) The lending policies vary considerably among the more than 440 companies across the country, but they provide both equity financing and long-term loans, as well as financial and management planning.*

To get anywhere with these companies, you must bombard them with cold, hard facts and financial forecasts covering every aspect of your business. Special emphasis must be placed on its anticipated success, with accurate accounting of how you will spend the money—down to the last penny.

For the most part, these and other venture capital companies are interested only in prospects that could turn into major national organizations within their industry in five to seven years. They expect a large rate of return on their investment, and most fledgling businesses simply don't qualify.

Additional Federal, State, and Local Funding

There is now much government money available for small businesses on the national, state, and local levels. This is because it is now recognized that *more than half of all new jobs* are generated by companies with twenty or fewer employees. It's not always easy to find this money, because there is no central organization for it. Your best information will probably come from other entrepreneurs who have had firsthand experience in getting these funds.

If you're planning to go high-tech, or if you have lots of ideas

*For more information and a list of SBICs, contact your local SBA office, or the National Association of SBICs, 1156 Fifteenth Street NW, Suite 1101, Washington, D.C. 20005.

for new inventions, the Small Business Innovation Research* (SBIR) program, enacted in 1982, awards grants for research and development. It offers consultants to help you with your SBIR proposal, and a SBIR newsletter. The money is hard to get. There are many delays before you get it. But there's nearly half a billion dollars of it available, if you have patience to deal with the bureaucratic red tape.

There are also hundreds of Certified Development Corporations (CDCs)† around the country that have money to lend. They are authorized by the SBA as part of its fixed-asset lending program, called 504. Again, there are complicated procedures involved, but many CDCs provide assistance in preparing the loan request package.

Almost all the states now offer some type of small business financing, according to the Washington, D.C.-based Corporation for Enterprise Development.‡ The majority of states have Small Business Development Centers (SBDCs) to provide management assistance. More than half the states have small business offices, toll-free hot lines, or small business advocates. If your state doesn't, try its departments of commerce or economic development.

There is a lot of help available on the local level as well. In small towns, contact the mayor's office or county government for information on these programs. In cities of more than 50,000, try the economic development office.

Finance Companies

At commercial finance companies the interest rates are exorbitant, but that is because they make higher-risk loans. Consider

*To learn more about the Small Business Innovation Research program, contact the SBA's Office of Innovation, Research, and Technology at (202)653-6458.
†To find the CDC nearest you, contact your SBA district office, or call the Small Business Answer Desk at (800)368-5855.
‡Many states now make loans available to small businesses, especially ones that are willing to locate in certain depressed areas and show job-creation potential. See the SBA's booklet *The States and Small Business: Programs and Activities* ($12, ordered from [202] 783-3238). It contains over 400 pages of program listings, not including programs available on the local city/county level.
    See also *The Directory of Federal and State Business Assistance: A Guide for New and Growing Companies* (NTIS order no. PB**-101977), a 170-page directory published by the U.S. National Technical Information Service, (703)487-4650 ($29, plus $3 shipping).

this option *only* if your business is in a position to repay yet still looks too speculative for more conservative institutions.

Feminist Credit Unions and Pension Funds

Women around the country have organized credit unions to make funds available to people who have trouble getting money from traditional lenders. For the most part, however, only small amounts are available, usually for individual borrowers, not businesses. Since these credit unions try to charge low interest rates and have little margin for bad loans, they must carefully evaluate a person's ability to repay.

Some pension funds are set up to lend money to small businesses as well. Ask your accountant for advice on locating and approaching them.

Business Incubators and Other Possible Money Sources

Business incubators * offer the newest source of entrepreneurial funding and day-to-day assistance. At this writing there are more than three hundred incubators around the country—centers for start-up businesses that feature low-rent office/retail space, shared business services, and counseling to help them grow. Most incubators are nonprofit organizations, getting their funding from state and local governments, although they have become so phenomenally successful that many entrepreneurs are starting up for-profit incubators (following the basic entrepreneurial code: find a need and fill it).

Some incubators, because they are backed by venture capital groups, provide start-up financing and revolving-loan programs. Others will lend money by taking a royalty interest in any product that a business develops while in the incubator. Still others will not actually lend money but will help you find financing.

All business incubators exist to help a business start up and grow to a healthy stage. Once you're ready to spread your wings, you'll be expected to vacate your space, to make room for another fledgling business.

*Contact your state's Commerce or Economic Development department to find out if your state has a business incubator center, or contact the National Business Incubation Association, Ohio University Innovation Center, One President Street, Athens, Ohio 45701, (614)593–4388.

Women's World Banking, * an international nonprofit financial corporation founded in 1979 by Michaela Walsh, guarantees loans made to businesswomen by lending institutions, rather than acting as a bank itself. (Typically, 50 percent of a loan will be guaranteed by WWB and 25 percent by a local WWB affiliate. The lending bank is then responsible for 25 percent of any loss.) WWB is supported by a capital fund formed by grants and long-term loans. Ms. Walsh founded this corporation so that women in all parts of the world can: (1) establish credit lines in local lending institutions in order to start their own businesses; (2) build within each country support organizations to assist female entrepreneurs in the running of their businesses; and (3) form a global support network for businesswomen to exchange ideas and techniques.

The *American Woman's Economic Development Corporation* (AWED)† holds seminars to help women put together loan proposal packages. In addition, the *National Association of Women Business Owners* (NAWBO) provides start-up assistance in the form of vital informational sources for the female entrepreneur.

Rounding up enough clients for your services who are *willing to pay you in advance* for their first job is another possibility for funding. This would not provide you with working capital, though, or anything to fall back on when you screech into your first slump.

The most unconventional way to start a business is with *credit cards.* This is *not* recommended, because of the high interest rate (average: 18 percent) that the cards charge. But more than one hungry entrepreneur, after unsuccessfully searching for funds, has gone this route. It involves establishing a good personal credit rating (borrowing money and paying it back on time), and

*Women's World Banking, 8 West Fortieth Street, 10th Floor, New York, New York 10018, (212)768–8513, has over a thousand worldwide affiliates—groups of lawyers, bankers, business and government people who know their countries' economies and who are committed to helping women.

†AWED, 60 East Fortieth Street, Suite 405, New York, New York 10165, (212)-692–9100, is the country's leading not-for-profit organization providing entrepreneurial women with a wide range of management training and business counseling. They also sponsor an annual conference in New York City for women in business (and those contemplating starting a business). In addition, AWED's ten-session loan package course teaches women entrepreneurs everything they need to know to get a loan.

NAWBO, 600 South Federal, Chicago, Illinois 60605, (312)922–0465, provides counseling for female entrepreneurs, has dozens of chapters across the country, and publishes a newsletter for its members.

amassing numerous cards offered by various banks across the country. These bank cards promise cash advances or lines of credit from a few hundred dollars to up to $25,000. (One entrepreneur started her successful mail-order business with $100,000 raised from thirty-seven credit cards.)

Most often, however, credit cards are used for occasional short-term working or expansion capital, rather than for start-ups. The important thing to remember is that you must pay off these cash advances as soon as possible. Taxwise, however, the same deductions are available with credit card loans as with any other business loan, and the interest becomes deductible at the point it's incurred, not when it's paid.

Factoring is another way of financing businesses. It is far from ideal, but some entrepreneurs have no choice. In factoring, you don't borrow money, you sell your receivables for cash. You send the factor the bills owed you and the factor pays you 75 percent (usually) of the total immediately, and the remaining 20 percent when the client pays. For this, the factor takes a hefty 5 percent (with the percentage going up a couple of points every thirty-day period the client doesn't pay). It's far costlier than a bank loan, but sometimes necessary.

HOW MUCH MONEY DO YOU NEED?

Use your accountant when setting out to raise money. Her professional evaluation of your idea will add credibility to your projections, in the eyes of the "money people." In addition, a good accountant has a track record with the local financial community, even if you don't, and can steer you toward lenders who may be sympathetic to your type of business. With your accountant's aid you can estimate accurately how much money you need to blast off from the launching pad.

And how much money *do* you need? The type of business you start will determine that to a large extent. But often, how much you *need* has to be geared to how much you think you can *get*, keeping your past business history in mind. An aspiring entrepreneur with no assets or track record is going to have to start small and look for expansion financing once she's proved herself and her business. In other words, when coming up with your entrepreneurial idea, keep in mind how expensive the idea is and whether you think there's a likelihood of getting start-up financing. If you have a strong background in the field of your proposed business, you'll fare better than someone who has a fantastic idea but no skills to trot out for the potential lenders.

Read the following chapters first, to get an overview of all the factors to consider. Next, figure out your basic minimum expenses (rent and utilities, business licenses, consultants' and legal fees, insurance, equipment and supplies, inventory or raw materials, and additional expenses such as advertising and salary for staff and yourself).* Then *double* them: expenses will always be higher than your original estimate. Unplanned crises and disasters, which inevitably occur, must be anticipated.

Next, write down your break-even point (what your sales must be to meet expenses) and the volume of business you must have to make a profit (e.g., how much merchandise must be sold, or what services performed). Income must be regular to meet overhead and expenses as they come due.

So, you'll need enough money to cover your expenditures for the amount of time you project it will take to get your business off the ground and attract a flow of steady customers. Depending on the type of business, you should be cushioned for *at least* the first six months. (Prestige businesses, like art galleries, take years longer to build a steady clientele than do stores, which are nestled right in the heart of the consumer mainstream. Likewise, if you are building a company around your newest invention, it's going to take a greater outlay of cash to get started and, therefore, longer to get into the black.)

PLANNING YOUR PRESENTATION

All potential moneylenders, whether they're bankers or private investors or friends, must be presented with facts. And you must have these facts ready to present, in black and white, and indelibly stamped on your brain as well. As a general rule, loan proposals should be at least ten pages long and cover the following information:

*When seeking a loan, don't sketch in a higher salary for yourself than that at your former job. Money people aren't impressed. Besides, business owners frequently have to put money back into their businesses during the first year (and often longer, depending on the business). If you take too much for yourself, your business doesn't stand a chance.

1. Detailed explanation of your business idea, including descriptions of all of the products/services you plan to offer. Description of your business's past history, if there is one, and a discussion of the market segment that you're aiming for, including how you propose to reach that market.
2. Loan purpose, i.e., how the loan will be used to bring your goals to fruition. Support this with market studies, descriptions of needed equipment, specific plans for expansion, etc.—as much "show and tell" as you can come up with.
3. How much money you need. List separately what you require for rent, utilities, office furniture and supplies, equipment, inventory, accounting and legal fees, insurance, business licenses (if necessary), qualified personnel, advertising, working capital.

   Back this up with your accountant's cash flow projections covering the entire loan period, including the interest charges. If the planned loan includes a line of credit, provide monthly projections for the first year and annual and seasonal figures for three to five years. This financial projection should include a balance sheet indicating what shape your company will take *after* the money is obtained.
4. How you are going to repay the loan. This should be backed up by financial projections, statements from the past (if the business is going for expansion financing), market studies, and any other factors you believe will impress the moneylenders that their loan is going to help your business grow significantly.
5. What you will put up for collateral—both company and personal assets. Include appraisals of real and personal property to be used as security, including a statement of your personal net worth and sources of income. (Include both savings and your outstanding bills and debts.)
6. Biographical sketches of you, the owner, as well as sketches of partners (if any), key managers, or employees. This should include: (a) your business background, and a resumé with special emphasis on experience and education in the field of your proposed business; and (b) financial and personal references. In other words, do you have experience and are you reliable?

In defining what your business will do, be sure to show why there is a need for your business, who your competition is, and how well they are doing and why. Then describe how you feel your company can successfully compete. Point out any unique qualities that set you apart from the competition. Round out the presentation with photographs and/or illustrations, if possible.

Indicate your potential market and your marketing plan—that is, how you are going to lure clients away from your competition and how you plan to advertise and promote your business. If you have already lined up some advance orders or customers, so much the better.

You have to persuade your financial sources that you are a good risk. Bowl them over with your confidence and enthusiasm, your ability to see both the forest and the trees. Emphasize your good health and flexibility; include alternative plans should problems arise, and your inclination to seize new opportunities.

Don't be discouraged. Financing is difficult to get, but it is by no means impossible. If one lender turns you down, try another. (Be sure to find out *why* you have been turned down, and use that information to strengthen your business plan.) If too many lenders turn you down, then consider taking another look at your proposed business. Try to modify your plans to suit the money people, or reconsider whether or not you have a viable business idea.

·3·

The Business Plan: An Overall Checklist

A bad beginning makes a bad ending. —Euripides

So you want to start a business. At least you think you do. Before you begin fantasizing about how you'll spend your first million, let your brain consider more realistic immediacies. You'll never again have as much time as you do now to spend on the tangibles and intangibles of your potential enterprise. The more you plan before you open your doors for business, the more successful you and your business will be.

It takes time to get a business on its feet. Many women defeat themselves by taking the plunge too quickly, swept away by their enthusiasm before they really know what they're doing. It's true that some businesses may be organized in a month or so, but most will take approximately six months of intense groundwork. Many advisors feel that a potential entrepreneur needs a full year's preparation before she's off and running.

ARE YOU READY TO BECOME AN ENTREPRENEUR?

This is a question that must be asked at the outset. Entrepreneurs are, by nature, risk takers. However, some entrepreneurs will readily admit that getting over their fear of failure was a major hurdle. This fear prevents many people from going into business. Nobody likes the idea of losing their money (or someone else's). Nobody enjoys the possibility of squandering their business reputation, or losing face with their family, friends, and business associates. But studies show that many entrepreneurs believe there is no way that they can fail. Their positive attitude gets them going and helps them over obstacles.

Are you afraid of failure? Sit down and consider it. Usually, the worst thing that can happen to an honest entrepreneur is that her business will fail. Think about how that would affect you. Would it depress you terribly? Would you have lost all your savings? Would it be so bad to have to go back to work for someone else? Would you be able to pick yourself up, dust yourself off, and start all over again?

The people who become entrepreneurs either conquer their fear of failure or refuse to admit its existence. They are able to risk the possibility of falling on their noses, and are undaunted by it. Successful entrepreneurs possess the following personality traits: self-confidence, commitment to their vision, the instinct for survival, self-discipline, motivation, and the ability to plan.

Before you take the entrepreneurial plunge, you must also have a realistic view of your strengths and weaknesses. If you haven't already analyzed your administrative adequacy, stop right where you are and take an objective appraisal of yourself (just like those fictional women who look in the mirror and *really see* themselves for the first time).

The owner of a business has to be in total control, a Jill who masters all trades (or at least oversees them), able to dazzle clients, be a sympathetic employer, fix the fax machine, and interpret profit-loss statements—all in the course of a day's activities.

Can *you* do it? Sometimes you don't know till you try. But to help you figure out how well you know yourself, here are some qualities that successful entrepreneurs must possess. Evaluate all your plusses and minuses, no matter how trivial. What do you have to offer, and what do you lack? Owning and running a successful business, no matter how small, takes a number of ingredients. Some things that help:

The imagination to come up with a good idea for a successful venture

The good health and energy to maintain physical and mental stamina

The enthusiasm to believe in your plan and to *enjoy* what you do

The drive or the will to work harder for yourself than you have ever worked for anyone else

The time, since there are numerous occasions when you will have to work overtime to meet deadlines, balance the books, etc.

The determination that your plan *will* work

The discipline to *make* it work

The individuality, flair, and creativity to set you apart from the competition

The facility to evaluate facts and make decisions, quickly and effectively

The ability to live with your decisions and not blame others if things go wrong

The poise to keep your head under pressure

The strength to endure the inevitable crises and fluctuations in the economy that will affect your business

The sense of humor to make the dark days bearable and the good ones even better

The understanding for *and* from others around you. If you have a family, they must be behind you 100 percent—or you may be forced to choose between them and your business

The experience necessary to succeed. Education and practical training in the field itself and know-how in dealing with the public. (If you are not qualified, start working *now* toward gaining the experience you will need to start a business sometime in the future. While obtaining educational and on-the-job training, be formulating your plans so that you will be prepared and will make as few mistakes as possible. Take courses—at night if necessary—on business and money management—finance, bookkeeping, business law, management, marketing and promotion, etc.)

No one should embark on entrepreneurship without knowing how much of herself she is willing to put behind it, both physically and psychologically. In other words, the more you know about yourself and your business before you start, the better. (Remember, when you set out to borrow capital, the moneylenders will look at you, the owner, to gauge your business's potential for success.) And talk to other women entrepreneurs. Learn firsthand about the sorts of obstacles you will be up against.

Then, if you are still convinced you want to own your own business, go out there and show them you can do it.

TAKING ON A PARTNER

It is difficult, to say the least, to keep a business going on either creative or managerial skills alone (although you stand a better chance with the latter). If you aren't batting close to .300 in both of these areas, then reevaluate your situation. Realize your limitations in the beginning, before you start, and consider joining forces with an expert who will complement your capabilities.

You can hire someone to manage your business while you're out charming customers or inventing new products, or vice versa. But experience of that magnitude generally cannot be budgeted into new businesses with limited capital. So the logical solution is to find a partner to co-own the business with you—someone willing to invest the money, experience, and dedication to make it succeed; a person who will provide yin to your yang, balancing the scales where you alone might tip them.

Finding a Partner

How do you locate this superwoman, your business mate? Many women go into business with close friends. This is not altogether a good solution, since friendships have been known to run off course with so much at stake. Some women link up with former business associates, which is a logical solution but feasible only if that person rounds out your total business picture. Sometimes women choose male partners, and as with all partnerships, some work and some don't, depending on the professional compatibility of the people involved.

If you don't have anyone in mind, go to your business colleagues, banker, lawyer, or accountant. One of these sources may come up with the perfect person, based on their evaluation of your needs. In addition, someone you approach as an investor may decide to invest more than money, and take a hands-on interest in your business.

Check out your competition. Not that you're out to ruffle feathers, but there are many experienced women anxious to step from behind the scenes, yet lacking the courage to go it alone.

No matter how or where you find your partner, don't make a

snap decision. This is a person with whom you will share a large chunk of your life, through ups and downs, year after year (if all goes well). Investigate this person thoroughly. Check her references. Make sure she's the person she seems to be, honest, trustworthy, *and* creditworthy.

Partnership is a great deal like marriage, and you both have to work out the problems as they arise, before they become insurmountable. Keep an open dialogue going all the time, so you don't let petty gripes build into major bitterness.

Husband-Wife Partnerships

Once dubbed "Mom and Pop" businesses, husband-and-wife entrepreneurs are now referred to as "copreneurs."* These partnerships are going stronger than ever, but they've come a long way from the sweet couple who ran the corner candy store.

In the past many husbands really ran the show while their wives worked not so much *with* them as *for* them. Things have changed considerably. Today a husband and wife can work successfully side by side as equal partners, as long as each has something to contribute to the business at hand. Certainly copreneurships are economically advantageous.

On the personal level, however, there are the potential pitfalls of any partnership. Each partner must have well-defined duties and areas of expertise in order to keep the partnership equal and the business stable.

It's difficult for any entrepreneur to keep business problems from spilling over into leisure time. That's one of the reasons entrepreneurs have a high divorce rate. Couples in business together understand that often the business has to come first. But copreneurs still must work hard to maintain a harmonious balance between their home and professional lives. If they don't the business as well as the marriage will suffer, and employees may be caught in the middle, making for a tense working environment.

Before becoming business partners, a husband and wife should analyze their personal relationship as well as their professional goals. Remember, both marriage and business have high mortal-

*For information on copreneurs, write the National Association of Entrepreneurial Couples (NAEC), P.O. Box 3238, Eugene, Oregon 97403, (503)341–6444.

ity rates. If you are considering taking on a spouse as a business partner, each of you should know exactly what you're getting into, and put it down in writing.

The Partnership Agreement

In the beginning, you and your partner(s)—this applies to co-preneurs, too—should write up an agreement stating your intentions, delegating responsibility, and including buy and sell arrangements should one of you wish to withdraw at a later date. The law does not require this to be written; a smile and a handshake will do. But to avoid any misunderstandings that could lead to future difficulties, get it in writing.

In addition, agree upon an impartial person, outside the business, who can serve as an arbitrator should any problems arise. This person can also act as a sounding board for new ideas or as a consultant, but she should be unbiased and have no vested interest in the business.

YOUR BUSINESS PLAN

A good business plan is the key to your future success. Even if you intend to start a small business with only yourself to answer to, a written blueprint will enable you to anticipate, and solve, problem areas in organization, marketing, and financing.

Once your doors are open to the public, you will be racing to keep step with your brainchild. Besides actually doing business with paying customers, you'll have to choreograph the background goings-on of your office, factory, or store. That means taking care of all the nitty-gritty details: keeping books and records up to date, handling payroll, paying bills, supervising your staff, constantly reevaluating goals, and mapping out new strategies. A business can't tread water; it must grow to stay healthy. And as its owner you are going to be very busy. (That's not a prediction; it's a fact.)

Before risking valuable time, energy, and money, you need to know how much profit you stand to make and exactly what procedures must be followed in order to manipulate the strings of success.

Besides steering you in the right direction, your written business plan will form the basis for proposals to banks and other potential investors. It will provide instant information to your accountant, banker, lawyer, and partners, should you choose to take on any. A detailed business blueprint can help persuade suppliers to grant you credit and might even convince future customers to place advance orders. In addition, it will become a constant source of reference, something by which you can measure your growth. A good written plan will also guide your decision making.

The rest of this book will unravel the mysteries of each specific area of business with which an entrepreneur must deal. But first, you must picture the whole forest. Below is a series of questions to be answered before you do another thing. Get out your pen and paper, and clearly and concisely analyze yourself, your potential business, and your goals.

The Concept

What will your business do? Explain, as specifically as possible, your idea, product, or service. Include: a physical description of the product, how and where it will be manufactured; a description of the services you will offer and how they will be administered; or, a description of your store, how it will look, what it will sell. What will you name the business?

Who is the potential user of your product or service? Describe your desired customers and the market in which they exist. (List the sources of information used to make your projections.) Is there a need for your business, and why? If your idea is innovative, explain why it will appeal to your market.

Who is your competition? Assess these businesses, and explain how your product or service represents variations and improvements over existing ones.

Marketing Your Business Idea

How will you reach your target market? Explain how your product or service will be sold: sales force, distributors, pricing, advertising and publicity, location, image and graphics, promotion, etc.

How do you propose to enter the market? What will constitute your selling tools? How will you organize a sales campaign?

Discuss these factors in detail. For example, if location is key, provide descriptions (and snapshots) of proposed ideal locations. If advertising will be your prime motivator, tell where you plan to advertise, how often, and why. How much will your ad campaign cost (both to create and execute)? What will your ads say? Who will write and design your ads?

What is the image you wish your business to project? Will you have a logo and other graphic identification (slick brochures, fliers, menus, etc.)? What about interior design? Sales force? Location? The aura with which you surround your business, and make it attractive to the buying public, will help clear a niche in the marketplace for you.

The People

Who are you? Why are you equipped to make this particular enterprise a success? As owner you will be your company's most important asset. Describe your background, strengths, and weaknesses: what talents/skills do you bring to the business; in what areas do you lack experience? Include your previous work and life experience, your skills and knowhow, and your analysis of what the job of running your company will entail.

Provide work biographies of your partner(s), if there are any, and other key people who will be involved with the vital operation of your business (managers, full- or part-time consultants). How many employees will you need at the outset? Indicate which areas of responsibility and authority within the business each person will cover, and how you will attract these quality people.

Outline the outside businesses or services that will be necessary to your company's smooth operation, e.g., wholesalers, suppliers, agencies, postal services, customs, business contacts, neighboring businesses, independent contractors, and so forth.

List the names (and firms they are with) of your lawyer, accountant, banker, insurance agent, and marketing and/or management consultant. What services do you expect to receive from them?

Financial Estimates

How much capital will you need to launch your business? Estimate all your costs including rent and utilities; equipment, decoration and fixtures; deposits and credit payments; supplies and inventory; printing costs for stationery, brochures, etc.; advertising; marketing survey; grand opening promotion; initial consultation fees; travel; insurance; and unexpected expenses. Investigate these costs thoroughly, but be generous with your estimates, because unforeseen expenses (such as repairs on equipment) always crop up.

How much capital will you need to operate your business for the first eighteen months? Include all of the above, plus estimates for salaries, taxes, and allowance for growth.

Show cash flow projections based on three growth potentials: low, expected, and better than average. With your accountant, figure your break-even points within each category. You must predict a profit within a reasonable amount of time if your market analysis has been accurate.

List sources for capital and terms of financing: personal savings, debt financing (money that is repaid, with interest), equity financing (money obtained through the sale of stock in the company).

Long-Range Planning

What are your motivations for going into business, and what do you expect to gain? It's important to analyze your reasons for wanting to launch this particular business and where you want it to go. Ask yourself where you would like to be in five years and whether you are willing to make a long-term commitment to your enterprise.

Will your business be your primary source of income, or supplementary? How much money must you realize from your time and financial investment in order for the business to be a personal success?

List desired standards and growth for the business. What new products or expanded services do you envision?

How will you handle personal and family obligations while running a business full-time?

Envision all the things that could possibly go wrong and affect your business (poor economy, loss of major suppliers or partners, ill health, etc.) and figure out how you will deal with every problem.

Write out your answers to all these questions. Once it's on paper, test your business plan on family, friends, and business associates. Their reactions can send you back to the drawing board or marching ahead toward fame, fortune, and independence.

Be realistic, but don't let anyone discourage you in this preliminary stage. Too often, innovative ideas disintegrate under stolid scrutiny; too much logic can ground your starship before it's even launched. At this stage, let your creativity and enthusiasm reign—just channel them in the right direction.

You may have trouble answering some of the above questions in detail because you lack expertise in a particular area. However, each element is covered in the upcoming chapters. After you have finished the book, return to your business plan and answer the questions again. You may be surprised to find that some of your perceptions have changed.

If the business you envision doesn't seem to have enough market and financial potential, you will have to revise your idea— or come up with another business that *will* work.

WHY BUSINESSES FAIL

According to Price Waterhouse, one of the country's "Big Eight" accounting firms, 20 percent of all new businesses go under in the first year; 50 percent are gone after seven years. Some statistics put the new-business mortality rate much higher than that. (These figures improve substantially, however, if you start out in a low-rent, shared-services business incubator.) The primary reasons for failure are inexperience, incompetence, mismanagement, and undercapitalization. A thorough business plan will help you stay on top of potential problems and setbacks.

Some of the more specific reasons for business failure are listed below. Read and beware:

Entrepreneur's lack of experience (and inability to keep on top of things)

41

Inaccurate record keeping (and records not kept up to date)
Poor management of money
Lack of advance planning
Misuse of time (not tackling duties in order of priority; not delegating responsibility)
Weak marketing plan
Owner's inability to grow with the company (to keep reevaluating progress and setting new goals)

Remember, don't rush it. Spend as much time as you need on the beginning stages of your business. Don't be in too big a hurry to open your doors to the public. Time well spent now will save you money (and headaches) later.

·4·

Mothers of Invention: The Birth of a Business

The vitality of thought is in adventure. Ideas won't keep.
Something must be done about them.
　　　　　　　　—Alfred North Whitehead

Of all the steps in preparing to do business, the idea stage is the most exhilarating. Beyond that the climb gets tough; opening your business and keeping it going, especially in the first crucial year, is a lot of work. At the beginning, however, you can luxuriate in the *concept*. What is it? Where do you find it?

Many potential entrepreneurs thrive on the excitement of starting up their own venture, with complete autonomy to run things as they wish. Coming up with the idea and setting it in motion is how they get their thrills.

But other people who want to strike out on their own are hesitant about the risks involved. These would-be entrepreneurs are more comfortable with the idea of buying a business or franchise, or becoming a dealer or distributor for an already established business-opportunity company. All of these options will be explored in this chapter, to help you decide what might be the best route for you.

GROWING YOUR OWN BUSINESS IDEA

When you think up a business idea, it's best to stay in an area where you have experience and contacts who consider you a credible professional. But there are exceptions.

For example, sometimes an idea *happens*. You're lolling in a hammock one sunny Sunday and presto! you conjure up the vision of a homemade-ice-cream parlor. In your mind's eye, you've devised recipes for Veggie Vanilla and Chile Chocolate, decorated your shop with ceiling fans and an 1890s soda fountain, located it near the high school, and you're proferring parfaits for profits.

Some entrepreneurs start out with a burning desire to strike out on their own, and scout around for a demand to supply. They *discover* the need in their town for an ice-skating rink or lighting fixtures store or a gourmet takeout.

Others come up with a terrific invention—yes, the better mousetrap or computer chip—and set out to market it to a public that may or may not yet realize how much they need it.

Some entrepreneurs forgo the area of their expertise and build a new business on a long-standing interest or hobby that they finally decide to market. One female attorney gave up her successful but stagnant law practice to travel the world, finding and importing antique silks and brocades for the to-the-trade-only fabric house that she founded.

Trend spotting is another way some businesses come into being. Looking around you, seeing what *you* want, what your children need, what your neighborhood lacks, what would make your life easier, more organized, more fun, is a viable way to come up with a unique product or service idea. Sometimes it can merely be a variation on an old theme, in the way that the yogurt and ice cream crazes combined to inspire frozen yogurt. Or it can be something completely innovative, such as nontoxic, educational toys that do something new and different.

Still other potential entrepreneurs, after a steady climb of education and on-the-job training, answer the call to solo with their special talent. Often they start out with clients already in tow, people who know their work and reputation and are willing to back them. This can work whether you become a consultant in a high-tech industry or decide to market the spicy seafood marinade that your friends have oohed and aahed over for years.

No matter how you arrive at your decision to go into business for yourself, you have to translate your idea into a practical step-by-step plan. Assuming the basic premise is sound and you're not trying to sell air conditioners to Siberians, your company's success hinges on a solid foundation and detailed plan of action.

Analyzing Your Community

For a start, take a look around you. Consider your area's economic base. Is it thriving; are new businesses moving in? Are large companies closing down or moving out? Does your business concept depend on good times when people become free spenders, or will you offer a basic product or service that your community needs and that can transcend hard times? Your business doesn't stand a chance if your community cannot support it.

Defining the Idea

Define your idea *on paper*. It has to make complete sense to you before other people can be convinced. If you can't explain what your business will do in twenty-five words or less, then rethink your concept. Ask yourself a few questions. Are you *supplying* a demand? (Your neighborhood needs a day-care center; art supply store; auto repair clinic; or taco stand.) Or, are you *creating* one? (A food shop featuring exotic delicacies from around the world; a nifty children's boutique with a play-yard in back; a game called "Widgie," destined to replace backgammon; an art gallery to display the work of local artists.)

The Quality of Your Idea

Some women have no trouble coming up with a business idea. In fact, they dream up more businesses than they know what to do with. If you are overwhelmed by the quantity of your schemes to make a million and don't know which to zero in on, what do you do? Simply put together a business plan (see chapter 3) for each of your best ideas and weigh them against the criteria set forth for a successful venture.

Evaluate the market potential of your proposed businesses. Besides making financial projections, really focus on your target market. Interview potential customers (strangers, not friends, for more objective replies). In other words, test your idea on paper before you plunk down any money on it.

CREATING A SOCIALLY CONSCIOUS COMPANY

Some entrepreneurs fill a need by founding companies to help the environment and/or the people of the earth. They start asbestos removal businesses, raise chemical-free chickens, or in the case of a Chicago woman, create a commercial bank aimed at bringing money into a poor inner-city ghetto and investing it there.

But even if the type of company you start isn't specifically socially conscious, you can maintain strong ideals in the way you run it and invest your profits. So, besides *what* you do, you also have to give some thought to how you're going to do it, not the specifics, but the intangibles. More and more entrepreneurs these days are attempting to make a contribution to society as well as pull in profits. The challenge, of course, is keeping these goals balanced.

If you are interested in helping others as well as yourself,* here are some points to keep in mind. Prepare a mission statement, a sentence or two expressing your personal and social goals. These goals don't have to be any loftier than merely wanting to create a pleasant and ethical working environment for yourself and your employees, creating a high-quality product that is designed to last, or using only preservative-free, organic ingredients in the pizzas you sell. Trying to figure out how to put your good intentions to practical application is the key.

Get advice and backing from outside support systems, such as the National Association of Women Business Owners.† Then make a commitment to place your working capital, pension funds, or profits into a fund that invests only in companies that are run according to ethical guidelines.‡

*The following publications aid and advise companies that are socially conscious: *Business Ethics,* bimonthly magazine, 1107 Hazeltine Boulevard, Suite 530, Chaska, Minnesota 55318, (612)448–8864; and, *Catalyst,* newsletter published by The Institute of Gaean Economics, 64 Main Street, Montpelier, Vermont 05602.

†National Association of Women Business Owners, 600 South Federal Street, Suite 400, Chicago, Illinois 60605, (312)922–0465, is dedicated to helping women entrepreneurs in all areas of business. Besides the national headquarters, there are thirty-six local chapters across the country. Also, Renaissance Business Associates, 4817 North County Road 29, Suite 200, Loveland, Colorado 80538, (303)679–4305, is an international association of business owners, including social entrepreneurs. The American Association of Responsible Business, 2605 Adams Mill Road NW, Suite 1, Washington, D.C. 20009, is a new trade association for ethical businesses.

‡To obtain a list of socially responsible investment funds and advisors, write The Social Investment Forum, 711 Atlantic Avenue, Boston, Massachusetts 02111,

Have your company contribute directly to worthy local and national causes. Not only will you be helping others, your reputation as an ethical employer will help you attract quality staff. And when your business reaches out to help your community, your community is going to support your business.

NAMING THE BUSINESS

A company's name must be memorable and pronounceable. Picture it up on a sign, there for the world to see. It should look good and convey the idea of what you do or make or sell. The name should establish the image you wish to project. Avoid trendy, up-to-the-minute names; they may be initially catchy, but inevitably become passé and you are stuck with an anachronistic name you loathe.

After you come up with a name, live with it for a while. Try it out on friends and business associates before you make your final decision. If it wears well and gets positive reactions, then stick with it.

If you use a made-up name (The Black Raven Construction Company) instead of your own (Meredith Hampton's Hardware & Haberdashery), you must file a *fictitious name statement,* also called *dba* (doing business as). This must be filed with your local county clerk, within thirty days after the start of your business. The registration fee is generally around ten dollars. (In some states the dba must be filed with the state's department of taxation; check with your legal counsel on this.)

In some communities you will be required to publish a notice of the intended name for four consecutive weeks in a local or legal newspaper. Your county clerk can give you information about this, as well as the name of the least expensive recognized publication in which to run the statement.

This does not apply to corporations. Incorporating a business carries its own spools of red tape, which will be unraveled in the legalities chapter. But when thinking up a name for a corporation, do not pick one that's too close to an existing corporation

---

(617)451–3252, and include $8 for a directory. For information on *Investing for a Better World* and *Insight,* two newsletters on social investing, write the Franklin Research & Development Corporation at the Boston address listed above, or call (617)423–6655.

in your state, or the state will reject your choice. You'll lose valuable time and have to come up with another name.

BUYING A BUSINESS

Buying a business* or franchise is a good way to go into business without having to start from scratch. However, you have to do as much homework as if you were starting from square one. You don't want to buy a business and inherit the former owner's headaches. Nor do you want to rush into a franchise until you have investigated the franchisor thoroughly.

There are a number of good reasons for buying an already existing business. You may not be able to come up with a lucrative new idea that will go over in your community. Or you may hear of a business for sale that is just what you're looking for.

If you are considering buying a business, ask your accountant, lawyer, banker, or business realtors and friends if they recommend any that are for sale. Look at the "business opportunities" section of your local newspapers, real estate giveaways, and business/franchise periodicals. Or you can advertise yourself: "Looking to buy . . . (special interest)." Usually an entrepreneur will have an idea of the type of business she's interested in, e.g., a restaurant or a travel agency. But sometimes, if you are savvy about business in general, you won't care what specific business you run. You'll want to look for an idea that appeals to you out of a large field of possibilities.

When you've narrowed down your list to businesses that interest you, be prepared to spend time and money on investigating the scene behind the "For Sale" sign. The transaction will involve negotiating a fair price, evaluating the seller's facts and figures, and closing the deal.

You have to find out *why* the owner is selling. Sometimes it is because of age, ill health, or because s/he wants to create another business (the true entrepreneur). But sometimes owners want to unload a mismanaged or failing business before they go bankrupt. This isn't necessarily bad *if you possess the skills* to come in and turn it around, plus the financing to keep it going. Keep in mind that it takes time and talent to revitalize a sick business.

Before signing on the dotted line, consult a lawyer and an

*See SBA Management Aids booklet no. 2.029 ($1), *How to Buy or Sell a Business*, by John A. Johansen.

accountant. A lawyer not only helps you arrive at a decision but must represent you at the final transaction. An accountant will not only verify the financial records of the seller, she will contribute valuable observations on market trends and the company's future profit potential. These professionals will also help you evaluate the answers to the questions that follow.

Why Is This Business for Sale?

Knowing the owner's real reasons for selling will help you negotiate the price and give you an idea of the degree of experience and skill needed to continue the business profitably. It is possible that the seller wants to move to Tahiti. It's also possible that a new superhighway is scheduled to cut right through aisle four.

Get the facts, and be wary if the seller seems to hedge on certain information. The fewer unknowns, the better chance you have for success. The things to check on and evaluate are:

Debts or hidden (or unrecorded) obligations

Accounts receivable—how long do customers take to pay?

Repeat business—what percentage of the billing is with steady clientele?

Back taxes or employee withholdings—does the company owe any?

Lawsuits—are there any pending?

Length of lease—is it renewable or transferable to the new owner? Property, fixtures, equipment—is there solid evidence of the seller's ownership of these things?

Trademarks, patents, copyrights—have they been granted, or are they pending?

State, federal, and city licensing—has the seller complied with all regulations?

Zoning laws—will any new ones affect the business? Any pertinent construction or demolition in the neighborhood?

Competition—who and where are they?

Distribution—are there any problems with outlets or suppliers? (Talk to the suppliers and to customers; make sure the seller has a good reputation.)

Managers and employees—to what extent are they important to the business? Are they willing to stay on with the new

49

ownership? (Spend time with them; decide whom *you* would keep or replace.)

Most times, though, a business is for sale because it's losing money through the owner's inadequate managerial ability. If you have experience and managerial skills, you're in a good position to pull off a success. But you have to work with what you have. Study the business thoroughly before you start reshaping and cost-cutting. Have a plan for how you're going to turn the business around (if it needs turning around) *before* you buy it.

Will This Business Make a Profit?

In arriving at a fair purchase price, the profit potential is the key factor in your negotiations. Check the records (annual profit-loss statements, balance sheets, tax returns) of past performance.

The simplest way to forecast profit trends is to assume sales will continue to increase or decrease at the same percentage rate as they have in the past. If the profit trend is down, then either new money or special skills will be needed to improve the picture. If profits are up, the seller is in the best negotiating position. The final sale price will strongly depend on these trends.

How Strong Is the Market?

Learn all you can about the business. Analyze the product or service. What is the demand for it; who are the customers? To what extent is the business affected by the overall economy? Is the location convenient to customers and suppliers? Is there enough parking space? Is the business seasonal? Does it thrive on word of mouth, or does it call for saturation advertising and active promotions? Buying a business without checking these things is like buying a house without looking in all the rooms.

What Are the Tangible Assets of the Business?

What is the actual physical property you will be buying? Have a qualified appraiser evaluate the inventory of goods, fixtures, equipment, supplies, furniture and decoration, lease of the space, and property ownership. All of these should be assessed at the real value to the buyer: are they usable or salable on today's market? (A computer system that may have cost many thousands in 1982 may be worth next to nothing on a trade-in today.) How much *additional* money—for inventory, supplies, salaries, equipment, etc.—will you have to put into the business? Calculate *everything,* including new stationery, logo, or brochures (if necessary), interior design, expanded line of merchandise, additional employees, and the like. Study the client list and see how active it is. The ongoing quality of the business is the strong determining factor in the cost appraisal of the tangibles.

What Are the Intangible Assets of the Business?

Often these are labeled the "goodwill" of the business, and it's much harder to place a price tag on that. It is the image under which the business operates: its reputation, financial standing, reliability of product or service, and favorable location. It also includes the company's relationships with customers, suppliers, creditors, and the community at large. It is of real value to both the seller and the buyer if the business scores well above average in these areas.

What Are the Liabilities?

Liabilities are the risks involved in operating any business. Investigate them just as thoroughly as you do the assets. (Check out the company's credit rating and whether there are current loans outstanding.) Naturally, the seller will minimize the risk factors. If there is hesitation or evasion on her part to supply this information, you can assume the risks are greater than the potential.

Negotiating the Price

The seller will have an asking price. It's up to you to determine how fair it is and to negotiate, using what you've learned about the business. Despite a favorable image, if the business's profits have been sliding downhill, then the purchase price can be little more than the physical assets. If the company is healthy in spirit

51

and profits, there are various formulas that can be used to determine a reasonable buying price.

One of the simplest is to estimate the resale worth of the *tangible* assets. Then set a value on the *intangibles*. First, figure the average annual net profit, based on the company's tax records and financial statements. Next, multiply that figure times *five* if the business is well established, with a favorable name, product, or location; times *three* for a moderately well-known business; or times *one* if the business has only a one-year profit picture.

Finally, add the tangible and intangible assets together for the total price.

Closing the Deal

Both your lawyer and the seller's lawyer will negotiate a contract spelling out every term of the transaction, including:

1. A clear title to all physical property.
2. Agreeable finance terms. Remember, you will still need operating capital, so purchase payments should not deplete your cash flow.
3. Protection against any false statements, inaccurate financial information, or hidden liabilities.
4. A provision giving you operating control between the time of agreement and actual takeover. This protects you from the seller's depleting assets with a "going-out-of-business" sale, or destroying the goodwill factor.
5. A statement of when and how the buyer is to take over the business, and specifications of the familiarization period.

Every buy-sell transaction has its own special and highly individual aspects that will dictate the negotiations. Money may not always be the deciding factor for the buyer or seller. For example, the seller may accept a lower bid in favor of the person she feels will best maintain the quality of the product or service. The buyer may rank the psychological factors of owning her own business (and not having to start it from scratch) far higher than the actual income of the business.

In the end, only you can understand and appreciate why you

are buying, and the final price will rest heavily on your motivations.

BUYING A FRANCHISE

Basically, a franchise is a licensing and distribution agreement between a parent company and an independent businessperson.* Franchising is a viable and often exciting way to get into business for yourself. There are pros and cons from both a business and personal angle; whether it is right for you depends on many considerations.

One usually thinks about fast food when it comes to franchising. But nowadays franchises are available in nearly every area of business, from fax stations to exercise studios, party shops to miniature golf courses. Costs of franchises vary, but most are more expensive (albeit safer) than start-ups, because you are paying for the parent company's recognizable name, good reputation, major suppliers, and practical expertise in the day-to-day running of the operation.

According to the Chicago-based Women In Franchising, Inc. (WIF),† more and more women—because of their lack of a solid business background and difficulty in raising money—are now looking into franchising as a viable way to become entrepreneurs. In 1990, woman-owned franchises dominated the diet, health, and exercise industry (80 percent), and the home furnishings industry (75 percent). In the leisure industry, 33 percent of the franchise owners were women; in business/financial services, 19 percent. And recently, women have successfully branched out into many fields formerly considered non-female, such as manufacturing, automotive, construction, mining, computer, etc.

WIF recommends checking out any potential franchisor in terms of whether or not it provides a good opportunity for women. Susan Kezios, the president and founder of WIF, urges women to examine the parent company for these four factors before buying: the percentage of women-owned franchises, the number of women in top corporate management positions, the

*See SBA Management Aids booklet no. 7.007 ($.50), *Evaluating Franchise Opportunities,* as well as the franchise issues of the monthly business publications.
†Women In Franchising, 175 North Harbor Drive, Suite 405, Chicago, Illinois 60601, (800)222–4943.

awareness of issues such as day care and flextime within a franchise, and the availability of financing or leasing programs.

Advantages of Franchising

Would-be entrepreneurs who have a real fear of failure (or losing all their savings) are often better off buying a franchise. That way, you can rely on the expertise and track record of an established parent company to cushion the risks. That's what you get. In return you pay the franchisor a hefty franchise fee and ongoing royalties.

For people with little business experience, buying a franchise can be a godsend. A franchise offers a proven success formula. The groundwork has already been laid in image, advertising, and publicity. Often the franchisor will tailor ads and promotional campaigns to your community. You buy equipment, fixtures, products, and supplies through a centralized purchasing system, so that long months aren't spent in establishing credit. The cash outlay is often lower than what is required to set up a business from scratch. And the franchisor may be able to help you with financing, either through its own credit system or by arranging a loan through your bank.

More important, the franchisor can offer you training and continuing marketing advice. You automatically join a business community made up of people who operate the same business, and together you can learn from each other.

Disadvantages of Franchising

What you give up when you buy a franchise is the freedom to do things your own way. Franchises have to conform to a uniform look, and be run by the book. Many franchise owners feel that there's no need to reinvent the wheel or take unnecessary risks. If that's you, then by all means consider a franchise. There's a lot of money to be made from a good franchise in a good location. Many franchise owners wind up owning multiple franchises.

The misconception about franchising is that it *guarantees* profits on your investment. But franchising carries no more guarantees of success than any other investment. Success or failure ultimately rests with you, and you must be qualified to run the business.

You will be expected to work hard—some women franchise owners think nothing of working eighty hours a week—and to follow systems and a set way of doing business. If you are a spontaneous person with strong innovative and creative talents, then franchising is probably not for you. Most contracts are restrictive and lean heavily on pretested methods and controls with no room for deviation. If you don't want to do business that way, then don't buy a franchise.

Finding a Franchise

First, assess how much money you have to invest. Understand that over and above the franchise fee, you will need financing for overhead and operational costs. (The parent company will be able to provide you with information on what that will cost.)

Next, what kind of business do you see yourself in? In selecting a franchise, a main concern is to make sure the business fits. It should place you in the kind of physical environment you like and bring you into contact with people with whom you feel comfortable dealing. What kind of service or product is needed in your area? Some services simply won't go over in a small conservative community the way they do in urban areas.

There are numerous ways to locate franchise opportunities. All the entrepreneurial publications run periodic issues on franchises, full of information and advertisements. Your local library should also have a selection of books devoted to franchising, as well as franchise directories. Check out local and nearby city newspapers: under "business opportunities" you will find listings of both businesses for sale and franchises. Other sources of information would be the International Franchise Association, Women In Franchising, trade associations, business organizations, and your local chamber of commerce.

Look up franchising in *The New York Times Reader's Guide,* and the *Wall Street Journal.* Look up "business opportunities" or "women in business" in your library's guide to periodicals. There are also franchise exhibitions held in major cities around the country. For information on these shows, read business magazines or write to convention centers in major cities.

Evaluating a Franchise

Once you've located a promising franchise operation, find out everything you can, not only about the company's franchise policy but about the company itself.* For instance, you will want to visit its headquarters, see its operation, meet the officers.

Also talk to other franchisees: those in their first and second year of operation can give you a good estimate of when to expect to break even financially. Those who have been in business longer can provide you with longer-term financial information. Talk out the pros and cons of the business and the terms of agreement; find out if the parent company is available when needed, if it provides the ads and promotions it promises.

This is not a one-sided proposition; the franchisor must accept you as well. The company will have a definite idea of the type of person and territory best suited for its product or service, and will start forming an impression of you from the very first letter of inquiry you write. Be aware of the image *you* are projecting; your letters should be clear, to the point, and typed. Correspondence should be answered promptly and appointments kept on time.

The Parent Company

Investigate the parent company, with the help of your accountant and lawyer. Federal and state laws regulate what franchisors must tell you about their franchisees' past sales, costs, and profits. At your first meeting with a potential franchisor, federal regulations require the franchisor to supply the franchise agreement and other related agreements (having to do with trademarks, for example), and the Uniform Franchise Offering Circular, or UFOC.† What you can expect to earn if you join the franchise family is called an "earnings claim," and is not required by law

*Contact the following organizations for advice or assistance in judging a franchise: International Franchise Association, 1350 New York Avenue NW, Suite 900, Washington, D.C. 20005, (202)628–8000; Council of Better Business Bureaus, National Headquarters, 4200 Wilson Boulevard, Suite 800, Arlington, Virginia 22203–1804, (703)276–0100; Federal Trade Commission (FTC), Room 238, Washington, D.C. 20580, (202)326–3128; your Small Business Administration district office; the U.S. Chamber of Commerce, 1615 H Street NW, Washington, D.C. 20062, (202)659–6000, or your local chamber of commerce; and Women In Franchising, listed above.

†In 1979, the Federal Trade Commission (FTC) Franchise Rule went into effect. This rule requires all franchisors to make full presale disclosure nationwide, even if there is no state regulation requiring such disclosure. In addition, the laws of

to be provided to the potential franchisee. (Many franchisors, however, provide this information voluntarily.) Never invest in a franchise without first trying to estimate how much you can expect to earn.

In addition, look at the franchise corporation from other directions. Does it have a good reputation? Is it known in your area? How long has it been in business? What are the histories and backgrounds of the principals in the business? How has the product/service changed since its inception? Is it a staple or a luxury, and how will the economy affect its marketability? How many other franchise operations are there, and are they successful?

The company should freely provide you with names and addresses of other franchisees. Any attempt on the part of the company representative to evade questions is highly suspect. So is the attempt to lay any pressure on you to sign on now. Reputable firms don't engage in high-pressure tactics. They don't have to.

For further information on the company, check with the International Franchise Association, an organization that screens all franchisors who join. The IFA will answer all your questions regarding the standards and ethics of a company.

If the company in which you're interested is not listed there, ask for references that you and your lawyer can check. A bank credit reference is particularly important as an indication of how long it's been doing business and the strength of its credit. Other sources of information are the Better Business Bureau and the Small Business Administration.

The Territory

This can be critical. What is the territory, and is it clearly defined? Will you have options to expand? What is the existing competition within the territory? How protected are your exclusive rights?

The Market

Has a market survey been done by the company? How does your territory measure up under that survey? Who is the con-

---

fifteen states and the federal government require that a franchisor give all prospective franchisees a detailed UFOC, outlining the franchisor's financial condition, history, principals, business experience, and franchise program.

sumer, in terms of age and income, and how is that consumer reached? Does the salability of the service or product depend on location? On advertising?

The Franchise Fee

Just what will you be getting for your money: is it clearly spelled out in the contract? Does the franchisor offer training, sales aids, national/local advertising, promotion, publicity? Does it help you pick your location and provide interior design and central purchasing of equipment? Does it offer continuing assistance and a strong operating system, and is it on call for unexpected emergencies?

The Cost

Discuss and consider the additional funds and operating capital you will need to get the business underway and to sustain it during the months when profits will be small and expenses will be high. Are there hidden costs? What professional help will you need—salespeople, managers, accountants, etc.?

Financing and Profit Potential

What percentage of the profits will you be required to pay to the franchisor, and under what terms? Is this percentage reasonable when weighed against profit potential? Will the franchisor assist you if you should need a loan? Will you be extended long-term credit on equipment and/or products? Ask to see the profit figures of franchisees who operate on the level on which you expect to operate.

Personal Evaluation

Rely on your instincts as well as the facts. Are you happy with the people you've met? Have you understood the terms of agreement, and are you still enthusiastic about the venture? What about your ability, physically and emotionally, to do the work necessary to build this business, now that you've had a closer look? This is going to be your business, so before signing any agreements or making any payments, be sure you feel right about everything. Any nagging doubts you have now may come back to haunt you later on.

The Contract

Your lawyer will see things in (or not in) a contract that will never occur to you. Choose a lawyer who is knowledgeable about franchising. She can uncover loopholes and can advise you on your own qualifications—both personal and financial—in terms of how the franchisor will view them.

Go over the contract with your lawyer point by point, and make sure you understand it thoroughly. Most contracts will read strongly in favor of the parent company. Remember, business relationships are not social ones, no matter how nice the franchisor makes it seem. You're buying *their* package, and they get to call the shots. In the business world, as everywhere, it's the fittest who survive.

Summary

The main thing when buying a business or franchise is to look at either from all directions. Turn to your consultants for their advice, and to make certain that the books and legalities are in order. Evaluate the product or service, check out the inventory and equipment, talk to employees and customers, find out the reputation of the seller. Remember to heed the old adage, "let the buyer beware," so that you, the buyer, won't be full of regrets.

CHOOSING A BUSINESS-OPPORTUNITY COMPANY

Becoming a dealer or distributor for an already established product falls under the category of a business opportunity. It's a way to strike out on your own, without starting from scratch *or* giving up the freedom of doing things your way. It enables you to go into business for yourself, using the name and products of an established company. Yet you avoid the strict operating criteria of a franchise, as well as the expense of the franchise fee and royalties.

Basically, you buy the program, equipment, or products from a specific company, accept some minimum guidelines, and go about marketing the business on your own. The cost is much less than that of a franchise, and you are completely independent. What you don't get is training or advertising aid or any of the support given by a franchisor.

Business opportunity companies advertise in newspapers and in all the magazines geared to entrepreneurs.* Check out the ads and see if one appeals to you. Then check out the company and its reputation, with the help of your banker or lawyer. It's perhaps the least expensive way of getting into business for yourself.

BECOMING A CORPORATE ENTREPRENEUR

If you decide you don't have the nerve, resources, or family situation to enable you to strike out on your own (yet), then consider creating more freedom for yourself within the company where you work. Carving out an entrepreneurial niche within an existing company has been done successfully by many women. These women, often called "intrapreneurs," gain autonomy without losing the stability of a regular paycheck; in fact, their salary may increase because of their ingenuity.

The key is to look around your company, find a need, and offer to fill it. One woman at a large New York ad agency did this by establishing a video newsletter that highlighted new equipment and techniques, profiled experienced technicians, and pinpointed new trends within the industry. Not only did she convince her own company that there was a need for such a publication, she ended up marketing it to other ad agencies as well. Her company rewarded her with a raise, a corner office, and her own screening room to view the work of new talent. Another woman who worked for a large magazine convinced her bosses that the publication could garner a lot of goodwill and free publicity by establishing an educational program that could be taken to elementary schools around the country. The upshot: she became the head of a new subsidiary and several years later left the company to strike out on her own.

The point is, there's opportunity everywhere and somebody has to seize it. It might as well be you.

*See bibliography, under periodicals, for listings.

·5·

Preproduction: Gathering It All Together

What we plan we build. —Phoebe Cary

ADVANCE PREPARATION

Assuming that you have now figured out what kind of business you want to start, you have to give much thought to how you're going to start it.* Launching an enterprise takes time and money. The more time you spend in the planning stage, the more money you'll save yourself later.

Some businesses can be started on a shoestring and expanded when the profit picture is rosy. Others require a large initial outlay of cash (for equipment and inventory, etc.). Before you withdraw your savings or try to borrow money, know exactly what you're doing.

And don't rush it. You won't be able to foresee all the obstacles that will invariably fall across your path, but find out everything you can about your proposed business—its requirements, problems, rewards—before you start.

Talk to other entrepreneurs who are doing or have done the same thing. Learn from their successes and their failures. Learn

*For additional help on figuring out your business plan, see the following booklets published by the Small Business Administration: *Business Plan for Retailers* (General Management, no. MP 9, $1); *Business Plan for Small Service Firms* (General Management, no. MP 11, $.50); *Business Plan for Small Manufacturers* (General Management, no. MP 4, $1); *The Business Plan for Homebased Business*, by Carol Eliason (General Management, no. MP 15, $1); and *Developing a Strategic Business Plan*, by Michael L. Policastro (Management Aids, no. 2.035, $1).

how to avoid pitfalls, and how to deal with crises that may crop up unexpectedly.

And remember Murphy's law: what *can* go wrong *will* go wrong. If you can unflinchingly face up to that in advance and still want to burst forth as an entrepreneur, then give it a shot. According to research conducted on entrepreneurs, most share a number of common personality traits, the most important of which is confidence. If you possess confidence in yourself, in your ability to sell your idea, to set up a business facing fierce competition, and can trust your intuition along the way, then you stand a good chance of succeeding.

OBTAINING PROFESSIONAL ADVICE

Although some women complain that the "experts" discourage them, professional guidance is essential for a budding entrepreneur. Just remember, consultants can only *recommend* courses of action. You, as the owner, have to evaluate, objectively and intuitively, what is right for your business. After all, it is *yours*. No one will care about it as much as you do.

Selecting Consultants

Shop around for professional consultants, including lawyers, accountants, insurance agents, bankers, and business advisers. Check out all recommendations from business associates and friends before making any decisions. Look for people who are knowledgeable about small business in general, and your type of business in particular. Seek advisers who speak your language and will take an interest in you. Beware of people with large egos; they won't admit it when they don't know something. Avoid those who appear patronizing. Beware, also, of consultants who have overextended themselves and are too busy to tend successfully to the needs of their smaller clients. If you don't get the results you want when you want them, then don't hesitate to find someone else to assist and advise you. After all, it's your business that's at stake.

Once you have established a working relationship with your advisers, keep in regular touch with them. Follow-up is essential. Make sure you both do what you say. Send a written memo or letter after each meeting, reviewing the topics discussed and stating which of you will handle each item.

However, don't overuse professionals or become dependent on them. Often you can deal with small crises yourself. If you call on your lawyer or accountant for these, you're wasting their time and your money. Consult with the experts only when necessary, after you've done your initial legwork.

Hiring Friends As Advisers

It's best not to hire friends, but if you do, handle the relationship as professionally as you can. Be businesslike, *especially* with friends. To avoid later feuds, draw up a written agreement, outlining the specifics (services and charges) of what they will do for you.

Fees

Establish all costs at the outset, especially for budgeting professional consultations into your business plan. Get a minimum fee and estimate it from there. Fees left up in the air may shock you when it's time to pay up (and if you've hired friends, it can ruin a friendship). Discuss charges for consultants' services first off. And don't be timid about shopping around for professional services. Look for quality, not bargain rates. An adviser with lots of experience in your type of business can save you money in the long run.

Finding Additional Business Services

If you can't afford to hire anyone in the beginning, there are free or inexpensive counseling services available.

The Small Business Administration has an Office of Women's Business Ownership (1441 L Street NW, Suite 414, Washington, D.C. 20416, [202]653–8000), which coordinates the SBA's efforts in support of women business owners and aspiring entrepreneurs. In addition, the Women's Network for Entrepreneurial Training, launched by the SBA in 1988, is a pilot mentoring program available in some states. It matches women mentors with women who need business guidance and support. Also, every SBA district office has a women's business ownership representative, to answer your business questions and inform you of the SBA's services for women.

The SBA has numerous programs of management assistance. Small business development centers (SBDCs) cater to start-ups and early-stage businesses and operate in conjunction with over five hundred local colleges and economic development agencies. Small Business Institutes (SBIs) are also based at colleges and universities but work with established businesses on market surveys, new product analyses, etc. The SBA also sponsors SCORE (Service Corps of Retired Executives) as well as ACE (Active Corps of Executives). Both these groups, made up of professional businesspeople, consult with new businesses on all facets of business training and management.

The SBA also publishes an extensive list of free and for-sale business advice booklets. Your library probably has most of them. If not, contact your nearest SBA office for information.

There is also the SBA Small Business Answer Desk, established in 1988, with two phone numbers. Call (800)368–5855 for a voice-response computer system that gives out information on start-ups, financing, SBA services, local assistance (if you punch in your area code), and business data. It can also put you through to a counselor who can answer questions about the SBA's guaranteed (7-A) loan program, the direct (504) loan program, and a wide variety of other queries. To bypass the computer and reach a counselor directly, call (202)653–7562 between 8:30 A.M. and 5:00 P.M., eastern standard (or daylight saving) time.

The American Woman's Economic Development Center (60 East Forty-second Street, Suite 405, New York, New York 10165, [212]692–9100 or [800]222–AWED) and the National Association of Women Business Owners (600 South Federal Street, Suite 400, Chicago, Illinois 60605, [312]922–0465) both offer counseling programs assisting women entrepreneurs—including seminars on various phases of business management, consultation on obtaining loans, advice, and specialized assistance.

The Economic Development Administration (EDA) of the U.S. Department of Commerce has research and development centers in a number of cities across the country, to provide management and technical assistance to small business owners. They also help in finding capital and in developing loan packages. The EDA works with universities to provide free assistance in setting up businesses. For information, call their hotline: (800)424–5197.

OMBE (Office of Minority Business Enterprise, U.S. Department of Commerce, Washington, D.C. 20230, [202]377–2000) funds several hundred regional business development offices, providing management, training, and technical services and occasionally holds regional conferences for minority women in business.

Many banks and large accounting firms offer booklets and free assistance to anyone starting a business. Consult your local Yellow Pages for listings.

Many cities have women's business development centers to aid women business owners. Check your state and local chambers of commerce for information on any WBDCs in your area, or check with your state's department of commerce and industry.

Trade associations, especially those composed of small companies, offer assistance programs, as do some large corporations, as a public relations gesture. To find trade journals and newsletters in your field, see *The Encyclopedia of Associations* (Gale Research Company), available at your library. For specialized information pertaining to business periodicals for particular industries, check the library for *Magazines for Libraries,* published by the R. R. Bowker Company.

Universities and many community colleges are a good source of advice, and many offer lecture series and courses in entrepreneurship. Several of the entrepreneurial magazines also offer videotapes on all aspects of business management, as well as booklets on how to start myriad types of businesses, and regular articles and advice columns on business start-ups and management (see the bibliography, under periodicals, for names and addresses).

Suppliers of your business equipment, inventory, or raw materials are key sources of useful information. As a goodwill gesture, they will become your grapevine of news on your competitors (their prices, new products, expansion plans) and can tell you of new businesses coming to town, national ad campaigns, etc. Suppliers are knowledgeable about styles and types of fixtures, what kind of work load certain equipment will take, what's selling in New York and growing moss in Minneapolis. Wholesale suppliers can advise you about inventory (how much you need, the breakdown of sizes, colors, and styles) for your shop. But keep your eyes open. Even though she is out to win you as a repeat customer, the salesperson selling you equipment for your shop, office, factory, or restaurant may try to oversell. Know what you need in advance by talking to owners of similar businesses. The most important thing to remember when dealing with suppliers: *ask and listen.* And negotiate prices. Get several opinions before settling on a supplier.

Sometimes, groups of small business owners gather for informal meetings and exchange of advice. The National Association of Women Business Owners currently has chapters in thirty cities and six statewide areas across the country. Talk to other women entrepreneurs and find out what organizations they belong to. Form a women's business group in your community if none exists.

Still another valid source of advice is entrepreneurs in another city who are in the same business as you. You can pay them an agreed-upon fee to visit them and study their methods, routines, and time-saving devices. Or, arrange an exchange program with a female entrepreneur from a different area: have her come to observe you for a day or so and give advice, then you do the same.

Finally, refer to part IV of this book for a listing of books, services, and organizations that aid women entrepreneurs. Check your local library and bookstores for all available up-to-date reading matter on your type of business. With entrepreneurship booming, there are books and magazine articles on all facets of company management as well as how to start all types of businesses.

ESTIMATING YOUR COSTS

After defining precisely what your business is going to do and before you consult with anyone else, figure out approximately what it's going to cost to get your plan on its feet. Estimate *all* your expenses—rent, operating cash, equipment and fixtures, parts and materials, starting inventory/raw materials, office supplies, decorating and remodeling, installation of equipment, deposits for utilities, legal and professional fees, licenses and permits, insurance, estimated taxes, salaries and payroll taxes, advertising and promotion, cleaning service, etc.

Be diligent about obtaining current prices so that your estimate will be accurate. Determine all your expenses for the entire first year. No business can expect to make a profit right away, and you have to begin with enough money to be able to ride out the dry periods without being thrown.

Starting on a Shoestring

Many small businesses, especially services, begin on a tight budget by keeping overhead, furnishings, equipment, and operating expenses down to the bone. This involves working from home or renting an inexpensive space (i.e., in an out-of-the-way location); buying secondhand office furniture and machines, or leasing equipment; avoiding regular employees by hiring temporary people only when needed, or by taking in partners.

Other small businesses, such as retail stores or restaurants or manufacturing companies, require substantial financing. They must pay for expensive equipment, for higher rent in a prime location, or for a space with many thousands of square feet. There are usually high initial costs for remodeling (building partitions, installing additional plumbing and electrical outlets, conforming to building code or board of health requirements, etc.). Expensive equipment and fixtures are basic requirements: air-conditioning, refrigeration units, adequate lighting, display cases, to mention a few. The furnishings, lighting, and decor must provide an attractive ambience. In addition, there are heavier costs for inventory or supplies, insurance, advertising, and the like.

Stores and small manufacturers also require additional capital to help them over seasonal slumps. If you anticipate all of these varying costs in the beginning, you won't be forced to shut down six months later because of undercapitalization.

Business Incubators (or Business Development Centers)

The newest boon to aspiring entrepreneurs is the business incubator.* There are hundreds of these nonprofit or for-profit incubators now. They are designed specifically for start-ups and provide low-rent office or retail space, shared business services, and counseling to help you grow.

Incubators are buildings (often in low-rent districts) with affordable space for a number of independent start-ups. The shared-cost services include (depending upon the incubator):

*For information, contact the National Business Incubator Association (NBIA), Ohio University Innovation Center, One President Street, Athens, Ohio 45701, (614)593–4388, and Canada Business Incubator Association, c/o Jeune Chambre de Commerce, The Montreal Inc., 555, boulevard Dorchester ouest Bureau, Suite 1100, Montreal, Quebec, Canada, H2Z 1B1, (514)866–5226.

consultants, receptionists, typing and secretarial services, phone systems, computers, photocopying and facsimile machines, notary public, translation services, conference rooms, business reference libraries, shipping/mailing/ receiving rooms, child day-care centers, and coffee shops.

Sound too good to be true? They have indeed become the equivalent of fairy godmothers to aspiring entrepreneurs. What's more, they're helping new enterprises beat the statistics of high business failure: most incubators have a success rate of over 80 percent! Many even provide in-house funding that will help you raise the capital you need to get started.

The downside: once your business is on its feet, you will be expected to "leave home" and make room for another fledgling business. (The time you are allowed to remain in an incubator varies, but it is generally up to three years.) By that time, though, both you and your business will be on solid ground and able to cope with the rents and expenses of the real world.

Because of their enormous success, most incubators have waiting lists, so you may be forced to postpone your start-up until a space is available. And a warning: the SBA's Office of Private Sector Initiative cautions that many privately owned incubators may be nothing more than industrial parks offering a few shared services for their tenants, but no counseling or financial assistance. So when you find an incubator, talk to the other tenants as well as the management, and make sure that the incubator provides all the services you want.

Sharing Office Space

If there's no business incubator in your area, or if there's a long waiting list, consider sharing an office suite in a prestigious location with other small business owners. In that way, you can share the expenses of a secretary or receptionist and reception area, a telephone system, office machines, and conference room with other professionals.

Sometimes a large corporation may have more space than it currently needs and will be willing to sublease it out under favorable terms. Place an ad in the newspaper stipulating the size space you are looking for, or ask real estate brokers if they know of any companies with extra square footage for rent.

Especially if your business relies on the image of a posh location, this may be the least expensive way to go.

Working from Home

If you work free-lance or deal in a cottage industry or service where direct customer contact is minimal, you might consider working out of your home or apartment, at least to begin with. As business grows, you will expand. Then, especially if clients begin coming to you on a regular basis, you may want to move into a more prestigious or convenient locale (or local zoning regulations may require it).

So long as you designate a specific business space, one that won't have to be set up and dismantled every day, starting off at home is often an economical and practical solution.

Many women are attracted to working at home because they will be saving money on the high cost of commercial rent. For women with children a home office is also an ideal situation. They can close the office doors to family interruptions, yet still be available when needed. However, if you work at home, you have to like *being* at home. Many people get cabin fever when working and living in the same quarters.

Aside from personal considerations, there are certain businesses where a high level of professionalism must be maintained. Working from home may be wrong for your business image or the type of client you want to attract. If your home office is in the suburbs, expect to find some clients who may not want to travel far for consultations or don't particularly like wading through a kitchen, garage, or family room to get to your desk.

As for the legalities of working from home, check into your local zoning laws to make sure you are situated in an area where you can operate a business from a private residence and where you will be allowed to display a sign, if necessary. Consult your local city and county authorities regarding licenses and permits required for your particular enterprise—for example, the board of health for food-related businesses. Talk to your insurance agent about any additional coverage you may need for your home office and its equipment.

The primary concerns for working at home are privacy and adequate work and storage space. Dusting the breakfast crumbs off the dining-room table and then hauling out the typewriter is a bad idea from an organizational, functional, and legal point of view.

Current federal tax law stipulates that in order to qualify for a home office deduction, "the portion of your home that you have allocated for your business purposes must be used exclusively and regularly for your business or employment."*

Many successful entrepreneurs have launched multimillion-dollar companies out of their homes. One woman started a computer business out of her second bedroom; another opened an ad agency in her garage. It can be an inconvenience to the rest of the family, but it can be done. Sometimes—if you have very limited start-up capital, for instance—it's the *only* way to start your business.

What to Spend on Rent

You want to keep rent as low as possible. One rule of thumb to go by: rent for *retail or service* businesses shouldn't run more than 10 percent of projected gross sales. For *wholesale and manufacturing,* your rent should not exceed 5 percent of projected gross sales. This figure should include maintenance, taxes, insurance, and janitorial expenses.

Selecting a Profitable Location
for an Office or Storefront

Opening a store or other business in which image and convenience are prerequisites for success requires planning.† Look around. Don't grab the first space you see because the landlord says three other people are panting to sign the lease. And remember, the most charming nook overlooking a flowered courtyard might as well be in Italy if no one can find it. Don't depend on word-of-mouth advertising. Unless you're selling gold bullion at a 50 percent discount, you are not going to attract a steady flow

---

*For additional information, see *Business Use of Your Home* (Internal Revenue Publication no. 587, $.35), available from your local IRS, or Superintendent of Documents, U.S. Government Printing Office, Washington, D.C. 20402.
†See the SBA booklets: *Choosing a Retail Location* (General Management, no. MP 10, $1); and *Locating or Relocating Your Business,* by Fred I. Weber, Jr. (Management Aids, no. 2.002).

of traffic by being chicly inaccessible. Aim to find the best space you can afford, smack dab in the center of the business action.

The type of business also influences your choice of location. If you deal with other businesses or depend on a heavy lunch hour trade, then the downtown business district is your target. A friendly little neighborhood bakery should be in the middle of a friendly little neighborhood; a college bookstore near the college. Or maybe you need the hubbub and clientele of a shopping center or mall to sell your wares. Match the location to the customers you want to attract, making sure you are near public transportation and adequate parking facilities. If you will be open at night, check for good lighting. Make sure there is access for the handicapped.

High-traffic areas mean higher rents, but they bring in more money, too. It's generally foolish to choose a second-rate location, unless your business is offering something so unique and necessary that people will flock to you no matter where you are. Talk to your banker and other business colleagues who know about profitable locations before making your final decision.

If you are renting a storefront, obtain the occupancy history of the location. Find out why stores have failed there in the past. Was the failure linked to the location or due to other circumstances? Talk to adjoining or nearby business owners.

After you've considered your locational requirements, explore all the available rentals to satisfy your spatial requirements. You obviously want the most square feet for your money, but the layout is just as important. It must be a workable space with room to accommodate all your needs, whether desks and file cabinets or dressing rooms and display cases. Moving is expensive, so try to find a space that will last you a good long time. If you plan to make additions or repairs, get your landlord's approval before you sign the lease, and then get checked out by the appropriate authorities (building inspectors, fire department, board of health, etc.) before you lift a hammer.

Study your lease (there are various types) before signing it, and have your lawyer check through the provisions. Points to be considered are:

What is your square footage? How much usable space will you be getting? (Some landlords include public space, i.e., hallways and bathrooms, in their calculations.) Finding out how a landlord measures the square footage helps you compare rents.

Who owns or pays for any structural changes made to the property, both during the lease and at its termination?

How long is the lease, and what are the provisions for renewal? How much will your rent increase when you renew? (Try to negotiate for a short-term lease, with an option to renew for a long period of time.)

Are there any restrictions in the lease (or the zoning) that may apply to your business? (In some parts of the country you can get a protection clause in which the landlord agrees not to lease adjoining property to an identical business.)

What compensation do you have in case of fire or property condemnation?

What insurance coverage does the landlord provide, and at what amounts?

What are the provisions for subletting or assigning the space? (Try to negotiate a cancellation option in case you need to vacate the premises before the lease expires.)

Who pays for what utilities—heat, air-conditioning, electricity? Who pays for repairs?

Does the landlord provide parking spaces? Janitorial services? Garbage collection? Handicapped access?

What happens if the landlord goes broke? Make sure your lease has a standard "recognition" or nondisturbance clause.

Try to plan your opening date so that you're not paying rent without an opportunity to recover the expense. Landlords sometimes take a "hold" deposit on space, with rental starting on a specific date. You'll be required to put down the first month's rent in advance plus at least a month's rent as a security deposit, returnable to you when the lease expires (assuming you haven't left the place an irreparable shambles). Utility companies also require an initial deposit, which accrues interest.

Buying a Building

Small business owners seldom get into buying buildings unless they're going into manufacturing, starting a business incubator, or planning to house the business downstairs and live above it.

But if you are considering this alternative, have a lawyer negotiate the deal and the buying price. This includes examination and certification of the deed to make sure that you are really buying what you are paying for. In addition, you must have the premises inspected for termites, faulty wiring, plumbing, heating and air-conditioning, etc. Make sure the building is in an area zoned for the type of business you plan to run.

An Office Abroad

For a reasonable per diem fee, small and medium-sized businesses may set up offices in foreign cities around the world. The U.S. Department of Commerce has launched a program setting aside office space at government trade centers abroad. The fee covers office space with typewriters and telephones, access to telecommunications, and areas where marketing displays can be set up.

The program is called the Product Marketing Service. Users of this service must alert the government three months ahead of their intended visits. The department will also arrange for secretarial help and will provide interpreters for an additional fee. For details, contact your nearest Department of Commerce district office. (And see chapter 16 for more information on expanding your business globally.)

ANTICIPATING YOUR OPENING

Equipment and Furnishings

By now, if you've tried to figure out exactly what equipment you'll need to start, you're probably tearing your hair out. If you've signed on with a business incubator or are sharing office equipment with other small businesses, then you're in better shape. The problem is, in these fast-paced, high-tech times, how can you possibly differentiate what you absolutely *need*—to help you run a more steamlined, efficient business—from what you can do without?

In the old days (not very long ago) one bought a typewriter and a few file cabinets and that was that. Now you have to sort out the vast telecommunications systems available to help you save time and make money (and the more money they save you in terms of efficiency, the more money they'll cost you up front). The variety of high-tech paraphernalia—telephone systems, computers, software, facsimile machines, and photocopiers, etc.—offered now is mind-boggling. It's enough to send any self-respecting entrepreneur back under the covers, trembling. But the nightmare won't go away. It needs to be interpreted.

The right equipment can pay for itself: it can save you hours of work. To get an idea of what you will need, consider these questions: Where will you be working (home, office, etc.)? How much space will you have? How many employees—right away *and* later on? What will your business be mostly based on: phone calls, writing, accounting and bookkeeping, lists of clients? What chores will be the most time-consuming? What kind of wiring or rewiring will be needed for installation? What can you afford to spend?

Make a list of the kinds of equipment you think you'll need most. Usually a personal computer heads the list, because it will immediately take care of word processing, accounting and financial spreadsheets, inventory, database management of client lists, etc. If you're going into retail, then obviously cash registers (computerized) will be necessary. But perhaps you won't need a fax machine right away and will be able to make do with a tabletop copier (you can always go out and have a large copying company do your color copies and reductions, if those things won't be everyday necessities).

Think in terms of getting by with the least amount of equipment you'll need; just make sure that everything you do get can be upgraded and expanded when the time comes.

The next thing to consider in terms of office equipment is how you'll afford it. What would be most advantageous for you—renting, buying, leasing, or using someone else's equipment (a fax station, photocopier, or business development center)?

Equipment—Buying versus Leasing

With the constantly changing tax laws, don't try to weigh the tax advantages of leasing vs. buying. There are some tax advantages to each. The most important thing to decide is whether a purchase or lease deal makes economic sense for your business start-up; if you also accrue tax benefits, so much the better. (Your accountant can advise you on up-to-the-minute tax laws concerning equipment deductions and depreciation.)

For long-term use, it is more practical to own your equipment. New equipment lasts longer than used, and also increases the fixed assets of your business. But with technology changing so rapidly, do you want to risk sinking a bundle on computers that may be considered Edsels a few years down the road? It's a hard business decision that cannot be made hastily. Expect to spend a lot of time looking at available equipment and evaluating it. If you decide to buy your equipment, make sure what you purchase can be expanded or upgraded when the time comes. Most large computer retailers (Computerland, Radio Shack, Entré Computer Centers, Sears Roebuck Business Systems Centers, etc.) have consultants on staff available to figure out the needs of your particular business. There are also independent computer consultants who can come in and design a high-tech office for you, based on your budget.

Sometimes you can assess brands of merchandise by renting on a short-term basis before sinking your earnings into a permanent purchase. But there are drawbacks to this, too. Unless you are a high-tech expert, it takes time to learn to use different machines to their full capabilities, and you may not want to spend so much time before making your decision.

Leasing* (everything from computers to laboratory equipment) will allow potential savings over buying or renting, and is often attractive to new or small businesses. By leasing you can get equipment immediately, with no money down and reasonable monthly payments. When the lease expires, you have the option of buying the equipment or returning it to the lessor. This means you don't get stuck with obsolete equipment.

Leasing also allows the financing to be tied to the life of the machine(s), and therefore frees up your business's capital. (Leasing doesn't affect the long-term debt or equity status of your company.) However, leasing is generally considered viable if you are planning to use your equipment for only five years before replacing it. Owning equipment is considered more advantageous if you plan to use the equipment for a longer period of time. Also, if your business falters after a couple of years you will still be responsible for the equipment for the length of the lease.

*See the SBA booklet *Should You Lease or Buy Equipment?* by Paul Lerman (Management Aids, no. 2.014, $.50).

There is also a new sort of leasing called venture leasing.* The venture lessor will rent equipment to a brand new company in return for a percentage of the company's equity. The drawbacks are that they charge high rentals and will not generally lease to companies that haven't already been funded by venture capitalists. On the other hand, banks and traditional leasing companies won't often deal with business start-ups.

Other factors to consider in leasing: being stuck with obsolete equipment, problems with repair and maintenance, the value of the equipment or machinery at the end of the lease agreement. There are various leasing agreements available: operating; net/financial; sale lease-back; automobile. Make sure you understand the differences between them before you agree to any deal.

New Equipment versus Used

When buying, consider secondhand office furnishings to save money, or talk to suppliers about arranging payment terms. Often you can find decent used furnishings at going-out-of-business sales (check the newspapers for announcements), auctions, flea markets, secondhand shops, even garage (tag) sales. Remember, you can acquire additional paraphernalia as you go along, so don't go overboard before you discover what you really need. Take it a file cabinet at a time. Before making major purchases, shop around for ideas as well as bargains.

The same advice applies to other office, restaurant, or store fixtures, not to mention decorative trappings such as ficus trees and wall-to-wall carpeting. Not that you have to resort to wooden orange crates, but better that than blowing your capital on a setting right out of *Architectural Digest.* Ingenuity can do more for your image than going into debt for the sake of authentic elegance. Clients and other businesspeople, including lenders, are impressed by a lean business that spends its money only on necessities that will improve profitability.

When it comes to computers† and fax machines, etc., should

*For a list of companies that do venture leasing, see "Gearing Up," by Ellyn E. Spragins, *Inc.,* October 1989.
†For information about used computers, see your local computer retail stores, computer users' groups, ads in local newspapers, or write: Boston Computer Exchange, P.O. Box 1177, Boston, Massachusetts 02103, (800)262–6399. See also the SBA booklet, *How to Get Started with a Small Business Computer,* by Michael M. Stewart and Alan C. Shulman (Management Aids, no. 2.027, $1).

you consider buying used equipment? Well, no and yes. You can save 50 percent or more on used equipment. But you get what you pay for. Fax machines, for example, have gone through four generations since their introduction in 1981. That means an old one probably isn't cost efficient because it simply won't do all the things that you'll expect it to. And the same applies to computers. The old bulky ones take up a lot more space than the new ones. And although an old machine may work fine in terms of word processing or bookkeeping, will it be compatible with the newer machines that you'll eventually want to acquire to accommodate the newer, faster, quieter printers and more advanced small business software?

It depends on the machine; you'll have to check it out thoroughly. It's true that they're practically giving away computers that cost many thousands of dollars five years ago. But are they really a bargain? Some are; some aren't. Check with a computer expert or consultant, friends, and other business owners before you make your decision. If a used machine does everything you need it to, then it might make sense to choose it, since even brand new ones will be obsolete before you blink three times.

OFFICE EQUIPMENT

You'll need specialized machinery to knead the dough for your bakery, ventilate your restaurant, take electrocardiograms at your health-care facility, etc. But every business has a central office that runs things, regardless of what the business actually does. And to run this office as efficiently as possible you'll need to know what exists out there to help you. As stated before, in this high-tech world there's more available than ever before in history. Things are changing fast, however, and you'll have to research the field like crazy before you buy, rent, or lease anything.

Telephones

For any entrepreneur, the telephone forms the hub of her business. Nothing can get done without it. Now, however, you don't merely have telephones, you have telecommunications centers. Since the divestiture of AT&T in 1981, it's become a free-for-all out there in telephoneland.

What will your business need when it comes to telecommunications technology? Often, when you start out, it's little more than one or two phones connected to one or two lines. But the decisions that have to be made have not only to do with what long-distance carrier your business will use. (Talk to AT&T, MCI, and US Sprint; they each have competitive services for small businesses, including 800 numbers [inbound service] and WATS lines [outbound service]. Get all the specifics before choosing one over the other.)

Your local phone company also offers myriad telephonic goodies for the small businessperson: call holding, call forwarding, call blocking, call transfer, three-way calling, call waiting, call pickup, voice mail, hunting, call tracing, call accounting, call selecting, auto callback, to name a few. Fortunately, all local phone companies have representatives available to advise small businesses on the services they can provide. But it's up to you alone to decide what's worth the money. In addition, some companies like BellSouth provide public relational workshops for small businesses, in conjunction with the SBA, that can help you with everything from writing a business plan to managing cash flow.

Do you want to rent the equipment, or buy? And who will be responsible for the repair and maintenance: you or the phone company?

Then there are the phones themselves. Some are mini-computer information centers; some have fax, copying, or answering machines attached; some have video screens; many will speed-dial (or automatically redial) preprogrammed numbers for you. Some instruments look straight out of 3001; others resemble McDonald's burgers and Lego blocks; still others are sleek designer models. There are cellular mobile phones (either hand-held or for cars), portable phones, cordless phones, speaker phones, headsets, intercom phones. . . .

And it's all up to you to decide what you need and how much you want to spend. Don't be too dazzled. Try to remember your resolution to operate a business that's run close to the bone.

Answering Machines, etc.

If you are free-lance or planning to work in and out of your office, you must invest in something or someone that will take calls for you when you're away from your desk. There are several alternatives besides a receptionist: an automatic answering machine, an answering service that picks up on your line, and the newest thing on the scene: the telephone company's voice-mail system.

The answering machine can come with its own phone or not, depending on what you want. It plays your prerecorded message to callers, and allows them to record their message. Some models enable you to call in from anywhere to pick up your messages.

Professional answering services that hook up to your telephone vary widely in price and quality, according to the hours you use them. Most services that offer bargain rates are usually basement quality, providing rude or indifferent personnel who give you scrambled messages. When you shop around for services, compare friendliness as well as prices. You usually pay more for charm and accuracy, but your business's image depends on it.

The telephone company's voice-mail system, the most expensive alternative for a small business, acts like a home-answering system. It allows you to record outgoing messages and receive incoming telephone messages in your own private "mailbox." This complex system will also enable voices, video, and data to be transmitted simultaneously over the same telephone line.

Computers—Hardware and Software

Computers. They're necessary to business, expensive (if you need to supply monitors and printers and modems to numerous employees), and they go out of date very fast. In addition, there are thousands of hardware manufacturers and software programs to chose from. How do you pick the right one for *your* business? And how do you and your staff learn to use it to its fullest capabilities? No wonder the new entrepreneur can contract computer anxiety syndrome before she even opens her doors for business.

For a start, computer retail stores have experts available to advise you. There are also private computer consultants* (who are knowledgeable but may be too expensive for a small business). Look into computer users' groups,† which offer (depend-

*To find a computer consultant, ask your local retail computer stores, or write: Association for Women in Computing, 134 West Thirty-second Street, New York, New York 10001, (212)244–4270; or ADAPSO, the Computer Software and Services Industry Association, 1300 North Seventeenth Street, Arlington, Virginia 22203, (703)522–5055.
†To find a computer users' group in your area, check newspaper ads or retail

ing on the size of the group): a hotline for trouble-shooting software programs; discounts on hardware and software purchases; classes for beginners and experts; a library of software, hardware, and books; and a newsletter updating the newest information. Ask friends and business acquaintances, but remember that they may be perfectly happy with a computer system that's not right for *you*. Take a computer class in a computer-equipped classroom. Ask members of your trade association what equipment they use. And read (regularly) both computer and entrepreneurial publications for the latest technology and software geared to small business owners.

The choices are staggering, enough to make you want to bite the bytes. Besides monochrome, one-color, or full-color displays, hard disks and floppy disks, laptops, keyboards, LANs (local area networks for computer intercommunication), and the various types of printers (including daisy wheel, dot matrix, and laser), there are mice and trackballs, modems,* graphics tablets, scanners, and much more.

There are software programs that will do: word processing and correct your spelling; financial spreadsheets and bookkeeping; small business accounting; mail-merge; flat-file data bases; graphing; inventory tracking; billing; check writing; date-book organizing; etc. And the desktop publishing software that's available enables you to have your own printshop: you can design and print everything from professional-quality brochures and booklets to stationery, newsletters, and presentations.

It's all out there to help you, but the costs mount up. Do your homework thoroughly before buying or leasing. Don't go overboard. Get what you need *now,* with an eye toward compatible add-ons later. Deal only with reputable companies. (Talk to some of their customers; get a list of referrals.) Make sure that what you

---

computer stores. Groups with a national following include: The Boston Computer Society, (617)367–8080; the Capital PC User Group, in Rockville, Maryland, (301)762–6775; and BMUG Inc., Berkeley Macintosh Users' Group, Berkeley, California, (415)549–2684.

*Modems attached to your computer have numerous purposes. You can: type and send messages over phone lines to other computers that have modems; deliver messages through designated E-Mail services (available from AT&T, MCI, and Western Union); subscribe to marketing data services (such as Dialog, NewsNet, Nexis, Compuserve, Dow Jones News/Retrieval). These services take the place of an in-house research team, and provide info and articles on specific industries and businesses, compiled from newspapers, magazines, and investment analyst reports.

get comes with training and a user support system, a good warranty, and a dealer nearby to take care of repair and maintenance.

Additional Office Equipment

Besides a personal computer and a good library of small business software programs, there are other items that you may (or may not) need, depending on the size and scope of your business.

Electronic typewriters have not gone out of date. In fact, the newer ones have many advanced features that rival those of a word processor. There are many times when you can save on a computer's complexity by typing envelopes, filling out forms, or writing a quick note or letter with a typewriter.

Facsimile (fax) machines transmit documents over the telephone to a fax machine at the other end. They are the wave of the future as more and more businesses are getting their own fax machines. But if you don't think you'll fax material more than a few times a week, then—at least in the beginning—it would make more sense to use a public fax station. They charge more per copy, but they have the technical expertise. If, later on, you decide that you can't live without your own fax, consider the fax/telephone or fax/copier/telephone combinations, to save space. When you buy, get the latest equipment and make sure that it can be programmed to lock out junk-fax mail. Make sure you locate the fax in the most convenient spot for all users, and establish guidelines for disseminating messages.

Copiers are smaller, cheaper, and have more features than ever, including color copying, image editing, and reduction/enlargement. For the small business, there are personal copiers that fit on a desk or countertop and are reasonable in price. If you need larger or faster copying capabilities, consider renting or leasing from a major company, or—in the beginning—frequenting a copy center.

High-speed calculators and *voice-activated microcassette recorders* are two other necessary office machines. The latter is ideal for letter dictation, or jotting verbal memos to yourself when you're in a hurry.

Videotape recorders, depending on your business, may be necessary for giving selling presentations, or for in-house training and communications.

Make sure that you catalog every piece of equipment you own, with its serial number, model number, and date of purchase. In addition, keep track of repairs and maintenance service.

Service Contracts

Whenever you buy a piece of equipment, the salesperson will try to interest you in a service contract that takes over when the warranty expires. Service contracts are expensive; for them to be cost-efficient your equipment will have to break down often. In many cases service contracts aren't necessary, because replacement parts may cost you much less than an annual service contract.

Some equipment is more prone to break down than others, or is more expensive to repair on a per-job basis. Portable desktop computers rarely need a service contract, but if your business expands to a mainframe computer, then you'll need a contract with a guaranteed response time. Large office copiers probably need a service contract, but small personal copiers don't. Depending on the complexity of your telephone system, you'll have to determine whether you need some sort of service agreement. Phone systems shouldn't break down often, but they are the lifeblood of your business. Fax machines and electronic typewriters shouldn't need service contracts.

When equipment breaks down, regardless of whether you have a service contract, save money by having it repaired instead of replacing it.

Paper and Supplies

The amount and description of office supplies you need will depend on your business. But when possible, buy supplies in quantity; this lowers the cost per item. Bulk orders save time as well: think three to six months ahead when placing your orders. (The more storage space you have, the better.) Buy from discount houses to economize.

In spite of computers, the business world is inundated by paper. In fact, one unsettling statistic: paper consumption *doubles* every four years. Only 1 percent of this country's information is currently stored in computers; 4 percent is on microfilm. It can be slightly more expensive, but why not consider using high-quality recycled paper products for your business?* Many consumers appreciate it, and your company will be doing something positive toward saving the planet.

And don't throw away used paper. If one side is still blank, cut it down and recycle it for office scratch paper, message pads, and memos.

Logo, Stationery, and Business Cards

The minute you have an address and phone number, have your stationery and business cards printed. If you can't afford a freelance artist, you can design your own. All you need is access to a computer with desktop publishing software, or a steady hand, art supplies, and press type. (This is pressure-sensitive type that's transferred onto another surface. It comes in predesigned letters, numbers, decorative borders, and line drawings. There are many brands available at any good stationery or artists' supply stores.) Do a layout, and have it photostated before having it printed. Or talk to your printer, who may be able to provide ideas by showing you samples of letterheads or styles of type you may wish to use.

You may wish to have a graphic designer create an individualized logo for you, but in general it's best not to spend the extra money, at least in the beginning. If you do adopt a logo, use it on everything you have printed—stationery, shopping bags, sales checks, order forms, labels, ads, etc. In the beginning, to save money, have a rubber stamp made up with your logo to reduce printing costs.

In any case, before making any final decisions check several printers, offset printers, copy centers, or lettershops for quality (which can vary considerably) and price estimates.

The least expensive printing is called one-color, which sends the paper through the printing press only once. A one-color printing doesn't have to be black and white; it can be brown ink on buff paper, maroon ink on gray, whatever combination appeals to you. Two-color printing, considerably more expensive, means that two colors of ink are used, and the expense stems from running the paper through the presses twice. The more

*For recycled paper catalogs, write Earth Care Paper (sells to small businesses and consumers), P.O. Box 3335, Madison, Wisconsin 53704, or Conservatree Paper Company (sells to midsize and large companies), 10 Lombard Street, Suite 250, San Francisco, California 94111.

colors you use for stationery or brochures, the higher the cost.

Line drawings are simple to reproduce. If you have a clever logo, plan to stick with it, and consider having a permanent plate made so that later supplies can easily be reordered by phone. For T-shirts, have a silkscreen made that you can reuse when needed (colors can be changed when reordering).

You might also consider having second-sheet stationery printed as well, using your company name and address in small type (usually across the bottom of the page). Besides its use as a second page for business letters, it can be utilized for such things as business forms and price lists.

Paper comes in many weights, measured in pounds. For example, sixteen-pound paper weighs sixteen pounds per thousand sheets. The heavier the paper, the more expensive. Select paper that looks and feels substantial but still folds easily.

Envelopes are featured in many sizes, but the most practical are: the standard business size for letters, and a smaller size, printed with your company's name and address, to enclose in bills. The envelope size should match your stationery. Have at least three times as many business envelopes printed as stationery, because they can be used for sending checks, brochures, and other enclosures besides letters.

The larger the quantity you have printed, the less expensive it is. One hundred business cards might cost you six dollars, and five hundred only ten dollars, because once the press is set up it doesn't cost proportionately more for a longer run. Order enough supplies to last for a reasonably long time, and reorder when supplies start dwindling.

Additional Costs

The budget for additional start-up costs (inventory,* specialized manufacturing equipment and raw materials, restaurant supplies and fixtures, etc.) depends on the amount of your capitalization and the scope of your plans. Again, your future suppliers are usually willing and able to furnish good advice, based on their knowledge of, and dealings with, other small businesses in your field of operations. Take advantage of their assistance.

*See SBA booklets: *Inventory Management* (General Management, no. MP 22), and *Buying for Retail Stores* (General Management, no. MP 18, $1).

·6·

Legalities:
The Strong Arm of the Law

*If you can't give me your word of honor, will you give
me your promise?* —Samuel Goldwyn

The American business system is a mine field of laws (and
interpretations of those laws). Trying to find your way without an
expert is business suicide. *Get a lawyer*—the sooner the better. It
will cost you some money now, but it will save you in the long run.
And be professional about it; don't rely on a cocktail party brief-
ing from a lawyer friend who hasn't evaluated your particular
situation in detail. That sort of offhand advice could end up
costing you more than legal fees. Business success or failure may
hinge on your attorney's knowledge, interest, and advice.

However, remember that lawyers are busy people, and it's hard
for them to be current on your business and its status. It will be up
to you to keep your lawyer posted on both your enterprise and
changing trends or court decisions within your industry. (Read the
trade magazines to keep yourself up-to-date.) And although it will
be necessary to seek legal advice throughout your entire business
career, remember that you needn't follow that advice blindly.

Don't ever be afraid to ask questions, and keep on asking them.
It is imperative that you understand everything your lawyer tells
you. She is being paid to advise you; but don't let her tell you
what to do. Get the facts, assimilate them, weigh the pros and
cons, then make your own decisions.

This chapter will give you an overview of the legal decisions
your business will require. The information presented here is
meant only as a general guideline. It is *not intended to serve as a
substitute for legal advice,* or to make it unnecessary for you to seek

85

advice. The legal world changes rapidly. In all situations involving local, state, or federal laws, get specific information from pertinent government agencies or a qualified professional.

WHY DO YOU NEED A LAWYER?

The legal decisions start long before you open your doors for business. First off, what kind of legal entity will your business be: A sole proprietorship? Partnership? Corporation? Your attorney can brief you on the merits and drawbacks in your case and draw up the proper papers. Then there are business laws, taxes, contracts, leases, licenses, labor, and dozens of other potential headaches that aspirin won't cure.

Other considerations may apply to your business as well: health permits, federal employee identification number (EIN), Occupational Safety and Health Administration (OSHA) requirements; regulations covering hazardous material; zoning laws; local ordinances on signs, snow removal, etc.; federal tax code provisions concerning small business; federal regulations on withholding taxes and social security; sales tax regulations; and state Worker's Compensation laws, to name a few.

Setting up a business haphazardly can be ruinous. In terms of time and money lost, hasty decisions are sometimes irrevocable. Suddenly discovering that there are taxes or licenses you weren't aware of, for which you now owe—with penalties for neglect tacked on—can run you right out of your working capital. This is not meant to scare you off, just to alert you to potential problems.

Aim toward establishing a continuing relationship with your lawyer. She should be knowledgeable and interested in your success and remain on the lookout for changing laws and license requirements that can affect your business. All through your business life your lawyer will be a soothing presence in the background, available for both crises and routine legal matters.

CHOOSING AN ATTORNEY

With so much at stake, you want to find the right person. A woman may be more in tune with your wavelength, but the most important requisite is to find someone interested in your project and knowledgeable about the type of business you're starting.

86

Shop around. Ask friends, business associates, owners of similar businesses, suppliers, trade associations, your accountant, banker, or local women's business association. Or contact the women's bar association in your state. You might also consult professors at nearby law or business schools, or librarians at law libraries.

Lawyers specialize in different fields: taxes, corporations, patents, litigation, criminal proceedings, and so on. Find one well versed in the problems of small business.

You'll have to decide what size law firm to deal with, too. There are large ones, with partners and junior partners and paralegals in abundance, and homey two-person operations where they empty their own wastebaskets. The big firms may offer you a wider range of expertise; the small make you feel more comfortable (and may offer everything you will ever need). Choose someone who comes well recommended, someone you trust.

Discuss fees up front. You won't have to put a lawyer on retainer, but you will have to pay for all the time she spends on you (lawyers keep time sheets including telephone calls), even for that initial session to discuss your business.

Before you do anything, reach an understanding as to how you'll be charged. Most lawyers charge an *hourly fee* that will depend on where she practices and her degree of skill. It runs generally from $50 to $150 per hour, plus expenses. Sometimes, however, a lawyer will charge you a *flat fee* for a specific job, such as incorporating your business, drawing up a specific contract, or representing you before a state administrative commission. This set fee is what you owe, regardless of how much time the lawyer spends. Occasionally, you can agree on a *contingent fee,* usually a percentage of a settlement negotiated through a trial. If the lawyer loses the case or recovers nothing for you, then you don't owe her anything. In general, try to get the most favorable fee structure for each particular legal job to be done.

WAYS TO SAVE ON LEGAL FEES

Get as much information for your money as possible. Before seeing your prospective lawyer, have a basic idea of the type of business structure* that is best for you. Define your business and

*See the SBA booklet *Selecting the Legal Structure for Your Firm,* by Antonio M. Olmi (Management Aids, no. 6.004, $1).

your goals clearly; be as well informed as you can. Come armed with all necessary papers (including your written business plan) that your lawyer should look at. Prepare a list of questions or points you want to cover during the initial session. That way you won't waste time and money going over basics you should already know. Also, this thorough preparation will help you evaluate the quality of the advice you're getting.

If you will need legal forms or contracts for operating your business, save money by having your lawyer design standard forms that can be used for all routine matters. Sometimes you can hire a fresh-out-of-law-school (therefore less expensive) attorney for easy legal tasks, e.g., collecting money that's owed you. Or find someone to share legal costs with you, such as neighboring business owners, if you have grievances with your landlord, or need to seek a variance from the zoning board. And always see your lawyer during normal business hours; some lawyers charge extra for overtime, i.e., weekends or evenings. Sometimes you can save yourself both time and money by handling legal matters over the telephone.

Know what's going on in your industry; if you come to your lawyer with your homework prepared you won't have to pay for her hours of research. Regulations concerning licensing and insurance for small businesses have been loosening. Consult a professional but also do some footwork yourself. Keep up with the changing laws through your local and state government agencies, Small Business Administration and U.S. Department of Commerce district offices, chamber of commerce, women business owners' association, trade journals in your particular field, and general small business publications. The more information you can gather on your own, the lower your legal fees.

When settling on a lawyer, get a number of recommendations. Find out their fees. But don't try to save money by hiring an inexpensive attorney who may lack skills. She may take hours to draft a contract that might take an experienced, more expensive lawyer only thirty minutes.

Once you have settled on a lawyer, keep her informed about your business. And stick with her; build a business relationship. The better informed she is about you and your business, the more quickly she will be able to perform future necessary legal tasks.

LEGAL STRUCTURE FOR YOUR BUSINESS

There are three legal forms that a small business can take: individual proprietorship, partnership, or corporation.* Each has different provisions regarding taxes, management, liability of the owner, and distribution of profits.

Often a small business will begin as a proprietorship or partnership (because of the ease of setting those up) and then later, when the business has grown, file for incorporation. The following is an explanation of the three business structures, to give you a preliminary glance at the pros and cons of each.

Individual Proprietorship

This is the most popular structure with entrepreneurs starting small businesses. It means that you are the high lama of your business. You lay down your own rules and make the day-to-day managerial decisions. A sole proprietorship is the easiest structure to create and the least complicated to dissolve. It is the oldest form of business, so the laws regarding it are firmly established. A free-lancer is considered a sole proprietor, since the same legalities and taxes apply.

Legality

Sole proprietorship is very flexible. You don't need government approval, although you must check with local city and county authorities to determine whether a license for your particular business is required. Also, if you are doing business under a name other than your own, you may be required to file a dba notice with the local authorities and run an announcement in the newspaper.

There is no legal time limit for a proprietorship. The business automatically ends when you stop doing it.

Liability

As sole owner you are *personally* liable for all business debts, to the extent of *your entire personal holdings* (your house, car, stocks,

*Other specialized forms of legal structures (but not considered necessary for small businesses) are joint stock companies, syndicates, pools, and Massachusetts trusts.

etc.). In addition, you don't have the full tax benefits of the tax-deductible plans (including pension and profit sharing) that are available to a corporation. Additional liability, such as personal injury lawsuits, may be lessened by getting proper insurance coverage.

Administration

All policy and day-to-day operations rest with you, as owner-manager. You're in full charge, in complete control of organization and profits.

Pitfalls

Many single ownerships fail because the person at the helm should *not* be steering alone. The business may sink from inexperience, inept management, or undercapitalization. And if something such as illness happens to you, the business could fall by the wayside.

Taxes

The business profits will be taxed as personal income. In addition, many states levy a state income tax on profits from an unincorporated business; so do some cities and counties. (Check with your local tax bureau, a tax attorney, or your accountant.) Individual proprietors have to pay federal self-employment (FICA) tax for social security coverage, and if they have employees they must also withhold and pay employment taxes. (If you hire any of your children, under age eighteen, you don't have to withhold or pay FICA for them; if you employ your spouse, then you do have to pay.) Obtain a federal employer identification number by filing Form SS-4 with the Internal Revenue Service district office where you will be paying your taxes. You will not need Worker's Compensation and disability insurance for yourself (because single proprietors are owners, not employees). (For more tax information, see chapter 15.)

Raising Money

A sole proprietor can raise money to begin or expand her business by borrowing, purchasing on credit, or investing her own money in the business.

Since you are solely responsible for your business debts, potential moneylenders will evaluate your personal wealth to provide collateral for the loan. For that reason, there is less available capital than in other types of business structure, and difficulty in obtaining long-term financing.

If you are considering a business that, by its very nature, will require a large investment in equipment or inventory to operate successfully, then you should probably not consider sole ownership.

Partnership

A partnership consists of *two or more* owners of a business. Although more complex than a sole proprietorship, a partnership is easy to set up and to terminate.

At the outset, the partners should (for their own protection—it is not legally required) write up an agreement stipulating intentions: how much money and/or property each partner is putting into the business; each partner's duties, rights, tax/expense/debt obligations, and share of income (or loss); what will happen in the event of death, illness, bankruptcy, retirement, or disenchantment of one of the partners, etc. An arbitrator should be agreed on and designated in advance in case irreconcilable differences arise between the partners. Even if your business's attorney does not write up this agreement, you should have her check it to make sure it covers all the bases. Your personal lawyer should also look at it to make sure *you* are thoroughly protected.

This agreement should also include a buy-sell clause. Under the partnership law in many states, the death of one of the partners automatically ends the partnership, unless the partnership agreement stipulates otherwise. The buy-sell agreement states what will happen in this event and which partners will buy the deceased partner's share, as well as a formula for determining the price. The partners should take out an insurance policy to fund this possibility. (The policy is not tax deductible.)

Legality
There is the same operating flexibility as in a proprietorship, except you have to determine clearly which partner will do what. There are no federal requirements for starting, although you must check with your city/county/state to see if a business license is needed. A partnership ends upon dissolution by the partners or the withdrawal of any one of the partners (unless there is a written agreement stating otherwise).

Some states require that partners file a Certificate of Conducting Business as Partners, which identifies all partners by name. This must be filed with either the local county clerk or the state. If the partnership is working under a fictitious name, then a dba (doing business as) form is required by some states.

Liability

The partners, or at least one designated partner, are responsible—and personally liable—for all business debts, the same as in a sole proprietorship. In a partnership, each member can bind the other so that one partner can cause the other to be personally liable. Also, there are not the tax advantages of benefit plans, such as pensions and profit sharing, that are available to corporations.

Administration

Each partner has an equal responsibility, with the various operating functions divvied up. The combined abilities and experience of two or more owners give the business a stronger chance of succeeding. New concepts and business policies need only an oral agreement by the partners before going into effect.

Pitfalls

The disadvantages are obvious, regardless of whether the partnership is made up of business acquaintances, friends, family members, or spouses. Each partner has to carry her own weight in the new business or major conflicts will arise. Many partnerships have dissolved over disagreements on basic business policies. And barring dissolution, the bad blood caused by these conflicts can make daily operations intolerable.

For this business structure to work, the partners must respect each other's talent and contribution to the business. They must be compatible and confident that they are working toward a mutual goal. They must be willing to settle differences before they escalate, and able to make personal compromises for the greater good of the business.

Taxes

The partners are taxed separately on their individual returns, as if they were proprietors. The business itself files a tax return that lists the income and loss of the partnership, although it pays no tax. Partners pay self-employment tax for social security benefits.

Each partner is fully responsible, and liable, for all debts and taxes incurred by the business, regardless of the amount of her investment in the business (with the exception of *limited partnerships,* covered below). Some cities/counties/states require a tax on unincorporated businesses, so the profits from the business are taxed. Check with your tax attorney or accountant.

Raising Money

It is easier for two or more people to raise money for their business than just one. There is more money to begin with if each partner chips in (either money or property), and the combined resources of the partners can make up the collateral when they apply for a loan or look for investors. Because of their liability for business debts, a partnership may be granted better borrowing terms than some small corporations. This full liability often makes outsiders more willing to extend credit, although long-term financing is sometimes harder to obtain.

Limited Partnerships

A limited partnership allows you to limit the liability of one or more of the partners, to the extent of the amount of *money they have invested* in the business. (Limited partners are required to invest either cash or tangible property; they cannot contribute services as an investment.) Besides the limited partners, at least one active partner must be designated to oversee the daily operations of the business.

Legality

Limited partnerships are more complicated to set up, since a legal written contract is required. This agreement is technical and must be drafted by your lawyer, then filed with the state according to your state's tax regulations. (Some states charge a filing fee.) This lessens the degree of flexibility, as the partnership must adhere strictly to the laws of the state in which it is organized.

Some states require you to file a Certificate of Limited Partnership, as well as a dba form if the business uses a fictitious name. There are special federal tax requirements regarding limited partnerships: consult the Internal Revenue Service, your tax lawyer, or accountant.

Administration

The limited partners are not permitted to advise in the active administration of the business. If they do, they become general partners and are thus fully liable for all business debts. Limited partners are, however, allowed complete access to information on the daily goings-on of the business, including the books and financial statements.

Raising Money

The same rules apply as those for a general partnership if additional capital is needed. The limited partners, though, are responsible only to the extent of their personal investment. In general, active partners will take on limited partners in order to raise money for their business.

Corporations

A corporation is a complete legal entity unto itself. In effect, it is an artificial human being, society's civilized monster. It can sue, buy property, and exercise many other privileges of living people. It cannot marry, but it can merge; it cannot vote, but it can influence votes; it cannot hold public office, but it can control those who do. You don't have to be a miniconglomerate to incorporate. There are many small business corporations.

Legality

A corporation must adhere formally to state laws. The scope of the company's activity, as well as its name, is restricted by a charter and is, therefore, more complex to establish than the other business structures. It must be set up according to the legal procedures of the particular state in which it is formed.* Require-

*In general, it is necessary to incorporate in the state in which you plan to do the major portion of your business. If you set up your business in another state, it will be considered a "foreign" corporation, and will have to pay additional fees/taxes. Sometimes, however, it is advantageous to incorporate in another state. For example, at this writing, many corporations are formed in Delaware because of that state's advantageous corporate laws (even though the owners may never set foot there). They hire, for an initial fee plus a minimum annual fee, a registered agent who files all necessary corporate documents. If a Delaware corporation is

ments vary from state to state, as do the filing fees, which can cost anywhere from $10 to $2,500. Legal fees for setting up a corporation generally run between $200 and $500.

In most states, it is legal to incorporate without the services of an attorney, which can save money. However, there is a great deal of work and skill involved, and unless you have confidence in your abilities along these lines, it is advisable to hire a lawyer.

To incorporate, one, two, or three people (depending upon the state) must organize and become officials in the new corporation. (In the case of a sole proprietor who decides to incorporate, the other two people do not have to be equal or active partners or major shareholders. For example, a lawyer or accountant could be designated.) Next, they file their "articles of incorporation"—which adheres to the state's information requirements—with the state's commissioner of corporations. (This includes: proposed name and main location of corporation, purposes of the corporation, names and addresses of owners and shareholders, stock type ["common" or "preferred"] and maximum amount to be issued, amount of capital required at incorporation time, plus other requirements that vary from state to state.) Afterward, a filing fee and an initial franchise tax must be paid. This must be followed by an official meeting, conducted with recorded minutes, to deal with the specific organizational and operational details.

Liability

The major advantage that corporations have over the other business structures is limited liability. The company is *generally* responsible for its debts only to the limit of its assets. Therefore you, as owner, are not liable for any of your company's debts, although you may lose what money you personally invested. (Exceptions to this would include liability incurred by the gross negligence of the owner[s].)

Termination

Since a corporation has a life of its own, the retirement, illness, or death of any of its key officials does not automatically end it.

---

not based in Delaware, then it must register in the state in which it does most of its activity as a foreign corporation and pay an initial fee, varying from state to state.

The certificates of stock, representing ownership or investments made in the business, may be transferred from one party to another without interfering with the company's operations. A corporation can be sold (through stock transfer), go bankrupt, or simply fade into the sunset (although it takes several years' worth of legal red tape for a corporation to die a natural death).

Because of the complexities involved in each method of dissolution, both your lawyer and accountant should be consulted so that it may be put to rest as painlessly as possible.

Freedom of Action

No other state is legally required to recognize a corporation except the state in which it is formed. However, every state permits out-of-state or "foreign" companies (with exceptions, such as utilities and common carriers) to do business within their borders so long as they comply with the rules and regulations of the state. This often involves filing legal documents with proper state authorities and paying specified fees and taxes. A corporation appoints (hires, actually, for a minimum fee) a representative, called a registered agent, in that state to take care of the legal red tape. To find a registered agent in the state in which you wish to do business, consult a lawyer or that state's department of commerce and industry.

Sale and exchange of corporate stock is governed by state "blue sky laws," which protect the potential investor. (The phrase was coined by a legislator who remarked that many companies sought to "capitalize the blue skies.")

The selling price of the stock relies on the current worth (assets) of the corporation. The amount of stock a person owns depends on how much money she is willing to invest in the business, according to its growth needs. The more money you invest in a new corporation, the more control you will have.

Administration

If a proprietor becomes a corporation, she does not necessarily have to lose control of her business. In many small corporations the sole proprietor can retain ownership by buying the majority of stock in the new corporation. The same applies to a partnership that becomes a corporation; the partners can divide the majority of the stock, according to the amount of capital they have each invested in the company.

Stockholders may participate in the policies and day-to-day operations of the company, but not necessarily. A corporation is not liable for the actions of its stockholders just because they have invested in it.

Pitfalls

There is extra, time-consuming paperwork in running a corporation, such as keeping the corporate records and filing additional tax returns. Also, if a corporation is run by people who own only a small percentage of the stock, there are risks, such as a "hostile takeover" (by another company, individual, or group that quietly buys up the controlling interest of stock, then takes over the company, often kicking out those who started or ran it). Another risk might be ineffective management, because those in control have very little personally at stake in the company's success or failure.

Taxes

Corporations pay taxes at different rates from individuals. The business is taxed separately, and it—rather than the owners—is liable for all the debts, one of the most favorable aspects of incorporating. But corporations can pay heavy taxes, and for a regular C corporation the income can also be taxed doubly, first as earnings and again when distributed as dividends to shareholders. (See "S Corporations," below.) Have your accountant or lawyer provide you with a calendar outlining all the responsibilities of the corporation, including the filing dates for all taxes. (See chapter 15 for additional tax information.)

Raising Money

A corporation is generally in the most advantageous position to raise capital. It can borrow by putting up corporate assets as collateral. A large corporation may start out with a "limited" stock offering and later "go public"—that is, sell stock shares to the public, to attract a wide range of investors. Money obtained from selling stock or a percentage of the company is called *equity capital.* There is no financial risk for a stockholder beyond her investment.*

*Any gain on a stockholder's investment will be taxed at preferential capital gain rates. But if a corporation elects to issue Section 1244 Small Business Corporation Stock, any loss a stockholder realizes from her investment may be deducted

However, if a corporation takes out a loan to finance its debts, the lender may require a personal guarantee from the owners. This eliminates the limited liability to the extent of the loan.

A stockholder is not liable for any of the company's debts should it go bankrupt; the only financial risk is the amount of money invested in the company.

S Corporations

The Internal Revenue Code (under the Subchapter S section) permits small business corporations to be taxed at individual rates. Thus, a closely held corporation (with fifteen shareholders or fewer) can avoid heavy corporate taxation by allowing each owner-shareholder to report her share of the company's profits (or losses, i.e., for deduction) on her personal income tax return, as is done in a partnership.

This election may be revoked at any time, and it is an ideal corporate structure for new or low-income businesses. Have a lawyer give you the specific details and S-corporation requirements as they apply to you and your business.

Corporation Filing Requirements

Many states require domestic corporations to file an annual statement identifying the company's officers and their addresses, as well as giving the corporate office address. This filing fee runs around $10.

Limited Liability Companies

Approved by the Internal Revenue Service in 1988, the limited liability company is the newest concept in business structure. It combines the individual taxation of a partnership with a corporation's limited liability, but without the special eligibility requirements of an S corporation. Unfortunately, as of now only Florida and Wyoming have adopted this business form. Check with your

---

as an ordinary loss (rather than a capital loss), to the extent of $50,000 ($100,000 on a joint return) in any tax year. To qualify for Section 1244, the stock must be "common" stock, issued only for cash or property other than stock/securities.

attorney to see where your state stands regarding this business structure.

Cooperatives

Another variation of the three standard business forms is the cooperative, a legal structure that can be set up as either a partnership or a corporation. Cooperatives are generally associated with agriculture, housing, child care, and crafts designers and artisans.*

A cooperative is created by any group of people having common economic or physical needs. The cooperative does not make money for itself. Net profit is shared among its members, according to a predetermined method of allocation. Cooperatives are managed by the members, board of directors, or, often, hired management. The cooperative is controlled democratically, usually with each member representing one vote.

A cooperative group may choose to be incorporated, or not. Some states have laws covering the incorporation of coops.† When it is incorporated, the coop members are not personally liable for any debts the cooperative incurs, and the taxes on profits are paid by the corporation.

If the group is not incorporated, it is viewed as a partnership. All members are responsible for business debts, and the profits are taxed as individual income. If your group is considering the cooperative alternative of business structure, be sure to consult an attorney.

Federal, State, and Local Licensing Requirements

Federal

Certain types of businesses engaging in interstate commerce are subject to federal regulations, licenses, and permits. Check with your lawyer or accountant, although generally these regulations do not apply to small businesses.

*For further explanation, see Program Aid Booklet no. 1001, *The Cooperative Approach to Crafts,* by Gerald Ely, published by the USDA Economic Statistics and Cooperative Service, available from the Superintendent of Documents, Government Printing Office, Washington, D.C. 20402.
†Some cooperatives incorporate under the District of Columbia Cooperative Law and then incorporate in their own states as foreign corporations.

State

Contact your state's department of consumer affairs to see if your specific business must obtain a license. Licenses are issued for a specific period of time, generally a year or two, and must be renewed periodically.

Local

Most small businesses are regulated at the local level. Check with your city *and* county to learn if you need any sort of license to do business. Sometimes both require one.

Find out about local zoning laws to make sure you conform. (Some city or county zones will not allow signs in front of a business. You should check zoning restrictions before signing a lease, and also if you plan to do business out of your home or apartment.)

Should you ever remodel or add on to your building, you will have to meet building code standards, as well as fire and police standards.

If you deal in food (making or selling it), you must meet the standards of your local health board.

Where to Get Licenses

For your convenience, here is a listing of legalities that must be dealt with (depending on the sort of business you wish to start):

License to do business	Local office of state tax department
Dba (fictitious name statement)	Local county clerk or state tax office
Certificate of partnership	County clerk's office or state tax bureau
Zoning regulations	County clerk's office
Seller's permit (sales tax resale number for retailers)	Local board of equalization
License for food sale or service	Local and state health departments
Health/safety requirements and labor information	U.S. Department of Labor

Information on federal taxes; employer identification number; social security and unemployment	Local office of Internal Revenue Service
Worker's compensation	State insurance fund, or state worker's compensation board
Disability insurance (for employees)	State department of human resources development or state disability office

ADDITIONAL LEGAL CONSIDERATIONS

Patents

Regardless of whether you've invented a better mousetrap or a mechanism to facilitate travel into hyperspace, you want to be protected from others stealing your idea and capitalizing on it: you'd better get a *patent.* Not that it's easy. Obtaining a patent can be expensive, because the procedure is technical and time-consuming and generally requires the assistance of a patent attorney or agent.*

A patent search of the millions of existing patents must be instituted. The patent application is complicated and difficult to prepare without legal help. All this is expensive and can cost generally from $3,000 to $7,000. And it takes nineteen months for the Patent Office to grant a *utility patent,* the most popular type.

Obtaining a patent gives you the power to prevent others from using, manufacturing, or selling the patented product. A patent is good for seventeen years and may not be renewed; anyone has the right to use an invention whose patent has expired. But receiving a patent does not necessarily stop others from challeng-

*A list of registered patent attorneys (booklet no. C21.9/2:974) is available from the Superintendent of Documents, Government Printing Office, Washington, D.C. 20402. For more information on obtaining a patent, contact: U.S. Patent and Trademark Office, Department of Commerce, Washington, D.C. 20231. See also SBA booklets: *Can You Make Money with Your Idea or Invention?* by John Tavela (Management Aids, no. 2.013, $.50); and, *Introduction to Patents,* by staff members of the SBA (Management Aids, no. 6.005, $.50).

101

ing it, or modifying the idea and manufacturing it. The term *patent pending* offers no legal protection. There are many restrictions on what inventions can and cannot be patented.

Many professionals advise an inventor to file her patent (for her protection) and then to find a financial backer to license it and pay royalties. The feasibility of this depends on how much you are willing to give up to see your invention get off the ground.

To save yourself some money before hiring an attorney, the patent office has a nondisclosure program whereby you can register your invention idea (to protect it while you have a prototype made) for only $6. It will be kept on file for two years, and the patent office becomes your collaborating witness. You can also do your own *free* patent search (lawyers charge lots for this) by going to a patent deposit library, usually located in your state's largest city or capital.

While working on your invention, keep a hardbound ledger (that can't be tampered with) listing all expenditures, with receipts stapled in, and notes on the research and development of the invention. Have someone witness it from time to time, and it becomes, in effect, the diary of your invention. To find a manufacturer for your prototype, check your library for state manufacturing directories, the *Thomas Register, Standard and Poor's,* and *Wards Business Directory.*

Trademarks and Copyrights

If your company has a *trademark* * (a name, logo, or symbol that identifies it), the first step toward protecting it is *using* it. Then you can acquire exclusive rights to your trademark by registering it with the U.S. Patent and Trademark Office. If your company does business across state lines, then you are eligible for federal trademark protection. The government charges a fee to register the trademark. It's good for twenty years, and renewable every twenty years after that.

If you are an author, illustrator, or composer you can protect each and every piece of work with a *copyright,* which remains in effect for your lifetime plus fifty years after your death, at which point it goes into public domain. The copyright gives you exclu-

*For information on trademarks, contact: U.S. Patent and Trademark Office, Department of Commerce, Washington, D.C. 20231.

sive rights to print, reprint, and copy the work, perform the work publicly, record and translate it, etc. When you complete a work, print the word *copyright,* the year, and your name on the illustration or title page of the work. Then register it with the U.S. Copyright Office* by filling out a form, paying a fee, and sending them two copies of the work.

Bankruptcy

There is no stigma attached to bankruptcy, although no one likes the idea of resorting to it. But sometimes bankruptcy is the only way to go when you need to get out of a financially unsuccessful business and creditors are storming your doors. It's not so bad. Bankruptcy laws are federal laws. The proceedings are conducted in an orderly way, enabling the people involved to make the best of a sad situation.

Individuals and unincorporated partnerships can file for bankruptcy without the services of an attorney. There is a filing fee that may be paid in installments by obtaining permission from the officiating judge.

Corporations must be represented by an attorney for bankruptcy cases. The legal fees are reviewed by the court, and a projected method of payment is set down. Sole owners and partners can be liable to the extent of their entire personal holdings. Owners of corporations are liable for their debts only to the limit of the corporation's assets.

There are two types of bankruptcy that pertain to small businesses. *Chapter Seven* is straight bankruptcy, when there is no possible way for the business to be reorganized in order to become profitable. *Chapter Eleven* is partial bankruptcy and can be filed when the condition of the business is not completely hopeless. The business is then given another chance to become profitable, but you must be able to show how and why you think you can turn things around.†

Among the forms to be filed, you must itemize all the debts you

*For copyright information, write the Register of Copyrights, Library of Congress, Washington, D.C. 20540.

†Chapters Seven and Eleven bankruptcy can be filed with forms provided in a kit published by Julius Blumberg, Inc., available at legal stationers across the country. Each kit contains complete filing instructions.

At this writing, one of the hottest areas in commercial lending is financing companies in Chapter Eleven to help them turn around.

owe and property or assets you own. Certain items (such as alimony and child support) are exempt from bankruptcy action. Get a list of exemptions from your state, to be used as a guide to filling out the forms. As the proceedings get underway, you will be expected to appear in court as well as to meet with your creditors.

Because of all the complexities involved, business bankruptcy should be handled by a lawyer, regardless of whether the business is incorporated. (Bankruptcy costs vary from state to state, and depend on the case.) Let's hope, however, that you will never need to use this information.

Litigation

Let's also hope that you will never be sued. But nowadays, unfortunately, lawsuits abound and the statistics grow worse every year. Some people, it seems, go out of their way to look for reasons to sue: that low doorway that they clunk their head into (major concussion, recurring headaches), the unraveling rug they trip over (broken bones, missing teeth), the vegetable oil that splatters into their face (severe burns, eye damage). The possibilities seem endless, and though you may try to protect yourself and your products, it doesn't always work. For example, in 1987 over 16 million civil cases were filed in the U.S. courts, involving *one of every fifteen people* in the country. Add to that the staggering figure that businesses spend over $20 billion every year on litigation. (That doesn't even include the cost of settlements and judgments.)

And what if someone copies *your* product or idea? What if you need to fight for your own rights and protection? Having to go to court can severely cripple a small business, in terms of cash flow and cutting marketing or product development budgets. The expense, however, is the fault of both the business owner and the attorney. Many business people are threatened and terrified by the thought of litigation. They dump the problem into their lawyer's lap and hope that it'll go away, the sooner the better. Then they accuse the lawyers of sitting on the cases, prolonging them so that their fees will escalate.

What can you do, besides praying that this will never happen to you? One thing is to make sure to include a clause in *every* contract you sign, calling for the alternative-dispute resolution

(ADR) technique.* Basically, it enables you to settle a dispute at an early stage of litigation, without having to go to court (and thus saving a bundle of money in legal fees). Besides settling the case through arbitration or mediation, there are newer ADR techniques that include: "renting" a judge to hear your case; or holding minitrials that bring the disputing parties and their lawyers together for one day to argue and settle the case.

In other words, if you are willing to settle without having your day in court, you can save yourself a lot of headaches and your business a lot of money.

SUMMARY

Choose a lawyer you trust, and trust your lawyer. But always make the decisions yourself, after having obtained your attorney's advice.

You're going to be in business for a long time. Over the years your attorney will advise you, handle your contracts and agreements, represent you in front of licensing boards, courts, and regulatory bodies. She'll counsel you on equity financing, purchasing inventory, choosing the best fiscal period for your taxes, interpreting new laws and regulations, working out credit assistance, negotiating leases, franchising, selling or terminating the business, and much more.

Listen to your lawyer; she knows the law. But listen to yourself, too; it's your business.

*For more information on the ADR technique, see "Contempt of Court: How to Avoid Litigation, Cut Legal Costs, and Get On With Your Business," by Stephen D. Solomon, *Inc.,* October 1989.

· 7 ·

Accounting: Setting Up and Setting Prices

Heaven knows how to put a proper price upon its goods.
—Thomas Paine

Great ideas must translate into financial language, and percentages and profits must be transformed into everyday patois. Accountants interpret, bookkeepers record; but it is the Certified Public Accountant who reads the numbers and turns them into facts and predictions. CPAs are the seers of the business world. You can show them what you have, and they'll tell you if it works.

Every business owner is faced with a barrage of decisions as the company moves from day to quarter to year. A new entrepreneur learns quickly that an accountant's assistance is invaluable.

Besides depending on your accountant, take time to educate yourself. Enroll in a good course in bookkeeping, accounting, and finance. Dun & Bradstreet, the business information and credit-rating service, reports that most business owners say that if they had it to do all over again they would have started out armed with this knowledge. It will help you relate better to your accountant and to the world of numbers and ledgers.

FINDING THE RIGHT ACCOUNTANT

Get firsthand recommendations from business associates or other small business owners in your field, people who have actually worked with the accountant and can vouch for her expertise

106

and trustworthiness.* If you receive recommendations for several accountants, talk to them all. You will work closely with your accountant on a continuing basis, so select someone who is knowledgeable and experienced in *your type of business;* whose advice, ideas, and judgment you respect; and with whom you will enjoy working.

When you interview a prospective accountant, find out which services are included in her basic fee, and which are extra.† Fees are generally quoted on an hourly basis, with an estimate given for time involved. Assume (but ask, to make sure) that for a quarterly or yearly fee she will take care of your quarterly reports, sales and other taxes, and trial balance sheets (or will recommend a free-lance bookkeeper who will). She should also do up a profit-loss statement at the year's end. Find out whether your accountant will represent you in case of a tax audit.

A verbal fee quotation is okay, but don't hire anyone without agreeing on the price ahead of time (and this applies to every other area of your business as well). Never accept a vague, "Don't worry . . . I'll give you a fair price." It may turn out to be fair, but if it's more than you intended to pay, resentment builds and all initial goodwill collapses. Remember, everything always costs more than you expect it to.

In short, when choosing an accountant, compare costs, and compare experience in the field and in your type of business. Choose the professional who is best qualified to handle your needs. At the outset, ask for an engagement letter, reviewing the services provided and stating how much the fees will be.

THE ACCOUNTANT'S SERVICES

With all of the revolutionary small business financial software programs available for your computer, don't think that they can completely take the place of a good accountant,‡ especially when

---

*For additional help in locating an accountant, contact: American Society of Women Accountants, 35 East Wacker Drive, Chicago, Illinois 60001, (312)726–9030.
†Tax returns for single proprietors or partners are usually extra, since they pay business taxes on their individual return.
‡Most of the large accounting firms cater to small businesses as well as large, and offer free booklets and brochures to help start-up entrepreneurs. For example, one of the booklets published by Price Waterhouse is *Planning and Financing for the Entrepreneurial Company.* (Price Waterhouse's national office is located at 1251 Avenue of the Americas, New York, New York 10019, [212]489–8900.)

you are setting up your business or going after financing. The software bookkeeping and spread sheet programs will help you enormously, and can save you money. But the person running these programs has to know what she's looking at. As a business owner, you must comprehend all the financial goings-on of your company, because finance is at the heart of a business. If you aren't savvy in economics, your accountant can light the dark path ahead.

An accountant is a truly multifaceted person. She will:

Compute initial costs, based on your estimates

Figure out your profit potential

Establish your break-even point

Help you set fees and prices

Set up your bookkeeping system (and/or give you recommendations as to which financial software program(s) would be best for your business)

Draw up (and teach you to read) financial statements

Advise you on the tax advantages of the three major business structures as they apply to your own situation

Introduce you to a banker who will be sympathetic to your business and your needs

Help with loans (by helping you with your business plan, and by preparing financial projections and vouching for you)

On your first meeting, be prepared to provide your accountant-to-be with an outline of the business. (This can be done orally, but anything written or visual will help her understand your vision.) Besides the concept itself, include any marketing surveys (no matter how informal) that you have conducted. Indicate your business's potential—your community's need for it, its competition, and its *distinctiveness* from existing competition. Include the estimated expenditures you have already itemized for overhead, supplies, and equipment.

The accountant will check your estimates for accuracy and suggest realistic costs where your initial estimates are low (and they probably will be). Then she will work out your profit potential, that is, how much money you must make to meet expenses and how much more to realize a profit.

She will help you establish fees by setting standards that are based on competitive prices plus your operational costs. If you are dealing in an unusual product or service, where there is no standard fee structure, she will set a pricing formula for you. Knowing what to charge for services is a major stumbling block for inexperienced entrepreneurs. Making a thousand dollars on one job is not necessarily something to gloat over unless you know that it is sufficient to cover the costs directly related to the job—including labor and billing time.

SETTING PRICES FOR YOUR BUSINESS

The Break-even Point

Setting accurate prices for your product or service cannot be done until you have established your break-even point. Tally up your overhead (fixed expenses and variable costs) and then hone down this figure to a time basis. For example, if your fixed monthly overhead is $4,000, then the weekly figure is approximately $1,000. Based on a five-day week, you will have to earn $200 per day just to break even. Anything over that, less additional expenses, is profit.

The Basic Formula

The next step is to find out what similar businesses are charging for their products or services. With this in mind, you can set your prices competitively, based on Labor + Expenses + Materials + Overhead + Profit = Price. The actual percentage you will tack on for profit fluctuates according to the type of business you're in—service, retail, wholesale, or manufacturing.

In figuring any prices, whether for products or services, you have to cover the time spent for selling (marketing, advertising), buying supplies, producing the product or performing the service, and bookkeeping. In general, you can figure that 50 percent of your costs will be for specifics (e.g., labor, direct expenses such as raw materials, etc.), 20 percent for nonspecific costs (e.g., general equipment, overhead, miscellaneous supplies, shipping, gas for your car, etc.), and 10 percent for selling costs. The remaining 20 percent will go for profit.

You must constantly reevaluate your use of time, cost of materials, etc., and what you charge. If you don't charge enough, your work will be undervalued. If you charge too much, people will flock to your competition. Stay current with your competition and their prices.

Estimates

For large-scale jobs or special orders, be prepared to provide the client with a price estimate, based on your estimated labor costs, raw materials, and expenses. Before pricing a job, however, try to determine the client's budget. (Often, clients keep this top secret, hoping you will quote them a lower price.)

Accurate estimates are difficult to assess until you have experience in similar jobs. Since unexpected costs often arise, tack on an additional 25 percent to your estimate to cover these hidden costs. The fastest way to lose a client is to end up charging a significant amount over the original estimate. (In mid-job, should you discover that your estimate was too low, inform the client right away and try to negotiate a new cost estimate.)

Advance Deposits

Sometimes the smaller the price, the harder it is to get paid. Anytime you take on a new client,* obtain a deposit for the service or product order. Waive it later on for good customers, unless you need partial advance payment to cover your own outlay of expenses connected with the job. In general, the amount of the deposit should be half of the total bill.

Consideration of Intangibles

For certain creative businesses, the higher your fees, the more apt you are to convince people that you are worth that much. (Of course, you have to be able to deliver above-average performance for the services you offer.) You must base the price of your

*To find out the credit worthiness of new clients, manufacturers, and/or suppliers, see the reference book used by banks: *Annual Statement Studies* ($54.50), published by Robert Morris Associates, 1650 Market Street, 23rd Floor, Philadelphia, Pennsylvania 19103–9734. It gives financial information on companies in nearly 350 industries. It's also a good reference for judging the performance of your business versus your competition.

service or product on its value to the *client,* an intangible which overrides your basic costs.

In setting fees, always balance psychological buying practices with economical ones. And remember, *in the beginning* all businesses need to build a clientele. Without losing money, you must still be flexible and offer introductory prices, hold a grand opening sale, or whatever is necessary to attract the public to you.

PRICING FOR SERVICE BUSINESSES

Since expenses are usually negligible in service businesses, you must calculate your costs in labor.* This time cost is generally doubled to cover overhead and general expenses. Then the total of these two categories is doubled, in order to make a profit: 2 + 2 = 4 + 4 = 8 (total cost including profit).

Services are highly competitive, but if you engage in a unique project for which there is no basic fee structure, then divide the hours you expect to work by the income you need to cover expenses and make a profit.

In computing labor costs, don't neglect indirect expenses. For example, electricity used in running a computer must be considered in pricing a job involving the use of a computer (e.g., typing letters, bills, etc.). Don't forget to charge for transportation if the job involves numerous meetings at your client's office. Keep receipts for every expense involved with every job. Unless you do, hidden costs can drain your profit.

Miscellaneous Creative Services

Examples of such services include landscape design, shopping services, creative agencies, event planners, etc. Many services establish their fees based on a percentage of the total job, including expenses. This percentage varies according to the exclusivity, individuality, or competition of the service, but it generally ranges from 10 percent to 20 percent. Discuss what your percentage should be with your accountant.

Also, be sure to establish a reciprocal discount (usually 10

*See SBA booklets *Pricing Your Products and Services Profitably,* by Judy Nye (Business Development Publications, no. FM 13); *Accounting Services for Small Service Firms,* by Irving M. Cooper (Management Aids, no. 1.010, $.50); and *Budgeting in a Small Service Firm,* by Phyllis A. Barker (Management Aids, no. 1.015, $.50).

percent) with other stores, suppliers, or specialized talent that you use on a regular basis in executing jobs for your clients. It is up to you to decide whether you pass this discount along or hold on to it.

RETAIL PRICES

The standard retail price* is a 100 percent markup *per item* over the wholesale price. If, however, you specialize in unusual crafts, artwork, antiques, groceries, or imported items, then your prices will be geared to the current market value of those items. According to the SBA, most retail profit doesn't begin to accrue until the second year, often longer.

Another essential part of retail pricing is seasonal markdowns. Unsold merchandise must regularly be marked down in order to reduce inventory and free both your cash and your shelves for new purchases. Monitor your markdowns so that you can spot a pattern in your unprofitable buying. Remember, the more skillful your buying in the first place, the fewer markdowns you will have.

CONSIGNMENT PRICING

If you are a craftsperson and want to sell your work on consignment, you have to set your price—what it will sell for retail. The store will take a consignment percentage (usually 30, 40, or 50 percent), and when the item is sold, you get the remaining percentage. If it doesn't sell, then you must reclaim the item.

Always sign a preliminary agreement with the store, stipulating the number of items you leave with it, the date, and percentage rate. Have the store send you a monthly check along with a list of items sold and any requests for more. Stay in touch with the store, and keep records of what has sold and the money taken in.

From the store owner's point of view, it's attractive to offer merchandise without having to purchase it. However, many retail stores shy away from accepting items on consignment because of the hassle of the extra paperwork and bookkeeping involved.

*See SBA booklets *A Pricing Checklist for Small Retailers,* by Bruce J. Walker (Management Aids, no. 4.013, $.50), and *Simple Breakdown Analysis for Small Stores* (Management Aids, no. 1.019, $1).

For additional information on retail costing, see *Financial Manual for Retail Stores,* Fairchild Publications, 7 East Twelfth Street, New York, New York 10003.

WHOLESALE PRICING

You have to know accurate up-to-date costs in order to set prices. The formula is generally Time (labor) + Expenses (including overhead, selling, equipment, and raw materials) + Profit (the amount you wish to make, usually 20 percent) = Wholesale Price. In other words, you must be able to make a profit by selling your product at 50 percent of the retail price.

Every item a manufacturer designs, reproduces, and sells must be costed separately. The original costing must be revised whenever any changes are made in the design or when labor, raw materials, equipment, or overhead costs escalate.

How much profit you can make per wholesale item is based on your own research (in stores and catalogs) of the potential market: how much you estimate the item can sell for at retail (which is, generally, double the wholesale price). If you cost out an item and decide that it cannot be produced to sell at a fair and competitive price, then you must revise your estimates. You must either consider less expensive raw materials or try to cut down on overhead costs. Don't, however, consider cutting quality or it will lose you clients in the long run. If an item is too expensive to produce to sell at a fair market price, then perhaps the world doesn't need that item. Go back to the drawing board.

CHANGING PRICES

Once you have set a price, you are not stuck with it. Although you don't want a reputation for fluctuating fees, you have to adjust them to match the seesawing costs of labor and materials. In addition, keep in step with your competition—lower or raise your prices accordingly. Read trade magazines in your field to keep up-to-date with price trends.

BARTERING

Bartering is a time-honored practice, and many individuals and business owners still engage in it. If you're a lawyer and one of your clients is a cabinetmaker, why not give free counsel for a wall of badly needed bookshelves?

The key is to make sure that the items or services to be bartered are of equal value to the recipients. And while bartering serves a purpose, your accountant will advise you that it never quite takes the place of money in the bank.

JOBS FOR PUBLICITY'S SAKE

Small business owners are sometimes talked into taking unprofitable jobs in exchange for "good publicity." Women's subliminal volunteering instincts often make them prey to this kind of pitch. But no matter how much you enjoy what you do, you are still in business to make money. If you don't, you won't *stay* in business.

Occasionally, however, there are times when it doesn't hurt to do a good deed—just so long as you don't lose money on the project. You will have to weigh the advantages before you take the job. Will it allow you to explore new areas you've been dying to tackle? Will it put you on a first-name basis with community leaders you've been wanting to meet? If so, then the experience gained and contacts made are worth it. Perhaps you want to attract publicity by having a celebrity on your client roster. (Stars often want discounts for gracing your business with their superstatus). Or you might decide to do a job at cost, as a favor to an adviser or friend, to repay a kindness.

More publicity can be gleaned by volunteering your service or product for charity benefits, ecological purposes, or community celebrations. "Paying your civic dues" creates goodwill, and your participation makes you feel good, too.

But what about *turning down* a job? The ability to make these discriminations comes with experience, and you will certainly make mistakes before you've developed the right mix of hard heart and soft touch. There are jobs that you can't afford to do and must refuse, in order to free up time to attract more lucrative accounts.

KEEPING BUSINESS RECORDS

Many innovative entrepreneurs are brought to their knees with fear of The Books.* But if "you gotta have a gimmick" is the first order of business, "you gotta have a plan" is the next. Write

*See SBA booklets *Recordkeeping in Small Business* (Financial Management, no. FM 10, $1); and *Analyze Your Records to Reduce Costs,* by Alfred B. Abraham (Management Aids, no. 1.011, 50¢).

everything down, and your books will tell you how your business is doing. You may think that you can carry everything in your head at first since it's a small business and yours. But it isn't that easy.

After you get going, a lot of facts and figures start vying for a choice location between your ears. Your daily, monthly, and yearly records turn into a memorandum of past events as well as a forecast of future trends. They help you accentuate the positives, eliminate weaknesses, and prevent costly mistakes in tax return preparation.

Bookkeeping has been referred to as "organizational common sense." Really, that's all it is . . . a place for everything with everything kept up to date.

The Bookkeeping System

Most small businesses can get by with reasonably uncomplicated record-keeping systems. Nowadays, there are many bookkeeping software programs available for the small business owner. Ask your accountant which she recommends. And if you aren't starting off with a computer, then have your accountant set up the *simplest* bookkeeping system for your needs, based on the following records:

Cash receipts—money taken in
Cash disbursements—expenditures paid out
Sales—to be recorded daily and summarized monthly
Payroll—the record of wages and withholding deductions
Equipment—assets in equipment, office machines, furnishings, and fixtures, etc.
Inventory—a record of the company's investment in merchandise or raw materials
Accounts receivable—a record of balances owed to the company
Accounts payable—a record of what the business owes its creditors and suppliers

And who runs this system, day to day? *You,* that's who. At least in the beginning, learn by doing it yourself. Don't allow your accountant to burden you with a time-consuming system of keeping records. Be sure you understand how it is done. So long as you keep track of what's coming in and going out, along with costs for labor and expenses, you'll be just fine. When money starts pouring in and things get more complicated, then you can hire a bookkeeper.

While you alone are shouldering the burden, don't neglect it. It's just a matter of setting aside a couple of hours regularly every week. It becomes a habit, like brushing your teeth. If you do it while the transactions are still fresh in your mind and the receipts within easy reach, it won't take long.

Bookkeeping Methods

All the data of daily business transactions must be recorded as each item occurs for later transfer onto a permanent ledger as a debit or a credit. These records are compiled monthly or quarterly into a financial statement: a balance sheet of assets and liabilities and owner's capital on a specific date; and a profit-loss statement of income and expenses covering a specific time period.

The Single-entry System

This system is a simple chronicle of the money going out and coming in: your record of every dollar spent—the date, amount, and purpose—and every dollar earned—the date, amount, and description of the item or client's name. Save all bills and receipts for everything, no matter how minuscule the amount.

Enter this information into a ledger page daily or once a week. On a monthly basis, total the columns of cash received and disbursed. If the money taken in is more than that going out, you've made a profit. If the opposite occurs, you'd better work twice as hard next month. If you have outstanding accounts receivable at the end of the month, then this profit-loss sheet doesn't tell the whole story.

The Double-entry System

In this system, you record everything twice—once under debits and once under credits. Every transaction is a balance of the two: if you spend $4,000 on a laser printer for your computer, you have depleted your cash, but you have increased your assets.

116

Standardized Record-keeping Systems and Software Programs

Stationery stores and office suppliers have various ready-made systems for keeping business records, and most small businesses can use standard account books.* Have your accountant recommend the best ones for your needs.

Always record transactions in pen, not pencil. If you make mistakes, cross them out, don't erase.

If you use a simplified double-entry system, then you'll need the following books: a sales-cash receipts journal; a cash disbursements-purchases expenses journal; a general ledger (to record assets, liabilities, and capital); an accounts receivable ledger; an employees' compensation record; and, of course, a business checkbook.

If you have a computer, then you'll want to use that for your bookkeeping. There are myriad software accounting programs available: bookkeeping/accounting (which—depending on the program—may do billing, check paying, inventory tracking, payroll, accounts payable and receivable, general ledger, etc.); financial spread sheets; and integrated software programs (which do all of the above plus word processing, flat-file database, mailmerge, etc.).

How do you find the right software package for your needs? Ask your accountant, owners of similar businesses, computer retail stores, computer users' groups, or a software consultant. Read the computer publications and *Consumer Reports*. Software programs are expensive, but they can save you a bundle of time. Make sure the one you end up with comes with a support system or hotline number to answer your questions and help you get the most out of the program's capabilities.

---

*Business checks may be purchased from office suppliers instead of banks. There are one-write check systems, which provide, along with your checks, an automatic accounting system. You write a check and carry it forward, and it takes the place of a cash-disbursements journal. Some banks offer these systems as well.

For additional information on all bookkeeping methods, see *Portfolio for the Small and Medium-Sized Business*, 2 vols. (Englewood Cliffs, New Jersey: Prentice-Hall).

Software packages are constantly being updated and the field changes fast. At this writing, several of the top bookkeeping packages are: Dollars and Sense, manufactured by Monogram; Managing Your Money (Meca); Quicken (Intuit); In-House Accountant (Migent); Great Plains Accounting Packages (Great Plains Software). The top integrated software packages are: Q and A, manufactured by Symantec; Works (Microsoft); Smart (Innovative Software, Inc.); and Enable (The Software Group). Check computer stores and magazines for new entries into the field.

The Profit-Loss Statement and Balance Sheet

There are two systems of recording income and expenses: cash and accrual. Whichever method you elect, you must use it consistently.

The *cash method* shows only the receipt of income (cash) and the actual cash disbursements (expenses). Many businesses rely heavily on credit accounts, so that the cash method of recording transactions is not a reliable reflection of profits and losses during a specified time period.

The *accrual system* reports all transactions that take place during a specified period, whether or not the payments have yet been made. In other words, you deduct expenses as they occur and add income as it is earned, even if you haven't been paid by the client.

A profit-loss statement based on the accrual method is the more accurate account of cash and credit transactions during a specific period, thus making business analysis easier.

To establish the realistic condition of your business, tally up the gross profit (money taken in); then subtract all your overhead costs and expenses. The resulting figure is your net, or actual, profit.

The balance sheet shows the ratio of inventory to sales (credits to debits), to indicate whether inventory is too high and sales too few. In a service business, it compares sales to profits to detect whether the profits are high enough to make a satisfactory profit.

Being busy from nine to five isn't enough. The productivity of your time must be measured in profits. Balance sheets and profit-loss statements are thermometers of your success or failure.

Profit Mix

There are additional ways of analyzing your financial statements.* Even if you are showing a profit, are there services or products that are losing money? You have to reexamine continually all areas of your business and sweep the dust out the door (not under the rug).

In some cases, however, a loss area may play a part in your

---

*Since 1973, Merrill Lynch, Pierce, Fenner & Smith has been offering a free thirty-page booklet, *How to Read a Financial Report,* which explains it all in detail. It is available at any of the nationwide Merrill Lynch offices.

company's image or prestige. Figure out why, and how much, it is losing, and decide whether its overall contribution warrants your continuing it.

Profit Trend

This is the overall picture of your profit. Is the profit increasing in proportion to your total business volume? Or is it simply holding its own or declining? The fact that you show a profit is not necessarily an indication that your business is growing.

Annual and Quarterly Expenses

Don't overestimate your monthly profits. Allow monthly allotments toward periodic or annual expenses like taxes, insurance premiums, licenses, equipment rental, maintenance expenses, and the like.

CASH FLOW

Cash flow* is the play between income and expenses—the amount of actual cash that is flowing in and out of your business at any given moment. It provides the money with which to work between billing and payment (order and delivery) and covers out-of-pocket expenses. Your creditors (money lenders, suppliers, landlord, etc.) demand that you pay your bills promptly, yet your customers often take several months to pay you. You have money, on paper, but the cupboard is bare in regards to cash on hand.

In order to *know* how much cash you can expect to have—cash to work with between billing and payment (order and delivery)— do a cash flow analysis, either monthly or quarterly. (Have your accountant help you in the beginning; you can take over from there.)

A cash flow statement covers three areas:

Source of cash—whatever brings money into the business, i.e., sale of products or services, payments by charge customers, capital from loans, and money earned on interest, etc.

*See SBA booklet *Understanding Cash Flow* (Management Aids, no. 1.006, $1).

Cash going out—whatever you must spend to keep the business operating, i.e., overhead, inventory or supplies, repayment of loans, etc.

Cash schedule—the comparison between this and other months (or quarters), i.e., a business barometer that shows whether you are generating more or less cash than in previous months. This will enable you to see where you need to cut back on expenses (and growth spending) in the coming months.

Knowing exactly how much cash you have on hand to spend will force you to develop alternative sales methods. In this way, you can balance your cash flow and compensate for slack periods and seasonal buying.

If you are owed money (and can prove it), yet need to meet impending bills, you can take out a short-term bank loan to cover expenses, as long as your credit is in good standing. But if you keep up with your cash flow, you should be able to avoid this kind of bind.

Financial Projections

Your accountant can assemble all pertinent information on your company's financial position for potential lenders and investors. This presentation will include a profit-loss statement and balance sheet, or projections if you haven't started in business yet.

Rely on financial projections. Putting them together entails identifying every potential cost, which is then entered on spread sheets for analysis. All costs are recorded in relation to specific time periods so that the cash flow can be computed. Your accountant's cash flow projections will help predict what amount of capitalization you will need to carry you along the inevitable rocky road down which every new business must travel.

Charting Financial Trends and Cash Flow

If you've computerized your bookkeeping, assign someone (either you or your bookkeeper) to do a quarterly search for trends and disturbing patterns as they apply to your financial picture, such as slow-paying clients and bank delays. Computerized records make it easy to evaluate the accuracy of your cash flow projections too, and you should do a cash-flow analysis every year or eighteen months, or whenever you're planning a change in your business. This will help you stay current with your finances; how well you monitor your cash flow will make or break your business.

STORING BUSINESS RECORDS

Metal file cabinets are not fireproof. Certain records must be stored in safety in case of fire, flooding, etc. The ones to be tucked away safely (in a fireproof safe, bank safety deposit box, or on other premises) are the ones that will provide the most information—current profit-loss statements, balance sheets, and tax returns—if disaster strikes.

Store any records that will help you collect insurance, report losses for tax deductions, and borrow money. Reestablishing a business also requires lists of customers, suppliers, inventory, equipment, and production information, so these items should also be kept in a safe place. Review your storage records periodically and bring them up to date.

Small business owners can suffocate under the amount of paper that must be saved. Since business records must be accessible, the most space-saving method is to store them in indexed, numbered, corrugated containers on metal bookshelves.

If you have computerized your record system, then the space you will need to store everything will be considerably smaller. Make sure that *all* of your company's records—financial and otherwise—are backed up on diskettes. Store one complete set of these backup diskettes in a safe place, away from your office.

Another way to save storage space is to microfilm your records, but it is time-consuming and costly. Also, microfilm must be kept in special humidity-controlled safes.

How Long Must Records Be Saved?

You can decide how long to hold on to routine records and correspondence, and your accountant can inform you of your state's statute of limitations for specific documents like canceled checks, vouchers, and receipts.* The table below is a general guide to the length of time one is required to retain records of certain business transactions:

Indefinitely	A copyright, trademark registration, letter of patent (even though they have a definite expiration date)
	Corporate by-laws, minutes of stockholders' meetings, annual reports
	Equipment maintenance records and warranties (for the life of the equipment)
	Certain correspondence, insurance policies, and contracts
	Annual operating records and the general ledger (balance sheets, profit-loss statements)
	Deeds
	Copies of ads, brochures, publicity, and business memorabilia
Six Years	Contracts and leases (unless renewed periodically)
	Records of lawsuits (these must be kept from six to ten years)
	Cash receipts and disbursements records
	State and federal income tax returns (and records corroborating them)
	Major-purchase receipts
Four Years	Payroll records (including wage payments and withholding deductions for income tax and social security)
	Accounts receivable and paid invoice records
Three Years	State and local sales and use tax records
	Routine purchase records
Two Years	Employee time sheets
	Petty cash vouchers
	Monthly bookkeeping records
One Year	*(until annual audit of the books is completed)*
	All production records and receipts
	Accounting records and supporting documentation

Poor record keeping kills more businesses than bad craftsmanship or marketing. Hire a bookkeeper as soon as you can realisti-

*The statute of limitations ranges from three to twenty years according to state but averages six years.

cally afford one. Nevertheless, at the beginning it's important to follow a system that can be maintained by you or someone with minimal experience or training in bookkeeping. All through the life of your business, you must review your books and financial records on a regular basis, so as not to lose touch with what's really going on.

Once you've found your accountant, keep her up-to-date on new developments. Rely on her advice, because she can see you from the other end of the telescope and focus on your potential problems before they explode.

· 8 ·

Insurance: Resting Assured

Oh, dry the starting tear, for they were heavily insured.
—William S. Gilbert

Yes, insurance is yet another expense, but one which should be thoroughly considered, since small businesses are least likely to withstand losses of any kind. Insurance premiums are fixed costs that become security blankets covering against fire, theft, and other losses that could not be absorbed by a small company. Insurance also provides additional financial stability, often making it easier to obtain credit. Later on, increased coverage, such as group health or life insurance plans, make it easier to attract and keep good staff members.

Before buying any insurance, figure out what you have to lose, whether you can afford to lose it, and how much it will cost to cover the risk. Then decide if you can cover the loss yourself, out of your company's general operating costs. For example, if the only item in your office worth stealing is a twenty-year-old electric typewriter, then it's cheaper to replace it outright than lay out money to insure it. On the other hand, if you stand to lose an entire inventory of antique birdcages, insurance premiums are negligible compared to your potential debacle. Insurance replaces a *possible* large loss with a small but continuing cost—the premium.

Talk to your agent and then buy what insurance you can afford. And then keep reevaluating your needs. What you do today may not be valid or meet the needs of your business in five years. There may be an increase in the value of your business, or a reduction, and your insurance coverage should be altered accordingly.

Discriminatory practices in underwriting, by the way, have been eliminated by law. A good agent will help you keep costs at a minimum. She will keep you abreast of changing regulations and laws (which vary between states) involving business insurance requirements and benefits.

FINDING THE RIGHT INSURANCE PERSON

The insurance person* you choose should be flexible enough to whip up a policy tailored to your budget. She should be knowledgeable and sympathetic to the needs of a small business. Insurance rates are high, especially for employee benefits such as health care, and you need an agent who will not bankrupt you by trying to overinsure your company.

In locating the right person for you, it is advisable, as always, to look for personal recommendations. Talk to other business owners who are satisfied with their agents (and have been dealing with the same person for *at least* three years). Ask your trade association, or your local women's business association. Perhaps your accountant can recommend someone who would be right for your business. The important thing is to shop around.

Even if you don't sign up right away, you should consult an insurance person before your start-up, so that you can budget the cost into your business plan. Once you've opened your doors, invite prospective agents to see your workplace. That way they can see for themselves the extent of the coverage needed.

But you needn't leave everything up to your insurance agent; you can get a clear picture of your needs before you consult anyone. Go through your working premises yourself with an eye toward insurance needs. Evaluate risks by observing your business (potential environmental risks, Workers' Compensation claims, dangerous machinery, product liability, storage facilities that might catch fire, etc.) as well as your geographical location. For example, if you work in a tornado zone or an area near a fault line, then you should get tornado or earthquake insurance. If

*In general, insurance *brokers* insure property and insurance *agents* insure people. An insurance *consultant* can consult with you regarding your needs, then recommend the proper agent or broker.

To locate women brokers in your area, write the National Association of Insurance Women, 1847 East Fifteenth Street, Tulsa, Oklahoma 74104.

your building is old, try to determine the things that could go wrong (e.g., the roof caving in after a severe snowstorm).

Many agents don't bother dealing with small businesses, but some make it their specialty. Try to get quotes from at least two different people. Even though rates are competitive among companies, there is often a disparity among benefits. And there are ambitious brokers who may try to sell you more than you need to begin with. Listen to their suggestions, talk to owners of similar businesses, then make your decision. As mentioned above, keep *reevaluating* those needs every few years, as your business grows and takes on new employees.

The Independent Agent

This person usually specializes in property or liability insurance and works on commission from several insurance companies. She can, therefore, put together all of your insurance requirements, and since you are her client, not the insurer's, you will receive better, more personalized service should you have a claim. Because she deals in different types of coverage, she has a greater knowledge of the various types of insurance. Just make sure she has extensive contact with several insurers who can supply all the coverage you will need, at reasonable prices.

The Direct Writer

The direct writer works directly for a specific company and is not an independent businessperson. The advantage of dealing directly is that because you are going to a specific insurer for a specific type of coverage, the cost is lower. Many insurance companies specialize in certain fields and can offer a great deal of experience in that type of coverage. Lloyd's of London, for example, specializes in unusual kinds of risks that no other company will handle—from marine research to movie stars.

SAVING MONEY ON INSURANCE

The *deductible* is the amount you must pay on an insurance claim before the insurance company pays up. For example, if you have insured your retail shoe store for $250,000 to cover inventory, business machines, interior design, etc., you would pay lower annual insurance premiums if you chose a $5,000 deductible rather than a $500 deductible. That means if you had a fire, you would be responsible for covering the first $5,000 worth of damages yourself, and then the insurance company would pay for everything over that. (Sometimes the deductible will be a percentage of the damage, or a time period, e.g., the first twenty-four hours of business lost after a fire might be the deductible in a business interruption policy.)

Make sure you're covered fully for any disaster, burglary, etc., so that you could replace everything afterward. But always save yourself money by choosing a higher deductible. It's often cheaper to cover the costs of a stolen fax machine yourself rather than pay the steeper insurance rates that come with a lower deductible and frequent small claims.

Etch each piece of stealable equipment you own with the name of the business, your business identification number, or your social security number. In the event of theft, these items will be easier for the police to identify, should they be recovered.

Another way to save money is to not insure everything. Think about what would be easier to replace out of pocket. Save on insurance by looking into loss-prevention programs such as fraud insurance and bonding. Fidelity bonds, for example, can guard against losses incurred by employee theft of funds or inventory.

Unless you live in an area prone to natural disasters there is no point in adding such expensive coverage to your fire insurance policy. The SBA has a loan program available if 40 percent or more of your business is destroyed in a natural disaster. (You are eligible, however, only if at least twenty-five other businesses or homes suffered from the same disaster.)

Save money by making sure your workplace is as safe as possible. Make sure there are enough smoke alarms and that the sprinklers are in good working order. Don't store combustible chemicals near the radiator or in a place that might catch a few rays of morning sun. Don't go for the homey look of that old oriental rug if the edges are frayed and a customer might catch her heel on it and trip. In winter, check outside walkways and steps for icy spots. Install adequate fire extinguishers, burglar alarms, and timers for night and weekend lighting. It's only common sense, and all of these things will help keep your insurance rates lower.

INSURANCE COVERAGE

Basic insurance areas to be considered fall into the categories of casualty (personal and product liability, fire, crime, etc.), accident, health, life, and Worker's Compensation. Besides getting the right coverage, you have to make sure that the company or companies insuring you are in good financial shape and won't go out of business, leaving you uninsured after you've paid out thousands of dollars in premiums. To check on the financial rating of an insurer, consult *Best's Insurance Reports* at your local library.

Some insurance companies offer package policies for small businesses. They are less expensive because you are insured for a number of things in one large policy, rather than several smaller ones. Some packages are designed for specific kinds of businesses. If you find a package that seems attractive, make sure that the policy spells out in detail all the areas that are covered, and the amount of coverage in each area. Make sure you understand from your agent any areas that are *not* covered.

Casualty Insurance: Liability

Liability, which includes general, product, and automobile, is about the most necessary type of coverage for a small business. General liability insurance covers you in case accidents are incurred by employees and clients on your premises. This includes both personal injury and damage to personal property. Unintentional negligence on your part (that old frayed oriental rug, for example, or unpacked boxes blocking an aisle) is no defense. One lawsuit, if you are found guilty, could wipe out the total assets of your company and force you out of business.

Liability insurance should also include product liability (if applicable) and auto insurance on cars to be used for company purposes (if not separately covered). Car liability insurance should be carried by any employee who uses her car for company business (if your state has not passed a "no-fault" automobile insurance law).

Product liability insurance is expensive (premiums have climbed as much as 1,000 percent in the past few years), and can be difficult or impossible to obtain because of the number of product liability cases to hit the courts in recent years. Many companies have been forced to discontinue certain products because insurance premiums and the risk of lawsuits are so high. State laws regarding liability also vary. Some companies operate without any product liability insurance (which is extremely risky). If you are dealing with a product, consider the product in terms of its risk and rethink whether or not it's cost-efficient to market it.

Casualty Insurance: Property

Fire Insurance
If you are renting an office or storefront, check with your landlord to determine the extent of her coverage that is applicable to you. (Generally, landlords' policies will not cover your equipment and inventory.) Then you may want fire insurance, which covers losses caused by fire and lightning. You have to purchase additional coverage for protection against boiler explosion, windstorm, hail, smoke or water damage, car damage, riots, earthquakes, and so forth.

Crime Insurance
This covers crimes committed by people outside the business. If your bookkeeper is pocketing company funds, for example, her pilfering constitutes an "inside job" and is not covered in this type of policy.

Robbery insurance covers the taking of property from a person by force or threat of violence.

Burglary insurance protects inventoried merchandise and safes, but there must be visible marks of forced entry—no sneak thieves.

A storekeeper's burglary and robbery policy is designed for small businesses and covers a small loss. Larger businesses need more complete crime coverage, at much higher premium rates—especially in high-risk locations.

Other Protection Policies

All-risk blanket policies designed for retailers or wholesalers; they cover one's entire inventory from all perils (flood, earthquakes, freezing, water seepage, landslide, war, radioactivity, dishonesty, etc.) except those specifically excluded by name on the policy.

Difference-of-conditions insurance protects you from miscellaneous perils not covered in your other policies.

Transportation insurance covers shipments of goods during transport.

Business interruption insurance protects a business if it is forced to shut down, either totally or partially, after loss from an "insured peril" (fire and such).

Glass insurance protects your plate glass windows, glass signs, glass doors, showcases, or countertops.

Power plant insurance covers against losses from explosions of furnaces, electrical equipment, engines, steam boilers, etc.

Rent insurance protects against damage from sprinkler leakage, etc., in rented buildings.

Accident Insurance: Disability and Worker's Compensation

If you have any full-time staff members, you are required by law to provide Disability and Worker's Compensation insurance.* This can be purchased from a state insurance fund or private insurer. Premium rates are determined by the employee's salary and the type of work involved, varying from 1 percent of salary in a low-risk job to 10 percent or more. It is tax deductible for corporations only.

In a corporation, the owners are considered employees, and they have the option to insure themselves, but not the obligation.†

A sole proprietor is not considered an employee of her business and is therefore not required to have Disability or Worker's Compensation (or unemployment, although she must have social security). Partners also are not considered employees, unless the partnership is incorporated. In general, Disability insurance for you, the owner, is a good idea. There are several types of policies available, including *Disability income insurance* and *business overhead insurance.* These will keep you and your business going (by paying

*Check your state's requirement, as the application for Worker's Compensation varies widely, and some workers are exempt. In some states, you are exempt if you have fewer than four employees.
†The Worker's Compensation Law requires the same treatment for executive officers as "employees." Failure of a corporation to provide insurance for executive officers would subject it to legal penalties.

130

part or all of your fixed overhead expenses) while you are temporarily laid up.

Health Insurance

Health insurance is coverage required for sickness and accidents—health and dental insurance, disability and sick pay, as well as life insurance. It is not required by law, but with the high cost of physicians and hospitals nowadays, it is risky not to have it. It is also the fringe benefit most employees look for these days, and a good health-care program can help you attract high-quality staffmembers. There are many plans available, and group health is less costly than taking out an individual policy. A "group," by the way, can consist of as few as two people, but every insurance company has its own definition of how many people make up a group. Medical premiums are tax deductible only for corporations.

There are different types of health insurance coverage offered by various companies:*

Fee-for-service provides eligible employees with a physician's and/or hospital's services: the employee can go to any doctor she chooses. The employee pays and is then reimbursed a percentage of the fee. Some insurance companies pay 80 percent of the costs and the employee is expected to cover the additional 20 percent. (Sometimes, depending on the insurer, the percentages run 70/30, or 90/10.)

Preferred Provider Organization (PPO) is a plan similar to the one above, but there are restrictions placed on the frequency of doctors' visits and the physicians whom the employee is allowed to consult under the coverage. In the PPO plan, a network of hospitals and doctors will agree to provide services at a 10 to 20 percent discount on their usual charges. The employee is sometimes required to co-pay an additional $5 or $10 for each visit; the rest is covered by the insurer. (Employees can use non-PPO physicians but it will cost them more.)

Health Maintenance Organization (HMO) is an option where the employer contracts with an HMO to receive a number of benefits

*For more information on health insurance, see the following articles: "Entrepreneur's Guide to Health Insurance Plans," by Kim Negron, *Entrepreneur*, April 1989; and "Help Wanted," by Stephen D. Solomon, *Inc.*, December 1989.

at a fixed price. The employee is sometimes (not always) required to pay a minimum contribution to the plan, but is required to go to the physicians and hospitals specified in the plan: no benefits will be paid if the employee goes to an outside doctor, regardless of the circumstances. The costs, however, for belonging to an HMO plan will be less per employee than under a major medical policy.

In order to cut costs, most insurers add a cost containment clause that requires a second surgical opinion. Each company differs to some degree in terms of benefits, deductibles, requirements, and options. (Dental insurance is optional on most plans, but not all; so is short- and long-term disability income.) Maternity coverage is available from most companies (and is legally required to be provided by employers in some states; check with your lawyer to find out laws in your area). Many insurers will not provide health insurance without your also purchasing a life insurance plan.

The main considerations when purchasing a health insurance policy are: How much will it cost if you (or a family member) needs medical care? What annual out-of-pocket expenses will you be expected to pay? Is emergency care provided? Dental care? Maternity coverage? Can you go to any doctor you choose, or will your choice be restricted?

It's important to compare plans to make sure you are ending up with the coverage you want for yourself and your employees.

Life Insurance

Small businesses can use life insurance to add to their financial stability, since it qualifies as collateral for a loan. Individual life insurance policies are available to sole proprietors and partners. For sole owners, it can furnish money for heirs who must continue or dispose of the business.

For partnerships and corporations, life insurance may provide the necessary cash for funding buy-sell agreements in the event of a partner's or major stockholder's death, and it can also be used to pay estate taxes.* In a partnership it protects the business, since

*In the event of the death of a partner (or major shareholder) the buy-sell agreement forces the estate of the deceased to sell and you, the remaining partner, to buy their share of the business. The money for this transaction comes from the proceeds of the insurance.

the partnership is legally terminated with death. Group life insurance policies are tax deductible only for corporations.

Any personal expense (such as medical or life insurance) that your corporation can pay for represents a tax savings. But consult the Internal Revenue Service, or your accountant or tax attorney, for up-to-date rulings in the ever-changing tax laws.

Term and Permanent Life Insurance

There are two basic kinds of life insurance and hundreds of variations.

Term life insurance means you are paying to cover the event of death; the company pays if you die, but it has no value as long as you stay alive. It's renewable every few years.

Permanent life insurance generates a cash value and it can be collected in twenty years, when you are sixty-five, or at whatever time the policy stipulates. You can hold on to the policy or surrender it for cash value. You can also borrow against the cash value at a low interest rate because you are actually borrowing your own money.

Key Person Insurance and Business Owners' Insurance

Key person insurance insures any person whose death could mean a substantial loss to your company. For example, if you manufacture the clothes of a specific designer, the loss of the designer could be disastrous to your business.

Business owners' policies can protect an owner against losses from disability or medical expenses or her dependents against losses from her premature death.

Wellness Programs

It is obvious that the better physical shape you and your employees are in, the less you are going to have to pay for health care. Because of this, many employers now prohibit smoking in the workplace and sometimes refuse to hire smokers.

Health insurance companies know that smokers, people with high blood pressure, and those who are overweight and underex-

---

See also SBA Business Development Publication, *Business Continuation Planning*, by Seymour Reitman and Donald E. Clough (Business Development Publications, no. MP 20, $1).

ercised are going to have more health problems than nonsmokers who watch their diets and exercise regularly. Therefore, some insurers now offer discounts to companies whose employees rate favorably on the major risk factors.

Wellness programs, then, are an obvious way to save money on insurance costs by giving your employees incentives to stay in shape and/or stop smoking or abusing other substances. First, you must make sure the employees want a wellness program and are willing to participate in it.

There are many ways to go about it. Install some exercise equipment in a back room—a stationary bike, treadmill, weights, etc. Sponsor a softball (volleyball, etc.) team. Offer an exercise class before or after work (there are many excellent exercise programs available on videotape). Urge everyone to use seatbelts, have their cholesterol checked, go to a treatment center for drug or alcohol abuse, join a stop-smoking class, etc. Local non-profit health organizations may provide booklets, speakers, or diagnostic testing for free or a minimal charge.

And give bonuses for weight loss, quitting smoking, etc. (The bonuses can be in cash, or in perks such as theater tickets, gift or restaurant certificates, and such.)

ESTATE PLANNING

No one wants to think about it but, if you own a business, estate planning has to be part of your general long-term business plan. It's necessary because estate taxes—currently up to 55 percent of a business's appraised value at the owner's death—can kill your business as well. Consult your financial advisers, and figure out what you can do to save your business in the event of your untimely death. Estate planning includes: writing a will and appointing an executor of your estate, choosing your heirs, buying adequate insurance, and coming up with tax-avoidance strategies and management-succession plans.

RETIREMENT/PENSION PLANS

Pension plans are another form of clever investment strategy for the business owner.* They offer tax advantages, and help you

*At the time of this printing, the fate of Section 89, a provision of the 1986 tax act requiring businesses to give high- and low-paid employees comparable fringe

(and your company) build and retain wealth. There are numerous plans available. They are:

Keogh Plan

The Keogh Plan is a pension/retirement plan for people who are self-employed (free-lancers, sole proprietors, or partners of unincorporated businesses).* This plan is not mandatory for self-employed people.

You may contribute annually up to 15 percent of your net taxable earned income. This money is tax deductible, with a ceiling ($7,500 generally, but check with the IRS for the latest tax rulings), but it must remain in the fund. The interest and dividends the money accrues each year are tax-free, too. When you retire you pay regular taxes on the money as you withdraw it from the fund, but by then you are likely to be in a lower tax bracket.

There are two types of Keogh plans: *defined* and *contributed.* For the self-employed, a defined benefit plan will allow you to decide how much you will receive per month (with an annual ceiling) when you retire at any age past fifty-five. A company-defined plan allows the employer to maintain a single account for the whole company that will provide a monthly annuity (based on a pre-arranged company formula) when you or your employee retires.

There are two types of contributed plans: *profit-sharing* (not the same plan that is found in larger corporations that pay employees a quarterly/annual share of their profits) and the *money-purchase plan.* For a very small company without employees, a contribution plan is most advantageous. The profit-sharing plan allows the shared company profits to be deferred into the employees' retirement accounts. (The employer must have a formula stipulating how these contributions will be allocated among plan participants.)

The money-purchase plan requires annual company payments based on a fraction of the employee's pay and the employee's contribution, with a limit of $30,000 or 25 percent of the employee's salary, whichever is smaller. For those under age forty-

benefits, is up in the air. For up-to-date information concerning Section 89, consult your accountant or tax attorney.
*The Internal Revenue Service, brokerage firms, and savings banks can give you further information regarding requirements for the Keogh Plan, as well as the other pension plans described.

five, this is generally the most appealing plan. Retirement benefits can be withdrawn any time after you reach the age of fifty-nine
and a half, and *must* be withdrawn before you turn seventy and
a half to avoid IRS penalties.

A brokerage firm can handle these plans. Or ask your accountant or tax attorney to recommend an independent professional
pension administrator.

401k

The 401k plan, also known as the salary reduction arrange-
ment (SARA), permits you and your employees to defer part of
your salary, tax-free—i.e., a designated percentage of your paycheck is withheld. The IRS does not require you and your employees to pay tax on the deferred percentage until you withdraw
the funds at retirement. The maximum deferment is $7,300 or 25
percent of a person's annual salary, whichever is smaller. This is
best for companies with over ten employees.

The Individual Retirement Annuity Plan (IRA)

The IRA plan covers individuals who are not usually covered
by an employer's plan. Basically, it is a voluntary contribution of
your own money (up to $2,000 per year) toward a pension plan,
before taxes are applied. Once completely deductible, it is now
based on your adjusted gross income (AGI). According to the
new tax laws, a single taxpayer whose AGI exceeds $35,000 is not
entitled to any IRA deduction, but if you've grossed less than
$25,000, you may take a full deduction. (If you are married, the
deductible point is $40,000 to $50,000; married couples filing
separately do not get IRA deductions.)

If your income exceeds the tax-deductible limits, you can
choose instead to place your $2,000 contribution into a 401k or
Keogh fund.

The Simplified Employee Pension (SEP)

The SEP plan is basically a "super IRA" (see above), designed
for companies with under twenty-five employees. To be eligible
for this plan, 50 percent or more of your employees must partici-

pate. Contributions are limited to $30,000 or 15 percent of the employee's salary, whichever is less.

Qualified Pension Plan (Profit-Sharing)

This plan is set up by a corporation for its employees and is tax deductible. It is not obligatory but is often a drawing card to attract qualified people to your company.

Triple Play

This is the maintenance of a Keogh, an IRA, and a 401k so that you can spread more of your and your employees' wealth around these tax-sheltered retirement plans. Discuss this with an estate planner or attorney.

"Cafeteria" Plan

This is also known as the "flexible benefits" program. It allows you and each employee to choose the various insurance and pension benefits that meet your and their individual needs.* A cafeteria plan can help control the cost of benefits, because you can choose to donate a fixed sum, say $500 or $1,000 annually, toward each employee. The employee can apply these pretax dollars toward the benefits she wants. This also helps employers save money from reduced social security taxes.†

BONDING

For a fee, a business can secure bonding, which shifts the financial responsibility for a *specific job or employee* to a licensed bonding company or insurance firm.

---

*Write for the free booklet, *The Best Benefits Program for Your Business,* published by the Touche Ross Enterprise Group (a nationwide firm offering services in accounting, auditing, tax, management, and benefits consulting), 1633 Broadway, New York, New York 10019–6754). Or call (212)489–1600 for the booklet and an explanation of the many other services they offer small businesses.
†Send away for the $4 booklet, *A Look at Social Security—1989,* prepared, updated regularly, and published by A. Foster Higgins & Co. (an employee benefits consulting firm), 125 Broad Street, New York, New York 10004.

Fidelity Bonds

These protect the business owner against employee theft and embezzlement. The employee (the "principal") is bonded by either a licensed bonding company or insurance company. There are three types of fidelity bonds: *Individual bonds* name a specific person; *schedule bonds* list all names or positions to be covered; and *blanket bonds* cover all employees but do not identify them by name or title, so that hirings and firings can take place without affecting it.

Bonds stay in effect until their cancellation. The limit of liability is always included, indicating the maximum sum to be paid.

Surety Bonds

These guarantee that the employee will carry out the specific job she was hired to do. If she is inept or quits, you can collect on the bond. (These are often used in the construction business, enabling bonded small contractors to compete against larger companies in bidding for jobs.)

ADDITIONAL INSURANCE COVERAGE

Depending upon your type of business there are many other special-purpose insurance coverages to be mentioned but not elaborated upon: business interruption insurance; credit life insurance; commercial credit insurance; accounts receivable insurance; valuable papers insurance; profits and commissions insurance; malpractice insurance; insurance for franchises and mail-order companies, and so forth.

Remember when you meet with your new insurance agent to describe the workings of your business fully with her. She will advise you on what specific coverage you need.

· 9 ·

Banks: Where Credit Is Due

Women, like princes, find few real friends.
—George, Lord Lyttelton

Banks are in the service business. In return for your money, via checking, money market, and savings accounts, their business is to serve *you*. As women have come into their own as managers and entrepreneurs, there has been a growing effort to make women feel at ease and to seek their business. But when it comes to applying for a start-up business loan, banks treat aspiring female entrepreneurs the way Dracula treats daylight. True, a large percentage of the nation's wealth is in women's names; much of it, though, is in name only. But women are gaining their ground and are now protected by law against credit discrimination.*

In order to use money effectively, women must understand it thoroughly. Instead of avoiding the subject, once the genteel thing to do, it is time to realize that the economy in general, and one's own economy in particular, are areas one can scarcely afford to neglect. Remember, a lot of U.S. Treasurers have been women.

To erase the fear of numbers—diminishing, multiplying, running your life—you have to learn to live with them. And if you're going into business for yourself, then your future success relies to a great extent on your ability to control the dollars with sense.

*The 1974 Federal Equal Credit Opportunity Act (ECOA) and subsequent amendments prohibit credit discrimination on the basis of sex or marital status in mortgage and business lending. Credit worthiness is now based on the ability to pay one's bills and is not bound to the credit rating of a spouse or ex-spouse.

No matter how fantastic your accountant and banker may be, it is you who must conduct the orchestra.

ENTER . . . THE BANKER

When you start your business, even if you're working freelance, open a business checking account. It is both professional and practical to keep business accounts separate from personal ones, even if they are with the same bank.

Have your accountant or lawyer introduce you to a banker at the outset of your business if you haven't already lined up someone you respect. (A recommendation will present your business in a sounder light than will your coming in cold off the street.) Since you will work closely, your goal is to establish both a banking relationship and a friendship with your banker. Listen to professional advice while you shop around, but make your own decision as to the banker and bank you feel will help you the most.

Rapport with banking people cannot be underestimated. Many male bankers are willing to help women, but they are often paternalistic. More and more women are becoming bank officers these days, and are even opening women's banks.* A woman may be more sympathetic to your project. Remember, however, that she is still a banker and cannot waive banking standards just because you are a woman, too.

No matter how small a business you start, laying the basic groundwork (for later expansion loans, etc.) is imperative. At the first appointment with your prospective banker, be prepared to present your business plan, your professional background, what you plan to do, and where you aim to go. After you've settled on your banker, keep her up-to-date on your progress. Call her every few weeks. It is not a waste of her time; she wants to know how you're doing, to participate in your growth whenever she can.

Besides the sympathetic banker, the bank itself must be consid-

*In 1819, the Bank for Savings on Chambers Street in New York City was the first savings bank to open its doors to women. In 1919, the first women's bank in the United States—with a completely female staff—was opened in Clarksville, Tennessee, by a woman named Brenda Runyon. In 1926 it merged with another bank, and there wasn't another women's bank until The First Women's Bank was founded in New York City in 1975. The First Women's Bank of Maryland, in Rockville, Maryland, began operating in 1979. There are also The Adams Bank in Washington, D.C., and The Women's Federal Savings Bank in Cleveland, Ohio, as of this writing.

ered. Banks are competitive businesses. They offer numerous services besides cashing checks and issuing loans. Some large banks are set up to help small businesses with payroll management and tax paying, thus saving you the expense of a bookkeeper. But in general, small businesses are best nourished by small banks, where there is close contact with the officers, easy access to the president, and the tellers know you by name. Most large banks simply cannot grant you the same personal attention.

BANK SERVICES

After your business is set up, you may want to look to your bank for a number of additional services. Large banks may offer a more varied selection of services in order to attract new customers, but all banks are set up to help you in ways you probably haven't required before. Banks, depending on their size, can provide some or all of the following services (and it is up to you to ferret out what your bank can do for you):

Provide personal service plans to help reconcile your monthly statement

Transfer funds anywhere, by wire or cable, saving the days it usually takes for a check to clear

Set up and keep records for employees' benefits, like profit-sharing and retirement

Establish Keogh (federal tax-favored retirement) plans for sole proprietors or partnerships

Provide a lock box system to pick up and process checks for faster payment if you do a lot of business in other cities

Run credit checks for you on any new client or supplier, both in the United States and overseas

Offer payroll management services, including taxes

Issue you a letter of credit, outlining terms of payment, for a supplier

Introduce you to affiliates in other areas of the country, or abroad, if you plan to expand

Act as your register and transfer agent should you (if incorporated) decide to go public

Help you find another business with which to merge, or a buyer if you want to sell

Sell tax-exempt bonds and notes

Become trustees of your estate

Guarantee a cash reserve up to $5,000 (for special accounts)

Issue charge cards, such as MasterCard or Visa

Offer (for a fee) an investment management service

Rent safety deposit boxes for your important records

Stop payments on checks (Don't reissue a check that has been lost until you have stopped payment on the original.)

Certify checks (until you have established credit)

Issue check-cashing convenience cards for a nationwide network of cash machines.

Find out what your bank will be able to offer you as you grow. Bank policies vary, but all work within the same basic framework.

OPENING A BUSINESS BANK ACCOUNT

Banks require a business or personal reference if you are not known to them or introduced via a respected businessperson in your community.

If you are doing business as a sole proprietor or under a fictitious name, you must submit a certificate of business (available from your county clerk for about ten dollars) to open an account. A business must also have a federal employer identification number in order to open a bank account. In order to get it, use your social security number if you are a sole proprietor, or file Form SS-4, available from the Internal Revenue Service. A partnership must also provide a list of partners and stipulate which ones are authorized to sign checks. If you are incorporated, you must hand over a copy of the corporate resolutions, a list of officers, and the names of those authorized to sign checks and negotiate loans. (This can change as the business grows.)

It is also possible to have a signature card on file for anyone else on your staff who goes to the bank for you. In this case, there is usually an agreed-upon limit for cashing checks.

It's an excellent idea to keep a separate bank account for tax monies, so that you won't inadvertently use tax money for day-to-day operating expenses. This is especially advantageous for retailers and services required to pay sales tax, so they won't be caught in a bind at tax time.*

*To obtain your sales tax resale number, apply to the state board of equalization for a seller's permit.

Your Credit Rating

Business life is a cycle of "creditability." What's happening now is based on the past, and your future credit hinges on now. When a new business seeks to establish credit, the creditors look to the owner's personal credit, since the business itself is an untried entity.

A single, working woman gathers credit when she opens a bank account, takes a personal loan, or acquires charge cards. A married woman must maintain her own financial identity, separate from her husband. (If you open a joint account with your husband, credit institutions regard this as establishing *his* credit, not yours. However, under the provisions of the Equal Credit Opportunity Act, all you need to do is notify your bank and creditors that you want the credit history on your joint account reported in *your* name, as well as your husband's, and the change will be made.) Credit cards must be in a woman's own name—married, maiden, or hyphenated. She should also keep her own personal checking, savings, or money market account.

An excellent way to establish credit is to take out a loan and pay it back (with interest) on time. (In fact, if you're planning to start a business someday in the future, it's a good idea to start taking out loans now. As soon as you've paid one off, get a new one—for an increasing amount of money. Over a period of years this will establish your creditworthiness. When you're ready to start your business, you will already have established a relationship with a bank/banker.) However, banks cannot grant loans just so you can establish credit; you must give a reason for taking one out—moving, home improvements, etc. If you are starting out on your own for the first time, someone may have to cosign the loan with you (a relative, spouse, accountant, etc.), but when you pay it back on time, the credit established is yours.

The key to financial independence is financial responsibility. Honor your loan payments, pay your credit card bills before interest accumulates, and never overdraw on your checking account, either on purpose or inadvertently. The same rules apply for your business—a company's history of debt-paying establishes its credit rating.*

*Business credit ratings are listed with Dun & Bradstreet and Equifax, Inc. However, you are not required to furnish your company's financial information. If you choose, these companies will list you, but not *rate* you.

The capitalist system revolves around credit references; if they're clean, the god of money smiles upon you. If not, you will be in for a lot of time-consuming hassles that sap your energy and your morale.

An amendment to the Federal Equal Credit Opportunity Act (ECOA) of 1974, set forth in the Women's Business Ownership Act of 1988, has eliminated the previous exemption regarding banks granting business loans to women, which is an enormous breakthrough. Under this amendment financial institutions are required to: tell you of your right to receive a written explanation for denial of loan applications; retain loan application records for at least a year; and refrain from inquiring into the marital status of an applicant. (The ECOA of 1974 prohibits banks, retailers, and other lenders from asking about your spouse's credit standing, and your childbearing plans [or birth-control practices]. Federal Reserve Board rulings prohibit a creditor's cutting off credit or requiring a reapplication upon divorce or separation. And the 1971 Fair Credit Reporting Act guarantees your right to see your credit profile.)*

Establishing Business Credit

If your business depends heavily on supplies—inventory, expensive equipment, raw materials, wholesale foods—then you have to establish credit. Even if you have more money than Scrooge, it is good business practice. Credit helps a business expand and cushions the blows in hard times.

Credit is simply others' belief that you can meet your bills. A creditor extends to you a certain amount of time (after delivery of the goods) before the payment comes due. This can vary from ten to ninety days (or up to two or three years for expensive equipment).

In retail or wholesale businesses, in which your suppliers associate with you on a continuing basis, the standard credit-establishing procedure is initially to pay in full for goods, at the time

*Your credit profile is generally on file with numerous reporting agencies in your area that have received credit reports about you in the past six months. If you've been denied credit, you can see your file for free, but if you're merely curious, there is a small fee. Look in the Yellow Pages for local credit information corporations.

After filling out the proper form, you can obtain a printout of your credit file, either in person or by mail, but not over the telephone.

144

you order them. The total cost of initial inventory or stock has to be figured in your start-up budget. The next time around, you may pay half on ordering and the balance within thirty days, or in full upon delivery. By the third buying excursion, you should rate full credit.

From then on, it's fairly easy to have a credit line run on your business through one of the big credit firms, such as Dun & Bradstreet or Equifax, Inc. They will research the list of suppliers with which you deal and record the manner in which you organize your payments—in thirty days, sixty days, etc. They will check your bank references, audit figures of the business, and investigate your past credit relationships. This information is then condensed onto a computer card and is available to any subscriber who requests the information. Dun & Bradstreet or Equifax, Inc. will make no recommendation, either positive or negative—it's up to the supplier to decide whether you are a good or bad risk.

The apparel business, however, is a special case. Here, Dun & Bradstreet will advise suppliers as to the amount of credit you merit. Another important source of credit information is the Credit Exchange in New York City.* It is the magic word on Seventh Avenue; if you want a season's inventory and the time to pay for it, establish your business with the Credit Exchange.

But what if you don't have a credit rating? No credit, no personal fortune—nothing but a bright idea and lots of drive. It's not a great position to deal from, but there are options. Probably your best bet is to draw up the solidest, soundest, most convincing presentation you can, outlining what your business will be and what it can do. Then use this to sell one supplier—the kitchen equipment dealer, say, for the restaurant you want to start. Make them see that they can't lose—the community is desperate for haute cuisine, and you're a Cordon Bleu chef of the first order. With your recipes and their stove and refrigerator, Chez Champignon is a surefire moneymaker. Then once the kitchen equipment people have come around, use your credit relationship with them as leverage to convince other suppliers. And—*voilà!*—you're on your way to a sound credit rating.

*Credit Exchange Inc., 229 West Thirty-sixth Street, New York, New York 10001, (212)760–7600; Dun & Bradstreet, Inc., 200 Liberty, New York, New York 10004, (212)945–0810 or (800)526–1003; Equifax Services, Inc., 747 Third Avenue, New York, New York 10022, (212)832–6800.

SUMMARY

Banks *want* your business.* And they want to see your business grow. Before selecting a bank, shop around for the right bank for your needs. Usually, the bank that feels right to you will be right for you. Some women entrepreneurs treat banks as any other major business purchase and put their account out for a bid. By presenting their business plans, financial history, and banking needs to several banks, they are able to choose the one that offers the most generous line of credit, best interest rates on long-term loans, and most extensive list of services.

Get to know your banker. She will help tailor her bank's services to your needs, no matter how large the bank or how small your business. Not all officers know everything, but they have access to any information you need. If you feel you are being shuffled to the bottom of the deck because you're a woman, or your business is too small to interest the bank with whom you've been dealing, then change banks.

But move only if you need to. It is easier to borrow working capital or get an expansion loan from a banker who has dealt with you over a period of time.

*Some banks are now recruiting new business by becoming known as socially responsible lenders. Conforming to the Community Reinvestment Act, the Vermont National Bank has set aside money for specific causes, with 25 percent earmarked for small businesses and nonprofit organizations. Other banks may be following suit soon, so check your potential bank for its social consciousness before giving it your money.

· Part II ·

Succeeding in Business

· 10 ·

Advertising and Publicity: Much Ado About Something

There is only one thing worse than being talked about, and that is not being talked about.

—Oscar Wilde

THE GRAND OPENING

Besides coordinating advertising and publicity with the opening of your business, you might consider throwing a party for potential clients and members of the local media. For added promotion, you might let it be known that you are going to donate the proceeds of your first day in business to a charity or community cause that you support. Grand opening bashes are especially important for prestige businesses, such as art galleries. But no matter what your business does, it's important to garner as much as attention as possible for your opening.

Hospitality wins admirers, and it doesn't have to cost a mint— nonalcoholic punch and homemade cookies will do. Have it at your store or office; talk other businesses into furnishing you with supplies for credit or at discount. Or get local entertainment to help you out for free publicity. Think of every angle. And reciprocate with other businesses throughout your career.

Other grand opening attention-getters might be a contest or raffle (give away a free product or service). You might have a car drive around town with a sign announcing your existence. Have T-shirts made up with your company name for you and your staff to wear. Have balloons or any other kind of inexpensive giveaway printed with the name of your business.

Many newspapers and local magazines have special sections or columns dealing with new products, new restaurants (reviews), or services. Find these and send press releases to the editors. New-product columns are great for mail order, as they will list your company name and address. And this publicity is all *free!*

ADVERTISING

The Making of an Ad

Advertising is an integral part of business. Like the neighborhood dowager who introduces newcomers to the community, an advertisement announces the arrival of your business. And advertising has a continuing function: to *introduce* a product or service; to *inform* the public of its features; to *persuade* people to try it; and, as time goes by, to *keep reminding* your public that you're still around and better than ever.

Advertising is only as successful as the product or service it is promoting. No amount of advertising will work if your shop is inaccessible, poorly stocked or staffed, or not open at convenient times. The point of advertising is to bring in new customers; you have to be equipped to handle them once they're there, or you'll lose them forever.

The Advertising Budget

The less you can afford an ad campaign, the more you probably need one. Without advertising, people won't know you're out there. Of course, many businesses can make a go of it from publicity and word of mouth, especially if they are situated in prime high-traffic locations. But sooner or later, business owners realize that they cannot drift. If they are to grow and to attract new clients continually, they must advertise.

Have your accountant help you plan a monthly advertising budget, projected at least six months in advance. There are no hard-and-fast rules for establishing an ad budget. Generally, it is anything from 2 to 10 percent of your estimated yearly gross. Keep at least 5 percent of that budget aside for special events (holiday celebrations, community activities, etc.). Spread the rest out in a consistent pattern (but don't spread yourself too thin).

Steady advertising brings in customers. The more modest your budget, the more carefully you must chart your long-range campaign. Ads must be repetitive to be effective; don't bother to advertise if you cannot afford to advertise regularly.

Your advertising expenses will fall into two general categories: production and media. Production expenses when you are dealing with print include creative labor, typesetting, photostating, art, copy, layout, and materials. (If you have a computer software program with desktop publishing, or access to one, you can save time and money by eliminating most of the above steps.) Broadcast production expenses run to things like studio time, equipment rental, tape, talent, and labor.

Media expenses are the cost of buying time or space in the medium that has been selected to present your message. Possibilities include television, radio, newspapers, magazines and periodicals, and others, which will be discussed in this chapter. In estimating your budget, make a list of the media available to you, and obtain rate sheets from them. Use these to determine the best places for *you* to advertise, and divide your monthly budget among them.

Make a chart, divided into months. Then list, in columns, the medium, cost of ad, size or length of ad, date ad must be submitted, and date ad will run. Later, include a description of the ad itself in order to keep track of what runs where.

Test your advertising ideas (and mock-ups of ads) on friends and business associates to get personal reactions as to which ads have the most impact.

Prepare several ads and rotate them, so that people won't tire of the same old thing. Budget for your peak season by allocating extra funds for heavier penetration at that time.

Cooperative Advertising

Ads jointly placed by more than one advertiser are cooperative ads. Often they are used by a store or service and its dealer/distributor, or supplier. Sometimes all the stores in a certain location will go in together on an ad. Many large manufacturers of brand-name merchandise often offer coop advertising packages to shops that buy from them. Sometimes the manufacturer will pay the majority of the ad space cost in return for a featured store location for the merchandise. For a new business, this kind of advertising helps associate your name with already established operations and saves money into the bargain.

Advertising Strategy

To create an advertising strategy, start by answering questions about the nature of your business and your market.

First, determine just who *you* are. In what price range are your products or services? Is your emphasis on price, or on quality and service? What exactly are you selling? Is it one thing, or many? Are you easily accessible? What extras do you want to tell the public about?

Once you're sure who you are, decide who *they* are. What consumer group are you going after? When you've defined your potential market, then focus your attention on a prototype. Visualize this person, and direct your ads to her or him.

Ads are the ambassadors of your business. They must attract, inform, and establish the image that you want to project. Keep that prototypical client in mind while you're reveling in creative brainstorming; remember, what strikes you as devilishly sophisticated and snappy might not be right for your market.

Since many small business owners handle their own advertising out of necessity, it's a good idea to take some evening courses in advertising and public relations. The more you know, the fewer costly mistakes you'll make.

The Copy

You have the choice of institutional or product advertising. The institutional ad is simply a general reminder to the public that your business exists, giving business name, address, business slogan (if you have one), and hours you are open. The product ad tells the reader about a specific service or piece of merchandise. In general, keep it simple. Those full-page ads chock-full of copy work only for certain very special cases. The quicker you can make your point, the better are your chances of getting it across. Go to the library, and check local newspaper ads for competitive businesses for the past year. Make note of how often they advertised, the size of the ads, how varied they were, etc. This will help you form your own campaign.

Your ad may vary depending on the medium you're running it in. Once you've picked the medium and decided on the size of your ad, look through the publication and see what ads catch your attention. Study them, learn from them: what makes them work? Many publications have media departments to help small advertisers create an ad, demonstrating what sort of message can be effective in the amount of space purchased.

A good format to follow is this:

Headline. An eye-catching succinct phrase or question.

Body. The sell. In as few words as possible, let the world know what you have and why they want it. Be believable and clear. Mention your product or company by name.

Wrap-up. Price (if it's a selling point). List any extra incentives or other details. Tell how to buy or obtain more facts about the product or service.

Finale. Mention any available catalog or brochure. Give company name, address, telephone number, and business hours. If you have a company logo, use it here.

For short-term ads (running in daily newspapers, weekly journals, local broadcast spots) you can tie in the weather, seasons, holidays, current events, or community activities with your copy. Keep tuned in to any special local or national happenings that are synergistic to your business. If you're writing broadcast copy to be delivered live by an announcer or disk jockey, keep her voice and style in mind.

In general, back up superlatives with facts, keep the name of your company up front, emphasize your advantages over the competition. Aim for impact and individuality in the copy and simplicity and consistency in the style.

The Art

In advertising terms, art is anything visual—drawing, painting, photography, even type style and layout. But a cluttered ad will defeat your message.

Art, like copy, should be kept simple. If you use an illustration, make sure it is persuasive and descriptive. Keep to simple line drawings, with no shading. Detailed sketches are harder to reproduce clearly. Check the quality of reproduction in the publication your ad will be running in. Photographs, for instance, do not often reproduce well in small-space newspaper ads. If you decide to use a photo (e.g., to advertise in the shop-by-mail sections in magazines), hire a professional photographer to take clear, well-lighted eight-by-ten-inch photos to accompany your ad. (The magazine will stat them down to correct proportions for your ad.) Omit illustrations unless they serve a purpose; otherwise, they'll just crowd the space and detract from the copy.

If you are having your copy typeset, choose a style that complements the message. Keep legibility in mind—you may be crazy about Old English lettering, but the public won't wade through a whole paragraph of it.

A publication's advertising or media department can advise you on typefaces and the use of borders. It will also inform you whether a cut (metal image) of your logo is necessary for its printer. If a cut is needed, you'll be charged a nominal fee for it.

Save money on illustrations and borders by using "clip art," copyright-free designs that you can cut out and use in your layout. Clip-art books are available at art supply stores or bookstores.

Design your ads so that they stand out from the rest of the page. Study the competition; see what's being done, glean the best points, and understand what makes them good. Then use that background to do something even better and *different*.

Production

Who will create your ads? You will. In the beginning, while your budget is small, it probably won't make economic sense to go to an outside agency. And who knows better than you what you want to say?

If you really don't feel up to it, then hire someone to do it as inexpensively as possible. Check art and writing classes at local colleges, or look for a talented free-lancer. Talk to friends, and pick their brains for ideas.

Advertising departments of many newspapers and small magazines offer help in preparation of copy, artwork, and layout. Talk to them after you have written up a rough ad, and take advantage of their assistance. But don't follow their advice blindly, or your ad will wind up looking like all the others.

For information on advertising in general and advertising ethics, contact your local chamber of commerce, Better Business Bureau, and trade associations.

If you're going to produce the ad yourself, start with the concept. Always stress the advantages of the product, never the product itself. For example, suppose you have invented a revolutionary little gadget. Don't say, "Introducing the Terrific Do-Everything Gadget . . . does fifty different things. Buy one today!" Vague claims don't leave a trail of afterimages. Present the facts: "Introducing the Terrific Do-Everything Gadget . . . it pops corn, cleans dentures, shreds cabbage, dyes Easter eggs, and make peanut butter sandwiches *in ten seconds!*" People must be able to focus on a product in relation to their needs.

When you've got your copy, have it typeset or varityped. (Discuss the various methods with your printer, along with costs.) Or do it yourself with a good desktop publishing software program or even a typewriter and press-on type. In some instances, even hand lettering may give the effect you're looking for.

If you are hiring an artist or photographer, look at her work first. Choose someone whose style complements your product and image. Make sure the fee is established in advance and fits your budget. Be clear as to whether there will be any additional charge for supplies and expenses. Young talent is usually the best for a small budget. Just be sure to explain exactly what you want, and keep an eye on the work in progress.

Do several rough layouts, to see what works the best. Experiment with different sizes for your headline; play around with ways of cropping and placing the artwork. Maybe you'll want to use a decorative border.

When you have done it the way you want it, assemble the ingredients on mat or illustration board or lay it all out on your computer. To work in different sizes, you can have your art and copy reduced or enlarged by photostat. Spread rubber cement on both surfaces, and let them dry before positioning.

For precision work, tear a piece of tracing paper or onionskin in half, and place the pieces slightly overlapping on the mat board after the cement is dry. The tracing paper will not stick to the dried rubber cement, and it allows you to see through to your layout markings on the mat board, so that you can position things exactly where you want them. Then place the section of art or copy you're working with in position, and slip out one of the pieces of tracing paper from beneath it. When you've pressed that securely in place, slip out the other piece of tracing paper and smooth out the rest.

When the layout is complete, have it photostated to size. Then you can keep the original and give the "camera-ready" copy to the publication. Don't have a printer make up permanent plates unless you plan to run the same ad often.

Free-lancers and Advertising Agencies

It is said that if you don't spend more than $10,000 a year on advertising, you probably don't need an agency. But what if you have two left hands (and two left brains) when it comes to putting together your own ads? This is an aspect of your business that can be time-consuming, and if you don't have the talent for it, why take the time away from things you *can* do well?

You can hire a free-lancer to come in and handle your advertising needs; it makes sense if you don't have a huge ad budget. Free-lance writers and artists work on a per-project basis and cost much less than an ad agency. Locate them through the Yellow Pages, your chamber of commerce, local printers, advertising clubs, trade associations, or the advertising, journalism, or art departments of your local college. *AdWeek* magazine, published nationally in regional editions, also includes a directory of free-lancers.

Most free-lancers will be happy to come and show you their portfolios for free. See what they have done for other similar businesses and whether their style conforms to your vision. Ask their fee, and what results their ads have had for their other clients. Before you hire a free-lancer, agree in writing exactly what services the writer or artist will provide, along with delivery dates and price.

Should the day come when you want and can afford an agency, how do you find the right one for your needs? Agencies pull together ads, but they do much more these days, from creative brainstorming to product marketing research. Some agencies handle direct-mail promotions and even answer customer inquiries about your product or service.

In general, it is wise to gravitate toward a small agency. Large agencies can handle your advertising globally and provide more services than a smaller agency, but this is probably overkill. Small businesses are often treated like ugly stepchildren at the large agencies. Besides, many small agencies were started by former high-level executives at big agencies. Small agencies generally charge less and can offer you more personalized service.

Before selecting an ad agency, talk to several. (Find them through business associates, trade associations, the Yellow Pages, or the *Standard Directory of Advertising Agencies* or *The AdWeek Agency Directory* at your library. Check also the advertising magazines sold on newsstands, such as *Advertising Age* and *AdWeek.*) Describe your needs (be prepared to provide background information on your company and the direction you see your company going), as well as your budget. Look at samples of their work, especially campaigns for businesses with budgets similar to yours. Follow the progression of ads for the same client, noting originality and continuity. Have them give you an idea of what they think they can do for you.

Before making your decision on an agency, run a credit check, compare rates, and evaluate the agency's reputation (talk to former and current clients). Settle on an agency that will give you the most attention and the best quality.

Ad agencies exist to inject professional creativity into your ads and to save you time and headaches. They conceive of, execute, and supervise the ad from start to finish. All you have to do is nod with approval and pay the bills.

When an agency places your ad, the cost to you is the same as if you placed it yourself. The agency takes a 15 percent commission from the publication or station. This is where the agency makes its money, so the more you advertise, the more enthusiastic about your account the agency is likely to be.

You pay the agency for its expenses in preparing the ad. If the ad yields more than $150 in commission, then copy and layout should be free. All additional expenses—printing, artwork, photography, etc.—are billed to you at a 20 percent markup.

An agency will save you time and mistakes and give your ads a professional look. But until you're in the bucks, learn about advertising by doing it yourself—or with a little help from your friends.

WHERE TO ADVERTISE

Evaluate all media, and decide which ones reach your prospective market most effectively. There are a lot of publications out there, and they'd all love your advertising dollar. There are: metropolitan, local, and weekly newspapers; national/regional/local magazines; special interest newsletters/magazines; and trade publications.

Where you will advertise will, of course, depend on your budget. Contact the sales departments of the publications that interest you and request their rate cards—fliers that list ad prices and circulation statistics.*

Newspapers

This category includes dailies, weeklies, biweeklies, Sunday editions, shoppers, neighborhood newspapers. Get rate sheets and circulation data on every publication in your area. See how well they report local news for a clue to the extent and nature of their readership. Look into special interest journals, foreign-language papers, publications of clubs, societies, and churches, theater and summer stock programs.

Display ads can be a fraction of a page (a half-page, an eighth, a sixteenth, etc.) or sold by the column inch. A column inch is one inch deep (fourteen lines) and the width of the column in the publication.

Rates decrease as you increase the number of ads you place. Classified listings are usually money wasters, unless the publication is particularly suited to them.

Newspaper advertising must be frequent. Consider what kind of schedule will be most effective for your business. Mondays and Tuesdays are good for services, Wednesdays through Sundays best for store advertising. Newspapers provide intensive coverage and quick response.

Before you sign a publication's space contract, make sure you understand the conditions, costs, and termination clause. Find out what it will cost if you decide you want to get out of the commitment.

*See "Put It in Print: Ten Easy Steps to a Profitable Print Advertising Campaign," by Shelly Mainhardt, *Entrepreneur,* January 1989; and SBA publication no. MT-11, *Advertising* ($1).

Check your library for *Consumer Magazine and Farm Publication Rates and Data,* and *Business Publication Rates and Data,* both published by Standard Rate and Data Service.

Magazines

Consumer Magazines

Many national magazines publish regional editions.* If your business has a large enough appeal, look into these. They may cover several states, a single state, or even a large metropolitan/ suburban area.

And look into special interest magazines. If there is one that ties in with your product or service, it would be worth considering.

Business Magazines

Business and trade publications are a good way of letting others know what you're doing. Consult *Standard Rate and Data* (both the business publications issue and the consumer magazine book).†

If you're not familiar with the magazine you're considering, have them send you circulation data,‡ rates, and a copy of a back issue. Evaluate it for quality, number of advertisers, and decide whether it will be a good platform for your message.

Local Magazines

Look into local business publications, sponsored by the chamber of commerce and local trade associations. Also check out club, alumnae, college organization, and visitor magazines.

Magazine rates vary widely. Many offer discounts based on volume, frequency, and continuity. Magazine rates usually go by pages and fractions of pages, although some offer classified and column-inch rates.

Magazines have a longer reading life than newspapers, and special interest magazines are often kept on file instead of being thrown out. General interest magazines attract more readers per copy, but their readership's interests are less carefully pinpointed.

*To acquire names, check your library for the following publications: *Gale Directory of Publications* (formerly *Ayer's*); *Ulrich's International Periodicals Directory; Editor & Publisher International Yearbook; Radio Annual and TV Yearbook; Bacon's Publicity Checker; The Gebbie Press House Magazine Directory* (lists house organs of large corporations); and *Standard Rate and Data*.

†Check your library, or try to get an old one from an ad agency—they usually throw out back issues after new ones arrive. The Department of Commerce also publishes a state-by-state list of trade publications.

‡Make sure the statistics quoted are audited or sworn-circulation statements.

Classified Directories

The Yellow Pages is the most famous of these. When you take out a business phone, you are allowed one free listing. But if you offer a variety of products or services, consider placing ads under more than one category. It costs extra, but people do use the Yellow Pages. A telephone company representative will give you a cost breakdown for bold-type listings, column-inch and display ads. (You can also pay to have bold type in your White Pages listing.) Instead of a flat yearly rate, you pay the telephone company in monthly installments.

Other classified media include general industrial directories for all industries or types of products. Nowadays, many cities publish private Women's Yellow Pages and neighborhood Yellow Pages. Listing in these can also bring in more local business.

Radio and Television

Many community public access and cable television stations offer reasonable rates for local time slots. Rates vary greatly, depending on the time of day and the length of the spot. Radio is apt to be less expensive, both in terms of production costs and media costs, but check with all your local stations for particulars.

Different types of shows reach different audiences. Aim for the market you want and the best time of day to reach it. A late-late-show time slot is inexpensive and fine if your product appeals to a college audience, but not worth the expense if you're trying to sell to preteenagers.

To have any impact, you must advertise regularly. Don't waste your money on a one-shot radio ad.

Broadcast advertising makes a strong impression. If you are seriously considering TV and radio, don't rush into it. Start timing ads to see how much you can get effectively into a minute, thirty seconds, or ten seconds. Study the messages that get across to you, and break down their ingredients. Count the number of times the product's name is mentioned during a commercial.

In preparing a commercial for TV, you can keep costs down by using a series of still pictures with a voice-over announcer. Or rent videotape equipment and stage a mini-production. Use the same guideline you use in print advertising: keep it simple. Don't try to jam in too much.

Make sure the announcer's voice is easily understood; the less colloquial, the better. For radio, you can either tape an ad or submit copy to be read by the announcer on the air. In some local markets this can also be done with television.

Mailers and Brochures

Follow the same thought patterns and physical steps for preparing a print ad and producing a brochure, catalog, mailer, or flier. Before you begin, talk to a printer about sizes. It's cheaper if the piece fits a standard envelope, preferably an envelope the size of your stationery. There are a number of shapes to consider, too—invitation, presentation, accordion, one page, etc. Ask to see samples of brochures, not only to evaluate printing quality but also to get ideas.

Get a price estimate. The printer will figure it for you based on the size of the piece, the paper stock you choose, the number of colors, and the quantity of the run. Standard sizes are less expensive, and the fewer colors you use, the less it will cost you (see chapter 5, under the heading "Logo, Stationery, and Business Cards"). Don't forget the folding, which is also done and charged for by the printer.

Some printers offer lower prices for four-color printing by running a batch of orders together on a large press. This is economical, but it takes longer (the printer will wait until she has enough separate orders), and often you won't get perfect color matching. There is also a three-color for two process, which applies to two-sided printing. (The printer can print black plus one color on the first side, for example, and then black plus another color on the reverse. When folded properly, it can be very effective.)

Consider the possibility of designing self-mailers. These are brochures or other mailing pieces that can be sent without an envelope; they are simply folded, stapled, stamped, and addressed.

Catalogs

If you provide a number of products or services, or sell by mail order, put together a catalog. Catalogs must be well organized, with items grouped according to category. (Some with multiple applications may be repeated in several categories.) Products can also be classified by price range, seasonal sales, etc.

In the copy, be brief, accurate, and catchy. Use clear, simple illustrations and an uncluttered layout. The cover of your catalog should be eye-grabbing and colorful, even if the inside contents are in black and white. If you offer many items, you might consider adding an index page for your customers' convenience.

Be sure to feature the company name and address, preferably on the front and back covers. If items can be ordered by mail, or additional information requested, include order cards or relevant instructions.

Print "catalog" on the outside of the mailing envelope. Make up a dummy catalog with the paper stock you will be using and have it priced at the post office; if you're just over one price plateau, maybe you can cut down the size a little. Postage adds up.

There is a lot of copy in a catalog and a lot of room for typographical errors. When you have your copy ready for the printer, check it over thoroughly. Make copies of it and give them to friends to proofread. Catch mistakes before they go to press in order to avoid expensive and time-consuming resetting.

Shop-by-Mail Advertising

If you are selling a product, consider advertising in the shop-by-mail sections located in the backs of many consumer magazines. In this way, you can offer your product via direct mail, prepaid with postage costs included. Be sure to include a clear photo or sketch of the product you're offering. Check with your post office to obtain accurate shipping fees for the product (including all the packaging).

In order to gauge success with your ads, instigate a coding system to monitor your ads. With your mailing address, have the customer write to Dept. A (B, C, and so forth). Have a different code for each magazine and each issue you advertise in. This is how you will be able to keep track of publications (and months) that are bringing in the most orders. Shop-by-mail advertising is expensive for the most part, so don't go overboard until you have determined the mail-order popularity of your product. Also, you must be set up to ship your product as soon as the orders start flowing in; current law stipulates that the order be filled within three weeks. (If there will be a delay on an item, you must inform the customer in writing, giving them the opportunity to cancel the order; you must also inform them of the new shipping dates.)

Direct Mail

This is advertising sent through the mail to a selected group of customers. It can be useful for soliciting mail- or phone-order business; announcing new products or services, and special events like sales; notification of price changes; and public relations via holiday greetings, etc.

Direct mail is expensive. An average piece of mailing costs up to twenty-five cents for paper and printing, plus postage. There is the chance of a full minute of someone's attention and the risk of an immediate throwaway. Keep it individual, personal, and never address it to "Occupant."

Direct Response Mail

The aim is to get potential customers to respond *now*, via return postcard for orders or more information. You could also enclose a questionnaire or a quiz. There are ad agencies whose specialty is determining the best kind of direct response mailing for your needs.

The Use of Mailing Lists

A mailing is only as good as its mailing list. It can be costly and ineffective if you don't hit the right market for your product, or if three out of five persons have moved.

You can either build your own list (preferable and cheaper) or purchase one (if you're looking for special groups of people).

To build your own, ask for lists from social clubs, or any organization you belong to, the chamber of commerce, charity groups, your child's school list, or the local college and church lists. Noncompetitive organizations are easier to approach than the business community. You can also check directories and newspaper notices. Once you're in business, get the names and addresses of all customers. Sponsor a contest or sweepstakes in which the participants must provide name and address.

The rental or purchase of names from mailing list houses (and some magazine publishers) provides you with general lists of names or specialized lists according to categories of people. But it is expensive, and the lists go out of date quickly. Make sure you get recommendations for a reliable company before laying out money.* And make one person on your staff responsible for keeping the lists up-to-date.

Postage
First class mail is automatically forwarded to a new address or returned to you (make sure to include the return address). It's expensive, so use it only for personalized mailing pieces. Third or fourth class (parcel post) provides cheaper rates, although you must pay an extra fee to have the mail forwarded or returned. Include on the envelope "Return or Forwarding Postage Guaranteed." For bulk mailings you must obtain a permit, and there are certain regulations to be complied with before you can get a bulk mailing license. Talk to the post office for current rates and rules.

Direct Advertising

This is distinguished from direct mail because it is distributed in person, from house to house (under doors or attached to knobs), or handed out in the street. It also includes "take-one" cards displayed by cash registers or on counters in stores. These handbills, fliers, and other types of throwaways are basically unsatisfactory and cause litter. Note that it is illegal to place direct advertising pieces in mailboxes.

Other Forms of Advertising

This category includes notices on bulletin boards, posters, billboard ads, transit ads, novelty giveaways (with your name imprinted) like matches, T-shirts, calendars, pens, memo books, buttons, ashtrays, and so forth. (Businesses put advertising on everything these days, from shopping carts to trash bins. There's

*The Small Business Administration publishes several useful booklets: *National Mailing List Houses* (Small Business Bibliography no. 29); and *National Directories for Use in Marketing* (Small Business Bibliography no. 13). Also, the Quill Corporation publishes a free forty-page primer, *How to Compile and Maintain a Mailing List,* available from Quill Business Library, 100 South Schelter Road, Lincolnshire, Illinois 60069.

Mailing lists usually charge per thousand names. Returns are about 5 to 10 percent for selective lists, 2 percent for more general lists.

the new Talking Poster, and one company is testing slogan-decorated eggs, while another is experimenting with ads on hot dogs.) The best novelties are the ones that tie in with your business. For example, if you run a summer stock company, you might send out calendars featuring your production schedules. This kind of advertising can be expensive, but if it seems to answer your needs, it could be worthwhile.

PUBLIC RELATIONS AND PUBLICITY

A business has to keep its name in front of the public. Advertising is a steadily building wave—publicity is the foam on top. It attracts attention, enhances your prestige, and it's free!

The snare is that people tend to become giddy in the limelight. Before they've used the publicity to their best advantage, it has floated away like a child's soap bubbles in the summer sky. People pay greatest heed to publicity when they can connect it with ads they've already seen. Publicity complements paid advertising but should never be a total substitute for it.

With ads, you are in control of what is said about your business. With publicity, you can be misquoted, or the wrong emphasis can be placed on your activities. It's rather like producing a play. When the reviews come out, they may be good or bad, but when you run ads afterward, you can assemble all the favorable quotes and present the show to its best advantage.

Visual Appearance of Shop or Office

The best long-term public relations for your business is the overall impression you give to your customers. A retail shop should maintain clean display windows, and see to it that displays are creative and changed frequently. The staff should be friendly and speak to each customer who enters. As the owner, make a point of introducing yourself and learning customers' names. The shop itself should be well decorated, clean, bright, freshly painted, with good layout and sound (the type of background music you use should conform to your image; keep it low enough so as not to be intrusive).

The same rules apply to an office. The environment should be attractive; the staff, friendly and accommodating. Clients should be made comfortable, especially if they have to wait. Offer coffee, and keep up-to-date publications in your reception area.

Public Relations

Public relations is relating to the public—for recognition. It can be as seemingly insignificant as a smile or a thank-you note or as complex as staging a parade. PR is the sum total of everything that creates a favorable character for your business.

Public relations must be planned. When handling PR, you or the person you designate must be confident, patient, friendly, and good with details and follow-through. This shouldn't be difficult; after all, you are selling something you believe in. There are seven basic steps to building a PR campaign:

1. Define your objectives (more specifically than "getting more clients"). What exactly are you after? What do people think of you? Exactly what can a campaign do for your business?
2. Create your central ideas. Then relate them to your needs, altering or expanding them. Keep in mind the people you are trying to reach.
3. Identify your public. Is it classified into age, sex, occupation, community, or a special interest group?
4. Select the media. Media does not mean just print or radio/television. It can be any form you use to reach your public with a message. Anything from printed brochures, special displays, door-to-door samples, contests, and giveaways to parades and press parties. *Always measure your ideas against your ability (and budget)* to execute them. A haphazardly planned, poorly executed scheme will work against your image. Be sure to notify the media well in advance of the event you want them to cover.
5. Set a timetable. It is important to know how much time the project will take, from start to finish.
6. Carry out the program. Schedule tasks with specific deadlines. Let each person know what she is to do and what it means to the overall project.
7. Evaluate results. Evaluation is the key factor to public relations. Check to see how effective your campaign has been and if it accomplished what you set out to do.

If you have information to share on any facet of your business or even an interesting hobby, you might consider writing an article or even a short weekly column for a small local paper.

You can participate in community events, ecological causes, beautification programs, and so forth. Every positive intangible thing that you do, whether directly connected with your business or not, improves your image. And that's public relations—communications (subtle or otherwise) reflecting the public image of your business.

Hiring a PR Agency or Press Agent

Like everything else, a small business owner must think in terms of getting her own publicity or hiring a talented freelancer. An agency would cost you anywhere from five hundred dollars a month on up. Besides, you have a key ingredient for success going for you: enthusiasm. No one will ever be able to love your business more, or sell your business better, than you.

Getting Publicity

Publicity comes in two packages. First, it swoops down from your lucky star: an editor or writer is intrigued by your ads or gets word through the grapevine that you're the only person in town who still weaves straw into gold. She calls you up for an interview or puts you on the local TV or radio talk show, and presto! Instant celebrity.

Remember, when you are interviewed, to accentuate your positives. This is no time for modesty. Make a list beforehand of things you want to emphasize, and stick to it. *You* control what you say during the interview; after that, the writer takes over. Don't say *anything* you wouldn't want printed. Good interviews come from good preparation—have answers ready for inevitable questions. You can psych out what an interviewer will ask by looking at your business as news. What aspects will make snappy reading?

Second, you can make your own luck. Come up with the most fascinating and newsworthy features of your business, and try to generate your own publicity. The points stressed might be you, what you do, who your clients are, or special announcements, like your grand opening.

Put it together into a friendly presentation, and call up every local paper and talk show.* Don't hesitate to take advantage of

*If you think you have national as well as local appeal, check your library for *Bacon's Publicity Checker,* which lists every magazine and periodical in the United

167

any personal contacts for introductions to prestigious people at these places. Contact news, public affairs, and special feature departments at newspapers and radio and TV stations.

Tell them, in capsule form, why they should be interested in your business. Don't be shy about mentioning your potential fascination to their readers. In general, editors, columnists, talk show producers, and talent coordinators welcome news. If they think you've got something to say, they will be interested.

Don't hit just one place; go to every publication and station in town. Don't omit company employee newspapers (house organs) and alumnae magazines. If you get turned down, go back in six months, to another editor or department, or with a new twist.

Be wary, by the way, of any publication that offers you free publicity for advertising there.

Press (News) Releases

Another way to get written up is to issue press releases to local media. Be organized, and send them out as new developments occur. Anything you do that can be turned into a juicy news tidbit should be typed up and sent out. Develop your own editorial contacts, so that the releases can be directed to the proper people.

Keep an up-to-date press file of names and addresses of every media person in town who might be interested in your business or event. Find out deadline times for publications, and jot down this information as well. Get sample news releases from your local newspapers, and use them as a guideline for setting up your own format.

How to Write a Release

A press release is news, not an ad. So you must present your business as news. The content must be subtle, accurate, and never overstated. Avoid superlatives. Outline the most interesting side of your business in a few sentences. Aim for attracting the editor's immediate attention (or your carefully constructed chatter will be chucked into oblivion). Keep your release *brief and concise.* In the first paragraph, include the who, what, where,

States and Canada, according to category. Or write H. R. Bacon and Company, 332 South Michigan Avenue, Chicago, Illinois 60605.

when, and how. Stress your major points, and back them up with facts. Then pep up the release with colorful descriptions, and round it out with minor details.

The release should be typed (double-spaced) on your company's stationery. At the top, type in caps "FOR IMMEDIATE RELEASE (date)." At the end, include your name as publicity director and a telephone number where you can be contacted for further information. Limit it to two pages, maximum.

Include a black-and-white glossy photograph whenever possible; the five-by-seven size is adequate. (Include a piece of cardboard in the envelope so that the photo won't be bent in the mail.) Type your name, address, and pertinent information (or caption) for the photo on a self-stick label, and attach it to the back of the picture. Don't write directly on the photo, or you may damage it for reproduction.

You would never let a child grow up without taking pictures of her development; the same should be true for your business. In general, think in terms of taking photos every six months or so. Never miss an opportunity to photograph a newsworthy business event.

Photographs can perk up your selling presentation and decorate your walls (people love to look at them). Often, a small publication will write about you but, lacking a photography budget, will request a picture from you to run with the piece. If you have one on hand, then you get twice as much space for the article.

Before a photography session, consider the most visual aspects of your business. Avoid sitting at a desk with telephone in hand. Action pictures are the most dynamic, even if the event has to be staged for the purpose of the photograph. And if you are hiring a professional photographer, plan your shots beforehand and don't waste time.

News Release Opportunities

Keep inventing newsworthy extras that your business can offer. A gift shop might stock scissors for southpaws, and a pet store could add an aquarium-decorating service. For publicity's sake, a caterer could demonstrate ethnic hors d'oeuvres on a TV talk show.

In addition to your own imagination, there are standard events that merit press releases:

Grand opening (or move to new headquarters)
Adding new products or services
Revealing a new business or manufacturing concept (for members of your trade or industry)
Contests of all sorts
Launching advertising or promotional campaigns
Hirings and promotions
Any publicity-worthy job or client
Extracurricular events or community projects you are sponsoring
Offering free brochures, informative booklets, or introductory kits
Predictions of new trends (backed up by facts)
Tie-ins with seasonal or charity events

Thinking up possible publicity angles should become as routine a consideration as advertising. Since publicity must be repetitive, like ads, it's a good idea to make up a yearly publicity calendar.

Maintain a relationship with your press and media contacts. Media people can change often—every six months or so. If you have specific names of contacts, call up every once in a while to check if they are still there or if they have been promoted. Be aware of their new titles, and always spell their names correctly.

Don't send one release and then forget it. Follow-up is important. The follow-up phone call should be short, informative, and cheerful. Remember, you're trying to make friends with another person. Keep up a dialogue with editors and media people. If they don't respond to your grand opening, hit them six months later with your expansion, after that with a new service, and later still, with a contest. Keep it rolling.

Once you have been written up or have appeared on a TV or radio show, call the person responsible to say how great the article or interview was. Or write a thank-you note.

Use your publicity and *keep on using it!* Have copies or tearsheets prepared for special mailings, enclosures in billings, ads (especially the headlines or good quotes), and future press releases. Include publicity credits in your selling presentation. Once an editor sees that a story on you has been done elsewhere, he or she is more inclined not only to believe the story's authenticity, but also to follow up on it.

Publicity Stunts

It's often effective to come up with an unusual event or stunt; the more visual, the better. After all, everybody loves a parade, or someone dressed up as a gorilla, or whatever crazy scheme you can dream up and have the budget to afford. An offbeat visual stunt has a good chance of attracting TV film crews and newspaper photographers. Now that many TV news programs have expanded their air time, they are eager for local color stories to use as fillers.

The stunt should be related to your business or tied in with a season or community event. For example, if you own an antique clothes shop, why not throw an antique clothing fashion show and invite your customers and the press? If you want to charge admission to the event and donate the proceeds to charity, so much the better. Charity functions will get announced on radio community bulletin boards and written up in local community papers.

As always, send out a news release in plenty of time for the press to arrange for coverage. Make sure you include the subject of the event, date, time, and location, along with background information about the business for the editor's use in preparing the story.

Be imaginative. Remember, you are competing for press coverage with many other businesses and associations. Timing, as well as thorough planning down to the last detail, is important. If the media covers an event that is poorly organized and doesn't quite come off, they are going to think twice about coming out next time. Again, remember Murphy's Law: what can go wrong will go wrong. Arrange for backup alternatives, including rain dates.

Publicity Checklist

Plan your publicity campaign well in advance, to allow the media enough time to arrange coverage.

Examine your campaign from every angle, to assure that it is zippy enough to attract coverage. Don't overlook any possibility for potential publicity. Be imaginative. If you can convince a local celebrity to attend your event, inform the press that he or she will be there. If you can tie your event in with another occasion or holiday celebration, so much the better.

Write a clear, informative press release, including the subject of the event, location, date, and time. Include the name and phone number of the person the press can contact for further information. (Try to designate one person to handle publicity and cater to the needs of the press on the specific day of the event.)

Compile a mailing list of every possible person who can give you coverage. (This includes TV and radio news departments, public-affairs departments, talk shows, daily and regional newspapers and magazines, including alumnae magazines and company employee publications.)

Follow up the press release with phone calls to everyone on your list. Check to make sure they received your release, and offer assistance in setting up coverage.

Once you have been written up by local publications, have copies made of the article, and include it in future press release packages. (Send it to customers as well, in catalog mailings or billings.)

ADDITIONAL CONSIDERATIONS

There are more subtle, ongoing ways of advertising your business. These have to do with the way your company presents itself in dealing with the public on a day-to-day basis, and how you—as owner—reflect your company.

Professional Image

Both you and your staff (when you take on one) must present a professional image when dealing with clients, suppliers, and moneylenders. Your competence and expertise are at the forefront of your business. But, as owner, the way you *look* also counts. You are the major spokesperson for your company, and you will form the first impression that many potential clients will have of your business. Always keep in mind the image you want your business to project, and project that image.

Not that business suits are always the answer. You have to dress according to your position and the situation. Miniskirts and purple hair may be perfect if you run a boutique that caters to an *au courant* clientele; jeans are fine if you're a contractor. They will be wrong when you go to the bank to apply for a line of credit.

If you need help finding the right professional image for yourself there are plenty of books and consultants to help you.

The business itself must also create a lasting impression. This is reflected not only in how the working premises look, but in how pleasantly the phones are answered, how professionally the customers are dealt with, and how expediently the job is performed. Your company's image must be apparent in your business cards, brochures, and correspondence, i.e., in all written materials; they must be neat, slick, and never sloppy.

Always do your homework. Never meet with a client unprepared. That way you will reflect confidence; potential clients *expect* it.

As for the workplace itself, decide on the image you need for your business: warm and cozy (with plants and comfortable couches), sleek and sophisticated (functional, non-fussy artwork and furniture), or whatever. What your business does will dictate to a great extent the right look to pursue.

Public Speaking

Communication, both written and spoken, is one of the major ways you will sell your product or service. Speaking well is another facet of your professional image, regardless of whether you are talking on the telephone, making a presentation one-on-one, or addressing a room full of people.

Your Voice

An entrepreneur must be aware of how she speaks, of both the pitch of her voice (the perfect tone for a woman, according to research studies, is G below middle C) and her speech habits. According to Professor Elizabeth Durrett,* of Vanderbilt University's communication studies department, women have a tendency to end statements with questions, or by raising the pitch of their voices, implying questions. Many women entrepreneurs like to use the words "we" or "our" when referring to their products or services. This is a no-no; always use "I," for more authority.

*See "A Way With Words," by Frank Mixson, *Entrepreneurial Woman*, Summer 1989.

Avoid unnecessary words like "just" and "only." Women are also more afraid of silences than men, and tend to use too many fillers.

All of these things are easily correctable. Listen to yourself, to the pitch of your voice and to annoying speech patterns. Leave a tape recorder on all day so you'll forget about it; you'll be amazed when you play it back. By becoming aware of how you sound, you can fix the problems.

Your Subject

If you are knowledgeable in your field, you will find that a great way to advertise your company is to lecture to local clubs and organizations. Figure out an angle that's special and talk about that. For example, if you own a nursery you might invite steady customers for tea and give a talk about the advantages of kelp as a nonchemical soil revitalizer. If you manufacture balloons, you might talk about creative and innovative ways to throw parties. Anything that will get you, the owner, in front of an audience will subtly enhance your business's reputation.

But what if the idea of speaking to a crowd makes your palms sweat and your throat tighten up? (According to a study published by the London *Times,* it is the thing people fear most in life.)* Speaking well is a skill; it must be learned through practice. The best thing to do is take a public-speaking course at a local college, or join Toastmasters International. Or have a few private sessions with a speech pathologist or public speaking specialist.

And be well prepared before you make your speech. Always try to shape your material for your audience. Make sure you have a beginning (introduction to your subject), middle (elaboration of all the points you want to make), and ending (the summing up). Have clear, concise notes in front of you for easy reference. Make eye contact with individual members of your audience. Attempt humor without making jokes. Move around; you don't have to stand planted in one spot.

Before making a speech, take some time to quiet yourself. Visualize yourself arriving at the lecture hall looking prepared. See yourself taking the podium and smiling confidently. Picture the audience, responding positively as you deliver your speech and clapping wildly at its end.

*See "Podium Panic: Speak without Fear," by Kevin McLaughlin, *Entrepreneur,* May 1989.

Written Communication

Well-written business communication is as important as good verbal communication. Good writing skills are good advertising for your business. These skills—whether you use them for business letters or interoffice memos—must be developed through practice, but here are some tips:

Say what you have to say as simply as possible. Avoid wordiness by using clear, precise language. Don't try to impress; present facts. After the initial greeting or introduction of yourself, get to the point as quickly as possible. Try to keep the letter to one page. Always proofread your letters by reading them out loud. Check for errors in spelling, typos, omitted or unnecessary words. Recheck details and dates. Make sure it's perfect before sending it out.

·11·

Marketing:
Selling It Like It Is

*Even if you're on the right track, you'll get run over if
you just sit there.*   —Will Rogers

There is an old saying that nothing happens until someone sells
something. Many women started young by selling Girl Scout
cookies door-to-door, or opening a lemonade stand. One woman
who now owns an internationally based design business started
at age three, picking flowers out of the neighbors' backyards,
then going around to the front door and selling them back.

Selling is what being in business is all about. Effective selling
doesn't happen by accident. It takes knowing your market, knowing how to position your business in the marketplace, and learning how best to "talk" to your market. Selling is analyzing your
competition, planning a campaign, sticking to the plan, and keeping records of the results. Selling is trial and error. It is learning
from failure and building on success. Most of all, it is hustle; i.e.:

Doing something that everyone is certain can't be done
Getting the order because you got there first, or stayed with it
 after everyone else gave up
Shoe leather and elbow grease and sweat and missing lunch
Believing in yourself and the business you're in
Doing more for the customer than anyone else
Getting prospects to say yes after they've said no twenty times

No matter what you are selling, be it a product or a service, you
are always selling yourself. See yourself as a product. Be person-

176

able. Be fun. Be nice. And smile: enthusiasm is infectious. It can make selling easy. Look for business opportunity in every situation. And never leave home without your business cards.

RESEARCHING YOUR MARKET

The root of all planning, selling, and organizing is information. The more you have, the more you'll be able to sell your product or service. Marketing is nothing more complicated than logic; it is the logical way to reach your customer or client. Just as market analysis helped direct the development of your original business concept and advertising, it is also the key to the future sales activities of your company.

Trends

Understanding your market is not just knowing who your customers are; you have to know where they're headed and their motivations as well. The way you position your business in the marketplace will be affected by geographic, economic, demographic, and social trends. Increase your awareness of what's going on around you, at all levels of activity. Relate trends to your business and your industry. For example, in the 1980s the high percentage of women in the marketplace spawned a booming market in personal services such as events planning, child care and entertainment, and specialty food. More women working also meant less time for leisure shopping, resulting in a major shift in buying habits. Catalog sales quadrupled. Writer Tom Wolfe predicted the eighties would be a decade dedicated "to the purple." He was right. The babyboomers came of age and became Yuppies, idealizing anything that suggested old money, old family, and the upper-crust way of doing things. Result? Upscale "to the manner born" home furnishings à la Ralph Lauren and Laura Ashley. Now look at the trends for the 1990s. They show the "hot" consumer group is over fifty. The home health care industry and home services are expected to soar. Designer labels are out and families are back in.

Researching trends is a matter of keeping your eyes and ears open. What titles are on the best-seller lists, what movie became the "sleeper" of the year, who are the trendsetters and what are they saying? Ad agencies spend billions every year analyzing the trends and second-guessing the psyche of the American public. Study the ads in a cross section of magazines. Study the fashion forecasts. Absorb the messages all around you. How do they relate to your business, your customer, your industry?

INVESTIGATING THE COMPETITION

Savvy business owners confide that the more you know about your competition and how they operate, the better off you'll be. Knowing your competition will help you to define your business strategy.

Identify your competition and estimate how much of the market you share with them. Are they doing well, and why? Is it only they, or is your whole industry thriving? The competition will help you identify your own strengths and weaknesses. A problem may be as simple as inadequate parking space, or as complex as lack of customer identity and loyalty. Your competitors will help you know what prices and fees to set. If you are bidding on a job, you have to know what the competition is up to. You may bid more than your competitor, but you can convince the client that yours is still the better deal—better delivery, better quality, better terms. Competitor awareness will help focus your graphics and display, and give you the central core of your pitch when selling one-on-one.

Never be lulled into thinking your competition doesn't affect your business, or that you have no competition at all. A successful product will immediately create its own competitor, someone else who is monitoring you and is determined to undersell or compete. Anticipate this and stay one jump ahead—have a patent or copyright on your product, make firm contracts with your suppliers. Analyze any rip-off and always reevaluate your original. It may be that your competition has come up with a better format. But don't be seduced into giving up quality in order to cut costs to meet knock-off products.

Competition can increase your business. For example, one art gallery in a town will have a hard time; five galleries located on the same street will create a "scene." Or perhaps a bigger company in your industry has the funds to run an expensive ad campaign, thus creating interest and demand for your competing product or service. Utilize this, and find a gap you can fill. You can compete successfully because you are a smaller, more personalized business, with more at stake than your corporate competitor.

Your competitors will keep you on your toes—which is exactly where you want to be. To learn more about them, you should:

Buy your competitors' product. Test it, take it apart, analyze its cost of production.

Stalk the competitors' territory. Look at their displays and showrooms. Meet their salespeople, their outside consultants—you'll be surprised at the information you'll pick up.

Attend trade shows and conferences. Collect your competitors' giveaway materials and visuals. They will indicate your competitors' latest product innovations, price changes, and marketing directions.

Talk to your clients. They are often your best source of information on the competition. Let *them* tell you what others are doing. Ask them to show you direct mail pieces you may not have seen. Listen to what they like about your competition. If you lose a sale or a client to a competitor, ask why. Send out a questionnaire asking potential clients to evaluate your business, your sales approach, your product. Find out what they do and don't like about you and your competition.

Reading about Competitors

Commercial Data Bases

These provide the easiest and fastest way to track a competitor, though the information is general rather than specific. Data bases contain articles from newspapers, magazines, and trade journals, reports from stock analysts, patent filings, *Who's Who* sources, and other biographies. Consult the *Directory of Online Data Bases* (New York: Cuadra/Elsevier).

Specialty Trade Publications

Within your trade, read all available material. This includes: newsletters, trade advertisements, new-product announcements and events calendars that list upcoming industry events and trade shows. To locate the magazines or newsletters concerning your industry, check your library for sources published by Oxbridge Communications (New York): *Standard Periodical Directory* and *Oxbridge Directory of Newsletters.*

179

Local News Clippings

Read local ads, PR and management announcements, and help-wanted ads. You can use a news clipping service, which will mount a search either by general topic or by company name. See the Yellow Pages headings: "news clipping," "newspaper clipping service," or "public relations."

Published Studies and Reports

Findex, published by National Standards Association, Gaithersburg, Maryland, publishes a directory of market research reports. These reports are also available through many data base vendors, including Dialog, (800)334–2564; NewsNet, (800)345–1301; and Nexis, (800)227–4908—all of which will act as your monitoring service, sending you the latest articles on your competitors and on your industry. *Wall Street Transcript* is a weekly newsletter focused in a roundtable discussion on a specific industry; consult your local public or business school library to see if they subscribe. *The Official Gazette* prints reports on newly patented material.

TARGETING YOUR MARKET

Who is your customer and why should she buy from you? What factors are most important to your customer: price, availability, special service, unique products, location, quality, originality? Is it a geographic decision (you're the only delicatessen for twenty blocks), or is she a customer at large (your homemade box lunches are delivered all over town)?

Perhaps you will have to educate potential clients as to their need for your service. A case in point is a creative graphics agency that recognized a need when they saw shoppers abandoning the local downtown area in favor of suburban malls. They created a poster campaign to lure shoppers back, then sold it to the downtown business association.

In targeting your market, ask: How do you satisfy the client's needs? What makes your business viable? How can you help customers define their needs? Be flexible; your products and services should address those needs.

Research Sources for Defining Your Market

Local census bureaus. They can provide useful information on everything from income levels to geographic studies. Also check with your local chamber of commerce, or your state's department of economic or industrial development, located in your state's capital city.

The Small Business Administration. Besides publishing a number of marketing booklets, it can provide marketing analysts to help you.

Libraries. These have numerous marketing reference directories.

Universities and graduate schools. These are excellent sources for assistance. You might interest a student in doing her project study on your business, or an entire class in conducting a market survey for you.

Finding Prospects

Previous Employers

If you are leaving a business in which you've done well, to go into business on your own, take back that previous employer as your first client.

Trade Shows/Business Conferences

Any function in which businesspeople gather is a good place to meet people who might use your service. Trade shows are often the only way you will be able to meet people in key positions, people you might not normally be able to get to. Collect names and write down personal observations, which come in handy later when you contact the company or person.

Use the trade show directory as a research source: it will contain the names of the companies participating and personnel at the booths, products displayed, cross-referencing of participating companies (by product), and lists of industry-affiliated publications and services. You may be able to order back issues of trade show directories by writing *Trade Show & Convention Guide* (Billboard Publication, Nashville). The show sponsors may also record all conferences and speeches and offer them on cassette or in written transcription.

Lists

Make a list of the companies you would like to deal with. Study trade journals, buyers' guides, membership lists, alumnae lists, organization lists. Ask friends and business contacts for names of people they think would use your service or product. Read the local newspapers for names of people and their activities.

Networks

Attend business, charity, and social functions. Work on political campaigns. Volunteer your services to organizations. Offer the services or products of your business in exchange for names. Join associations and special interest groups. And remember, never go anywhere without your business card.

Brainstorming: The Focus Group

Many ad agencies and marketing companies conceive of new ideas, invent products, and evaluate services by putting together group panels—a cross section of the right age, sex, and economic group, usually from eight to ten people—to discuss a specific project. The panel includes a moderator who tosses in leading questions and keeps the participants from digressing. Moderated panels, or focus groups, provide an efficient method of amassing relevant insights into particular problems and strategies.

This method can be adapted to solve some of your own business problems and chart new courses for selling your product and service. Assemble your selected group in a comfortable environment, give them coffee or tea, and let the ideas flow. Tape the discussion so you can mull it over later. Ask thought-provoking questions rather than those that can be answered by yes or no. You can glean valuable clues to refreshing every facet of your business, from prices to colors, new products to client relations.

Government Contracts

The government needs services and products that are furnished by outside businesses—food, supplies, clothing, printing, writing, artwork, ad campaigns, coordinators of focus groups, special events planners, and much more. Securing a government contract could provide the entire financial base for your business; the jobs are generally large and can bring substantial income to your company.

It sounds ideal. But to work for the government, you must submit to rigid requirements, strict time limitations, and masses of red tape. If you're interested, head immediately to your nearest Small Business Administration office. The SBA keeps a running file of the names of eligible women-owned small businesses (any service or retail business that grosses under $1.8 million annually, or any manufacturing company employing fewer than five hundred people) that wish to seek government contracts. Specialists are available to advise business owners on how to obtain government contracts and how to prepare bids for major contracts and subcontracts.

The National Association of Women Business Owners and many local women's business associations also work to help women secure these prime contracts. At the local and state levels in some areas in the country, there is legislation guaranteeing a certain percentage of government contracts be granted to women-owned and minority businesses.

Personal Objectives

Your sales campaign should be compatible with your personal objectives for the business and for yourself. Visualize where you want to be next year, in five years—not only within your business, but in your life. Create a one-year plan and a five-year plan. Let your sales campaign grow within these guidelines. Communicate your objectives to your partner(s) or key staff members. Think of yourself as a gardener, seeding today for tomorrow.

THE MARKETING PLAN

Having researched your market, it's time to dive into all your statistics and come up with a marketing strategy. There are numerous approaches; by now you should have an indication of the best ones for you. Your sales campaign might take a concentrated one-to-one selling approach, or could involve stepping up your ad campaign by blasting out thirty-second radio spots around the clock. It might take a clown passing out balloons to children to lure their mothers into your toy store. Or you might decide to hire a graphic designer to create a sophisticated new image in your brochure or catalog.

Part Three of this book, Women in Business—Interviews, highlights marketing techniques important to each industry. Retailing outlines ideas that successful merchandisers universally say attract customers and boost sales. Direct Mail Marketing takes you step by step through the vital components of reaching your market via direct sales. Services details the skills required for one-on-one selling. Food focuses on the special requirements it takes to sell food and drink. Manufacturing and Wholesaling deals with sales representatives and trade shows as a viable way to reach a large territory. Within these chapters, interviews with successful women entrepreneurs around the country lend interesting insights into the sales techniques employed by women in each industry.

All businesses will ultimately find sales avenues best for them. Though broad rules on selling can be illuminated, ultimately the way *you* do it, the way *you* talk to your customer, the way *you* position your business in the marketplace will be highly personal. You must do what feels right, according to your budget. In his book on baby care, Dr. Benjamin Spock relieved millions of nervous first-time mothers from a great deal of anxiety by assuring them, "You know much more than you think you know." Fledgling entrepreneurs, too, have instincts that are right—for them, for their businesses. Trust yourself. Follow your instincts. No one will ever know your business as well as you do.

Selling is, after all is said and done, an ongoing system in need of refinement. "What did I do right?' "What did I do wrong?" "How can I do better?" The answers to these questions will become the ways and means of selling your business.

CUSTOMER RELATIONS

In all businesses, the key to selling is backing up your sales with service. Always deliver what you promise, without delay, even if it means working overtime to do it. Once you've achieved a reputation for honest dealings, fair price, and prompt delivery, references from satisfied clients will help your business grow. It is said, one satisfied customer will net you ten.

Never underestimate the value of an old customer. When looking for ways to build your business, look first to your steady clients. Ask yourself how can you increase their business. Business advisers across the board say most entrepreneurs overlook this potential gold mine. Advise steady customers on new ways to utilize your product or service. As valued customers, offer them special incentives. This is the inner core of your business. Keep it strong and healthy.

You, as the owner, are the best salesperson for your business. Keep in touch with your public. Be friendly and ask your customers' opinions about your business. Find out if there is any product or service you should add. Act immediately to rectify complaints. Build your business by increasing your rapport with the public.

Provide extras whenever possible—that extra something generates goodwill. You have to make people *want* to see you and your business succeed; that's the key to reaping the rewards of word-of-mouth advertising. If you lose one person's business, you will usually lose other people's as well.

As a business owner, be visible in your community. Give talks, lead seminars, write articles, join trade associations. Let people regard you as an expert in your field. Get involved in community activities. Support charity drives by contributing your time and your business services. If you have a display window, give space to posters for worthwhile causes, or provide a community bulletin board. Salute the local rescue squad with a special window display, or congratulate school students on special achievements. Take the initiative for mini-events. But remember, you can't do everything. Support the causes that are near and dear to you, and don't feel guilty when you have to say no.

When seeking more markets for your business, keep your mind fertile. Think of new ways your business can interact with the public. You will reap the rewards of satisfied customers and increased business.

·12·

Procedures and Paperwork: Running True to Form

"The horror of the moment," the King went on, "I shall never, never forget!"
"You will though," the Queen said, "if you don't make a memorandum of it." —Lewis Carroll

A side from the fulfillment and satisfaction, part of the reason you are in business is to make money. (According to research, no successful entrepreneur is in it *strictly* for the money.) Besides your actual day-to-day endeavor, profits result from organized management. Plan. Organize. Direct. Control. Too often, business owner-managers get bogged down in the daily routine. They are so overwhelmed by the "now" of things they can't tell whether they're situated on solid ground or teetering on the side of a cliff.

An owner has to develop her own visionary business bifocals. One minute she is dealing with a slothful supplier, the next with a crazy client who takes up an hour's time with nary a thank-you. Meanwhile, she is trying to keep track of receipts, balance the checkbook, reorder supplies, write ads, answer phones, and oversee the staff (if there is one).

All this is exhilarating, and not nearly as impossible as it sounds, so long as some commonsense procedures are developed and followed. The complexity of organizational methods varies according to size and type of business. This chapter deals with a potpourri of basic guidelines to keep your feet on the ground and you on your feet.

First of all, set aside one day a week (or a couple of hours each day) for the behind-the-scenes running of your business—billing, answering mail, reordering supplies, checking progress on current jobs, keeping the books up to date, planning your advertising and selling campaigns, and returning phone calls.

Live your business from day to day, but plan ahead in blocks of time—three to six months or a year.

Periodically, reevaluate your systems and keep files and forms up-to-date. Know what everyone involved with your business is doing, and keep everyone advised on your activities.

TIME MANAGEMENT

Many women starting out in business make the mistake of trying to handle everything themselves in order to save money. Obviously, you have to pinch pennies, but time is money, too. You have to establish your priorities and stick to them. If you are going to manage your time prudently, you must be organized and map out a strategy. Here are some time-saving hints:

Know your goals (daily, weekly, monthly, yearly), and keep them constantly before you.

Make a list every morning, as well as an overall weekly list, outlining everything that needs to be done (including telephone calls, correspondence, record keeping, drumming up new business, and such). Arrange the items in order of priority, and get things done in that order. Lists mean nothing if you don't refer back to them constantly.

Delegate responsibility. It may sometimes take longer to explain what you want done, but you must learn to differentiate between what must be done by you and what can be handled by others.

Generate as little paperwork as possible. Many office forms are genuine time-savers, but don't get bogged down. Have a place for everything.

File papers immediately; don't let things pile up.

Use your business consultants to help you solve problems quickly.

Get as much done by phone as possible (ordering supplies, etc.). Or send a quick note to avoid a lengthy phone call with a chatty supplier or client.

Set specific times for specific tasks, e.g., telephoning and bill paying. Don't procrastinate.

Use waiting or traveling time to catch up on reading, thinking about solutions to problems, etc. Take taxis instead of buses (the Time = Money theory).

Go to lunch for pleasure. Business lunches are expensive and time-consuming and accomplish little. An office appointment takes less time and gets more done.

Don't spend precious office time making up your lists. Work on them on the way to work or the evening before.

In general, avoid busywork. Someone else should be doing it for you.

Everyone who has a lot to do and gets a lot done works from her own personal organizational system, whether it be a top-of-the-line Filofax or entrepreneur's Day Runner, a yellow legal pad, or pieces of scrap paper. Basically, whatever works for you is perfectly fine. But some people get so obsessive about writing things down and cross-referencing that nothing gets accomplished except lists. Don't let the details bog you down.

What wastes time? It's different for each person. The best thing to do is make a list of things that waste your time; knowing what they are will help you eliminate, delegate, or prioritize them.

THE COMPUTERIZED OFFICE

There are computer software programs that can run (with your participation) every aspect of your business, from organizing day-to-day appointments or tracking your inventory to bookkeeping, preparing your taxes, and filing all of your business and client information. This software is being updated and improved constantly. For the best program(s) for your business consult with other small business owners, computer users' groups, or retail computer stores. Read computer and software publications for reviews of the newest programs available.

But some small businesses don't need a computer, at least in the beginning. When you don't have an overabundance of information to store, the old-fashioned way of storing information is still the most expedient.

FILING

As your business grows, so will your need for additional filing space. Secondhand filing cabinets can be found cheaply at auctions or sales of used office equipment or can be floor samples from office supply stores.

Filing should be done alphabetically in manila file folders. Besides the alphabetical cataloging of clients and suppliers, there are general categories to be arranged: expenses, advertising (rate sheets, copies of ads, etc.), printing, publicity, photographs, bank statements, accounts receivable, paid bills, time sheets, general correspondence, and other informational sources related to your particular business.

Certain records must be stored safely, in case of fire or flooding. (Metal file cabinets are not fireproof.) You are also required by law to retain certain records for specific periods of time— financial records, tax returns, and so forth. (For a specific listing of what must be kept, for how long, see chapter seven, page 122.) Keep these tucked away in a fireproof safe, in a bank safety deposit box, or on other premises.

Index Card Files

Index cards and Rolodexes are an easy method of keeping track of various information: supplies and inventory, selling contacts, advertising and publicity sources, clients, and so forth.

Keep a card file by the telephone containing the names, addresses, phone numbers, and miscellaneous information on all clients and suppliers. Do up a card on your business, containing often-used information, like your sales tax resale number, Dun & Bradstreet number, tax employer's identification number, insurance policy information, and so forth.

Look at your business, and make up your own forms in areas where standardized information will be expedient. Visit office supply houses for preprinted forms of various types.

But don't bury yourself in forms. They are time-savers and memory aids, but too much paperwork can be counterproductive.

FORMS AND TIME-SAVERS

Everything should be written down and filed in its proper place. As your business and staff grow, it becomes more and more necessary for all participants to have access to vital information.

Organization of the constant inflow of information is the only possible way to keep your business running efficiently.

Job Forms for Service or Manufacturing Businesses

Organization forms keep business flowing. Free-lance people or tiny businesses often get by in the beginning by using file cards. However, printed job forms grow with the business and eliminate the helter-skelter method of jotting down notes that can be misplaced or incomplete. Several copies should be made: the original should be kept in the master job form book or file, the copies in individual client folders and the bookkeeping record file. Until a job is completed, keep the client copy in a central location (on a bulletin board, for example) for quick reference.

No matter what sort of job data sheet you use, it must include the following information: date of call (order), date of job (or delivery), who took the call, client's name, address, and telephone number, where/how the client heard of your company, the price quoted for job, form of payment, plus any other necessary description.

Each form should be numbered for reference, and a separate invoice number attached when the job is completed and billed. After that, it should be stamped and dated upon payment.

The master job file provides an at-a-glance record of past and current progress. If a job is canceled, the reason should be noted on the job form. If a client is difficult to deal with, it should be jotted down. The more people you have working for you, the more important it is for everyone to have access to this information.

Retail Business Forms

Stores must keep track of their orders from manufacturers and receipts to their own retail customers. If you don't own a computer and an inventory-tracking software program, you can purchase standard forms, or have them made up with your own logo or letterhead. Keep track of current stock with index file cards, and itemize all inventory purchases on a columnar pad (give every line of merchandise a number for easy identification), so you know when to restock and reorder. When inventory is replaced, keep track by entering the information on monthly on-order forms, listing the order number, date, manufacturer's name, style number, quantity, price, and shipping charges (if any).*

Daily Time Sheets

Any business whose fees are based on hours (services, crafts-makers, and the like) should rely heavily on time sheets for an accurate cost analysis per job and to see how time is being used. Both for yourself and others working with you, it is necessary to detect if you are working at capacity or wasting too much time.

Break the day down into hours, the hours into ten- or fifteen-minute slots. And write in everything—phone calls, coffee breaks, and details on activities for each and every job.

Petty Cash Records

A petty cash fund (a fixed amount of dollars) should be set up to make small payments in order to avoid having to write many checks. Every time money is taken from petty cash, a slip should be filled out, listing date, amount, purpose, and person to whom the money is given. Any invoices or receipts should be stapled to the slip. Every day the total of the petty cash slips should be balanced against the remaining money in the fund. Later, the slips are summarized according to type of expense and entered into the cash disbursements book.

CASH AND CREDIT ACCOUNTS

Cash Sales

If you run a store, you must write up the sales receipts for each sale (or use a cash register with tape receipts). Always give a copy to the customer. At the end of the day, all but a specified amount of money (for making change) should be taken out and deposited in your bank account. The cash should be tallied against the sales

---

*For more information on retail record-keeping forms and stock-control systems, check with a computer software consultant (or other retail business owners). See also Leta Clark, *How to Open Your Own Shop or Gallery* (New York: St. Martin's Press). Fairchild Publications (7 East Twelfth Street, New York, New York 10003) publishes informational books on all aspects of retailing.

receipts to guard against errors. Try to go to the bank at different times of day so you won't be carrying the day's jackpot for deposit every afternoon at the same time.

Credit Card Sales

If you are willing, and nowadays it is generally expected by customers, to pay a small percentage (generally, 3 to 6 percent) of sales to credit card companies, you can allow your customers to use major credit cards. In exchange, they may make higher purchases. A drawback is that you don't get paid as fast and your cash flow is slowed down. Talk to your banker about setting up an association with credit card companies.

Charge Credit Sales

Some small retail stores and service businesses choose to boost business by establishing credit to regular customers. This is generally not advisable because of the time and expense. However, should you consider it, be sure to open every new account, according to a standard procedure. Obtain the following information from the customer (you can buy printed forms or make up your own): full name, address, home and work telephone numbers; place of business, job title, length of employment; former employer, if present employment is less than six months; names of companies/stores that already have extended credit.

Clear all applications through the credit bureau. Check with other creditors (some people promptly pay certain accounts and leave others in arrears). Some businesses limit charge customers to both the amount they can charge and the amount that must be paid on their monthly bill.

Accepting Checks

A retail business should place a ceiling on checks, require identification (usually two types), and compare signatures. In addition, make sure that (1) the customer's name, address, and home/work phone number are printed on the front or written on the back of the check; (2) the check is accurately dated, not postdated or more than thirty days old; (3) the bank's address and branch are on the check (never accept a blank check); (4) the check is made out for the exact amount of purchase (and not more, in exchange for cash); and (5) the numerical amount agrees with the written amount.

After you have received a check, stamp it immediately with your rubber bank deposit stamp—make sure your bank provides you with one—so that a thief can't cash it if you are robbed.

Your local Better Business Bureau, police, or bank may have a list of bad-check passers working in your area.

Most checks returned because of insufficient funds will clear the second time you deposit them. Notify the customer that you are redepositing the check. (Some banks will not allow you to redeposit more than twice; they also charge a service fee.)

If the check bounces a second time, call the client and request immediate payment, by cash or certified check. If you get an evasive response, then call a collection agency and have it get to work on the case.

Sources of Credit Information

Certain types of information are sold by credit agencies; some are available from them as a service. Find out about the available services of your local retail credit bureau, and talk to your banker. If you need daily credit information, then consider buying the services of a credit bureau. Acquaint yourself with the International Consumer Credit Association and general mercantile agencies, like Dun & Bradstreet and Equifax, Inc.

BILLING AND COLLECTING

Credit sales are as insubstantial as cotton candy until they have been paid. Often the most likable customers don't pay their bills. And small businesses are the most vulnerable prey since they can least afford loss. Nevertheless, extending customers credit usually peps up sales (especially for certain types of service businesses). Just remember, your company's success depends on your ability to collect.

Send out bills at the beginning of each month, with terms of payment (due on the tenth of the month, or whenever). If a bill is unpaid, send a statement a month later, with another one following fifteen days after that. Next, two months after the original bill, send a letter politely requesting payment.

Follow up with a phone call, explaining that you must be paid in order to pay your own bills. Inquire if the service, merchandise, invoice, etc., are in order and if there is any reason payment is being withheld. Ask for a date by which you can expect payment, and call back if it hasn't been received by that time. Remain polite during the second call, but find out what the matter is. (Be prepared for "The check was mailed several days ago; haven't you received it yet?" or one of the standard stalls.) Arrange another schedule for repayment. If that isn't met, call and say you must be paid immediately or you will be forced to turn the matter over to your lawyer (or collection agency). And then do so.

Close off your credit line to deadbeats who will not pay on your terms. No client is worth the extensive time you spend cajoling and threatening her to pay up.

Only as a last resort will you want to hassle with a lawsuit or a collection agency to force payment. Discuss these methods with your accountant and lawyer. Collection agencies take a percentage of the monies they collect, but winding up with some of your money is better than none.

Should you have to sue a client for payment, represent yourself in small-claims court. This avoids exorbitant legal fees if your claim is under the designated monetary limit (generally, five hundred dollars or less).

PAYING BILLS

A new business establishes its credit rating by paying its bills on time. Be especially diligent about this the first six months you are in business and always with new suppliers. However, guard your cash flow, and never give up all your cash at once.

There is a priority of bill paying. In general, wait thirty to sixty days before paying bills in order to collect maximum interest on the money in your account. After that, banks and insurance companies must have the first consideration, since loans or policies can be foreclosed or canceled. Next, pay your rent and utilities. From then on, pay according to commitments. Generally, the last people to be paid are creditors who are easy on you, and professional consultants—accountant, lawyer, etc.

If you are caught in a bind, be honest with your creditors. Tell them you are waiting for accounts receivable, but *always honor your commitments.* Banks offer short-term loans (for thirty, sixty, or ninety days) to carry you over while you are waiting for a large payment.

After a check is written, mark the bill "paid," and add the date and check number. When a check is spoiled, mark it "void," tear off the signature portion, and staple it onto the back of its stub.

Every time you write a check, note the purpose as well as the date and amount. Keep a running balance, with deposits and check deductions up to date. Always reconcile your checkbook with your bank statement at the end of the month.

If a check is lost, call your bank immediately. Always stop payment on a check before issuing a duplicate.

PRODUCTION AND INVENTORY

If you manufacture products or make them by hand, keep an up-to-date inventory on all finished products as well as raw materials and tools. Your inventory of finished goods should provide a backlog of ready-to-sell items.

For retail, get advice from your suppliers on inventory. Stock small quantities, and see what sells best. In the long run, you will learn from experience what to stock in quantity, what to eliminate, and which are image items (not fast turnovers, but worth keeping in stock all the time). Aim toward a good merchandise turnover—have a variety of items so that customers can discover something different every time they visit your store. This involves organizing an active buying campaign on your part. The smaller the town, the more general and varied your merchandise will have to be.

Production Sequence (Manufacturing)

The physical layout of your working space should be planned for maximum efficiency. Plan each step in logical sequence, and have ample storage space for raw materials and finished products. The faster you turn out products, the more money you will make. Make sure you are performing every step the most expedient, logical way. Avoid wasting time; keep up a steady work rhythm.

Stock Control

Know when to reorder so that deliveries are made before you are depleted of standard merchandise. Store stock on shelves with index cards showing amounts, sizes, colors, in front. As items are taken out of stock, write in the change on the index cards. Keep track of all inventory (when not using a computer software inventory-tracking program) on a columnar pad, and give every line of merchandise a number for easy identification. Write down all transactions so that you will know when to restock and reorder. Physical inventory should be taken periodically to verify the balances you have on paper.

Keep track of raw materials and tools in the same way so that you don't run out. Always reorder when you get below a certain amount to allow time for shipment. A file card index is another useful way to keep track—every time you take an amount out of stock, write down the amount you take and subtract it from the original. Have a separate card for each line of merchandise.

INTERIOR DISPLAY (RETAIL)

The decoration and display of merchandise in your store should be unique—colorful, well lighted, and imaginative. It should be functional as well as decorative; don't leave your merchandise tossed around as an easy mark for shoplifters, but don't keep it out of reach either. Look at other businesses for ideas on interior display. When you go on buying trips to other cities, look around while you're there. Pick up ideas you can adapt to your own location. Change interior displays periodically and window displays often, to attract attention.

Window displays should be original and imaginative. Wrap bracelets around loaves of french bread in picnic baskets; turn hardware supplies into objets d'art. Display the local sixth grade's art project, and throw a few of your products into the foreground.

Go to the window display decorator of a large department store and make friends with her. Stores like this always have leftovers and throwaways. Theaters and university prop shops have items to lend or rent. Borrow large plants from the local nursery in exchange for a free plug. Get Broadway or movie posters by writing away for them. Supplies and tie-ins are limitless. If you're too busy to deal with it, hire a free-lance display person to keep your store looking exciting and novel.

Protection against Shoplifting

Shoplifting can be a major drain on the finances of any store.* With experience, you will intuitively spot potential shoplifters by their behavior. Of course, beware of shoppers with bulky coats and large pockets, umbrellas, and bulky packages. Many stores request that such paraphernalia be checked upon arrival.

There are a number of precautionary techniques: uniformed guards; convex mirrors in strategic locations; receipts stapled to bags; electronic pellets attached to expensive clothes, which must be removed by the cashier with special shears. Shoplifters also switch price labels; effective safeguards here are tamperproof gummed labels, plastic string on tags, and prices written in with ink or a rubber stamp.

Your shop's layout can discourage shoplifters. Keep small, high-priced items in locked cases. Allow only a certain number of garments in dressing rooms at one time. Don't leave enticing pocket-sized merchandise in unattended nooks. Inspect your store from a shoplifter's point of view, and rearrange any tempting displays.

Protection against Burglary

Take out insurance. Keep up-to-date records of all inventory or equipment (when purchased, price, etc.). Talk to other small business owners about their precautions. Sometimes a group of merchants will get together and hire a private guard to patrol their block.

If your business warrants it, you can have a buzzer system installed with which you can unlock the door to let people in and out. This sort of thing sometimes discourages the casual customer, however, and is not recommended for a business that thrives on browsers. It is most effective for stores that specialize in small, high-priced merchandise, such as jewelers.

*Contact your local SBA office for the following booklets: *Reducing Shoplifting Losses*, by Addison H. Verrill (Management Aids, no. 3.006), and *Curtailing Crime— Inside and Out* (Management Aids, no. 5.005, $2).

There are security systems ranging in price and sophistication that you can have installed in your office. Some are available that connect directly with a nearby police precinct. A simpler and less expensive idea is to set up a secret buzzer with your next-door neighbors to enlist their aid in the event of a robbery while you are there. If you have an office, install a peephole on the main door, and keep the door locked when you are there alone. Another good deterrent is a guard dog. Even though it's dear old Fido, the family pet, if he's big enough, robbers will think twice about taking the chance of arousing his ire.

Protection against Computer Crime

Once you've gone to all the time and expense of putting your financial records, client lists, inventory, etc. on your computer, you don't want to risk losing it all. Yet there are "hackers" and "viruses" out there that could steal your company's vital information or wipe out your entire system of stored data. According to research conducted by the 3M Corporation,* twenty megabytes of lost sales and marketing information takes nineteen days to re-create (at a cost of about $17,000); the same amount of lost accounting information would take longer to replace and cost even more.

Computer tampering is a crime on the books in all but two states (Vermont and Virginia), at this writing.

Some computer disasters are caused by human error or acts of nature (power failures, earthquakes, fires, floods, etc.), of course, but many are the result of deliberate sabotage. Computer viruses are unwanted program commands that enter systems through contaminated software and, like human disease, can spread (from one system to another by network connections or infected disks). These viruses can even destroy hard disks.

Computer hackers are experts who search the world—via a PC, modem, and telephone lines—for unprotected computer systems. When they find one, they can enter, gather information and change it, or destroy whole files.

You also have to watch out for your employees who create, manage, and operate your computer system. A technique called

*See the SBA booklet *A Small Business Guide to Computer Security* (Life Line no. LF-001, $1), and also "Preventing Computer Disaster," by Mikkel Aaland, *Working Woman,* November 1988.

"salami slicing" is a form of embezzlement; "data diddling" is another scam that alters computer records. And then there's the fired or disgruntled employee out for revenge. She can do major damage before she goes, by deleting or changing crucial data.

According to experts, being aware of the potential dangers is the first step toward avoiding them. Education is important when it comes to human error. Get advice from computer users' groups. Make sure employees understand their security responsibilities. Physically secure equipment, especially hard disks and laser printers, by using lockpads to attach machines to desks; keep computer areas locked. Work out contingency plans in the event of natural disasters: back up all data and keep copies in a safe place away from the office. Use passwords and access codes, and change them often. Bar fired employees from computer access immediately. And ask a computer consultant about the latest in computer and software security measures.

PACKING, SHIPPING, AND POSTAGE

Pack your merchandise well. Use sturdy corrugated containers, reinforced gummed tape, and address labels with your company name and address printed on top. Stuff inside with newspaper, tissue, and—preferably—other biodegradable forms of packing, to prevent sliding and breakage. Always enclose a list of contents inside the package or in an envelope attached to the outside.

For *parcel post,* the maximum weight is forty pounds, and the maximum size is 84 inches (length and girth combined). Rates depend on weight and destination. Insurance is extra but provides the only means of tracing a lost package.

Other private delivery, second-day delivery, or overnight delivery companies deliver almost everywhere in the continental United States. Maximum allowable size and weight of package varies between shippers. Prices vary according to destination and desired speed of delivery, and every parcel is automatically insured for a certain amount. (For valuable parcels you will want to purchase additional insurance.) Nearly all of the companies provide a pickup service for packages.

Postage meters are office time savers but more costly than stamps because, in addition to the postage, you must pay a monthly rental on the machine itself. Nowadays, instead of taking the machine to the post office for postage refills, you can leave money on deposit with the leasing company and call them when the meter is empty. They will give you a code to punch into the meter that resets it. Postage meters cost around $150 for installation; rental runs from about $20 to $70 per month. Because of the expense, unless you deal in mail orders or send out myriad catalogs, brochures, and correspondence, it's cheaper for a small company to stick with the personalized look of stamps.

QUALITY CONTROL

It's not enough to do something well. You must keep on doing it well to stay ahead of your competition. Quality control means saving money by doing things right the first time. It means keeping your quality high and your prices as reasonable as possible, so that the customer will be satisfied and keep coming back. Quality control is looking within your company and making sure that it's running at optimum efficiency, that everyone knows what they're doing and what's expected of them. Quality control also means caring about what you're doing and taking pride in doing the job well. What's the point of manufacturing a shoddy toy that will break an hour after a child's opened it on her birthday? Women entrepreneurs—all entrepreneurs—have a responsibility to themselves, their companies, their employees, and their public to try to add to the quality of everyone's life.

Whether you're dealing with a product or a service, success depends on your ability to deliver to your customers what you've agreed to deliver, on time, and consistently.

SUMMARY

Once you have become organized, don't let things slide. Reevaluate your systems as you go along; decide what to keep, what to drop, and what to add. Every business is different from every other one because of the individual personalities of the owners. Remember to keep setting aside those few hours every day or week to feed the home fires. It's much easier to spot trouble and avoid it than to deal with it after the fact.

·13·

Hiring: The Staff
of Business Life

Woman is woman's natural ally.   —Euripides

As your business flourishes, the day may arrive when you just can't do it all yourself. You need help, because it is no longer feasible, practical, or pleasant to go it alone. Sometimes it happens as suddenly as receiving an order too large to handle yourself. Or perhaps you've been letting some projects coast because you can't fit everything into the twenty-four-hour day.

Don't, however, take on any permanent workers until you are sure you are busy enough—*all* the time—to warrant the extra expense. Your increased business must be well established, not just seasonal. Employees mean not only salary but withholding taxes, Worker's Compensation, social security, and the increased bookkeeping that goes along with these—not to mention the additional space, desks, telephone equipment, and supplies.

Before hiring anyone, figure out exactly what the job will entail and what duties will be included. Then, determine whether they can be performed by someone working full- or part-time. In general, small businesses can cut down on time wasting by hiring free-lancers, temporary workers, or part-time or "flextime" workers, who tend not to loaf because of their shortened hours or per job duties.* You also save money in salaries and benefits.

---

*Flextime, or flexible time, allows employees more flexibility in their work hours. For example, they could come in between 8:00 A.M. and 10:00 A.M., work eight hours, and leave between 4:00 P.M. and 6:00 P.M. Employees who do much of their work independently—computer programming, bookkeeping, etc.—could work their forty-hour week according to a special schedule that they plan with you.

Job sharing, when two (or more) people share a full-time job, is another viable

201

FREE-LANCE WORKERS

Free-lance help is a good way to save money if you have a temporarily heavy workload but cannot justify taking anyone on full-time. Generally, you will pay on an hourly basis, although in some cases you may choose to pay a per project salary—a percentage of the profits of the job equal to the value of the free-lancer's service to you. State laws vary according to their tax and benefit requirements for free-lance or temporary workers.

WHOM TO HIRE

The job itself answers this question: What degree of experience is needed to fill it? Highly qualified people require high incentives—large salary, ample fringe benefits (longer paid vacations, hospitalization insurance, profit-sharing, etc.). And about the only way a small business owner can afford to bring this sort of additional experience into the company is to take on a partner and give up a percentage of the business.

If intelligence and common sense are qualification enough, then look for these qualities in a less experienced, energetic person willing to buckle down and learn—for example, recent graduates of commerce schools, college students, older people, a parent whose hours must coincide with school time, etc. The more flexible the hours, the more categories of workers open up.

It is good policy *not* to hire friends if you want to keep the friendship. At least evaluate the friend's ability to view your role as boss seriously and take orders without resentment. Before hiring a friend, consider whether you could *fire* her (without unpleasant repercussions) if things didn't work out.

HOW TO FIND HER

First of all, spread the word around that you are hiring. Announce what kind of person (and qualifications) you are searching for to business associates and friends. This word-of-mouth network is often the most satisfactory way to find someone.

Using the services of an employment agency costs a fee, and

possibility. It is especially helpful for young parents or semiretired people. There is also *new-time,* designed for working mothers; this is part-time work that coincides with school hours.

if the person doesn't work out, there's no money-back guarantee. To save time, contact several recommended agencies and interview people from all of them. Sometimes talking to a number of qualified applicants helps you to clarify your requirements.

Other sources for tracking down people are school placement offices, help-wanted notices on public bulletin boards, and paid ads in newspapers. Keep an ongoing file of people you meet whose qualifications impress you. You may not have a place for them now, but they are people to consider when a need develops later.

The Description of the Job

Before you start looking, chart your requirements. List every duty you will want your staff member to perform. Try to envision what the job could grow into as business increases. That way, when interviewing, you can evaluate whether a person will grow with your company or is suited for only one level of activity. Also, the more room for advancement, the more qualified the people you are likely to attract. As a woman employer, you should try to redefine secretarial and other jobs that have traditionally been dead ends for women.

Besides delineating job requirements, you must decide on salary, hours, number of sick days and vacation, plus fringe benefits (group health, discounts, etc.). Do this for every job to be filled, and make sure that every person you hire knows and understands exactly what she is to do.

What the Job Will Pay

The salary you offer will depend on the job to be filled and the going rates.* Check your balance sheet, and discuss this with your accountant so that you know exactly what you can afford to pay. Contact your state's departments of labor and industrial relations or your local office of the U.S. Employment Service for minimum wage requirements, as well as contract and wage stipulations should you have to deal with a union. Talk to other business owners or members of your trade association for further guidelines on salary. To attract top-notch help, you must offer

*See SBA publication *Employees: How to Find Them and Pay Them* (Management Aids, no. 5.002, $1).

reasonable salaries, adequate benefits, pleasant working conditions, and room for advancement.

For retail businesses, the amount spent on payroll should represent 15 percent of the store's total volume.

INTERVIEWING

No matter how highly recommended a person comes or how qualified she seems to be, you must interview her, formally or informally. Find out her experience and qualifications for this particular job. Ask for references and *check them,* no matter how excellent a judge of character you are.* There are discriminatory questions that are *illegal* to ask—questions regarding race, creed, sexual orientation, age, ethnic origin, marital status, number of children, and so forth. What *can* you ask? Basically, any question relating directly to the job or to your specific needs.

When conducting an interview, don't be too chatty. It wastes time and does not necessarily relax the interviewee. Ask thought-provoking questions, not ones that are easily answered with a yes or no.

You might want to include a bit of on-the-spot improvisation, where you see the interviewee relate to the work she must do. (Have her wait on a customer, take an order over the phone, check out your products, give an impromptu sales spiel, etc.).

Before hiring anyone, check to make sure that the information she has given you is true. Don't hire anyone on the spot; take time

*With the rising number of defamation-of-character lawsuits, former employers have become reticent about giving job references. Yet studies show that up to 25 percent of all job applicants embellish the truth in terms of their education and former business experience. Checking references has never been more important: in many states an employer can be held liable for injuries that an employee may inflict on anyone while on the job.

So, how do you get candid references when you do your checking? Have the job applicant sign a release stating that she knows her former employer will be contacted (and also that any false information she gives you could result in her termination from the job). Use your network, i.e., develop relationships with professional organizations so you can obtain off-the-record information. Or hire a professional reference checker, such as Equifax Services in Atlanta or Fidelifacts in New York City.

See these articles: "Reference Checks: How to Get the Information You Need," by Magaly Olivero, *Working Woman,* May 1989; "The Employer's Burden," by Marisa Manley, *Inc.,* September 1989; and "Information, Please: How to give useful job references without getting into hot water," by Marisa Manley, *Inc.,* June 1989.

to mull it over. And always trust your intuition. Even if someone appears ideal, if you have any nagging doubts, heed them. It's much easier *not* to hire a person than to have to fire her later on.

When interviewing, check each possible candidate for her knowledge and experience (does she know *how* to do the job?), her motivation (does she *want* to do the job?), and her ability (is she *able* to do the job?). If she speaks freely (and negatively) about her former employer, watch out: she may willingly share secrets about your company, too. If she tries to overjustify items on her résumé she may be covering up something. A job applicant who drops names to impress you is someone else to be wary of. Interviewees who squirm, appear tense, blink their eyes excessively, or avoid eye contact may simply be nervous, but be aware these mannerisms may also indicate that they are lying. People who blame everyone else (or outside circumstances) for past failures may lack proper motivation.*

In general, as the interviewer, be pleasant but professional. Explain in detail what the job is all about. Then settle back, ask questions, and *listen* to the answers. The more the other person talks, the more you'll learn about her.

The Job Application Form

Have printed application forms ready to be filled out before you begin the interview. The basic information you need is:

Name
Address and telephone number
Social security number
Previous job experience—where employed, for how long, and
    specific responsibilities
References (other than previous employer)
Any other skills, unusual qualifications, or pertinent informa-
    tion. (A person's marital status is not important, yet time

*See the following articles: "Anatomy of a Successful Interviewer: Open Mind, Closed Mouth," by Holloway McCandless, *Working Woman,* November 1988; "How to Hire the Right Person for the Job," by Johanna Hunsaker and Phillip Hunsaker, *Working Woman,* January 1989; "Hire Smart, Hire Right: The Artful Interview," by Phyllis Martin, *Working Woman,* March 1989; and "The Competitive Edge: Hiring Smarts," by Fran Tarkenton and Joseph H. Boyett, *Entrepreneur,* October 1989.

schedules in relation to home life may be. A woman with children may need to arrange flexible afternoon hours.)

Any other questions relevant to your specific business.

Be sure to leave adequate space for answers.

This should be filled out by all applicants as they arrive so that you can refer to it during the interview. Hold on to the applications, even after you have filled the job, in case you need someone else at a later date.

The Interview Procedure

After the prospective employee has filled out the application, explain exactly what you're looking for, what needs to be done. Besides experience, look for motivation—will she really enjoy the job or stay just until something better comes along? (Even so, you may still consider hiring her on a temporary basis.) The applicant's responses can help you predict her reliability and interest.

It is difficult to find perfection. Often, the person you intuitively like lacks certain skills that you require. You may have to compromise a bit and rely on on-the-job training to get what you want. If a person doesn't work out, you can always fire her, but that can be difficult (and expensive).

Don't rush the interview, unless you perceive immediately that the person has nothing to offer you. The more time you spend now, the better it will work out later. Interviewing becomes easier the more you do it. Just remember, trust your instincts as well as your intelligence. The right person will add a new dimension to your business and help you to increase sales and expand. The wrong one can waste time and materials, and lose customers.

ON-THE-JOB TRAINING

When a new person joins your staff, plan to take time from your own work to spend exclusively with her. Give her on-the-job instruction on every facet of her duties.* Don't ever be too busy to answer questions. Explain the workings of the entire business,

*See SBA publication *Checklist for Developing a Training Program*, by Leonard J. Smith (Management Aids, no. 5.001, $.50).

where things are, any rules and regulations, who the regular clients are, and other pertinent facts. Then keep observing her work and refining your instructions.

Each staff member must understand her job and how she relates to the overall scheme of the business. She must know her responsibilities, authority, and relationships. She must have the confidence that she can accomplish her assignments and that it is in her best interest to do so.

Everyone has different working methods. So long as a job is well executed according to schedule, don't be upset if a staff member does it her way. Don't smother your coworkers nor give them free rein to run amok. Be there to guide, but stand back and give your carefully selected associates the freedom to do things their own way.

SUPERVISING

Nearly 70 percent of all customer losses can be attributed to bad service by indifferent employees. At the root of most problems with employees is a business owner who is inept at handling personnel and delegating work and responsibility.

Throughout your entire working relationship, communicate what needs to be done, and when and how you want it. Be consistent in pointing out what's wrong (and what's *right*) about a person's work.

Don't forget that you are at the helm—giving instructions, gauging your success, building business, seeing clients, ordering supplies or inventory, charting new directions. After all, you are risking your money, and you have to make the decisions. Supervising your employees is just part of supervising your business. You must be willing to spend considerable time in hiring, training, and managing your personnel. You must emanate confidence in order to inspire it and to keep things flowing and growing.

Delegating Work and Responsibility

Once you have delegated authority, allow key associates to take the initiative to run things, even during your absence. It is difficult for small business owners to sit back and let anyone else shoulder responsibility, but you must resist the urge to thwart your staff and keep them from flourishing.

Be available constantly for encouragement and guidance. There must be individual motivation as well as team enthusiasm, but try to encourage cooperative, noncompetitive attitudes among your staff. Reward people for a job well done. If they have to work overtime or extra hours during a busy period, give them a bonus, not only in pay but in thoughtfulness, such as a new toy for their child or a certificate for a dinner with their spouse or friend. In some businesses where there is a regular period of the year that is busier, you might consider giving bonuses *before* the work crush begins.

Switch perspectives periodically, too. Listen to your associates. Find out what *they* want out of their job. You may not be realizing their full potential. Ask for advice and suggestions—and act on them. (The old concept of a suggestion box hasn't gone out of style: install one, and encourage your staff to use it.) Earn your employees' loyalty and respect by respecting them. And remember, many entrepreneurs are driven and work themselves hard; don't judge others by the standards you set for yourself.

Don't forget to promote people, and raise their salaries as your business makes more money. Give each job a title.

Firing

Since the standards (and ethics) of the business are yours, its ultimate success lies in your lap. If the quality starts faltering because of an indifferent or untalented employee, then you will have to let her go. Be kind to people, but not at the expense of your company's reputation and profits. If you do fire someone, try to be helpful in steering her into work for which she might be better suited.

When she applies for a new job and the potential employer calls you for a reference, be cooperative but protect yourself from a possible defamation-of-character lawsuit. Tell the truth; give an honest evaluation of the former employee's abilities. Don't volunteer any information that is more than a prospective employer needs to know for the job at hand. Don't say anything malicious or provide any false information, especially if you had conflicts with the former employee.

Staff Meetings

Keep well informed on what everyone is doing; let everyone know what *you* are doing. The most effective procedure is to hold regular meetings, either daily or weekly, to review new jobs, policies, production, sales, and suggestions. But don't waste time with meetings when a memo, one-on-one conference, or phone call can serve the purpose.

Before every meeting, plan what you are going to cover. Be sure to start and end on time. Keep the meeting as short as possible; everyone's busy. Reschedule a meeting if one or more key people can't be there. Let everyone know the agenda of the meeting beforehand, so they can bring necessary information and be prepared to discuss it. Allow for give-and-take, but don't let meetings veer off the subject at hand. Always know ahead of time what you want the meeting to accomplish (e.g., to provide information, solve a problem, make a decision, etc.).

To keep everyone's attention, stand up or move around the room from time to time. Stimulate discussion, and call on quiet people to offer their opinions. Keep the pace flowing.

A small business must encourage camaraderie among the workers. As your business grows, so will you—from both the additional customers and the fresh ideas and opinions of your staff.

Maintaining Good Office Relations

Personnel management experts offer these tips for keeping behind-the-scenes office harmony:*

Publicly praise the good work of staff members, and discuss grievances or criticism in private.

Actively solicit suggestions, opinions, and ideas from your staff. Adopt good ideas, giving full credit where it's due. Explain why other suggestions are not feasible.

Respect differences of opinion. Obviously, everyone views each situation differently.

*Adapted from "Avoiding Management Pitfalls," *Small Business Reporter* (no. SBR-121, $5) available from Bank of America, Dept. 3631, P.O. Box 37000, San Francisco, California 94137. See also their booklet "Personnel Guidelines" (no. SBR-115, $5).

Keep reassessing each job, with an eye toward keeping it interesting and challenging. Bored workers will not enhance your business's image.

Admit your own mistakes; your staff will respect you for it.

Keep your staff up-to-date with what's happening with the business, especially with matters concerning them.

Always explain why new policies are being put into effect.

Give promotions when they're due. Whenever possible, promote from within, rather than hire someone new. It's up to you to train employees so that they will be equipped to handle additional responsibilities.

Set up personnel guidelines, but don't be rigid. Deal with individual problems as they occur.

Be honest when dealing with your staff. Be consistent. Above all, be fair.

PAYROLL PAPERWORK PROCEDURES

Payroll Record Keeping

There are no legal requirements as to *how* employee records* are to be maintained. There are numerous payroll record-keeping systems and computer software programs, and your bookkeeper or accountant can advise you on the simplest method for your needs. The following information must be recorded:

The employees' names, addresses, and social security numbers

Amount and date of salary payments subject to withholding taxes, and the amounts withheld

The periods of employment, including payments to employees during their absence owing to illness or injury

W-4 forms (income tax withholding exemption certificates)

Your employer identification number (File Form SS-4 with your Internal Revenue Service district director in order to obtain this number.)

Duplicate copies of tax returns that have been filed

*See SBA Business Development Publication "Managing Employee Benefits," by Iris Goldfein and Melinda Lopes (no. PM 3, $1).

Dates and amounts of deposits made with government depositories (your bank or a Federal Reserve bank)

Employment (Payroll) Taxes

From the moment you hire your first full-time employee (excluding consultants, free-lancers, or temporary workers) you have taken on an added responsibility (and added bookkeeping procedures). Every business with one or more employees is required to withhold federal income taxes and social security (FICA) taxes. The amount is taken out before the paycheck is issued.

First off, file Form SS-4 with your IRS district director to obtain your employer identification number (not to be confused with the social security number required on individual tax returns). Obtain specific information from the IRS on your type of business, as well as Circular E in the IRS's *Employer's Tax Guide,* which indicates the up-to-date deductions to withhold (taxes and social security) from every paycheck, based on the total salary amount. Contact your state's department of labor if you have any additional questions.

Withholding returns are to be filed quarterly on Form 941, available from the IRS or your bank.

At the beginning of each year (calendar) and when hiring someone new, you must furnish every employee with a W-4 Form (or W-4E, in some cases—check with the IRS to see who qualifies). This form, called the Employee's Withholding Allowance Certificate, also indicates the number of exemptions affecting deductions from her taxable income.

Social Security Taxes

Social security taxes (also known by their legislative initials FICA) must be withheld and matched equally by the company; the amounts change yearly. The IRS and Social Security Administration offices provide tables showing the exact amounts to withhold and match for different salary levels. File (quarterly, in general) these taxes on IRS Form 941. (If you are a sole proprietor or a partner, your social security is paid with your federal income tax.) You will receive all the appropriate IRS forms, along with an explanation booklet, when you obtain your employer identification number.

City and State Withholding Taxes

Contact your local and state tax authorities for information about any payroll and withholding tax requirements under their jurisdictions.

State and Federal Unemployment Taxes

When you take on employees you must register your business with your state's department of labor. They will assign you an identification number, which you will use in your dealings with them. The amount you will be required to pay into your state's unemployment fund will relate directly to how often you hire and fire people. The better you are at keeping your staff members, the less you'll have to pay.

Federal unemployment tax (FUTA) is less than the state tax. File Form 940 one month after the close of your calendar or fiscal year, and enclose the tax money owed if it is less than $100. If it is more (generally, if you have more than three full-time employees), file Deposit Form 8109 and pay the tax to an authorized bank. (Your accountant/bookkeeper will set this up for you, if you wish.)

Pension Plans, Profit-sharing, and Disability Insurance

These are covered in detail in chapter 8.

Disability benefits are deducted from the employee's paycheck, along with withholding and social security. This provides compensation for illness or injury unrelated to the job.

Worker's Compensation and Unemployment Insurance

Once you take on full-time employees, you are required to take out Worker's Compensation from a state insurance fund or private insurer. The applications of Worker's Compensation vary widely between states. (See chapter 8.) This insurance is mandatory once a single employee is hired.

For unemployment insurance coverage, apply to your state's department of human resources development within fifteen days of hiring your first employee.

· 14 ·

Surviving and Thriving: Day-to-Day Management

Nothing succeeds like success.
—Alexandre Dumas, père

BUSINESS AS A GAME

It's not enough that your business grows from day to day, with everyone getting the job done. There has to be excitement to it, to keep both you and your staff stimulated and looking forward to coming to work. Research conducted on entrepreneurs shows that many of them love the creativity involved in starting a business but grow bored once things have settled down into a routine.

But things don't have to settle down. For you and your business to thrive, you have to constantly reevaluate and set new goals. The goals should be specific, and all of your employees should be informed so that they can work toward them.

If you look at business as a game,* you'll realize that there's nothing to stop you and your employees (the players) from being creative while you play the game. But in order for everyone to participate fully, everyone must learn the rules: it's up to you to teach them. (Education keeps people growing; if they're constantly learning new things they won't be bored.) How do you teach them? You explain how the business works (the game board). The best way to do that is to teach them how to read financial statements. If everyone knows where the money is com-

*See "Being the Boss," editorial interview, *Inc.,* October 1989.

ing and going, they have a clearer idea of how to achieve the goals that you set (winning the game).

Once they know the rules, your employees then become an integral part of your business. Not only will they perform the job for which they were hired, they will become educated about the workings of business in general. (Most employees have no idea how a business functions; they do their job and that's that.) If everyone understands how to read the company's financial statements, then they can see for themselves how the business is doing and how *their* participation is affecting the big picture.

Women entrepreneurs have learned the value of team playing as much as men. It's important to put together a working environment where everyone performs together and knows what's going on. But that's not enough: there must be rewards besides the weekly salary. If you are willing to provide incentives, such as quarterly bonuses for profits exceeding X amount, then people are going to bend over backward to make more sales, produce additional widgets, or bring in new clients. They are going to work together as a team and inspire one another to go the extra distance.

A business becomes bogged down only when the fun goes out of it. If you and your employees enjoy what you are doing, your customers will appreciate it and respond in kind.

PLANNING AND GOAL SETTING

As head of your company you have to run the business itself, participate in and oversee what the business actually *does,* and create plans to pursue your goals.* It's time-consuming, but as the chief executive officer you have to keep on top of it all, delegating what you can. There are five functions of business management that you must tend to: planning, organizing, directing, controlling, and coordinating.

Goal setting—in terms of sales, profits, growth within your market—must be divided into two categories: short- and long-range. The short-term goals will contribute to the long-range ones. It's time to refer back to your original business plan and revise it according to where you and your business are now.

How is your business standing up in terms of the current

*See SBA booklet *Planning and Goal Setting for Small Business,* by Raymond F. Pelissier (Management Aids, no. 2.010, $.50).

market? Have global economic trends changed the picture? Are there products/services that are obsolete or not making enough money to warrant their continuation? Is it possible to update certain products and services, to remarket them for a wider audience? How has your original target market changed, and what do you have to do to reach a wider market? Are you keeping abreast of changes within your industry and the expanded needs of your customers? Are you growing too fast? Too slowly? Are you continuing to keep costs down so you don't become overextended?

You must constantly look at your company's strengths and weaknesses, and as the old song goes, accentuate the positive, eliminate the negative. (This applies to your staff, too.)

Once you have reevaluated where your business stands within its market and against its competition, you have to set new goals. Make a list of five to ten *specific,* attainable goals. Discuss them with your employees and decide which you will focus on first. Write down the goal and keep it in a place where everyone can be reminded of it. In addition to focusing on the goal, you must come up with the steps necessary to complete it. At the end of each quarter you must determine how you stand in terms of your goal. If there are problems, they must be identified and you must figure out how to eliminate them. Everyone must be kept informed as to what's going on and how close/far you are from attaining the stated goal. When a goal is achieved, celebrate. Praise (and reward) the participants. Then proceed to the next one on your list.

Workers should be encouraged to set their own personal goals. Try to provide incentives for everyone to work at peak performance level. People who do a good job should be rewarded regularly, both with bonuses and praise. Always compliment employees on jobs well done. If something goes wrong, work with them on trying to correct the problem.

There are different kinds of goals, and there is a place for all of them within your business:

Work goals have to do with increasing sales, quality and efficiency of production, developing and conducting marketing research and sales programs, improving the quality of a product or service, expanding the total amount produced or marketed, etc.

215

Problem-solving goals define major problems and eliminate them—an ongoing process.

Innovative goals sometimes address an existing problem, but often have to do with coming up with new ideas for products or services, new ways of running things. Make sure everyone within the company makes suggestions.

Development goals recognize how important developing your employees' skills and knowledge is to the growth of the company, i.e., they come up with ways to educate everyone.

Goals mean nothing if you don't chart your progress regularly and review your progress in terms of achieving them. This should be done monthly or quarterly; some owner-managers feel that it should be done on a weekly basis to keep everyone revved up.

PROBLEM SOLVING

No matter how hard you try, problems have a way of cropping up continually. The important thing is to realize that all problems have a solution. Some solutions are easier to find, but there's always an answer out there.

The best way to solve a problem is to anticipate it and avoid it, if possible. The way to anticipate it is to plan ahead. Yes, you've heard it before: plan, plan, plan.

And when a problem rears its ugly head, try to solve it as expediently as possible.* The way to go about it is to:

Identify the problem. (Define it specifically, *all* aspects of it.)

Analyze the problem. (Seek the cause and the effects; what happened and why? Who/what was involved? What policies/ procedures came into it? Has it happened before, and what were the consequences?)

Focus on objectives that any solution must incorporate (including ways to avoid its occurring again).

Come up with possible solutions. (List different plans that might solve the problem. Brainstorming with employees or a problem-solving committee can help. Talk to other business owners and get their input.)

Evaluate possible solutions to find the right one. (Come up

*For more information, see "How to Make the Right Decision," by Connie Sitterly and Beth Whitley Duke, *Working Woman*, August 1988.

with the pros and cons of each alternative and try to eliminate them objectively.)

Pick the best solution. (Sometimes there is not a 100 percent perfect solution, so you go with the one that will best solve the problem.)

Act on it. (Pinpoint specific timetables and goals to put the new plan into action. Review the new plan regularly to make sure it is working.)

CRISIS MANAGEMENT

All good business plans should allow for unexpected interruptions in your daily routine. No matter how hard you try, something is going to go wrong sometime. Being prepared for this unpleasant eventuality is called crisis management.* If you're not prepared, a crisis could turn into a disaster for your business.

What sorts of crises can happen to a business? There are many: theft; fires; floods, earthquakes, and other natural disasters; losing a major client; the death of a partner or key employee; economic downturn in the market; increased competition, both locally and internationally, and so on.

Experts say that it's not the problem that's important, it's how you handle it. And if you deal with it *before* it happens, so much the better. The first step is to put together a crisis management team composed of you and key employees or outside consultants (your lawyer or accountant or a crisis management consultant). Then you sit down and think of everything that could possibly go wrong and what to do when it does. Next, compile lists of people (clients, media people, public officials, etc.) who would need to be contacted if a crisis occurred.

But what if the crisis happens to you, the owner? What if you are unable to work for a period of time because of illness, for example? Many small businesses fall apart without the owner at the helm. To get around this, sit down and think about how to delegate authority and give your employees the knowledge to keep the business running without you.

Write up an operating procedures manual, detailing each area of the business and how it's run. Include a page outlining your business's policies, i.e., if A occurs, the whole company will re-

*See "Crisis Management," by Scott Matulis, *Entrepreneur,* November 1988.

spond by doing B. Draw up a delegation plan, outlining who will handle what extra duties in your absence.

A crisis doesn't have to put you out of business if you're prepared. And if you can withstand the crisis, your company will be stronger for it.

COST CUTTING

You're growing fast and growth is expensive. All of a sudden there's not enough flow to your cash and you're in trouble. This scenario is a common one for small businesses. The answer, of course, is to cut your costs. But that's a hard thing to do when you've got a staff to support, a bunch of new clients, and a desperate need for more office space and more equipment. But when you have to do something, it can be done.

Cost reduction is basically a logical process. The first step is to make sure your employees understand the problems (if you've taught them to read the company's financial statements, they'll see what's wrong before you have to explain it). Everyone must understand that if budgets aren't cut they may all be out of a job.

Next, you have to figure out *how* costs will be cut. Look at each area of your business in detail, with the key employees of each area. Analyze all your expenditures and the reasons for them. Look for any opportunity to save money, remembering that you still have to keep the business competitive. In some areas, cutting costs will involve some risk, but nothing can change without risks.

You also have to take a hard look at all of your employees. This isn't easy, especially when you like the people with whom you work. But with the company and everyone's jobs at stake it is sometimes necessary to weed out anyone who isn't pulling her share of the load. You have to look at each employee in depth: what job does she perform and is it really necessary? How well does she do that job? Can the job be eliminated or combined with another? (Sometimes jobs were created to solve problems that no longer exist; the person, no matter how good she is, is no longer vital to the company.)

Now write up your cost-reduction goal for each area of business. This must be specific, e.g., cut staff by 10 percent, lower advertising budget by 20 percent, etc. In each area, you also have to estimate the potential savings in relation to the probability of success. Generally, the areas that can be most effectively changed are:

Controlling quality (Eliminating quality problems can have a positive effect on both customers and staff. If fewer mistakes are made, then more work can be done per day. Volume will improve and customers will come back. In larger companies, consider implementing a quality-control software program to isolate problems and costs.)

Meeting deadlines (Customers are disgruntled when they are promised something by a specific date and then it's not ready. Try to meet schedules by making more realistic estimates and by making sure the most qualified person is handling each job.)

Controlling spending (Over the years it's easy to become lazy in watching the money you spend, especially in the areas of office supplies, phones, advertising, and staff and salespeople's expenses. It is often possible to cut these types of expenditures by 10 to 30 percent. Establish a system where all expenses must be approved beforehand.)

Raising productivity (By having everyone committed to working harder, by planning better and following up, and sometimes by adding new technology, you can raise productivity levels as much as 30 percent. But this takes time, and everyone concerned must be willing. You must also explain in detail how each person can function more productively. If new technology is the answer it will cost you money, but sometimes you have to spend money to make it. Choose carefully what you need and don't overbuy, or you'll end up back where you started.)

The bottom line in cost cutting is communication. Everyone involved must understand why it's necessary, and they must understand exactly how they are to go about it.

STRESS MANAGEMENT

According to a five-year study conducted by the University of California–San Francisco Medical School and completed in 1988, 93 percent (!) of all executives suffer from health-threatening levels of stress. Entrepreneurs, even though they enjoy being their own bosses, are every bit as prone to stress as executives in large corporations. The entrepreneur has a lot of responsibility: the moneylenders are looking for repayment of their loan or high returns on their investment, the employees are looking for salary increases, the customers are looking for quality, the suppliers want to be paid on time, and so forth. It's the entrepreneur who must keep it all going. In a large corporation there's always someone to pass the buck to. But the buck stops with the owner of a business.

Stress is a real factor of life in the latter part of the twentieth century. There's so much to do, and never enough time to get it done. There are deadlines and presentations and budgets to meet. Entrepreneurs, high achievers that they are, are prime candidates for experiencing the stress-anxiety syndrome. And today's superwomen have it the worst of all. Not only are they running businesses, they are running families as well.

So what do you do about it? In a study published in 1989 in *American Health*,* Dr. Suzanne Ouelette Kobasa found that some people handle stress better than others. The three characteristic traits that help people overcome stress are: seeing crises as *challenges*, situations for which to find a solution; having *control* over your own life; and being *committed* to yourself, your family, your values, and your work. (Entrepreneurs fare well in all these categories.)

Stress can be controlled, even eliminated. First, you have to figure out what stresses you out (which situations, people, etc.). Then you can work at avoiding the types of conflicts or confrontations that cause your major anxiety. But it's hard to eliminate ongoing worries, so experts recommend that you allot a fifteen-to thirty-minute "worry time" each day (but never before going to bed): don't allow yourself to dwell on any problems except during the proper time.

Often, you have to look hard at yourself and your life. Identify faulty thought patterns that lead to anxiety; learn to delegate more responsibility; make changes in routines that cause stress. Be open: air your gripes. Harboring anger can affect you physically; be assertive with those who hassle you. It is said that you can bring on stress yourself, but you can talk yourself out of it, too. Other ways to relieve or reduce stress are: physical exercise,

*See "Aftershock: Learning to Cope," by Andrew Slaby, *Woman*, October 1989.

massage, hot baths, sex, stopping smoking, cutting down on caffeine, watching your diet, practicing relaxation techniques, and enlarging your social circle. Creativity also cuts down on stress.

There's good stress, too, such as creative deadlines, or too much business. These are a part of one's working life. Good stress keeps you pumped up; it won't make you sick.

In general, try not to worry about problems: come up with ways to solve them. Entrepreneurs are good at that.

GOOD LEADERSHIP

Women make good leaders and good bosses. By nature they are cooperative, flexible, nurturing, and enthusiastic. Women entrepreneurs have a great opportunity to bring these characteristics to the corporate marketplace.

Women are good at networking, helping each other to succeed. Female entrepreneurs can help other women by caring about their success and caring about those commitments to family that sometimes conflict with work. Maternity leave, day care, job sharing, flextime—all of these options are there for the woman entrepreneur to choose for her staff.

There are dozens of qualities that make an entrepreneur a good leader. Narrowed down to the most important, they are: self-confidence, skill, enthusiasm, a caring personality, the ability to share the spotlight, being able to make decisions (knowing when to mull and when to move), having a deep commitment to employees and the business itself, and maintaining the courage to surround herself with people who are more skilled (in some areas) than she.

A good leader can be supportive and nurturing to those under her. Strengthening others does not weaken a strong entrepreneur. It makes those under her willing to work harder because of the trust and support she has given them.

A good leader must be consistent in dealing with policies concerning both customers and employees. Consistency is imperative for an organized, professional business. You have to think about how you want to run your company, then set the rules. Stick to the rules, always allowing for flexibility and creativity in future policy making.

A good leader understands that she can never know enough. Keep educating yourself (and your employees). Advice on trends can be gleaned from research centers, TV, radio, magazines, newspapers, and other entrepreneurs. Education will give you the edge you need to keep ahead of the competition. Network, too; there's a lot to be learned informally.

A good leader is sensitive to her business. She doesn't leave town during peak times. Smart entrepreneurs, however, recognize the restorative necessity of rest and relaxation. Whether they want to or not, they schedule regular vacations, even if they're just long weekends.

Most of all, a good leader is a person who loves what she does and, even in tough times, wouldn't trade places with anyone.

· 15 ·

Taxes: The Bottom Line

The weight of this sad time we must obey.
—William Shakespeare

Every business owner is responsible for her company's federal, state, and local taxes, regardless of who actually does the bookkeeping and filing. Ignorance, as always, is no excuse; if you don't pay a tax, you'll have to pay a nasty penalty or answer ominous summonses. Have your accountant or tax attorney explain your obligations and provide you with a yearly tax calendar as a reminder of those deadly due dates. Consider having an extra bank account for tax monies (especially retail businesses with sales tax payments due quarterly), so that you won't accidentally spend money that should be allocated toward taxes.

Keeping accurate, up-to-date business journals is the first step to computing taxes. The Internal Revenue Service (IRS) requires that a company's tax information be backed up by permanent records (for auditing, if need be). These records must verify income, deductions, credits, inventories (when applicable), and any sales or rentals subject to excise taxes. They must also include names, addresses, and social security numbers of owner(s) and staff, as well as your employer identification number.* (Taxes relating specifically to employees are covered in chapter 13.)

Since paying taxes is like walking a tightrope at best (especially since the Tax Reform Act of 1986 went into effect), check with

*To obtain your taxpayer's identification number (also called Employer's Identification number), get Form SS-4 from the Internal Revenue Service.

the following sources for assistance and information on which taxes your business is subject to: the IRS, your state and local tax agencies, the public library, trade associations, your bank, your accountant, or a tax information service. These can fill you in on the ever-changing tax regulations and offer suggestions on how to go about keeping the necessary tax records. There are also computer software programs available that will calculate and prepare your taxes for you.

Major assistance will, of course, come from your accountant,* but, as in all other areas, the more you yourself know, the better off you'll be. Even if you plop these duties completely in your accountant's lap, make it a point to understand your company's tax situation. If you do your own bookkeeping, you should obtain professional advice in the beginning on the accurate computation and filing of tax forms. Penalty fines on late- or nonpayment of taxes can be frustrating as well as costly, and they *are* avoidable so long as you know what's doing at the IRS.

First of all, sit down and read publication no. 334, *Tax Guide for Small Business,* published annually and obtainable from the IRS.† This guide will unravel all the mysteries of federal income taxes. It is, in fact, a mini how-to book, explaining bookkeeping systems, tax laws, etc. for sole proprietorships, partnerships, and corporations, and it includes sample tax forms and all pertinent information required for the filing of your business tax returns. Whether you fill out the forms accurately yourself is another matter, but at least you will learn what forms must be filed, why, and what deductions you can make.

FISCAL VERSUS CALENDAR YEAR

The following is a rundown of the taxes that each business structure is required to file. The filing dates depend on whether

*If you are ever faced with a complex tax issue, you may require the advice of a tax attorney or a tax consulting firm. This can be expensive, but if there is a lot at stake, it may be worth it.

†As the tax laws are ever-changing, also consult with your accountant before paying taxes. In addition, several other publications that contain useful tax information, updated regularly, are: J. K. Lasser Tax Institute: *How to Run a Small Business* (New York: McGraw-Hill); Bernard Kamoroff, *Small-Time Operator* (Laytonville, California: Bell Springs Publishing); and *The Price Waterhouse Personal Tax Advisor* (New York: Pocket Books). See also "Guide to Tax Reform," *Small Business Reporter* (no. SBR-209, $5), Bank of America, Department 3631, P.O. Box 37000, San Francisco, California 94137.

you register with the IRS by the *calendar* or *fiscal* year. A tax year is twelve consecutive months, ending on either December 31 (a calendar year) or at the end of any month of your choosing (a fiscal year). Your lawyer or accountant can advise you as to which date is most advantageous for your business. In general, filing returns fiscally allows the end of your fiscal year to coincide with the low point of your annual business cycle. Almost every business has a slow period, having to do with the very nature of the business. If you choose a fiscal year, ending at this point of least activity, then you will have more time to work on closing your books for the year and filing your tax returns. (Sole proprietors and unincorporated partnerships cannot file fiscally because business taxes must be paid on your personal income tax returns, due April 15 every year.)

TAX PLANNING

It is important to review profits and expenses toward the end of your tax year. In that way you can monitor your cash flow. You might want to accept payment from a client *after* the year's end, so the income will be taxed on the next year's return. Another way to get a deduction in a high-profit year is to prepay your loans or mortgages. In general, if you anticipate higher profits for next year, defer whatever *expenses* you can to that year's return. If you anticipate lower profits, defer whatever *income* you can. Your accountant should be on hand to advise you about your tax planning.

The more your company grows, the more essential tax planning becomes; if venture capitalists become involved they will probably insist on it. Basically, at this point tax planning becomes a business plan for taxes. It will help you anticipate and reduce taxes. When your company's big enough, hire a tax expert to advise you. She will analyze what's going on with your company (by delving into your accounting and recordkeeping methods and going over tax returns from previous years). Then she will work out your growth plan while trying to reduce the tax bite. (For example, if you aren't already, she might advise you to become an S corporation, providing your company meets the required standards—see chapter 6.)

If your company is planning to expand into the global marketplace, international tax planning will be essential.

Every year or so review and reevaluate your tax plan in regard to how your company is doing in general, in terms of the timing of purchases/sales/other business activities, and possible new tax-reduction strategies.

Tax Planning Services Offered by the IRS

The IRS provides a toll-free number, (800)424–1040, to answer your questions regarding tax laws and the preparation of tax returns.

If an accountant or tax attorney isn't preparing your taxes, tax forms can be obtained from the post office, banks, or libraries. Or call the IRS's "Forms Only" toll-free number, (800)424–FORM, to order tax forms and instruction publications with information relating to specific areas of the tax law.

TAXES FOR INDIVIDUAL PROPRIETORS AND FREE-LANCERS

Federal Income Tax

For sole proprietors and free-lancers all business income and deductions* are to be filed on your individual tax return, Schedule C (Form 1040), available from your local IRS office. This is due on April 15. If you need more time to prepare your taxes you may use Form 4868 to request a four-month, no-questions-asked extension. However, you are still responsible for paying 90 percent of your taxes on April 15 (and the additional 10 percent when you file your Form 1040). But if you need the extra time to calculate your taxes, how can you figure out what 90 percent will be before you calculate them? Count on the IRS for fun stuff like that, and if you get it wrong they hit you for more money, in the form of penalties.

You must also file estimated tax returns quarterly during the tax year.† (If you underestimate your estimated taxes you will

---

*A full explanation of the status of, and difference between, part-time and free-lance people is available in the Internal Revenue Service *Tax Guide for Small Business.* Also consult the guide for up-to-date specifics on deductions and what constitutes taxable income for each business structure—the proprietorship, partnership, or corporation.

†Check with your local IRS office for updated information on estimated tax requirements.

have to pay a penalty. There are a few exceptions to this, but they probably won't apply to you.)

Since the Tax Reform Act of 1986 came into effect, tax paying, never fun or easy, has become a lot more difficult. Unless you're savvy in this area, you'd be better off paying an expert to untangle all the gibberish. The IRS puts all the responsibility on you to file correctly. If you make a mistake because of misinformation or negligence, you will be expected to pay for it.

State Income Tax

You must pay individual state income tax (if your state requires it) to the franchise board of your state. Check with them for filing procedures, and when to file. (State income tax due dates vary from state to state.) In many states, your reported federal income tax will be used as the basis for calculating your state income tax.

City, County, and Local Taxes

Depending upon where you live, you may be required to pay various local taxes. Check with your accountant and/or your city and county governments to see which of the following is applicable to your business, and obtain the proper filing forms: individual city income tax, sales tax, business licenses, city and county real or personal property taxes.

PARTNERSHIP TAXES

Each partner must file her individual share of the company's income on her personal tax return (Schedule C, Form 1040). The credits/deductions passed along to individual partners are explained on the K-1 Form that every partnership must issue annually to its partners.

For informational purposes, partnerships are also required to report the company's income. This is to be filed on Form 1065 (U.S. Partnership Return of Income), and there are stiff penalties for failure to file this form. Since the partnership itself is not subject to income tax, no estimated tax returns are required. Filing dates (and extensions) are the same as those for sole proprietorships.

State Income Tax

Partnerships are required to file an informational return to the state franchise tax board (if your state requires it). In many states, each partner must file an individual state income tax return. Contact your state's franchise board.

City, County, and Local Taxes

Check with your accountant or local city/county government to see what taxes are required for partnerships. (See tax listing for local taxes for sole proprietorships.)

SELF-EMPLOYMENT TAX
FOR SINGLE OWNER OR PARTNERSHIP

Owners or partners are not subject to federal payroll taxes (withholding taxes—see chapter 13), but instead are required to pay self-employment tax along with their federal income tax. Based on their business's net profit, this is Social Security tax for self-employed individuals; single owners or partners pay the highest Social Security rate of all. This computation is done on Form 1040-SE and accompanies your federal Schedule C, Form 1040, even though the self-employment tax is not an income tax. (And even if you owe no income tax for a particular year, you are still liable for the self-employment tax.) For more information, get a free copy of IRS publication no. 553, *Information on Self-Employment Tax.*

CORPORATE TAXES

Federal Income Tax

Corporations must file their income tax returns on Form 1120 (and application for extension on Form 7004), as well as estimated tax returns, due quarterly. The actual estimated tax payments are to be made to your bank (or any authorized commercial or federal reserve bank); payments are to be accompanied by Form 503. Form 1120-W gives complete information on figuring and filing the estimated tax. By the end of the tax year you will have to have paid 100 percent of your estimated taxes, which has to amount to at least 80 percent of the taxes you actually owe. If, at that time, you owe more than 20 percent, you may be penalized for not having paid enough.

If a corporation is on a calendar year, then the federal income tax is due on March 15. For a fiscal year, the return must be filed on or before the fifteenth day of the third month after the close of its fiscal year.

S Corporations

Small business corporations opting for the S status must file Form 2553, obtainable from your local IRS office. It's a one-page form, indicating your corporation's election to be treated as a small business corporation for income tax purposes. (As explained in chapter 6, this election enables the company to be taxed at individual rates. The owners may then report their share of the company's profits or losses on their personal tax returns. If they have income from other sources, their whole tax may be reduced as a result of their business expenses.)

S corporations must file their actual income tax return on Form 1120-S, according to the same time schedule as regular corporations.

State Income Tax

Every corporation is required to pay an initial minimum franchise tax (the amount varies from state to state), due on the date of incorporation. Thereafter, the tax is paid annually, based on the company's net income for the preceding year. Contact the franchise tax board of your state for information on filing franchise tax returns.

Besides state income taxes, corporations are subjected to some or all of the following taxes, according to the nature of the particular business: gross receipts and sales taxes; inventory taxes; business real and personal property taxes; capital stock taxes; business car or truck licenses and inspection fees; death taxes; "foreign" state business taxes; unemployment taxes; and Worker's Compensation insurance premiums.

City, County, and Local Taxes

Check with your accountant and/or city and county governments for specific corporate tax requirements. Corporations are subject to business real and personal property taxes, rental occupancy taxes, sales taxes, business license fees, etc., depending on the type of business.

ADDITIONAL TAXES
AND REQUIRED FORMS TO FILE

All businesses with employees must pay payroll, employment, state and federal unemployment, and social security taxes (see chapter 13 for elaboration).

Certain manufacturers and retailers are subject to federal excise taxes. Corporations must also pay stamp taxes and death taxes, when applicable. Check with your local IRS office to find out if you are obligated to pay excise or stamp taxes imposed on the sale or use of certain items (such as liquor, firearms, certain equipment, etc.), and usually filed quarterly.

If your business imports or exports anything, you will be subject to customs duties, both in this country and/or abroad. Contact the U.S. Customs Bureau and the foreign embassies or consulates of the countries in which you conduct business for information regarding fees and restrictions.

Although there will be no taxes owed, your company will be required to file certain additional forms (e.g., if you have a pension plan you will have to report on it annually). In addition, you are required to provide a W-2 Form to every employee and send Form 1099 to other businesses or subcontractors that your company utilized over the year. A copy of each W-2 and 1099 form must also be sent to the IRS annually. You must also keep on file a W-4 Form, for withholding allowances, on each employee.

Sales and Use Taxes

All retailers must have a seller's permit. This allows you to purchase tangible property for resale without paying sales tax. To register, apply to the board of equalization for a seller's permit (resale tax) number. (Sometimes, the board requires a security deposit at the time of registration, the amount depending on the company's size.)

Taxes are paid to the board *after* the item has been resold.

Wholesalers or manufacturers must record transactions on

resale certificates. These certificates, plus instructions, are available from the board of equalization.

Property Taxes

All businesses must pay annual personal property taxes on tangible personal property, including equipment and inventory. Real property taxes (on land, buildings), if applicable, as well as rental occupancy tax, must be paid semiannually to your local tax authorities.

BUSINESS TAX DEDUCTIONS AND DEPRECIATION

In general, legitimate, reasonable business expenses (not personal expenses)—considered by the IRS as "ordinary" and "necessary"—are deductible. The list of possible business deductions is extensive, but what is actually allowable depends on the nature of your specific business. IRS regulations concerning deductions change constantly, and there are extensive stipulations concerning allowable deductions. For example, all business insurance premiums *are* deductible (for fire, extended coverage, theft, liability, Worker's Compensation, group insurance for employees, unemployment insurance, fidelity and surety bonds, etc.). However, personal life insurance premiums are *not* deductible, and health insurance premiums are *partly* deductible.

Start-up expenses (incurred before you actually open your doors for business) can either be *capitalized* (which means you will not deduct them until you quit or sell the business), or *amortized* (i.e., you can depreciate them over a sixty-month period beginning the month you actually started your business). Discuss this and all possible deductions with your accountant or tax adviser. Basically, it's a good idea to start your business (i.e., make your first sale) *before* you buy all the equipment and furnishings that you will need for your business.

Assets used over a period of years are treated differently from things like raw materials and inventory that come and go rapidly. The rules for depreciating assets (equipment, tools, machinery, display cases, fixtures, computers, and so forth) change often, but generally the rule that applied when you bought the piece of equipment is the one you go by for depreciating it.

Materials, supplies, and inventory are not considered assets and cannot be depreciated. If you have a home office,* part of that can be depreciated. Have your accountant or tax adviser fill you in on current depreciation-of-assets rules.

The IRS imposes further restrictions on the depreciation of cars, computers, and certain other equipment. Keep a record of everything you purchase and use for your business, when you bought it, how often you use it (especially a car or truck), and so forth. These restrictions, like the others, change frequently.

REPORTING TAXES:
CASH VERSUS ACCRUAL METHODS

You have the choice of reporting your taxes via the *cash* or *accrual* method. (If you have an inventory, the accrual method is automatic.) On the cash basis, you must report all income received and take all your deductions for expenses in that particular tax year. (This way, you can, to some extent, control the income you report, for example, by putting off certain billings or postponing paying certain expenses until the next tax year.)

If you use the accrual basis, you must report income as earned, even if it has not actually been received, and you must deduct expenses that have been incurred in a tax year, regardless of whether or not you have paid for them. If you sell goods on the installment method, you must report your profit in the year of the sale, and not spread it out over several years.

HOW TO HANDLE A TAX AUDIT

Only a percentage of people are audited, but it can happen, and you should be prepared. What triggers an audit? Generally, it's your having reported suspicious (or too many) deductions—especially in those red-flag areas of travel and entertainment, business mileage on a car, and a home office (the IRS may want to come and see it: to make sure it really is an office). Not that you shouldn't take the deductions you're entitled to, but be careful to keep complete, detailed records (and receipts) of all business expenses. Other reasons for audits include carelessness,

*If you work out of your home or apartment, see IRS publication no. 587, *Business Use of Your Home,* for deduction requirements.

232

incomplete reporting of income, new rulings in tax laws, and so forth.

The Taxpayer's Bill of Rights, passed by Congress in 1988, requires that taxpayers be provided with clear and complete information, and be offered fair payment plans. Taxpayers can sue the IRS if they can prove that the IRS acted "recklessly" in collecting or assessing penalties. (For a copy of the free booklet explaining it all, call [800]424-FORM.)

There are different types of tax audits.* The mail audit will require you to send in substantiating information (canceled checks, receipts, etc.) regarding a specific query. (Send copies, never originals, through the mail.†) The office examination will require you to show up at an IRS field office with your records for the year to be audited, prepared to answer detailed questions. (Bring along the person who prepared your taxes, if you wish, or give them power of attorney to handle it instead of you. Remember, however, the IRS considers *you* responsible for your taxes, not the person who prepared your returns.) The third audit is the field audit, which takes place *chez vous*. For this, you should definitely bring in your tax adviser to help answer questions.

When dealing with the auditor have your records (and receipts and invoices, etc.) at your fingertips. Answer questions clearly and *don't* volunteer information. Be logical and organized, never chatty; the tax auditor is not your friend.

After an audit you'll be required to sign a paper agreeing to what the IRS examiner claims you owe. If you disagree, there are a number of things you can do, ranging from meeting with the auditor's supervisor to going to the U.S. District Court or the Court of Claims. For more information, get a free copy of IRS publication no. 556, *Examination of Returns, Appeal Rights, and Claims for Refunds*.

Of the people who are audited, 12 to 14 percent emerge unscathed. Most people wind up paying additional taxes. And, of course, if you've been intentionally fraudulent, you may go to jail.

---

*See "How to Avoid a Tax Audit," by Gretchen Worth, *Working Woman*, March 1989.

†It's a good idea to send all correspondence by certified mail, return receipt requested, in order to prove that it was received by the IRS. This is especially important if you are responding to a request for information, or if there is a deadline involved.

SUMMARY

Everyone is familiar with Benjamin Franklin's pithy maxim, "In this world nothing is certain but death and taxes." He was probably ruminating on taxes again when he wrote, "The first mistake in public business is the going into it."

Taxes must be reported on time every year. If you make a mistake you will not only pay for it but have penalties and interest added on as well.

The responsibility here as elsewhere falls on the business owner, even if she's merely supervising her bookkeeper or accountant. There is no salve to relieve the pain of taxes. The only way to alleviate the discomfort is by accurate recording, reporting, and remitting.

· 16 ·

Marching Forth: What Next?

Christmas is over and Business is Business.
—Franklin Pierce Adams

Everything's in place. Your business is humming along. You have contented customers, a satisfied staff, supportive suppliers, and mollified moneylenders. Yet your consultants are telling you that you've got to grow or you'll stagnate.

Well, this is one point on which many entrepreneurs disagree. Many women (and men too) reach a plateau where their businesses are easily manageable. They're happy and making enough money to suit their needs. They don't *want* to get larger.

Other entrepreneurs see growth as an additional outlet for their creative, pioneering entrepreneurial instincts. They stay awake nights conjuring up new products or services to attract new business. When they finally fall asleep, they dream of filling their office with the latest technological breakthroughs to give them an edge over their competition.

The right answer for you and your business is up to *you.* Staying small doesn't necessarily mean treading water. As Lewis Carroll said, you have to keep running to stay in the same place. Even if you don't aspire to steering your company into the *Fortune* 500, you must stay current and competitive.

But if you choose to grow, there are many ways. You can borrow expansion capital to buy more equipment, hire additional people, or enlarge your work space. If you want to grow really big, you can go public and sell stock shares in your company.*

*See "The Dark Side: Will Your Worst Fears About Going Public Come True?," by Joshua Hyatt, *Inc.,* May 1990.

235

If your business is based on an innovative idea or product that you feel would be a nationwide success, you can open branch offices or sell franchises. If you think people around the world can use your product or service, you can compete in the global marketplace.

And there's another alternative. What if you're the sort of entrepreneur who thrives on the start-up, then wants someone else to take over the business and run it? If the everyday routine is sapping your creative strength, then you might consider selling your business. (Whether you start another is up to you.)

These are the possibilities that will be explored in this chapter.

TO GROW OR NOT TO GROW

You've gotten through all the snags of the first few years. Your business is running along quite nicely. Then you start to get itchy, or one of your consultants suggests that what you have isn't enough, that you should shoot for the stars. Well, it's up to you. Perhaps the business is the right size as it is: you're generating enough income and enjoying the fact that you still have time for both tennis and the children.

But perhaps you do want more: the business has a track record and now you want to take it places. You want to Make It Big.

Some basic reasons to grow* (besides your ambition) are:

Your business is increasing. To accommodate new customers you need more employees, expanded inventory and equipment. For this you need more capital for expansion.

The thrill is gone: you want new challenges.

Your key staff members can't advance if you don't grow. If there's no opportunity for them they'll move on.

Your target market, you now realize, is too small. Expansion can help you reach a wider audience.

You need more time for yourself and your family. More employees would allow you to delegate more responsibility.

Your overhead is too high: growth can lower your expenses proportionally.

*Adapted from "Entrepreneur's Soliloquy," by Louise Sagalyn, *Working Woman,* August 1989.

Now, some factors to consider when trying to decide whether or not to expand (assuming your business is healthy and attracting new customers):

You will face more financial risk. Growth requires a substantial amount of money for more staff, equipment, inventory, day-to-day running expenses, etc. This means going out and borrowing more money. You have to analyze whether this increased overhead will result in substantially increased profits.

You will have to delegate more responsibility, and therefore lose a lot of the control you had over the business when it was small. It also means that you may be stuck with more administrative duties and have less contact with the customers or creative side of the business. The business will become less familylike.

You will need to grow, too. You'll have to learn new management skills to run a larger company.

You will have less time. Even with delegated responsibility a large business will keep you busier than a smaller one.

So, at what point do you go from busy and comfortable to risking overextension? Some businesses grow day by day, and the owners handle it in stride. But often it isn't that easy. Counseling can help. Get together with your consultants and hash out the pros and cons of expansion. Or perhaps put together an informal group of friends and business associates to brainstorm about your business, i.e., help you look at things up, down, and sideways. This is the time to get as much input as possible on all facets of growth versus staying put.

Think about your dear customers, too. How will they perceive your growth? Will they enjoy the expanded services, or feel lost in the middle and move on to one of your competitors? Remember them as you grow; after all, they got you to this point. Stay humble, and keep in touch with yourself.

And consider *all* the expenses involved with growth besides expanded overhead: more payroll and increased benefits, higher insurance premiums, need for more equipment and furnishings, redesigning office space (tearing down or putting up walls, painting), more heating and ventilation, additional phone lines, more electrical circuits for more computers, etc.

Before deciding to keep the status quo or make your move to grow bigger, consider all the angles. Change is risky but so is staying the same.

EXPANSION

The major reason for expansion is to handle increased sales and reach for a larger slice of the market. Often this involves bringing out new products or offering expanded services. But another way to grow is to take what you already market and add frills. (McDonald's expanded the basic burger into the Big Mac and McDLT; Ford Motor Company's Mercury Sable is simply the Ford Taurus with classier appointments.)

When you're considering growth, talk to your customers. Ask them what *they* want and they might come up with some interesting answers.

When it comes to expanding the business, entrepreneurs differ in their methods. Some go with intuition and risk and thrive on it. Others rely on their skills and plan to the nth degree.

Of course, planning is necessary for all business owners. Growth will be chaotic if it isn't choreographed, and this planning involves everyone in your business, not only you. You have to make sure your staff is behind you when you decide to move the business forward. Don't ever think of yourself as a one-woman show (unless you are one literally).

One of the most exciting things about growth is that it creates new jobs and opportunities for people.

Expansion Financing

Whether you need capital for expansion or working capital while you wait for customers to pay their bills, second-round financing is easier to get. Your business has established a track record. The moneylenders can look at your records and financial statements and see what's actually happening.

At this point, seek out your local banker. Invite the loan officer over to see your business. If you've been diligent and provided her with your financial statements right along, she'll know when you're ready to ask for help. Banks are usually willing to lend money for expansion, since the risk involved is greatly reduced.

Venture capitalists also provide growth money because the

business is established. They will take a smaller percentage or less stock than from a new enterprise.

The SBA also helps with expansion or assistance capital, as does Women's World Banking. (Review chapter 2 for the myriad money sources and how to put together a proper loan proposal.)

SAVING A TROUBLED COMPANY

But what if growth is a moot point? What if your financial picture isn't rosy and there's the danger that you might have to call it a day? Before you hang up the funereal wreath, realize that even sick companies can get well again.

As mentioned earlier, most businesses flop because of mismanagement or undercapitalization. Putting more money into your business isn't going to save it if proper attention is not being paid to how judiciously the money is being spent.

What are the symptoms of a sick company? There are many; losing money consistently is the most obvious. Other indications: being short of cash and barely making ends meet; losing customers; employees who are dispirited and quitting; the workplace itself becoming shoddy (peeling paint, broken machinery, messy and dirty office areas).

But it can turn around. The first thing to do is to realize that everything can be fixed (by you and/or someone else). The next thing is to separate yourself from your business. Sure it has problems, but don't let them get to you personally. Don't hide in the closet. Dust off your self-confidence. Get the support of your family and friends. See a counselor, if need be. Do anything to stoke your entrepreneurial fires.

How can you save your company? Talk to your consultants and put together a crisis plan. Then roll up your sleeves. The first thing to do is to get the cash flowing again. Monitor your incoming funds and watch every penny that goes out. Pay only for the things that will keep you going, in this order: payroll, utilities, key suppliers, withholding taxes. Once you've got control of your cash, you have a chance.

Listen to your employees, customers, suppliers, consultants. Now is the time to glean as much advice as possible. Show that you're taking charge. Exude optimism.

Figure out what areas of your business are losing money and drop them, even if they are your personal favorites.

239

Be positive, and try to improve attitudes. Let everyone know that things are looking up. Do anything you can to boost morale among the staff. Come up with something new that you can sell and publicize (a new product/service/way of handling customers, etc.). Get everyone's enthusiasm flowing again.

Plan a new business strategy, now that you know your company's strengths and weaknesses. Revise your company's values, if need be. Write up a new mission statement and make sure that everyone sees it.

Bring in a turn-around consultant, if necessary. But as with all of your consultants, check her out thoroughly. Beware of someone who promises you a quick fix.

Reevaluate your staff. Make sure each person is doing the job she was hired to do. Make sure each job is necessary. Retrain people, if necessary.

Reestablish credibility with your customers. Let them know you've made a commitment to quality and to making them happy. Try to come up with ways to garner favorable press attention. (See Advertising and Marketing, chapters 10 and 11.)

Raise new cash any way you can: collect receivables, liquidate inventory and supplies, sell unnecessary assets (unused machinery, equipment, company cars, etc.). Sell part of your business. Sell your patents. If you own your building, sell it and lease it back.

Communicate every new step with your employees. Build an enthusiastic team that cares about saving the business.

Fix everything that's broken. Give the shoddy workplace a facelift, even if it means painting it yourself on weekends.

Set out to develop new products or services and win new customers.

Saving your business can be done. And you can do it, with the help of your employees and consultants. The key is to *want* to save it. Even if you think you might want to sell it, you have to get it into shape to sell at optimum profit.*

GLOBAL EXPANSION

You've thought about widening your market. Have you considered reaching out to the rest of the world? Did you know that by

*See *Inc.* magazine's *Guide to Small Business Success: "Nine Steps to Save Troubled Companies,"* by John Banaszewski, published in 1987 by *Inc.*, 38 Commercial Wharf, Boston, Massachusetts 02110.

dealing globally you could increase your business by a staggering 95 percent? Foreign earnings can also hedge against recession in this country, because if things are slow here, you still have your products selling in other countries.

Foreign countries have become enormous consumers, and the world market is expanding much more rapidly than the national one. In fact, there is a worldwide demand for made-in-America products. Economists predict that the 1992 unification of the European Community will open up more new markets for foreign companies. In addition, the 1988 free trade agreement between the U.S. and Canada has eliminated many tariffs and barriers and opened up trade between the two countries. The technological breakthroughs in communication and transportation have also put the entire globe within easy reach. But according to a study conducted by Price Waterhouse, only 10 percent of the American companies that could export actually do so.

This option depends, of course, on what you sell. There's a large overseas market for toys, sports equipment, jewelry, lumber, etc., but the market is certainly not limited. Look at your product or service in terms of how universal (or American) it is. If you think the rest of the world will be interested, there's a lot of help out there. The Small Business Administration's* Office of International Trade and Office of Special Programs, for example, are working hard to encourage small companies to become involved in exporting. The SBA's international trade experts, through special programs and joint ventures with the U.S. De-

*Two publications of interest, available from the Small Business Administration, are: *Exporter's Guide to Federal Resources for Small Business,* published by the Interagency Task Force on Trade (and containing an excellent bibliography of other publications available on global marketing, including overseas buyers and representatives, general export information, export regulations, and financing); and *International Trade State and Local Resource Directory,* published in most states by the SBA's Offices of International Trade and Business Development. It contains, per state, names and addresses of local offices of the SBA and U.S. Department of Commerce, state agencies, small business development centers and other university or college programs, chambers of commerce, private organizations, foreign consulates and embassies, banks with international departments and other international financial services, export management and trading companies, international trade consultants, legal consultants and law firms with international departments, customs house brokers, international freight forwarders, export packing and crating, and translation services. For additional aid and information on global marketing contact the U.S. Department of Commerce's International Trade Commission, U.S. Foreign and Commercial Service, 3412 Federal Building, 230 North First Avenue, Phoenix, Arizona 85025, (602)379–3285.

partment of Commerce, have compiled an enormous amount of data that they make available to small businesses.

In addition, the SBA sponsors: periodic trade missions (delegations to individual countries for small companies looking for export opportunities); conferences and seminars across the country on all facets of how to market your product or service overseas; the Matchmaker program, which matches companies here with companies in the same industry in other countries, to develop long-term relationships; and the Export Revolving Line of Credit (ERLC), which guarantees 85 percent of loans up to $1 million for small businesses that want to export. It also publishes numerous periodicals, including *Exporter's Guide to Federal Resources* and *The State and Local International Resource Directory.*

There are numerous state and local assistance programs available for would-be exporters (for information and funding, in some cases). For example, the California Export Finance Office (CEFO) offers loan guarantees for small exporters. Also, several states or cities help small exporters with their applications to the federal guarantees program of the Export-Import Bank of the U.S. The National Association of Women Business Owners, which has joined forces with Les Femmes Chefs d'Enterprises Mondiale (FCEM), an international women's entrepreneurial association—also provides its members with export information and sources.

The main challenge for small business exporters—besides the fact that language, laws, regulations, and business and social customs differ from country to country—is finding distributors for their products. Some use foreign sales representatives; others hire an export-management company. Depending on your contract with them and how much you pay, they can handle everything from getting the right licenses to handling shipping documents and making sales calls. There is also a network of independent distributors that is geared to companies whose products require special installation and/or customer service.

There are disadvantages to be considered in exporting. Sexism is prevalent overseas, so you must be content to work in countries where women are accepted. Exporting can also tie up your finances because of delays in payments. And the costs of travel and promotion overseas can be very high. Remember that many products need modification for foreign regulations, technical standards, electrical current. You will also have to print labels, directions, and packaging in other languages, and convert to metric standards.

Exporting is not a move to make lightly. It can be expensive, for one thing. In most cases you must establish relationships with businesses in other countries first, and this takes time as well as money. Introducing a product or service overseas can take twice as long, and cost twice as much, and your business must be well-established here first. Experts say that small business owners must be willing to make a long-term commitment to exporting: foreign companies must be able to count on you.

On the plus side, there's a great deal of opportunity and assistance out there for companies seeking to do business on a worldwide level. And once you are doing business globally, experts say that overseas clients tend to be more loyal than American clients.*

SHOULD YOU FRANCHISE YOUR BUSINESS?

People love your product or service and business is terrific. Business associates across the country assure you that you've got a good thing going. You've considered expanding into other locations, but that will cost a lot of money and undoubtedly cause a lot of headaches. So now it's time to consider another option: franchising.† By doing that, you (the parent company) will grant each franchisee the right to offer your products or services in their part of the country. You will also provide them with training and a marketing plan that will tell them in detail how to run your business your way. (They will not be allowed contractually to run your business their way.) In return for using your name and your modus operandi, and for having a protected territory, they will pay an initial fee plus ongoing royalties. The trademark and operating instructions are granted to the franchisee for a specified number of years.

What your business does really dictates whether it's a good candidate for franchising. It must not be overspecialized and it

*See the following articles: "Globe Trotters," by Dee McVicker, *Entrepreneurial Woman,* May/June 1990; "Over There," by Paul B. Brown, *Inc.,* April 1990; and "Innocents Abroad," by Jill Andresky Fraser, *Inc.,* May 1990.
†See "Time to Franchise?" by Kevin McLaughlin, *Entrepreneur,* January 1989. For an excellent bibliography and resource information, write: International Franchise Association, World Headquarters, 1350 New York Avenue NW, Suite 900, Washington, D.C. 20005.

must be easily learnable. You must be different from your competition, i.e., offer something that's uniquely yours. You must be able to teach an inexperienced owner-manager how to run your business from top to bottom so that she will understand it and be able to duplicate it.

There is another type of franchising: product distribution. Under this method a franchisee is granted the right to distribute your product within a specified geographic location and under certain conditions. And a third type: granting other people the right to use your trademark or brand name.

Your business has to be strong to franchise. You must be organized and have the technological, financial, and human resources to expand. You have to keep your own company solvent during franchise expansion, because it's very costly in terms of marketing, training, administration, and legalities. You'll have to take on additional staff. You will have to deal with: putting together a complete operations manual for franchisees; tax planning; trademark registration; and qualifications for foreign or domestic corporations in different states. You, the parent company, must comply with state registration requirements, federal and state disclosure requirements, as well as other state and federal regulations involving your particular industry. You must adhere to strict regulations set forth by the Federal Trade Commission (FTC) requiring presale disclosure of certain information. You must be prepared for your franchise program to take up to a year to set up.

Consult a franchising attorney. There are many changing legal requirements and state franchise laws involving a franchisor. On your first meeting with a prospective franchisee, you must provide her with:

The Uniform Franchise Offering Circular (UFOC), a disclosure document that provides certain required information such as an audited financial statement and other presale information having to do with the performance of the parent company and its other franchises, the company's compliance with state and federal regulations, etc.;

The franchise agreement, and any related agreements;

An earnings claim document, if you make any claim about potential sales.

Although it can be tedious, franchising can allow you to expand your business idea with a minimum of capital. It is less risky than expanding your own company, in terms of financing, liability, and other obligations concerning property rental and equipment payments. You will also be relieved of the day-to-day responsibility of managing branch stores or offices. The buying power of a franchise network saves money for all concerned. More money can be put into local and national advertising through the collective efforts of all the franchises. More money will be available, if necessary, for research and development.

As in every other aspect of business, franchising will take a 100 percent commitment from you.

SELLING YOUR BUSINESS

There are lots of reasons for selling a business*: you want to move on to new challenges; your business has grown too large and time-consuming for you; you're ready to retire; you want to relocate; you and your partner can no longer agree and want to part company; you're simply burned out; and so forth. You should not consider selling a business that you've mismanaged to near bankruptcy, not if you expect to make any money from the sale.

Analyze your business from a potential buyer's point of view. If any areas of it are weak, work at strengthening them *before* you attempt to sell. To get the best price, you want to sell from strength. You have to look at your business in terms of its image, assets, competitive position, people (key employees who will be willing to stay on with new owners), organizational structure, day-to-day management procedures, and financial fitness.

To figure out what your company is worth you'll have to consult with your accountant. Basically, you will put a price on your assets as well as your business's reputation and goodwill with customers.

*For more information see the following: SBA booklets, *How to Buy or Sell a Business,* by John A. Johansen (Management Aids, no. 2.029, $1) and *Buying and Selling a Small Business,* by Verne A. Bunn, available from Superintendent of Documents, U.S. Government Printing Office, Washington, D.C. 20402; "Strapped for Expansion Cash?" by Ellyn E. Spragins, *Inc.,* December 1989; "Fit be Be Sold," by Ellyn E. Spragins, *Inc.,* April 1990; and *Inc.* magazine's *Guide to Small Business Success: "What's It Worth to You?"* by Jim Howard, available from *Inc.* magazine, 38 Commercial Wharf, Boston, Massachusetts 02110.

How to go about selling? You can hire a business broker, but in general no one is going to sell your business as well as you because no one knows it as well as you. You can place ads in the newspaper under "business opportunities," and in trade journals and business periodicals. Let your business associates and friends know you're selling; they may know of someone looking to buy. You might even talk to your competition: they may be looking to expand. Your employees (individually or as a group) may be interested in buying.

There are also leveraged buy-out experts. They are often interested in buying companies and linking them together synergistically. They provide a way for you to grow your company by selling out. Talk to your consultants and local investment bankers who are knowledgeable about venture capitalists looking to acquire different types of companies.

No matter why you sell, it is often a difficult decision to make. After all, your business is your baby and it's hard to let go. But often, it's the best decision. You have to think about what you need and what your business needs. Sometimes there comes a point when the needs no longer coincide. If that has happened to you, sell.

SUMMARY

A successful business can grow large or not. Even if you decide to stay small, your business will keep changing, because these days nothing can stay the same and survive. Regardless of the direction in which you decide to take your business, remember to enjoy the perks of entrepreneurism. If you are moved to wear an "Are we having fun yet?" T-shirt, then maybe you haven't set yourself the right goals.

As your business grows along, keep referring back to—and revising—your basic business plan. Nothing positive happens unless you make it happen, by being organized, loving what you do, and doing it well.

· Part III ·

Women
in Business—
Interviews

·17·

Introduction

*If you don't have a good idea—don't. If you don't have
enough capital—don't. And if you think you're going to
work at it part-time, for heaven's sake, don't. Because
there is no more demanding job known to man—or
woman—than working for oneself.*

   —Guin Hall (former director of the Woman's
     Bureau, New York State Department of
     Commerce)

Nobody ever asks a man how he *manages a career and
family.*   —Gloria Steinem

Across the country women are turning the flash of inspiration
into the hard cash of business success. Along the way they're
forging new ways to do business and creating new role models
to learn from.

What makes a successful entrepreneur? What are the day-to-
day realities of starting and running a business? What are the
high points and pitfalls? How has the whole process affected
entrepreneurs and their families? In this section you will hear,
first person, the answers to these questions and more.

For many women the least considered reality of being in business is the repercussions that business will have on home, family,
and social life. For most business owners there is no cutoff at five
o'clock. Problems spill over from work to home, time becomes a
precious commodity, and careful planning is essential if home life
and professional life are to work together smoothly.

Married women and those with children all agreed that the
support and backup of the family were essential as priorities,

schedules, and duties dramatically shifted when a new business was added to the family. Many women found that including their families in the day-to-day operations of the business was the answer to surviving the pressures of managing a public and private life. This mingling of two usually separate spheres, career with marriage and parenthood, seemed to benefit everyone.

Women start businesses for a variety of reasons—to fulfill a dream, to put children through school, because someone said they should (or shouldn't), because they hated their jobs or didn't have a job, to prove a point or to make a point, because they wanted some fun, because their backs were to the wall, because they had to take a big risk and prove something to themselves.

The women who are profiled here speak for hundreds more. Their inspiration, hard work, energy, and dedication are infectious. The businesses profiled come in all shapes and sizes: women overseeing operations involving three hundred employees, women who work alone from home, women who have gone national, women who keep it cozy on Main Street, women in high tech, and women in haute cuisine. All of these women were novices once. No one was "trained" in business (although nowadays many women are taking advantage of entrepreneurship courses offerred and the fast-growing network of women business owners). They trained themselves; they made mistakes and suffered setbacks. But they all seem to have these things in common: hard work, perseverance, determination, and the ability to learn from their mistakes.

Part Three is divided into chapters by industry: retailing, service, food, direct mail marketing, and manufacturing and wholesaling. Each chapter is introduced with specific information and resources pertinent to those fields, followed by interviews with women doing business in that field.

You are urged you to read *all* the interviews. Today's successful retailer, for example, knows that service is as important an aspect of her business as the product she sells. Manufacturers look to mail order houses to market their products, events planners depend on food people, wholesalers need to understand the problems of the retailers and vice versa. No business operates in a vacuum. The more you know about different kinds of businesses and the professional demands on all business women, the easier it will be to focus your own energies. You can learn from other women's successes in order to create your own.

• • •

General resources, in addition to NAWBO and AWED, for women entrepreneurs.*

> *Small Business Sourcebook,* edited by Charity Anne Dorgan (Gale Research). An indispensable source guide for new entrepreneurs profiling 163 small businesses with start-up information associations, reference works, supply sources, statistical sources, trade periodicals, trade shows and conventions, consultants, franchises and computer resources specific to each business. Additionally, it lists federal and state government resources, educational institutions, venture capital firms and incubators pertinent to various small business enterprises.
>
> *Entrepreneurial Woman* magazine. Entrepreneur, Inc., 2392 Morse Avenue, Irvine, California 92714. An exciting spin-off bi-monthly periodical for women in business. Additionally, Entrepreneur, Inc. publishes how-to-books, financial software, and video cassettes for hundreds of specific businesses. Write for listing.
>
> International Franchise Association, World Headquarters, 1350 New York Avenue N.W., Suite 900, Washington, D.C. 20005. IFA is the world's leading source of information about franchising. They sponsor seminars and forums on all aspects of buying a franchise and publish special reports about specific franchise operations.

*Part IV of *The Woman's Guide to Starting a Business* lists a full range of resources on general and specific business interests.

·18·

Retailing

There is no happier sound to the merchant's ear than that of a constantly ringing cash register.
—F. W. Woolworth

More women head into retailing than any other kind of business. Maybe it's because they're the number one consumers, maybe it's because they've honed their shopping skills to a fine art. Whatever the reason, merchandising is something women think they know about—the latest styles artfully displayed, books neatly filed by author and category, artworks lit by subtle track lighting, colorful baskets and tidy bins of toys, exotic flowers at the peak of their bloom in fine imported crystal. When a purchase is made, you jot down the sale, collect the money and hand over the goods. What could be easier?

A lot of things. The mortality rate of retail businesses is high, and the Small Business Administration computes the failure rate of women-owned specialty shops at 75 percent. Indeed, according to Dun & Bradstreet, 58 percent of all business failure in the United States in 1989 was in the retail trade. Why? Inexperience and undercapitalization are the reasons most often cited.

Most stores fail because the owner doesn't know anything about the retailing business. It's a common fallacy to think a clothing shop, for example, would be fun and easy to operate just because you love clothes. A flair for dressing yourself does not guarantee success in dressing other people. The trick is to look at it from a merchandiser's point of view.

Successfully merchandising goods is knowing what will sell, and how to make it sell, in a continuous cycle of buying from one source and selling to another. Trends, competition, and wholesale resources count for as much as image, style, organization, and customer relations. The retailer is dependent on the wholesaler, who must depend on the manufacturer, the mail, strikers, and sometimes the weather. Even in the best of times orders can arrive late, damaged, or incomplete, or be left to mildew under miles of customs red tape.

The merchandiser strives to appeal to her customers' individual needs while increasing her market by attracting new customers. Behind the scenes, the retailer is wading through inventory control systems, timed delivery dates, credit extensions, billings, security systems, and employee training. Up front, she must build an interesting, positive ambience through display, promotion, service, and attitude.

Retailing rises and falls on fashion, economics, and demographics. The small business owner must be flexible in the face of these fluctuating factors. You must be willing to go with the flow of change, to pay attention to the forecasts, to offer your customers new products and services. For example, ten years ago it was desirable to talk about where you bought an item, but what's important today is what you paid for it. This has given rise to discount specialty stores selling brand names. In today's market, the only thing that competes with low prices is good service. A talented retailer will integrate these trends into her merchandising philosophy.

Opening a retail store takes money as well as talent. A good location, inventory investment, buying trips, operating capital, store design, promotion, and fixtures are all costly. For many store owners, a computerized inventory system and the need for security systems will add yet another major expense onto the initial outlay.

If you don't have large sums to invest, there are other ways to go. Booths in mini-malls, kiosks in large malls, and stalls or display vans at fairs or in flea markets can cut overhead to a minimum while offering high-traffic locations and maximum security. Advertising becomes a collective effort, and you can test your merchandise with minimal investment risk. If permitted by local ordinance, even sidewalk vending can be highly profitable. The legendary vendor of all times still sells his peanuts near the public library on New York's Fifth Avenue. He's put a son through medical school, another through law school, and lives in splendid style in a big house on Long Island.

Consignment is another possibility. It can save money on rounding out a basic inventory line or be the foundation for an entire operation. Consignment can mean everything from a high-tech art gallery dealing in top artists, to local artisans and crafts, to resale goods and antiques.

Location

This can't be emphasized enough. Almost without exception, the most powerful key to successful retailing is location. Never spend less than you have to on location. Believe that you *will* make up the extra expense every business day from the additional walk-by traffic. Exceptions to the high rent/high traffic rule are these: discount stores, antique shops, stores that specialize in something so unique their customers will go anywhere, and shops that purposely locate in offbeat locations because the location itself is an attraction. For example, the old town jail, the renovated train station, the ship in drydock down by the pier.

Ideally, since your store sells a specialty, it should be the only one of its kind in the area. But competition isn't always a bane. Your store can succeed in attracting customers by stressing things your neighboring competition lacks—better pricing, better displays, more services. You may find that a cluster of similar businesses will bring in more customers. An atmosphere or a "scene" can serve to stimulate and develop customer traffic.

Display

You need to signal to the customer what kind of shop you have and the price range of your goods. People want a fast take. They want to see immediately what the store is all about.

The quality of your store, price, and style will be announced by the strength of your window display. Go for the best, most dramatic effect you can. You're vying not only with your competitors but with every other display on the block or in the mall. Window shop; study other stores as well as trade and fashion magazines. Pick up merchandising and display tips from Madison Avenue, Fifth Avenue, Rodeo Drive, or Michigan Avenue. Use the seasons, the holidays, local events, popular movies, unusual props, memorabilia, collectibles, theatrical lighting—almost anything has possibilities. If you're not artistic, find free-lance designers, guest artists, interior decorators, promising students, commercial photographers, and the like to help you.

Inside the store, the mood and ambience set by the window display should follow through. Lighting, music, in-store displays, color schemes, shopping bags, fresh flowers—all should complement each other.

Sales Staff

Your sales staff are your primary key to customer relations. Make sure they project your image and are knowledgeable in the product. Schedule regular staff meetings. Find out how they feel or what difficulties they may have in selling the product. Share your thoughts and plans for the store. Appreciate your employees; listen to their ideas and act upon them when you can.

Customer Service

Customer service is meeting the customer more than halfway. It's staying open late, it's arranging payment terms, it's making special orders or deliveries, it's listening to a customer's ideas and being honest and generous with your knowledge of your merchandise. It's hot coffee, and a play area for children. It's having friendly, agreeable personnel. It's maintaining a smile—even in the face of complaints, returns, and Junior's sticky fingers on the prized porcelain figurines. In the end, the customer *is* always right, because if she isn't, she goes away—and she takes her money with her. Shopping should be fun. It should be an experience. It should linger in the customer's mind so that she wants to return.

Retailing is an intensely people-oriented kind of business. Ideas quickly become tangible displays; activity and constant interaction with others make up every business day. Indeed, the heart of American business rests with the small specialty retailer.

As one store owner put it, "When a customer buys something

you've especially picked out—and I don't care if it's a dress or an original painting—it's exhilarating."

For further information:

National Retail Merchants Association, 100 West Thirty-first Street, New York, New York 10001, (212)244–8780. (Their book department publishes a catalog of books, films, and periodicals.) See your library for additional listings for specific retail associations in *The Encyclopedia of Associations* (Gale Research) where over 25,000 national and international organizations are listed.

Directory of Conventions. Successful Meetings Magazine, 633 Third Avenue, New York, New York 10017. Lists exhibitions all over the country of interest to retail merchants (i.e., gift shows, toy shows, home furnishings, etc.).

Trade Directories of the World. Croner Publications, 211-05 Jamaica Avenue, Queens Village, New York 11428. Lists all industries (gift, toy, apparel, fancy food, etc.) with information on their publications.

Bottom Line in Retailing: The Touche Ross Guide to Retail Management, by Randy L. Allen (Chilton Book Co.).

Independent Retailing, by Harold Shaffer and Herbert Greenwald (Prentice-Hall).

PENNY WHISTLE TOYS

They call it New York's hottest toy store. Anyone who loves lacquered wooden puzzles, top-of-the-line teddy bears, and the original Jukka trucks, trains, and airplanes from Finland, loves shopping at Penny Whistle. With stores strategically located on Madison Avenue, Columbus Avenue, in Soho, in Brooklyn, and (summers) in trendy Bridgehampton on Long Island, the key to its success is the careful editing of selection. When you walk in, you know you're going to walk out with a great toy.

Meredith Brokaw opened her first store in 1978, at a time when neighborhood toy sellers were being steamrollered out of existence by such giants as Toys R Us. Yet Penny Whistle thrived. As the mother of three children

> **in New York, she knew that she was hungry for good toys and better service without having to trek to midtown to find them. She banked on the notion that other parents felt as she did. She was right. Last year, sales were over $2 million.**

I wanted a small neighborhood toy store that sold classic toys. I knew I had a good idea, but I could sum up my retailing experience in one word—none. So, before my partner and I started the business, we enrolled in an accounting course and a series of seminars in how to start a business sponsored by the Small Business Administration for women at Hunter College. It was a tremendous confidence builder. We found out what exactly went into starting and managing a business and by the end of it, I felt prepared for at least half the pitfalls.

Meanwhile, we shopped the annual Toy Fair, and at the same time we were looking for a location for the store. We commandeered our kids, with promises of toys to come, and stationed ourselves on upper East Side street corners at noon and from three to five in the afternoons. For days we counted the strollers going by and the number of schoolchildren, and finally identified Ninetieth and Ninety-first streets on Madison Avenue as a prime location. With all the private schools within eight blocks, this area was teeming with families. It couldn't be better suited for a toy store. Demographically, it housed the families most likely to spend a little more money to get high-quality, educational kinds of toys. I really credit that whole year-long process with getting off to the right start.

To start a business you have to have a focus and a point of view; then you have to carry it through. Taking the courses was a very important ingredient. But finding the right location was even more important. You go for location. It was the main advice I got and it's the main advice I give. The perfect shop, a plumber's storefront, was empty and available at Ninety-first and Madison. Everybody wanted the space but the only trouble was, no one could locate the owner, an Indian millionaire who lived in Kuwait. My partner's husband worked for a firm that did business in Kuwait, and the next time one of their executives went there, he delivered a letter from us. We got the space and opened our shop October 1, 1978. No toy seller can afford to miss Christmas. We do at least 40 percent of our sales in the last quarter.

We called the store Penny Whistle because I had learned that Robert Louis Stevenson had originally selected that name for what later became *A Child's Garden of Verses*. It seemed to match the type of toys we wanted to sell: Classic. Quality. Educational without being overbearing. Maybe a little old-fashioned. We gave away little tin whistles on the day we opened to lure customers into the shop.

The initial investment was $50,000. (Today, I would estimate a small retail toy store would take a minimum of $100,000 to open.) Of that initial figure, my partner and I each put up $12,500 of our own, and we secured a loan from the bank for the rest. I have to say both of us were in the fortunate position in that opening Penny Whistle was a minor financial risk for us. I mean our children weren't going to go hungry if it didn't work. But I wanted it to work. I wanted to put together one great toy store that would work.

We were able to pay back the loan within the year. In 1981 my partner and her husband moved to the West Coast, and I was able to buy her out on the profits of the business.

I didn't consciously plan to open five stores, but I think anyone who has been in business will tell you that once you're operating, the business takes on a definite life of its own. It begins to change from the beginning so that what you thought would happen, what you may have planned for, often changes as your business develops.

My second store came about because sales were good, the feelings were good, and an excellent location came available. So while I hadn't planned it, the life of the store demanded it. No matter how successful you may think your business is, you have to keep it moving. It has to be flexible and open to change. It's like a human life. It starts out as an infant and then it goes through adolescence and then into adulthood. I would say that the middle age syndrome starts setting in about five years into the business. Your sales go down and all sorts of things that worked for you in the beginning don't work later in the life of the business. So in order to remain youthful and energetic and exciting and full of life, you have to keep your toe tapping. You have to bring in new things, you have to build in excitement and urgency.

I've found that the most complicated thing about a growing, expanding business is people management—finding the right people who can grow with you and take on the responsibilities you had when the business was small. They are your representatives, and they mean everything as far as the success or failure of the store. Your managers must feel closely tied to the store, part of the ongoing process.

I have four year-round stores and one seasonal one in Bridgehampton. Each store has a manager. All the managers operate as a management committee, and we meet once a week without fail. In those meetings we communicate problems and creative ideas, share product information, talk about future plans and promotions and sales goals. It's been a workable and healthy way to run the business, but I'm totally dependent on these people to manage their stores well. They are the key to the success of the whole operation. If there is a weak link, the whole group feels it.

My job now, day to day, is in overseeing. One day a week I go to each of the stores and I work with the manager on the displays and merchandising. I have one person who designs the windows for the stores, and he and I work out in advance what the windows are going to be. I work with all the people who make up the stores but I don't have anyone's job. It's only now with this many stores that it's possible to do it this way.

In the beginning, my partner and I did all the buying. I discovered that the Toy Fair is set up for the big guys—Toys R Us controls that place. But the smaller community-based stores, like Penny Whistle, which don't deal in mass merchandised products, are a different business completely. We deal with a different sort of vendor. We go to The Toy Building and the fair to see what's out there in the market, but it's not representative of what we carry. I go to Europe to buy, and more than half of my merchandise is imported. We carry Italian rubber farm animals and striped doll strollers from Spain, Brio wooden trains from Sweden, lacquered Greek music boxes, Steiff animals, Japanese robots, English puzzles, Austrian card games, and building blocks from a half dozen countries.

Now I no longer do the ordering but have one person in charge of the buying. I have a lot to do with what gets ordered, and I go out into the various markets to see what's happening, but since the addition of the newer stores, my buyer handles all the vendors directly.

Looking back over the twelve years I've been in business I would say that starting a business was not the most difficult part of it. The most difficult thing about being in business is sustaining it. After I had been in business for a while, I took another series of courses offered by AWED.* Once a business is off and running you begin to understand where your weak points are, what you need to know more about.

I make mistakes all the time. I think that being able to learn from your mistakes and learn fast is a key ingredient of building a successful business. You cannot be afraid to fail if you want to be a success. One of the biggest mistakes I made was buying deep—buying more than I could sell. I was very careful in the first years of the business but then I got overconfident. In a small retail operation this can mean trouble. But I try new things all the time and many of them don't work. We've tried children's furniture, mail order, and one Christmas we opened a tiny boutique in Bendel's. None of these made money.

Happily, other ideas do work. Of major success are the three Penny Whistle books I've coauthored with Annie Gilbar. The first one, *The Penny Whistle Party Planner,* has sold over 50,000 copies nationwide. We followed that with *The Penny Whistle Halloween Party Book* and *The Lunch Box Book.* The books have been a natural outgrowth of what we're doing at Penny Whistle. Particularly the party planner, because we do so much business that has to do with birthday parties. We try to stock a lot of toys in that lower price range so that they are good party presents. And we do a big business in party favors and prizes.

I think a large part of our appeal comes from the service we offer. Last year we packed over two hundred mail packages to kids at camp. We offer a telephone service whereby customers can call us and we will suggest appropriate toys for various ages. The store is arranged by stages of child development, and the staff is trained to advise customers on toys for each age group. We've also been known to truck the floor model swing set over to a birthday party as a loan when the ordered set was delayed. These extras mean a lot to our customers.

I watch the sales figures all the time. Our inventory control, cash flow, and where we are on a day-to-day basis is on the computer so that I can have figures when I want them. I want to know exactly at all times what we owe and what we have to sell, and where we're going to be if we don't do the sales. It shocks me how many people operate their business without having these

*American Woman's Economic Development Corporation.

figures close at hand. You have to work out a system whereby you can know at any time where your business stands. Business is a financial endeavor, and its success depends on being able to work the numbers so that you don't get caught in a bind, so that you come out ahead.

I've been quoted as saying, "Profits are my report card," but for me there's more than just the profit motive behind my commitment to the business. It's an enormously creative process and intriguing to build a name for yourself. In the past, when people talked about me, it was "Meredith Brokaw, comma, wife of news anchorman Tom." Now they just say, "Meredith Brokaw, comma, of Penny Whistle."

THE LEFT BANK and AMANDA

Mary Sue Morris is a born entrepreneur. "If you sat me down in outer Mongolia," she says, "my first thought would be, hmmmmm, let's see what we can do here." Her career background included advertising for a firm in Dallas and she also served as Director of Women's Marketing for American Airlines in New York. Then, when she married and moved to Cincinnati, Ohio, she worked with her husband developing small European-type shopping villages in Kentucky and Indiana. A chance tip from a friend alerted her to a bank building, circa 1920, for sale in a chic shopping area of Cincinnati. She bought it, renovated it, and four months later opened The Left Bank.

The Left Bank contained eighteen tiny specialty boutiques selling everything from imported coffee to designer shoes.

Basking in the glow of financial success, she bought and renovated an old police precinct built in 1901 and soon opened a nightclub called Amanda. There she met her Waterloo. "If you try enough things," she says, "you're going to find something you really can't do. And what I found out was, I couldn't run a restaurant."

Hyde Park Square is the oldest shopping village in Cincinnati. It's the only area that has maintained its quality, and all the shops on the square are excellent specialty stores. The bank had been empty for years. It was a wonderful location but so expensive no one business could afford to go into it. I looked at the building and loved it immediately. It was in pretty bad shape, though. The bank had put in three false ceilings, but it still had all the original fixtures, the bank cages, the old vault, and the original moldings.

I developed the idea of dividing it up so that a number of little specialty shops, each about twelve by twelve, could go in. The first step was to take an option on the property. This would give me time to go out and sell other people on the idea, people who would agree to lease space and open shops after I had renovated the building. I have to say my background in marketing and construction was invaluable to the venture.

To find people I first called every person who was already on the square, told them what I was trying to do, and asked them to spread the word. I found out there was a pent-up demand among people who had wanted to have a shop in Hyde Park for years but found it too expensive.

I guess the trickiest part was getting the right mix of shops. I encouraged the shop owners to be very, very specialized. I wanted each shop to be unique. I had this stated in the lease. It was a strict policy that no two shops could carry or sell the same item. As a result, the Left Bank customer knew that if she saw one thing in a particular shop, she wouldn't see it again.

As soon as I had a commitment on 50 percent of the leases, I felt I could afford to buy the building. And that meant going to the bank. My husband was not investing any money in this venture, but the bank insisted he cosign for me to buy the building. I felt it wasn't right, since he was not the one out leasing space and pulling this whole thing together. And my business credentials were very good on my own, but in the end I didn't fight it because it was so necessary for me to get the building opened in time for Christmas. In retail, the Christmas season can mean up to half your yearly sales, and to open a new place and miss Christmas would be foolish. So, with my husband's cosignature, I got my loan and bought the building.

I saw the building in June and bought it in July. Four frustrating months of construction followed. I laid out the basic interior design myself. Then I brought in an architect for exact proportions, special interior design, and, most important, to decipher building codes.

The architect I hired came highly recommended, and when we

initially sat down to talk, I thought I made it clear how I wanted the place to look. Everything in there was to remain: the old feeling, the charm, and the classical facade. Well, we ended up in the biggest damned fight; it was just a nightmare. He came back with *Lucite*! His plans had the entire front of the building ripped out and replaced with glass and Lucite. The inside plans were equally contemporary. It was as if we spoke two different languages. The whole time you're in that position as a woman you're wondering if it's because you're the "little woman" that they're not hearing what you're saying. In the end, I had to pay his bill and mark that off as lesson number one.

It's almost impossible when renovating an old building to get anyone to say definitely what it's going to cost. It's hard to estimate, and a contractor doesn't want to lose money. On big expenses like plumbing, electricity, heating, and air-conditioning it is difficult to get a bid that will stick. *Always* assume it's going to cost more than the estimate. Budget for it. My contractor turned out to be like 99 percent of the contractors you ever deal with; they assure you that you haven't got a thing to worry about, but during the last four weeks of the construction I was on the phone at 4:00 A.M. screaming about plaster, stairwells, bricklaying, and everything else. Contractors somehow never meet a deadline, and the pressure on me was tremendous because the shop owners had all been guaranteed the Christmas season. Their stock was arriving, and they needed to get into their spaces to decorate. In the end, I paid triple time to get the place finished.

My rents were the highest in Cincinnati because I paid all the utilities and provided all the services in the building, including creative service for advertising and promotion. Practical services included insurance, security, trash removal, cleaning, window display cases, and all maintenance, repairs, and storage. The shop owners' only concern was their merchandise and sales.

The Left Bank advertised as a whole. Each shop chipped in an equal amount to cover costs, but the first two years my budget for advertising and promotion was very small. At first I ran small newspaper ads each month, but I wanted to reach a much larger audience. I already had the upper-income bracket in Cincinnati by virtue of our location, but I wanted people in surrounding areas to know about us and make the excursion to Hyde Park. So, instead of spreading the dollars out over the year, I decided to go first class and shoot the works between November 1 and

Christmas. I concentrated the money on television and ran our ad in the local time slots on the "Today" show, "The Tonight Show", and the afternoon soaps. And it worked; we had people coming in from more than a hundred miles away.

I did the ad in the cheapest way possible. I had a good amateur photographer take a picture of each shop. Then I asked a friend in advertising to help me with the copy. The final product was a shot of each one of the shops shown in quick flashes while the voiceover recited a verse touching on all the different aspects of the bank, "Pots and pans and coffee beans/Socks and shoes for tennis teams . . ." and so on, for one minute. It ended with a shot of the bank from the front and the address.

To launch the business, I held a huge press party when we opened, and got local television and news coverage. I appeared on all the local talk shows, displaying some of the unusual things you could buy in The Left Bank, and whenever a new shop opened, I sent out a press release.

It took me a year to get the building running smoothly. In the first year there was no profit because I had to pay off the construction bills, and there were the inevitable hidden costs and finishing touches. But after that, the business was not only very profitable, it took only one day a week of my time to run it.

Along about then I spotted an old police precinct that had been empty for decades. I fell in love with the building and decided I wanted to renovate it and open a nightclub. People told me the location was terrible but I didn't think so. It was close to downtown and right off the main parkway. People said they would never go there, but the night we opened it was a smash hit. Amanda taught me more business lessons than I care to recite.

We were a smashing success the first year, and I should have sold the business while we were on top, but I didn't and the reason I didn't was I fell in love with it. I loved the building, I loved the idea of owning a nightclub, I loved the people who came to Amanda, I loved the people who worked for me. Lesson One: never fall in love with the business. Because of that I worked around the clock, I was exhausted by the business, I was blind to its faults. I felt like if I left the business for thirty minutes some enormous catastrophe would happen—and I was right. Something awful always happened.

It was a tough, tough business with built-in problems that I never could iron out. And yet, people would come up to me on a Friday night and hug me and say they had had the best time of their lives at Amanda. To this day I have people who tell me Amanda was the best thing that ever happened to Cincinnati's night life.

Lesson Two: never go in undercapitalized. The Left Bank had been such a success I thought it would be easy to raise money and launch Amanda, but when you want to do another kind of project from the one you're known for, it doesn't ensure that people will invest money in you. I found that a great jolt. I ended up selling two-thirds of The Left Bank to finance Amanda. But when things started to go wrong, it wasn't enough.

The building was really just a shell. We did a fabulous historic renovation on it. My downstairs was a restaurant and the upstairs was a bar—music, dancing, and gaming tables. I hired a wonderful person who had run a four-star restaurant in Colorado to set up the bar and the kitchen. I hired a food consultant. I bought beautiful glassware and tableware. I leased surrounding space for parking. Amanda was located in an area of town that had a large Appalachian population and, at the time, unemployment was high. My plan was to hire and train these people in the restaurant business. I was singlehandedly going to solve the unemployment problem. On the surface, it seemed I was doing everything carefully and correctly.

We were the first "members only" club in Cincinnati. I sent out invitations to join and something about the idea just clicked. It appealed to everyone. The night we opened we had the single worse snowstorm in the history of Ohio. The Ohio River froze solid. And people were standing ten deep trying to get into Amanda.

So what went wrong? First of all, I knew nothing about the food business. I knew what I wanted when I went to a restaurant, but I had no idea of how one worked. I never got a handle on the food. That part of the business was like a runaway train. We had the most erratic food. One day it would be the greatest food on the North American continent and the next day it was awful. The secret to any restaurant is consistent food—even if its consistently *bad,* at least it's consistent. I must have gone through forty chefs in the three years Amanda was open. That part of the business was awful. You need to know about food. You need a partner in the kitchen. I look at restaurants now and it seems to me in the most successful ones there is a partner out front and one in the back. If I had worked in a restaurant, even as a waitress for a few months, I would have known what I was up against. But I went into it blind.

I was good at promotions. I discovered that you've got to manage your space to make up for slow nights. Friday and Saturday I could have used twice the space. Monday was dead, the other weeknights almost as bad. I tied The Left Bank into events at Amanda with fashion shows. I did private parties. I instigated a guest chef night and invited a local celebrity to cook at Amanda every Monday night. It packed the place. I was good at making the place fun, but I wasn't good at staying on top of the real inner core of a restaurant. The bar, however, was probably the most successful bar they've ever had in Cincinnati. So the bar saved us.

Employee turnover in the business was the next worst thing. We were always desperate for employees. Always. My plan to train the unemployed did not work. They didn't show up, they left on the job, they didn't care. I don't care if you have the greatest chef in the world, if the dishwasher doesn't show up, the plates don't get on the table. In the end, I hired kids who were in private schools as my busboys and dishwashers. They were the only ones who were reliable because their mothers made sure they were reliable. They made sure the kids got there.

Theft was a problem. I found this very discouraging. Whole hams would disappear out of the icebox. Enough glassware and ashtrays were stolen off the tables to have stocked an entire store. They say theft is epidemic in the restaurant business, but I just didn't want to know about it.

After two years I wanted to sell the business but that proved to be very difficult. We had started to lose money. That's when I learned lesson number three. In this business, you want to get in and get out fast. If I had sold the business in the first year I would have made a lot of money. But I didn't. I hung on because I loved the business. Amanda's popularity triggered competition. People with much bigger resources and better knowledge of the business opened other clubs in town. What saved me in the end was the value of the property.

I think everyone in business must go through what I call the cold night sweats. It's all on your shoulders. You've got to meet payroll. You've got to meet payments. You've got to orchestrate the running of your business every day. No one else is going to do it for you. There is no fairy godmother.

266

The choice for me has always been what business to go into. I'm an entrepreneur through and through. But it doesn't always go right. You read a lot about people in business and it starts to look easy. But I'm here to tell you there are bad days. There are days you just don't think you can stand to do the things you have to do. But that's all a part of being in business. Through all my business experiences I learned that real estate is the field that I understand and love the most. In 1983 I opened my own company in New York, The Sheridan Group, Ltd. We buy, sell, and manage occupied apartments for investors from all over the world. Today I own over $6,000,000 worth of apartments in Manhattan and manage $25,000,000 worth of apartments for investors. But, you know, it takes just as much work to sell a $50 meal.

MURDER INK

Nobody, it seems, shops in plain old bookstores anymore. Book enthusiasts now head off to children's book stores (the fastest growing of the specialties), biography shops, how-to bookstalls, science fiction bookstores, cookbook emporiums, or any of a dozen or more other types of specialized bookstores. There they can find extensive titles, information, and even entertainment, on specific subjects.

Take a step into Murder Ink on Manhattan's Upper West Side, and you will discover a world of mayhem and murder. Dilys Winn conceived of her shop in 1972 and thus can take credit for being one of the first of the success stories in this field. Her unique mind for marketing expanded the life of the store beyond the boundaries of bookshelves into a series of related special events and writing projects. When she eventually sold the shop, Murder Ink was known internationally for its titles, its travel tours, its mail order, and its owner, whose own compendium of mystery lore, also called _Murder Ink_, has been revised three times.

The most successful specialty bookstores are those in which the owners are devoted to serving their public. Mystery buffs are among the most demanding, dedicated, and ardent genre lovers around. I know. I was one of them. I had been in advertising for ten years and I was really bored. I had turned into one of those professional malcontents until one day it struck me that everybody said the same things and nobody got off their ass to take action. So I said, "Okay, I'm going to open a bookstore that specializes in murder mysteries." I was an avid reader of mysteries and ever since I was a kid, I loved the idea of bookstores.

The next day I looked around my neighborhood and found a small storefront on a side street off upper Broadway. I envisioned a cozy shop with old wooden shelves and a rather worn English study feel to it—the sort of place Miss Marple might live in—and this little shop seemed to have that ambience. So I signed a lease. I opened Murder Ink six weeks later on my savings of $15,000. I know it sounds incredible, but it was easy once I decided to do it.

My friends thought I was throwing away my money but what they didn't understand was that I knew it was the right idea for me. Even if it had closed in six months, I would have felt I'd spent my money very well. Some people can't handle that. I think maybe if you go into business just to make money, you might be in trouble.

Today a small bookstore like mine would cost anywhere from $35,000 on up depending on size and location, but specialty bookstores can, and do, succeed in offbeat places. Often your customer is more word-of-mouth than walk-by. Plan on spending approximately a third of your investment on inventory, a third on rent, fixtures, and supplies, and the remaining third on operating expenses. And remember, a business always costs more than you think it will. Things go wrong. In my case, I tore up the linoleum floor expecting to find a wooden one; instead, I found rotting timbers. It's one of those little caveats of business that's really true: you can never bring it in for your original estimate.

I registered the name of my business with the city, opened a business bank account and began writing the publishers for their catalogs.* I also requested to be put on their regional salesmen's list. Then I went to all the big bookstores on Fifth Avenue and copied down every mystery title they had. That became my basic resource list. Small store owners should always snoop the big

*A complete listing of publishers and other practical information pertaining to the publishing and literary trade can be found in *Literary Market Place (LMP)*, the Directory of the American Book Publishing Industry. New York: R. R. Bowker. Check the reference section of your library.

bookstores for new titles and publishers. If you're small and unknown, you don't get the routine mailers the big stores get and you can miss out on the more obscure publishing houses. I also subscribed to *Publishers Weekly*, which aside from the reviews, gave me resources for fixtures and supplies plus ideas on display techniques. Later on, I went to the ABA (the American Booksellers Association) convention, which is held once a year, in order to find new resources as well as to meet publishers and authors.

The bookstore business is one of those fantasy businesses. I had envisioned myself running a literary salon, serving up glasses of sherry to my clientele but then the reality hits. Someone has got to cart those crates of books around, dust the shelves, keep up with the orders, scout for new titles, and stay on top of the billings and payments. Mail order became a large part of my business once I had gotten some national publicity and on an average day, opening mail and shipping books took up about three hours of my time.

The mortality rate of the book business is very high because, I think, bookstore owners are notoriously bad managers. They walk into the business the way I did, thinking it will be nice to sit and read a book and chat with the customers, but you have to be organized. It's not a genteel business at all.

The thing that hit me right off was how badly the publishing business is run. You think you're dealing with urbane, bright people—well, forget it. They're in as much of a hassle as everyone else. Shipments come in wrong; best-sellers are out-of-stock; billing is fouled up. I was dealing with about forty different vendors and I carried over five thousand titles. Every book went on an inventory control card that listed the title, the publisher, the number shipped. Now, of course, computers make inventory control less cumbersome to manage but then I was operating under a mountain of paperwork.

With an adequate balance in your business account, most of the publishing houses will extend credit. Otherwise, you pay for two shipments before you get credit. Credit allows you up to ninety days to pay your bill although you pay a slight increase every thirty days. In the book business you have a return policy with the publishers. You lose 20 percent on a return, but at least you're not stuck with inventory you can't move.

Reordering, I found, eventually became second nature. I hate to sound like the cook who says, "You'll know when the dough is right by the way it feels," but it was true for me in running the business. Each time I sold a book, I marked it on the inventory card and when I got to a certain low number, I reordered. You get a feel for the rhythms and flow of the business after a while, especially for your regular sellers.

Publicity was what made my shop as successful as it grew to be. I made a profit in my first year of business, which is incredible for a bookstore, but it was all because of publicity. The day I opened, a *New York Times* reporter happened to stop in because he was trying to find a Laundromat. As it turned out, he was a great mystery buff, so he wrote up the shop for the *Times*. Three weeks later *New York* magazine did an article. That launched a whole series of out-of-town articles, which launched the mail orders. I made a point of maintaining a friendly relationship with the people who wrote about me so I could call on them again as I developed the business. I wrote thank-you notes, and called them up from time to time just to say hello. I had no press contacts when I started the business but soon had them all over the country.

A small bookstore is usually a marginal business. You can't make big money on 40 percent mark-ups of books unless you do a volume business or expand the stock. In my case, there were no more mystery books to be stocked including my out-of-print books and first editions. So I figured out other ways to expand the life of the business.

First, I organized the Murder Ink Lecture Series. I held it twice a year for six weeks. I went after fun, offbeat topics and the kind of speakers who could generate publicity. For example, the lectures in one series were advertised in the following tantalizing ways:

"Want to buy the only Rembrandt painted in ball point?" I invited the art critic for the *Times,* the head of the Wildenstein Gallery, and the head of the New York City Police art squad to speak on art fraud and forgery.

"Ten fun things to do with arsenic." We heard from a toxicologist and a botanist about suspicious soufflés, and mordant mushrooms.

"The urge to kill." A psychotherapist and the chief of psychiatric services at Sing-Sing discussed mass murders, mind murderers, and would-be murderers.

"Meet me at the Morgue." This was a visit to the Specimen Museum and Office of the Chief Medical Examiner with a forensic doctor and an Interpol consultant.

I also organized Monday mystery nights, literally, and billed them as secret comings and goings. The mailer I sent out said: "Wear walking shoes and carry a big flashlight. Not for the timid. Smelling salts provided."

Next came the Murder Ink Mystery Tours of England. These included walking trips on the moors, visits to haunted castles and to famous mystery sites, special English lectures, and shopping for rare mystery books. Then I turned to writing and created a *Murder Ink Quarterly* containing mystery reviews and other related articles. Out of that came a book, *Murder Ink,* published by Workman Press, which is a compendium of mystery lore. It has been revised three times. All of these activities opened up the life of the business for me. I had become the expert on mysteries.

Special events is definitely the way to go with specialty bookstores. It keeps the concept fresh. And bookstores are automatic meeting places for like-minded people. The store owner should capitalize on this with autograph signings, seminars, poetry readings, cooking demonstrations, puppet shows, special celebrations, demonstrations—really anything that relates to the genre of the store.

Ultimately, I sold Murder Ink because I had done everything I wanted to do with it short of committing a murder myself. In much the same way I had opened the shop, there came a day when I realized it was time to move on. The business had become too small and too confining for me. And I think, one too many customers had come in and asked me to giftwrap. So I ran an ad in *New York* magazine, which read, "Publicity prone specialty bookstore for sale." The first person who called was a customer of mine, Carol Brenner, whose dream it was to own Murder Ink. When she found out it was indeed "her" bookstore that was for sale she didn't hesitate. She bought it, doubled the space, increased the inventory when, a few years later, the mystery field mushroomed, and ran the shop for twelve years. In 1990 she sold it to a new owner who will, no doubt, expand the store in new directions. But I'll always think of Murder Ink as my child. A child I brought up well because it exists independent of me and continues to be a healthy, growing business.

LINDA DURHAM GALLERY

Newsweek **magazine called New Mexico's Santa Fe art scene "pretty tame" except for one gallery and one gallery owner. Linda Durham, representing emerging contemporary artists, is the exception they noted. With vision and perseverance, her gallery, now ten years old, shows artists on the cutting edge of today's art scene.**

I didn't start this gallery because I thought there was a need. I started it because I wanted to do it. People far more experienced than I told me it couldn't be done, but I had in my head a little jingle I had learned as a child: "the world would stop / if it were run / by those who say / it can't be done." I could imagine my gallery. I could see it working. The two assets I had going for me in the beginning were enthusiasm and naiveté. Not everyone considers those assets, but I do.

I had virtually no art background but most of my close friends were artists. I found I was interested not solely in the art they produced, but in the way in which they saw the world. If a work was too strange for me, or beyond me, I would study it. I would think, "I know this person is intelligent and serious and that the work he or she is making has value. I just have to find that value." How do we know about past cultures except through the art they left? Isn't that the best way to find out about our own culture?

In the beginning, I learned from other people. I knew who "knew" and I asked them and I listened to them. There was a gallery in town, one that had gone from being little more than a trinket shop to a major factor in the art business, and I was curious as to how that had happened. I figured the only way to find out was to be an insider, to work there.

After working for the other gallery for about a year, I realized I had come up with all sorts of things I would do if it were *my* gallery. I wanted to take an exhibition on the road and I offered the idea to the gallery owner, but he didn't like it. So I put my own show together of works my artist friends were doing, and took it on the road myself. I picked Toronto as my first city because it was cultural and international. I went to Toronto and through one good lead found a space to do the show. Then I came home and raised $25,000 by putting up some property I owned for collateral at the bank.

I called the show "New Mexico in Toronto." I handled everything—curating, printing, mailing lists, customs, posters, advertising, shipping. The day I mailed the invitations was the day of the great Canadian postal strike. Almost no one came to the show. I ended up losing all my money, but doing the show gave me instant credibility in the art world. People talked about it and I got a lot of press coverage in Santa Fe. I was offered the opportunity to do a second show in California. I called this "New Mexico in the Bay Area." This was picked up on by the Scottish Arts Council, whose members gave me the opportunity to produce "New Mexico in Edinburgh."

My press releases and the invitations all said, "presented by the Linda Durham Gallery." Naturally people thought I had my own gallery. For a while I turned my living room into a gallery, but when a prime space came on the market in Santa Fe I went into very deep debt to get it. I simply *had* to have that space. It was worth the risk, the fear, and the sweat at night. I proved myself right. I have one of the best buildings and best locations in town.

It then took me three months to fix things up and get organized for the opening. I did all the painting and renovation myself because I had no more money. My opening was a group show featuring many of the artists who had been in the traveling show. Opening night came and it was scary. My dreams were all so much bigger than the realities that followed. But that's still true today. My dreams grow as the realities grow.

The first year I was in business I grossed $50,000, which was on a par with my mortgage payments. The professionals—the people who drew charts and graphs and made projections—all told me it wasn't working, that I couldn't make it go, that I should close or make compromises and show certain artists whose work was selling. But I wanted to create a market for work I loved rather than join a market. I wanted to sell important, contemporary art, not souvenir art.

Understand, there is valuable information even in negative advice. Answers and ideas come from everywhere. Even if someone is telling you to go out of business, you can get ideas on how to stay in business. Don't be intimidated. A so-called expert may be knowledgeable in figures and percentages but may know nothing about being a good salesman or communicator.

I continued to mount new shows every month. I remember my first August in the gallery, traditionally the best month in town, and I didn't have one sale. But the artists gave me great inspiration and encouragement. They wanted to see a contemporary gallery run in a great way. They stayed with me. I had thought that the artists would want to leave me and go somewhere else if they weren't selling, but I've found out it's just the opposite. They're afraid I'll drop them if their work isn't selling.

It took me seven years to turn the gallery around. I had to educate my public, teach them about contemporary art. I had to develop prospective buyers. The collector must have confidence in the dealer and confidence that the business is solid. It *is* now, but it was all a struggle. When I was in business three years, and doing badly, people said it takes five years. After five years, they said seven. I set myself hard goals. And when I was feeling the most broke I'd challenge myself by committing to some big expense—improvements, an ad, a brochure I couldn't afford—knowing that since I'm a person who honors commitments, I'd find a way to do it. At one point I took on a partner, intoxicated by the money she was willing to pay me to buy in. But after six months I realized the money wasn't enough and I couldn't share my vision of how things should go around here. I needed control of everything. I bought her out and sold stock in my company, retaining 75 percent for myself.

I'm aggressive about advertising, publicity, and marketing. I advertise internationally and in publications like *Art News, Art in America, Art Forum, Art and Auction.* I participate in the big contemporary art shows, such as the Chicago International Art Expo and the Los Angeles show. I work with museums and sell pieces to them. I sell to corporations and interior designers. But the thing that is the most fun is working with individual collectors who love art and who are building collections.

There are many ways to attract corporate clients. If you advertise in the right places, your reputation builds and they will come to you. You can solicit the corporations, but if you're not known it counts for very little. A personal contact helps a lot. The big corporations hire a consultant to build a collection, so you get to know those people and stay in touch with them.

As with many businesses, word of mouth is a major sales factor. People can read about you and see your ads, but if a friend tells them "Go see Linda Durham" that's the best kind of business to get. You never know who the buyers are going to be. The woman with the show-stopping ring on her finger may be a joke. The person with torn jeans may have a trust fund that just won't quit.

Artists come to see me with their work all the time—as many as ten a day. My heart goes out to them because it's tough. I feel it's my business to see what's out there, what's coming along. I see any artist who is working in New Mexico. I ask only that they make an appointment first. During the peak season I schedule very few appointments, but I see as many as I can in the off-season.

My commission is generally 50 percent of the retail price of a work. This is standard and includes: advertising, printing, parties, openings, and insurance. I also employ three full-time employees. Our day is filled with making calls, sending out information, dealing with inquiries, making contact with potential buyers, working with graphic designers, planning openings and press programs—and selling! The business grossed a million dollars this year, but believe me, I earn what I make.

I think my biggest problem in the beginning was my fear of business. I thought business was the enemy, the opposite of creativity. But now I know business offers a great opportunity for creativity. Even getting a bank loan can be an exercise in creativity. Now I know that business is not something foreign and masculine. I have adapted it to my own needs and utilized it on my own scale. Even so, sometimes, if I'm not feeling sure of myself, I have a secret remedy. I get in my car by myself and I sing really loud. It's like a jolt of energy, it restores my confidence.

THE KENTUCKY COFFEE COMPANY

The Kentucky Coffee Company specializes in imported coffees, teas, spices, and hundreds of related gift items and kitchenwares. In a country store atmosphere of wooden barrels, hanging baskets, spice jars, pottery, and utensils, customers browse while sampling the many exotic beverage blends. Janine Shaw was inspired by a similar business she saw on a trip to Dallas.

She has since opened three shops, the first in a low-rent location, the second in an upscale downtown galleria, and the third in a large regional mall.

I had wanted to start a business, but nothing clicked until I saw the coffee emporium in Dallas. I wrote to the owner and asked her if she would help us set up our store for a consultation fee. This was the smartest thing I did, because she shared with me her business experience. She gave me the names of reliable wholesalers, coffee, tea, and spice merchants; advice on what to order in giftwares, how much to order, when to reorder; suggestions on display, advertising, and promotion; and general advice on management. All of which might have taken me a year or more to learn for myself—but this way, I learned from her expertise and mistakes, not mine.

This is a family-owned business. My mother-in-law, Betty, was my partner until she retired a few years ago. My husband shares in the ownership of the store, and my son and daughter have both spent a lot of time working with me in the operation. We opened our first store in an out-of-the-way shopping center, where rents were cheap but there was little in the way of walk-by traffic. We opened the doors in 1976 on an investment of $20,000 (it would be double in today's market). It was a unique idea then, and publicity in the local papers really launched the business. Those writeups saved us the initial money we would have had to spend on advertising.

In a year we had shown a profit, and I decided to move the business to a prime location in a newly opened exclusive shopping pavilion downtown. Our investment in the second space was $35,000 (again, double those figures today), but our sales immediately tripled because of the walk-by traffic. The first shop grossed $40,000 in sales per year. The second shop grossed $140,000 in its first six months. That's why you go for location.

My start-up costs ran half for inventory and half for design, equipment, operating costs, and overhead. The first store was in excellent condition, and most of our money went for display and design. I bought coffee and tea barrels from the wholesalers and went to garage sales for old shelves, antique jars and bottles. Most of the design investment went for a very expensive espresso machine imported from Italy, an electric coffee grinder, a cash register, and the tables, chairs, and utensils we use to serve our customers coffee and pastries.

In the second location, our building costs were high because we were coming into a new building and had to install our own flooring, bathrooms, and electrical wiring. By that time our credit rating was excellent and we didn't have the cash outlay for inventory. The kitchen and gift items account for more than half of our profits, but it's the smell of freshly brewed coffee and the spices and teas that bring people into the store. I do all my buying through catalogs and sales representatives. I subscribe to *The Tea and Coffee Trade Journal, The Gift and Decorative Accessories Magazine,* and *The Gifts and Tableware Reporter.*

We make a nice profit in selling pastries and coffee by the cup. The only drawback is that by selling food we are classified a restaurant by the board of health, which means rigid inspections regularly and compliance with special laws that really don't apply to us since we don't cook in the store. But again, a cup of coffee and a place to sit brings the customers in, and most don't leave without buying.

The business is hard work and it doesn't run itself. In the first years I worked every morning, seven days a week. While my children were at home, I spent the afternoon and early evening with them and then came back and worked until our ten o'clock closing. My husband and son and daughter worked with me during the busy season. My mother-in-law took over afternoons, and we hired high school and college students for evenings and weekends and during the holidays. I did, and still do, all the bookkeeping and ordering for the store. I check the inventory and I do the taxes. Ordering takes up a lot of time, because I don't have the space to keep inventory and can't order a lot at one time. Also, I don't want to tie up large amounts of cash in inventory. Everything has to be carefully timed and watched, because there can be shipping delays or orders that come in only half filled. It keeps you on your toes.

After we had been in business seven years, I opened a third store in a regional mall about fifty miles from Lexington. This was quite a bit different from what I had done with the two stores in Lexington. There were 145 stores in the mall with large anchor stores—Sears, Penney, and Lazarus. The mall operators sought me out. They saw my store in Lexington, liked the concept, and convinced me to locate in their facility. The only available space they had was more than double what I have here, which is 600 square feet. In retrospect, that's the appeal of my store—to be small and crowded and cozy. But I thought that the mall would have so much more traffic that I could handle the larger space. I was very disappointed. The investment in the mall store was $60,000, yet my store in Lexington did double the business.

Malls are a thing unto themselves. If you go in at the construction level, as I did, it costs a lot to go into raw space. Sometimes you're given just a dirt floor. You have to pour cement, build the walls and the ceiling, wire, plumb—everything. The mall has final approval of what you build and how you design, including interior color scheme and decoration. But this was the least of my worries. The mall was situated on an interstate highway, which was still under construction when we moved in. The site was supposed to bring in customers from Cincinnati and Indiana, but the highway took years longer to complete than estimated. As a result business was not good for five years. We hung in there and finally did well in the last three years, but by that time my mall lease was up and they decided I wasn't profitable enough to stay on.

Malls require that you sign on at a base rent; then, when your profits reach a certain level, you pay a rent based on a percentage of the profits. If at the end of a certain amount of time you haven't moved into a high enough profit margin, they weed you out. Their profits come from the ones who are making it big. Unfortunately, by their standards, we weren't. They tripled my rent and I pulled out. It turned out to be the best decision I ever made. But my biggest mistake was going in in the first place. Knowing what I do now, I would have stayed with my two small stores in Lexington, and then if I had wanted to expand I would have stayed with this formula and not tried to change it. My shop appeals to the affluent shopper. People come here because of its character. In a regional mall you have a lot of people who aren't there to buy. Yes, the walk-by traffic seems high, but when you analyze it you have a lot of teenagers hanging out, the elderly on their mile walks, young marrieds who are just window shopping. Take all of them away and you don't really have as many potential customers as you might think.

Also, running a business from a distance is not easy. I had hired a good manager whom I trained, and I went to the store once a month, but it's not the same as being in the store all the time.

The best investment I made besides my second location was paying for the advice and contacts I got from the store owner in Texas who inspired this business. I avoided a lot of trial and error, and it gave me confidence in the beginning. I now charge a fee of $2,500 to anyone who wants to consult with me. I introduce them to reliable suppliers, give out my trade secrets and catalogs, and work with them in ordering, designing, decorating, and building a store. I always say you're only ninety days away from bankruptcy and you can't afford to make mistakes. It's well worth it to pay a consultant who knows the business.

The reason I started in business was to educate my kids. My oldest was in high school then. My purpose was to put my kids through college . . . and I did it! One year I had my daughter *and* son in college and my youngest son in a military school. That was a tough year, but the business managed to pay all the bills. My being in business has made all of the children aware that you have to work hard to achieve the goals you set. Nothing is handed to you without work, but the rewards are fantastic.

· 19 ·

Services

Everyone lives by selling something.
—Robert Louis Stevenson

The service industry is the baby boomer of the business world. Born and bred in the postwar years of specialization, the need for special services and professional consultants escalates yearly. A service business is one of the few types of business that can still be started on a shoestring—often for the price of a brochure and a telephone. It is a natural arena for the self-starter, the person with a talent or skill.

Service businesses can be divided loosely into two areas: creative services, which include everything in the realm of ideas, design, and the planning and coordination of events; and practical services—anything having to do with skills, organization, and placement.

"I let my imagination run wild," is how one woman defines her events-planning business in Chicago. A theater major in college, she now produces mini-Broadway shows for corporate conventions. Another woman, a pioneer in the personal services market, cites the growing number of professional/and managerial women in the workplace as the basis for her success. "Women used to do it all," she says. "Personal services were looked upon as luxuries. Today, working women see these services—shopping, party planning, driving kids to appointments and classes—as necessities, a way to keep some sanity in their lives."

Launching a service business starts by answering these questions:

Will it work? Define your skill, talent, or training in terms of an ongoing business. What qualifies you to offer this service?

Who will buy? Identify your potential market—its needs, desires, and problems.

How will it work? How will you deliver or administer your service? How will you reach your market—recommendations, visuals, one-on-one sales calls, advertising, publicity?

Will it make money? How much can you charge? Is there competition? Is your potential market limited?

Image

People who buy services must rely on intangibles to guide them. After all, you can inspect the inseams of a garment to see if it's well made, but how do you know whether the person who has just sent you a brochure can *really* launch your product, plan your wedding, or staff your trade show?

Credibility in a service business begins with the image you present. The naming of your business is perhaps more critical in the service field than in any other. It's what people hear about you first. Unless your own name is recognized in your field, your business name should illuminate the activity you perform. Communicate what you do rather than who you are. A case in point: Audrey Smaltz began her business of providing a free-lance styling team to designers and manufacturers in presenting their fashion lines as Audrey Smaltz, Inc. But one day she heard a speech by Martin Luther King, Jr., pointing out the importance of the ground crew in getting the jumbo jets in the air. In an instant she had the name for her business—The Ground Crew. Clients loved the name and got the message immediately.

If you plan to keep your overhead low by working from home, give special attention to the quality of your brochure, your logo, and the letterhead of your business. It should state clearly and attractively what your business does. If you must use a post office box, list an address as well. It lends credibility.

Selling

Most service entrepreneurs must spend a good deal of time seeing clients and selling one-on-one to them. Some people are gifted in the art of persuasion, but if you're not one of them, a selling strategy will make selling easier.

Creating a Strategy

It is essential you know *who* your clients are before you plan *how* to sell to them. (Targeting clients and listing prospects is outlined in chapter 11.) Once your sales targets are identified:

1. Organize them into "ABC" lists.
   A = top prospects. (This is where you will spend the bulk of your time.)
   B = secondary prospects. (Why do they fall into this category?)
   C = least likely prospects. (But not to be forgotten or overlooked. "C's" can eventually become "A's.")
2. Plot your time. Spend 40 percent of your time on selling and half of that on your "A" list.
3. File all prospects on cards, or in your computer, with as much information as you have, including: name, address, and telephone; mutual contacts; reasons you think they may be a hard sell (or easy one). Include information on their products, services, suppliers, ad agency, bank, or anything else pertinent to your needs. How your product or service fits with the client is crucial to your selling strategy. Do your homework. Constantly update your cards.
4. Recycle all information into a succinct verbal and/or visual presentation. Polish your pitch. Work it out on friends and associates. Don't make speeches; tell stories.

Sales Letters/Making Calls

There are no second "first times." Your first call, your first letter, your brochure must have something of YOU in it. Stand out.

The Letter

Each letter must be typed on your letterhead and directed to the specific person to whom you want to make your pitch. Be succinct; keep the letter to one page. Link yourself to your reader. Do you have a mutual contact or recommendation? ("Jane Doe suggested I contact you . . .") If not, find another way to form a bond. Be an expert, e.g., "I've done some research and I know that you . . ." Or ask for advice: "We are a new company and we would like to know . . ." Or, show you've done your homework: "I have followed your XYZ campaign with interest . . ."

Follow with a brief explanation of your business, names of satisfied clients, an indication of what you believe you can offer your prospective client (alluding to ways you can help her improve her business). You can include a brochure, but generally it's best to save it, leaving it with the client after you've met.

Close assertively. "I will telephone your office to make an appointment."

The Call

Often your target won't see you right off and will tell you to see someone else. Do so. See anyone this key person wants you to see. Sooner or later someone will open the door wide enough for you to get through. Don't forget the squeaky-wheel philosophy. Try calling before regular office hours, or offer to meet after business hours.

Cold Calling

This means calling on a client without a prearranged appointment. Go with information—an article you've clipped that should interest your prospective customer, or your brochure. Leave this if the person can't see you. Follow up with a call or letter requesting an appointment.

Persistence

Develop your contacts from the bottom up if need be. The secretaries, for example, can be your best ally. Send them notes, remember their names. Seasoned salespeople say that 80 percent of business gets booked after the fifth call. Most people get discouraged before that. If you stick with it, chances are you'll get to your prospect.

Making the Pitch

Before entering the meeting, pause and compose yourself. Even if you've had a rotten day, you have to radiate energy and confidence. Remember, being a woman who owns her own business is a great qualifier. People are impressed.

Look good. Let your appearance conform generally to the situation; be comfortable with what you're wearing. Make an entrance. Try to get some personal rapport going. Do a quick take on the office; play into it. But don't dwell on idle conversation.

Set a time limit. Ten minutes is a good rule of thumb. Respect the fact that most people are busy.

List your products or services. List reasons, in order, why the potential client will want your service or product.

Props and visual devices are good sales tools provided you know how to use them. Complement your rhetoric by illustrating your product or service with photographs, graphics, or video. Present these in a neat, clear, easy-to-handle way.

Be a good listener. Pick up signals. Be prepared to switch gears if the client wants to stop and talk over a point. Don't be a know-it-all. Don't be a stand-up comic. Be friendly but professional. React and interact.

Be prepared to handle objections. (Anticipate them in advance and think them through.) Look on objections as opportunities. Don't argue with the client. Answer their objection briefly and professionally.

Closing the Deal

Your own attitude is most important in sales. *Expect* to be successful. Be assumptive. Weave positive phrases into your sales pitch, such as "When you buy . . . When you hire . . ." Not *if* but *when.* Close your pitch with conviction and sincerity.

People will not act unless you cause them to act. Therefore:

Have your order form handy with the client's name already filled out. Hand her your pen and ask her to make the order and sign. If she says no, ask why. Use this as the basis of a discussion.

Be direct. "Will you be placing an order?" (Don't use the word "give." "Give" is a giveaway word.)

Relate a success story about someone else. ("The campaign we did for XYZ brought in these results." Or, "Call Jane Doe at

XYZ and ask her how our product sells.") Show letters of recommendation.

Use inducement. Talk about a special feature that happens only once or by a certain date.

Leave the door open for continuing contact. Plan another meeting or phone with an estimate, send a brochure or memo—do anything that allows for a follow-up.

Analyzing the Results

At the end of the pitch, you've either made the sale or you haven't. If you have, then you must solidify the relationship.

Send a thank-you note *immediately.*

Press their "hot buttons." Send PR articles or pertinent information on business topics that you may have touched on. If client has just had a baby, send a baby gift. If she's about to take a vacation, track down an article on the place she's going and send it. It shouldn't be elaborate, just a message to signal you're paying attention and you appreciate her trust.

Don't ever neglect your old customers. Old customers are like old friends: never underestimate their importance. Acknowledge their successes with personal congratulations. Advise them on new ways to utilize your product or service.

If you haven't made the sale, analyze why and use that knowledge to improve your techniques. Always look on the positive side. Don't accept any loss of business as final. Periodically return with new ideas, new information approaches. Often the client's needs will change, or a different person in the company may be more receptive. (Rapport has a great deal to do with it.) Hang in there, but never to the point of obnoxiousness.

Negotiating Price

Since you've already learned how to figure your basic fees (pp. 109–13), you must also learn how and when to negotiate a fee. Estimate the time it will take you to do the job (include traveling and administrative time) and expenses you will incur on the job (labor, transportation, telephone, supplies, equipment, and so on). Establish the very least fee for which you can do the job. Then, think what you would like to get for the job; aim as high as you dare. You now know your negotiating range.

Think of negotiating as a give-and-take process, a bartering of your ability versus their money. Break the job down into its components. If the originally stated fee is too high for the client, reevaluate the job minus one of its components. Always build into your proposal negotiable factors such as delivery dates, design variations, quantity of supplies, labor, or service. Be positive; do not make it seem as if the overall quality of the job is being jeopardized.

Much of negotiation is based on how badly you need the job or want the client. If you're new in business, often it won't hurt to let the client know how much you value his or her business. Keep it relaxed. Have fun with it. If you need to think it over, do so. Be friendly but firm when negotiating; don't get backed into a corner and, as the saying goes, never let them see you sweat. No one wants to do business with someone who seems unsure of herself.

Performance

Selling won't count for anything if you don't deliver what you say you can deliver. Performance is key in service. The show must go on—and go on without a hitch. Plan for problems. Be prepared for any eventuality. Don't make promises you're not sure you can keep; work overtime to get the job done by the due date. Be honest, be credible, be the best. You'll reap the rewards in additional business.

For further information:

AWED. American Woman's Economic Development Corporation. 60 East Forty-second Street, Suite 405, New York, N.Y. 10165, (212)692–9100. Write or call for information on specific seminars and advanced training in: How To Start a Service Business, How to Sharpen Negotiating Skills, Marketing Techniques for the Service Entrepreneur, and others.
Supergirls: The Autobiography of An Outrageous Business, by Claudia Jessup and Genie Chipps (Harper & Row). This is the authors' own personal saga in the creative service business.

How To Succeed as an Independent Consultant and *The Consultant's Guide to Winning Clients,* by Herman R. Holtz (John Wiley & Sons).

Getting Organized: The Easy Way to Put Your Life in Order and *The Organized Executive: New Ways to Manage Things, Paper and People,* by Stephanie Winston (W.W. Norton Co.).

THE ORGANIZING PRINCIPLE

Stephanie Winston turned her talent for organization into a lucrative business in 1976. Then, she was paid $200 a day to organize other people's messy lives. She cataloged private libraries, decoded complex filing systems, set up billing systems for professional consultants, helped free-lancers carve out work space in the home, even organized kitchens, drawers, and the hopelessly shambled closets of New York's harried housewives.

Then in 1978 she wrote *Getting Organized: The Easy Way to Put Your Life in Order* and the wheels were set in motion for the Stephanie Winston of 1990. Today, her focus is on corporate time management, a field in which she has become a leader.

I'm not obsessive about order and organization, but I do believe it's an instrument and technique for saving time and living more easily. Being organized is not necessarily being neat. Being organized is being able to find what you want when you want it, and being able to do what you want efficiently. I had no idea how many people felt truly uncomfortable because some system in their lives wasn't working. Some people just don't know how to go about getting organized; others simply let things get out of hand. The trick is to come up with solutions and systems so simple and helpful that people will stick to them.

I had no special credentials when I started my business, but I found the concept of organization fascinating. Some people fear it because they think it threatens their individuality; some people find cleaning up and keeping order a mundane task; others are unable to cope with mess. Whatever the reasons for disorder, I saw that bringing order into people's lives helped to ease tensions; it was definitely a positive business.

My clients in the beginning were individuals, many of whom

appeared orderly. One client was a psychotherapist working from her home. Her office was meticulously neat, but she hadn't any idea of which patients had paid their bills, nor was she able to keep up with her own monthly bills. All her correspondence—business and personal, bills, and professional materials—was stuffed into bags in her closet. The disarray was causing her considerable distress.

I started from scratch, going through everything, piece by piece. Then I set up a simple filing system and method of checking off client's names as they paid their bills.

Another client, a doctor, had everything in order including his library, which was neatly shelved and alphabetized by author. Yet the book he needed most often was out of reach on the top shelf simply because the author's name began with "A." I set up a special, easily accessible shelf for frequently consulted books.

I reorganized an office for a client so the secretary and the boss could see each other. Before, they had to constantly get up to talk to each other. I also did a lot of unscrambling of filing systems for my early clients. The most common filing mistake is excessive complexity. One company had a system so complicated, you needed a code book. There were markings like "PO-33." The secretaries were in tears because they could never find anything. So I simplified everything. If it started with "A," I put it in the "A" file. Nobody had ever considered this before.

Household organization was always a particular fascination of mine. It's been so neglected. People may sniff at housewifery, but I'd like to see the reactions of a typical male executive were he suddenly faced with coordinating the activities of three to five people and maintaining life support systems for them, and all of this most likely on top of a regular job. And so my initial jobs were in time management, family logistics, messy closets, household paperwork—whatever the client felt disorganized in.

My system was to work with the client solving the immediate problem and then set up a maintenance system so that the person wouldn't slip back into old habits. My average fee was $200 per day. Of course negotiation came into it, but those were the figures I tried to stay with. Setting fees is a primary problem when you're just starting out, especially if you have no credibility. In my case, I was starting a business that was unique and there were no competitors I could judge my rates against. I started with a fee of $100 per day and quickly realized there was so much of a need for my services I could raise them. If you find you're in a business that has no rate guidelines, then compare yourself professionally to others. For example, if you call yourself a consultant, then base your fees on what other consultants charge, though maybe not in your line. Design and graphic consultants, personal services consultants, information and reference consultants, editorial and training consultants, events planners and so on. Ask friends and associates and eventually you'll come up with something that fits your arena. Test the waters, then go up until you meet resistance. When you do meet resistance, you have to make the decision to go after a more upscale market or shift the focus of the business.

In launching The Organizing Principle, I found that a brochure and mailing did no good because I was unknown. Through personal contacts, friends, and word of mouth, I began to build up a clientele. I soon discovered my business was a novelty. I wrote the *Village Voice* and told them who I was and what it was I did, and they did a small piece on me. It got a great response, and I was encouraged so much I wrote to the *New York Times.* They wanted a full feature. On the morning it came out, my phone started ringing at 9:00 A.M. and didn't stop for four days. It was incredible. I was booked for months.

That article was syndicated all across the country. I appeared on the "Today" show as well as many other talk shows and soon found I was becoming a celebrity in my field. Then, when the *Wall Street Journal* profiled my business, it brought in corporate clients and I decided to move in that direction exclusively. I began giving staff seminars in personal management and now work with CEO's and business owners exclusively in time management and organization.

I've since written three books on the subject. My first, *Getting Organized,* was on the *New York Times* best-seller list for five months. This led to national speaking engagements and seminars. So, gradually my name recognition became my best asset.

Today, I consult, write, and lecture. I've observed that it is very hard for women to get beyond a certain point in the corporate world. They do, of course, but proportionate to the numbers of women in the marketplace, most don't get past middle-management positions. Women entrepreneurs, however, seem to have a better shot at success, because in running your own business, you can assert yourself and your creative skills to the fullest. Assertiveness in the environment is critical for success. I think women stand a better chance at success as entrepreneurs than they do in the corporate world.

RELOCATION ASSOCIATES

Every year thousands of families throughout the country transfer to a new corporate location. In Chicago, Anne Battle and her staff of five are dedicated to making that transition as trouble-free and informed as possible.

Relocation Associates has developed a simple and efficient way to address the needs of people moving to a city as complex as Chicago. They're experts on housing, financing, schools, weather, commutes, and recreation. Through unique audio and visual tools, plus personal counseling, relocated families can learn about the Chicago area and how it relates to their specific housing, lifestyle, and financial needs.

I had worked for a relocation agency on the West Coast and then, when my husband was transferred to Chicago, I suddenly found the shoe was on the other foot. I quickly discovered there was no relocation business in this area. It was frustrating for me. I was used to handing out precise information, counseling clients on everything from housing to the specifics of commuter trains. I could tell them down to the minute how long a commute would be and which station had the best parking. But here, at best I got information like "Oh, the train is great. It's not a problem."

Once I was settled, I decided to do some market research. I hired a young woman to help me, installed two telephones in the spare room, and began by calling fifty companies headquartered in downtown Chicago. Typically the people who handle relocation are the director of human resources or a vice president in personnel. I presented them with my idea, told them my qualifications, and asked if they thought there would be a need for a relocation service in Chicago. I also asked if they would use such a service and in what volume. Concurrently, my assistant was researching schools, commutes, new housing developments, recreational facilities, and so on in Chicago and the six counties that surround it.

It took us about eighteen months working from my house to gather sufficient information for relocating people. Then came the problem of translating that information out of file folders into interesting sales tools. In the initial marketing research calls, many corporations had wondered why they should pay for such a service when they could get it free from the real estate agencies. Their doubts became the basis of my selling program.

A visual presentation became crucial to my business. When I make sales calls I can't get any business unless I go in there face-to-face and have them see the materials we've developed. They are what sell my business. The problem is, we and the real estate agents all use the same vocabulary. An agent can talk about schools and commute distances, the weather, and local health clubs, but real estate agents, as helpful as many of them are, only know one territory—their own. And they are going to try their best to keep you in it. This is great for the agent but frustrating, discouraging, and often disastrous for the family relocating.

Pinpointing the areas that answer specific housing needs is time-consuming and confusing. It would take months to investigate and document on your own what we can provide in a matter of hours. Most people need more information than price brackets. They have questions and concerns and worries that require a sympathetic ear as well as information. We provide that. Every client is assigned a counselor, who works with them providing options and answers.

Our services are contracted for by the corporations. They pay an hourly fee, per relocation. I make my sales calls to the corporate representatives with the same material we use to counsel our clients. That way I can show them exactly how we will be dealing with their people. We have an audiovisual film that gives a broad overview of Chicago and the four major suburban areas: the weather, the cultural events and institutions, the schools, the recreational facilities. Then we use large, very stylized maps with color Mylar overlays to get down to specifics. Visualize a huge map of the greater Chicago area. A red-coded overlay might be where housing costs are $200,000 to $300,000. An orange overlay may indicate new housing. Another color will show in concentric circles the commuter distances from each area. Depending on a client's specific needs, we can pop these overlays on the map and all of a sudden it becomes visually apparent where he or she should be looking. For example, if the client has a $250,000 house budget, wants a new house, and doesn't want to commute more than twenty minutes a day, then we can show the possibilities immediately and visually. It's a very positive presentation; it's simple and direct.

We also present our clients with a packet of materials that address more detailed concerns and costs. Our computers have information broken down into specific areas. We have listings of health clubs, tennis clubs, golf courses, yacht clubs, schools, all the religious affiliations, property taxes, day care, new housing developments, and other appropriate information almost any family will need for the places in which they're going to look for housing.

Typically we talk by telephone to the families before they visit here to learn what their needs are. We spend up to an hour talking to both husband and wife. Sometimes we talk more than once. We try to get as complete a picture as we can of who they are, what their needs are, what they would like and not like.

Then, when they come in, we show them the film, work with the overlays, provide all the information they will need according to their interview, and help them to focus on all their options, narrowing it down to two or three areas that will meet both financial and lifestyle needs.

Occasionally there is a special client, a VIP or a foreign national or someone with a special need, and we may have to dig deeper for more specific information. For example, I have a client coming in tomorrow who has a learning-disabled child. The company really wants him for the job, but he doesn't have any interest in coming here unless he knows that the special program exists that meet his child's need. So, the company has asked me to do in-depth research on learning-disabled programs in the specific schools that are in the areas that meet the client's other needs.

Once we've seen the relocating family, we place them with realtors in the areas selected. They're not bound by those agents, but it gets the ball rolling. We have realtors we've screened in each area. This took us longer to put into place than all the research and all the marketing research we did. Finding top professional people in real estate is hard. We go beyond that. We try to match personalities as well as expertise. The older person who has seen an area change and whose clientele is part of the old guard is not the right person for a young, hip couple just coming into the housing market. You have to be adept at matching people up: that has been the main part of our success.

The business is difficult at times and very challenging. Relocating is such an emotional time. For some people it's a time of great excitement and anticipation, and for others it's really a wrench, leaving friends, uprooting children, moving to a whole new area of the country. A lot of people don't like change. They're intimidated by the size of Chicago. I remember one day I had two clients back to back and both women burst into tears. It was horrible. You know intellectually they're not upset with you, they're upset with the situation, but you can't help but feel terrible.

We see the emotions intensely but we don't see them for very long. We dread calling clients the first night after they've looked at houses. Usually they are distraught. The prices are so high, and unless they're coming from the Coasts, where real estate is also high, they are totally unprepared for it. It takes a while to get used to what you're seeing. Chicago is flat. In the new areas, you don't get big trees or two-acre lawns or woods. It takes people's eyes a while to adjust to that. So you get all the anger and frustration the first night, but after that everything calms down.

We are available to our clients while they are looking for housing, and for any and all additional consulting and support. A lot of questions can arise after they've seen us initially, and you never know when you might have misread the situation. People might tell us they want an older house that they can renovate, but when we call, they'll say, "I didn't mean *that* old." If we've got them lined up for similar areas, we may have to change gears. Or they might not like the realtor. Or maybe, after seeing what they're getting for their money, they may come up with another $100,000 to spend. Follow-up is everything when you're dealing with people.

Most people have positive feelings about us because we're not trying to sell them anything. They know we're being paid by their company, they know we receive part of the commission from the realtors if they buy from someone we've recommended, but we don't have any reason to direct people into one area over another. We are an information source with no ax to grind. We're not the boss who's going to be upset if they don't take his advice. We're not a real estate agent who is pressuring them to buy in his or her territory. Our clients feel good about us. And this sends a powerful message back to the corporation.

My staff consists of four counselors. In the summer I hire a college student whose job it is to update all of the research. Basically, I hire people I like. They come to me through word of mouth. I look for people who have a knack of putting things together, who have a bird's-eye view and can stand back and make comparisons, and certainly I look for people who are sensitive to people. When I started there were just the two of us working full-time. Later, I took on part-time employees, who worked on an ebb and flow basis depending on how much work we had coming in. But this proved an inadequate way to manage things. If one worked with a client on Monday but wasn't in the office on Wednesday to follow through, then it fell to me to see or talk to the client. It got crazy. I had no time to makes sales calls. So I hired a person to be full-time office manager and senior consultant. It frees me up to concentrate on selling our services to the corporations. And if the business is going to grow, that's where I'm most needed.

This is a big-city business. You have to have numerous options and many different price levels before it can work. It just wouldn't pay in the smaller cities. I'm a member of a loosely formed national organization called the International Relocation Consulting Association. We meet once a year and share ideas, and offer each other advice on particular problems we might encounter. We send each other clients. For example, a relocation company in New York put me in touch with the Pepsi people when they opened their Midwest regional office here. We pay the New York people a percentage of what we get.

I hired outside consultants when I first started the business—a computer consultant to work with me to set up our data base, a film maker to shoot the video presentation, and a cartographer and graphic designer to do the maps and overlays. In each case, I knew what I wanted but let the expert figure out how it could be done.

For me the secret of being an entrepreneur is not to think about it a whole lot. Otherwise, it can get overwhelming. I think about each day and I know I can handle what's on my desk for that day. If I had known how hard it was going to be in the beginning, I might not have started the business. And sometimes I can't believe what we've accomplished. I look around this office, which is located in the heart of downtown Chicago, and I think, my god. We've got fifteen hundred square feet, we've got three computers, we've got three printers, we've got all this audiovisual equipment, we've got a good amount of money in furniture, and five years ago we had an empty file cabinet in my house. You do a business one day at a time. And it happens.

PORTFOLIO ASSOCIATES, INC.

Beverly Harper has carved a prominent place for herself and her creative consulting firm in Philadelphia. In 1969, when the business was founded, she was an unknown entity in the business community and decidedly unfunded. Today she is in the forefront of that city's cultural and business scene.

Her creative consulting firm, then and now, specializes in graphics, design, communications, and special projects.

My basic idea was to put together a team of highly creative people who could act as problem solvers. Our skills collectively cover visual design, media development, video arts, research, selling, and a general account executive.

We started with a post office box and an answering service. I worked out of my apartment for the first year and took a minimal salary, as did everyone who worked here. If you're unfamiliar with business operation, especially with the long period of time it takes to get work on a regular basis, the last worry you need is meeting the expenses of a heavy monthly overhead.

I never went to anyone for financing, and this was a conscious decision. I felt that being black, a woman, having no business background, and needing money were four big strikes against me. I would have had to work four times as hard just to get to some neutral point, and I wasn't willing to do that; I didn't need negatives.

My appointments were always outside the office (my apartment). If you're cutting corners in the beginning by working from home, you should be doubly concerned with the image you're projecting and compensate for the lack of facilities in other ways. We concentrated on our image through graphics—the letterhead, business cards, and written proposals. They have always been very exciting and very professional. After a year and a half we were able to move into an office, and then I suggested all initial meetings with a client here because it let them know immediately that this was an established, ongoing business.

I incorporated the business from the start, and I had a lawyer and an accountant help set up the corporate structure. In looking for a lawyer and accountant, your special consideration should be to find people willing to work along with you. Don't go to anyone who is going to slap you with a big professional fee. No new business needs that.

To launch the business, we sent out letters explaining our services and concepts to prospective clients. Then, I followed up with a phone call and hoped to get appointments. It is vitally important for a young company to look at its sales approach with an objective eye. Put yourself in the shoes of the person you're trying to see. Think of the mail he or she sees every day: how can yours stand out and represent your company in the best possible light? A letter or a brochure is often the person's first impression of your company, and it should be easy to understand, to the point, friendly, but professional, too.

Various business associations and service organizations are good sources for business contacts. The local chamber of commerce can be extremely helpful in providing mailing lists of people in the business community. The United Way is another good source; many businesses belong or contribute to that organization, so by getting involved you begin to make contacts. These kinds of contacts are vital to getting a new business off the ground.

Sales efforts for this business fall into two basic categories. First, if we see a need, we try to sell the client on a solution. For instance, we initiated a citizen's participation program for a bank that had just opened an educational financing counseling center. We sold them on the idea of letting the consumer identify his or her own individual needs. The bank was not soliciting ideas from us or anyone else; we just called them up and said we would like to meet with them.

Secondly, we look for clients by making sales calls and general presentations. The secret to selling is to be organized before you go into a meeting; have as much background on the company and the person as you can; and know exactly what you can do for them. The government has something called the General Services Administration (GSA), which publishes a list of approved private sector businesses in various categories. This list goes out to regional government offices. To get on the list, a company has to write a proposal including its services and prices.

Once we were listed, I did a mailing to all the regional government offices in the area, sending a letter and samples of our graphic work. I followed up with a phone call and perhaps a meeting. Out of all of this, the post office said that it wanted a campaign developed to promote letter writing. We came up with a tremendously successful headline for a poster campaign: "When you say it in a letter it lasts a long, long time."

We've also worked at the federal level with the Social Security office. They wondered why people who were on disability were not using their "return to work" incentive program. We conducted a series of focus groups with people who were on disability to talk about the various issues associated with returning to work. Those discussions then became the basis of a series of recommendations to the Social Security Administration that focused on better communications.

One of our most fun creations was a black film festival. Working with a man I had met whose idea it was, we jointly produced the festival: he screened the films and I provided the organization and planning, the fund raising, and the graphic image for the festival. It was such a success; in subsequent years we sent it on the road to six states. For the past two years we've helped to organize and promote the first-ever international conference on black dance companies. Working with cultural activities and cultural organizations is high on my agenda.

When we first started out, about 90 percent of our business was for community associations with a great many needs but not much money. It gave us experience in planning, costing out jobs, timing, and finding out what service organizations needed. These projects became our "track record" when we started going after clients with bigger budgets.

Over the past ten years, I've explored ways in which women- and minority-owned businesses can get their fair share of the economic pie. In 1981, I helped to establish a minority business organization in Philadelphia called The Brain Trust. We were successful in getting legislation passed that would guarantee women and minority businesses 25 percent of the contracts from the municipal government.

A few years ago, we began researching the convention and tourist industry. This is a healthy and growing, $2.5 billion industry across the country, yet in Philadelphia, few women- and minority-owned businesses were involved in it. So we got the local hotel association to cosponsor, with a minority advisory committee, a series of seminars to educate these small businesses in what they could do for the convention, hospitality, and tourism industry.

I set yearly financial goals for my corporation. All businesses after they've been operating for a year should do this. Sit down and say, "This is what I've done, and this is where I want to be next year." Establish your fixed expenses for the business, then set a range of what you personally need to live on, a rock-bottom take-home salary. Both of these costs will tell you what you have to sell per year just to survive. Then, identify in categories where your business is coming from and decide in what categories to increase your efforts.

Once a year I rent a conference room in a hotel for myself and the staff—we are eight—to meet and plan the activities for the next year. We set goals and objectives and schedules for reaching them. The important thing is to get out of the familiar office environment to a place where you can really focus on ideas and schedules.

New businesses don't realize the amount of time that goes into planning and evaluating. I spend perhaps a full day planning and organizing my time each week. I keep a detailed list of what must be done and I check each thing off as it's done. I constantly evaluate the good and bad of all aspects of the business. Once you're able to isolate what these are, you can start improving them or using them to better advantage.

Recently I was elected president of the board of directors of the Philadelphia Dance Company, which is one of the top dance companies in the country. They're celebrating their twentieth year in business. It was not only an honor but a pleasant coincidence that I too am celebrating my twentieth year in business.

INSIDE OUT

Inside Out is the perfect name for this business. Sole proprietor Zina Glazebrook creates window displays for retail stores. She draws on her art background, her PR background, and her merchandising background to fuel

> the dynamics of her business. Her work is intense, dramatic, whimsical, and often surreal.
>
> Like many creative people, Zina finds talent comes easy. It's the budgeting of time, tracking the paperwork, dealing with clients, and staying on top of schedules that takes getting used to.

Windows are great merchandising tools. There are two kinds of windows. those that draw you into the store and those that sell the products displayed in the windows. One is a billboard and the other is a selling device.

I'm so sick of what I call True Value Hardware windows—things all piled up in a jumble with the price tags. To me there is so much more fun that can be had with a pile of paint cans. It's a matter of taking everyday products and looking at them differently in order to create a little fantasy, a little fun, a little thoughtfulness. That's the most exciting element of my job. Creating something extraordinary out of the ordinary. Stopping people in their tracks, making things look so yummy, they have to come in to the store and buy. Good window displays do that. So my business is more than design, it's really public relations, advertising, and merchandising.

I was in the retail business for many years, mostly in the kid business. My first jobs were all for toy stores. I loved being in retail. I loved buying. I loved spending other people's money. I loved putting the displays together. Toys, of course, are wonderful material for display.

In 1975 I went to work for Creative Playthings and tripled the sales of one of their stores in six months. When CBS bought them out, the executive bigwigs booted me up to vice president in charge of all their stores. I was twenty-five years old. It was extraordinary. But it was hard on me being an executive. I couldn't bear that this once wonderful European-style toy company was being destroyed by financial barracudas. The wooden toys were now made of plastic to look like wood. I felt I was prostituting myself. I quit.

I went to work for a much smaller retail toy business. They had two stores in New York and more were opening. I worked on promotions and merchandising and public relations. I increased sales dramatically. But after three years, I started to resent the fact that I was doing this for someone else. I felt like Cinderella, scrubbing the kitchen while everyone else went to the ball. I wanted my own business.

I moved to Sag Harbor, on Long Island, which is an old whaling town close to the more fashionable Hamptons, and I began to sell my promotional and PR services free-lance to shop owners in the area. Because of the sophisticated nature of the Hamptons there are a lot of very savvy retail people. My first client was a woman who owned a business called Kitchen Classics, which sold good kitchenwares, imported pottery— very upscale merchandise.

Her second store was just opening in East Hampton, and in the course of working with her, getting it ready, sending out the releases and PR materials, it just happened that I took on the job of arranging merchandise in her window. The store opened Memorial Day weekend and most everything that was in the window sold, including two copper stock pots that cost $350 each.

My client said, "Zina, you can help with my PR but you'd better keep on doing my windows, too." I was excited. Here, at last, was a playing field for my artistic side. My work for Kitchen Classics built up my credibility as a display designer. It made me feel accomplished at it. I felt I knew what I was doing. That job led to other jobs. And all of sudden I had a handful of clients.

One of my favorites continues to be the Cut-Rite liquor store. Visually a standard liquor store, definitely not the designer wine shops you see elsewhere out here. The owner called me up and said he admired what I had done for other people and that the liquor companies (who until then had done his displays) did boring windows. He wanted me to work for him.

A recent one I did was called "House Present." I borrowed a number of different kinds of small houses—doll, bird, ceramic, tin—and then displayed various gift-wrapped liquor bottles in and around them.

I called one window "High as a Kite." I silk-screened those words onto little kites and then strung them to half-gallon vodka bottles so that it looked like the bottles were flying the kites.

The ice cream parlor in East Hampton is another client. The owner decided to turn June into Kids' Month. We created story hours every Saturday, she put free sprinkles on kids' ice cream cones, we had placemats you could color on, and she held an art show—things like that for the month of June. I created a window that looked like the greatest kids' party ever, with hats and confetti and balloons. Inside we created a little party department selling favors and party gifts, plus you could order birthday cakes. The PR side comes in often. We'll create a program and then follow it through in the displays and attractions in the store.

One of my favorite windows was for a clothing store, also in East Hampton, that sells very pretty and romantic women's and children's clothing. I asked everyone who worked in the store to bring in pictures of their mothers and grandmothers, and I did a window called "For Mom" on Mother's Day.

In the beginning, I built my business through word of mouth. In the creative fields, you have to *have* work to get work. But one of my biggest jobs was with F.A.O. Schwarz, and that was a matter of being in the right place at the right time. The old store at the corner of Fifty-ninth and Fifth was closing and the new owners had decided to go for broke and open a new store across the street. They wanted it bigger and better than ever. They brought in top talent from every source.

I sold them on the idea of re-creating Eloise's bedroom at the Plaza in the big corner window. I found an artist to paint a three-dimensional canvas backdrop of one of the illustrations in the Eloise book written by Kay Thompson and illustrated by Hilary Knight. We created her bed and a life-size Eloise herself and then went about putting all sorts of things from the store into the room. We had a life-size stuffed turtle, a line of Eloise clothes, a goldfish bowl with live goldfish, Eloise's dog, plus the room was strewn with all of her toys. The Plaza Hotel gave us marvelous things, including a replica of the key to her room, and I even found an original Eloise doll, which was part of the display.

It was a celebrated window. In New York, of course, window display is a very heavy, intense marketing tool. Paul Stuart, for instance, does fantastic display for Barney's. One I remember was a murder mystery—you could follow as it developed from window to window. My idol is Gene Moore at Tiffany's. His windows are extraordinary.

My favorite part of my business is coming up with the concepts. What I do first is work with the clients to find out what they're trying to promote. I get a feel for the image of the store. Then, I establish a budget. Each client is different. Some want to know exactly what's going in, others give me carte blanche. I usually feed off an idea that they're trying to promote. I take my themes from anything and anywhere. I tie in with local events. I did something called "Classic Foods" for one of the specialty food stores to tie in with the Hampton Classic Horse Show.

I don't have a contract with anyone. I think oftentimes those can be the beginning of the end of business relationships. People start to feel hemmed in and anxious. So I have open-ended contracts. I work on a daily retainer fee of $500, plus my expenses for materials and props. I review this fee on an annual basis. Some stores I do for less if the store will be a good showcase for me. I'm usually given a budget for each window, and that fluctuates with the seasons. My Christmas windows are much more expensive, for example, than the off-season windows.

I let my portfolio sell my service to potential clients. I have all my work photographed professionally in eight by ten or twelve by fourteen color glossies. These are mounted in a spiral book. I take this in when I see clients. I also send out the portfolio to people who call with inquiries. This way I can sell myself at a distance.

Publicity has given me a tremendous leg up in getting business. First the local papers did an article and then, through a client, the *New York Times* did a feature on me. I reproduced the *Times* article and sent it out on my letterhead to everyone I could think of.

A graphics designer designed my cards and stationery. He came up with the idea of a see-through letterhead with the name of my business printed inside out. If you're in a creative field, I think terrific graphics will give you a certain kind of credibility. It makes a strong statement with people.

My biggest problem is cash flow. People don't pay on time. Clients often see me as their pal, and not someone who has to pay her own bills at the end of the month like everyone else. I may budget for income on a certain date, but quite often I won't get it until six weeks later. Then I'll have to scramble from another source. That scrambling is terribly time-consuming. It's difficult to have to nag people. Everyone in business for themselves should have six months' living expenses as a cushion in the bank to get them through the tough times.

Another problem I ran into in the beginning was arriving at a new client's store and finding I had to put in an extra five or six hours just getting the display area cleaned and ready for installation. It can be difficult to make the client see the problem and, of course, they don't like it one bit if you bill them for more hours than they've got in the estimate. You have to learn from all of this. Now I have it in my agreement that the area will be clean, and I spell out what clean means. I am also paid my retainer fee up front. As the saying goes, everything's funny but the money.

DIMENSION TALENT

Joan Solomon was just twenty-one when she started her business. Her strong sense of promotion, and ability to build and expand on the original concept, made this business the number one talent agency in Minneapolis.

After six years, her experience propelled Joan into a lucrative television production career in Los Angeles, where, among other things, she is writing a script about her days at Dimension Talent.

First of all, let me say: never start a business thinking you're going to get out of work. I thought if I started my own business, it would be just great—set my own hours, come and go as I please. Believe me, you work twice as hard as anybody else, and your hours are set by the demand of the business. You are committed to respond to that demand.

I was just out of college and looking for a job, an exciting job, something stimulating, and I wasn't finding it in the Minneapolis job market. In my search, I registered with the one and only model agency in town. The owner had been in business for fifteen years and wasn't doing anything creative in the field because she didn't have to. Some of the biggest corporations are located here—General Mills, IBM, 3M—and models were in demand; but she would send out the same five models on every job that came in, and you would see their faces over and over again.

My intuition told me that a creative, young, innovative talent agency would go over in a big way. My initial plan was to find ten new models and see if I could get them work. I dreamed up the name for the business and ran an ad for models in the paper.

The response was tremendous. Over two hundred models called for appointments. There I was alone in my apartment: it was time to get organized. My initial investment amounted to the advertisement, the application forms, pencils, and my telephone.

Soon after, I had business cards printed up and a composite brochure designed and printed with my best models pictured in it. I launched my business for under $1,000.

A well thought out application form is the essential tool of any placement agency. You need to know a lot of specifics to match a model to a client's needs. There are shoe models and hand models, for instance, high fashion, all-American, character models, swimwear models, young mothers, and fifty-plus. I went through all the fashion magazines looking at the photographs to see what kinds of activities a model is required to do. Does she play tennis, ski, ride, dance? All of these things can be important to the job.

With enough qualified models registered with me, and my brochure ready to go, I made a list of advertising agencies through the Yellow Pages. Then I called the creative art directors and made an appointment. I also sent my brochure to every company and person I thought might be hiring. It took me six months to build the business to a point where jobs were coming in regularly. At that point I eased up on sales calls and put my profits behind promotional techniques.

The first thing I did was come up with a huge calendar with a photograph of one of the models for each month. The photographs were spectacular. Each month I brought in a new photographer who did the work for free because these calendars went to every art director in town. It was a great promotion, because the calendars hung in every office and were a reminder for the whole year of Dimension Talent.

I made sure that every promotion I did was new to this area. I tried new ideas all the time. A lot of them flopped, but you can't limit yourself or try to protect yourself. You have to expect some things to fail. The point is, a business has to take risks and it has to be experimental. Otherwise, you're static—and that's death.

Once I had saturated the print market, I turned to radio and television. I found a gold mine. The Guthrie Theatre and the Walker Art Center had pulled in a great deal of big East and West Coast talent, but there was no one here in Minneapolis organizing and representing that talent for commercial work. I rounded up thirty-five actors from the Guthrie Theatre and rented time in a sound studio to make a demonstration tape. Each actor did two minutes of voiceover. I made quite a production out of all of this by inviting several directors from the advertising agencies to come and take a turn at directing the actors.

I called the newspapers, and a columnist came to the studio and did an article on the whole event. Clients heard and read about this tape, and suddenly I had added a whole new area to the business: radio and television commercial work.

From this broad talent base, I started to venture into other areas. I set up a photography studio and a props and styling service, designed and staffed conventions and exhibits, and put together rock concerts.

In the meantime, I developed a staff of four women to be in charge of various aspects of the business: the talent agency, prop finding and styling, the convention market, and day-to-day office management. Once a new area of the business opened up, I found the best person I could to run it.

I was gutsy when it came to setting fees. I knew what the other agency charged and I charged double. We were better than they were and I knew it. My fees were a jolt to the client, but it got their attention. I did the same with my actors. No one had ever paid more than minimum AFTRA scale, but talent from the Guthrie was major talent. I charged double scale. You have to take chances. It's better to negotiate a deal down, if you have to, than trying to negotiate up. I had nothing to lose and everything to gain.

I started making a profit after a year. I moved the business into an office that was a storefront. The space was large and fun and I turned the front area into a club for the actors and models. I decided to throw my first business party. I wanted all the ad agency and media people to meet the actors and models in an informal atmosphere rather than the awkward interview/audition basis.

Behind the scenes, I had all the proper advisers—a lawyer, accountant, banker, and insurance broker. I got a tremendous amount of help and advice from my bank. In the beginning I had gone to the biggest bank in town, and really, they couldn't have cared less. I never got to talk to anyone higher than the second clerk, so I went to a small neighborhood bank and it was all on a first-name basis, even with the president; they leaned over backwards with service and advice.

I always wanted a partner, desperately. But when I found one,

305

it was a disaster. I made a serious error in judgment and went into partnership with a personal friend, a man who had been in business before. He was interested in the administrative side of the business, which suited me fine because my strong point was innovation. I made him a full partner and things took a nosedive.

The adage that a business partner is a marriage partner is true. Conciliation, compromise, and flexibility are all things women are pretty good at, but you can't get steamrollered in business, just like you can't in a marriage. You have to stand up for your ideas.

It didn't work. I'm the kind of person who has to go it alone. I started taking more and more time away from the business and it suffered. Eventually, I decided to sell out. I finally realized there was no way to make the business work for me anymore. I had always maintained a sense of humor, which to me is a very important part of running a business. I laughed my way through six years; the seventh year I cried, and that was it, I knew it was over.

I had my lawyer and accountant figure a rate of profit based on the previous three years of the business. I took the average of those figures and made a projection on the future probability of income. I negotiated the buy-out based on that projection. The business was on solid footing. I got my price.

Going into business is a matter of timing and doing what feels right. Women have great instincts, and we shouldn't limit ourselves, especially at the beginning of a career. I would say the best thing I ever did was to start a business directly after college. You have strong ideals and a lot of gall at that age. It's a golden time to try your luck as an entrepreneur, and it just might be the only time you'll have the nerve. Youth and enthusiasm and, really, an overall lack of experience can be the things most strongly in your favor.

Starting a business can open up a flood of possibilities. No matter what the business does, it can provide you with a limitless world of people, places, and adventure.

VIRGINIA MOBILE ULTRASOUND, INC.

Remember the bookmobile, the library on wheels? This same idea has become the basis for transporting all manner of professional services—legal, accounting, health care—to individuals, businesses, and institutions.

Based in Charlottesville, Virginia, Carolyn Dawson and her team bring high-tech medical services to rural hospitals. Her mobile units specialize in detecting heart disease and testing cholesterol levels.

Small rural hospitals don't have the funding for state-of-the-art equipment and the technicians and physicians necessary to make diagnoses. My business provides that service. We travel over a wide area in Virginia and West Virginia and provide up-to-date health care to people who would otherwise have to travel far away to get it.

I knew there was a need for this business because I had spent many years in medical sales, but I got tired of making money for everybody else. I had a friend who was doing something similar in another city, and with my partner I went to see what his operation was like. We then came back to Charlottesville and structured this business based on some of his ideas and methods. I talked to many people in the medical field and verified that this was definitely a service that was needed.

We put together a team of physicians and technicians and invested in the equipment and the mobile vans. In the beginning, our service was built around echocardiography, which is detecting heart disease. We have a regular schedule of hospitals that need our service, and we visit them on a specific day of the week. We are on call for emergencies as well. Built into our service is the assurance that we offer the most advanced equipment for testing available. As technology changes, so do we. Small hospitals couldn't possibly afford to stay on top of the technology. Nor could they afford to recruit the qualified technicians or physicians that we provide.

Now we've added cholesterol screening as part of our service. We go into pharmacies and to companies that want to provide that service for their employees. In the future we will move more into corporate health. Americans are much more health conscious than they used to be, and so are the corporations that hire them. So there is a lot of opportunity in this field. In fact, health care businesses have a much higher success rate than other businesses. It's definitely the wave of the future, and I feel I was at the right place at the right time.

The initial investment in the business was over $150,000, which came out of our own pockets. I went to a bank, but they didn't want to take a risk on a new venture. I could have gone the SBA route but that seems to take forever so, to start, we took on a third partner, someone who was in the health care business and who helped us out a lot because he had a strong business background. We began making a profit after two years and were able to buy him out. Once the business got established, we had no trouble getting loans from the bank. And now, when we need new equipment, we either finance it ourselves or finance it from the bank.

When we started, we worked out of my house and my partner's wife did the bookkeeping, but about a year later, we were accepted by the University of Virginia's Business Innovation Center, here in Charlottesville. It is a program designed to help new business ventures for a three-year time period. They provided me with a small office, access to office equipment such as fax and xerox machines, and, most important, consultations with top businesspeople who are on their advisory board. We can call them with problems or use them as sounding boards to help us with new ideas and directions. This has been invaluable. If I need help, I know where I can go to get it.

I go after business by doing extensive background work on the areas we'd like to go into. Then I put together an individualized sales package based on my research. I have a brochure and all sorts of printed materials to give to potential clients, but the one-on-one selling approach is the one that gets us the client.

I work seven days a week, especially now launching the cholesterol units. My whole drive for doing this is so my kids can have a better life in the future. My children love my being in business. It's made them realize you have to go after things you really want. They see that Mom can do it and it gives them confidence. They're real proud of me. My goal is to work really hard for several years and then enjoy the rest of my life. Then I'll be able to do fun things with my kids and eventually with my grandkids.

Because we sell the latest in technology, I have to keep up with what's happening. I belong to the National Heart Association and I go to all their meetings. I talk to the sales representatives and, of course, the salespeople know me, so they keep me informed on new developments in the field. The technicians I hire and the physicians I subcontract to are all very good, and they also supply me with new and advanced developments.

One thing you never cut corners on is the people who work for you. Pay for a good accountant. A good accountant will help you stay in business. Hire the best employees. Give them benefits. Pay the premiums. You need good people working for you. If you're lucky enough to find someone who is loyal and hardworking, treat them right. Good employees reduce your stress level and make life easier. Support your people because if you don't, you're sunk. They're your business. If you don't have good people, you don't have a good company.

Business is also paying attention to the bottom line. I can get through anything as long as I know what I'm up against. The only way to really have a handle on your business is to know where you stand in the books on a month-by-month basis. It blows my mind that so many small companies don't do monthly financials. I want to know every month where I stand. I want to know what's coming in and what's going out. If you can see you're going to be in a big cash flow bind in a month, you can do a lot of things to compensate for it. You can cut back, work harder, delay buying equipment, adjust, try different routes—whatever. There's a lot you can do about a cash flow problem *if* you see it coming. If you don't, you can go under real quick. Being a good business manager has to do with financial control—and that means knowing what's going on all the time.

Business is ethics, too. I don't have a lot of competition, but I pride myself on our service and the good quality of work. If we can't do it right, I don't want to do it. In every business, mine included, you see dishonest things going on around you. I deal with Medicaid and Medicare, the health department, and a lot of insurance companies. I want to be able to sleep nights. I don't want to end up in jail five years down the road because I screwed up. So you pursue what you want as hard as you can, you're honest, and you don't let anyone get you down.

Most of all, business is common sense. If you've got that, then it's not as hard as you might think to manage a business. I have a high school diploma and that's it. I think it's important for women to know you don't need an M.B.A. to start and run a profitable business. You have to be persistent. You have to find the information you need, but it's out there for anybody to find. You have to know your own strengths and weaknesses. I knew I was good in sales; that's my background. I started with that and then I found the people qualified in their fields with the expertise my business needed. I don't say I'm an expert at echocardiography. I say my company is an expert.

·20·

Food

Cooking is like love—it should be entered into with abandon or not at all. —Harriet Van Horne

Everyone loves food. Food seems to have supplanted baseball and moviegoing as the all-American pastime. Americans are now indulging themselves in foods from the far reaches of the globe and redefining the basics here at home. American chefs are the new celebrities. "Nouvelle" has put regional fare on metropolitan menus. Gourmet is out, specialty is in, and take-out can mean everything from sushi to posole.

It's no wonder that the selling of food and drink is the number one business in the United States. The past ten years have seen a number of women gain superstar status in the culinary heavens. Sheila Lukins and Julia Rosso parlayed specialties sold in their small upper West Side food shop, The Silver Palate, into a multi-million-dollar global wholesale operation. Sophia Collier, of Soho Beverage, created a natural soda and then sold it to Seagrams for $15 million. Chef Alice Walters of Berkeley's Chez Panisse was one of the initiators and preeminent practitioners of the new American cuisine that now has a countrywide following.

The most important factor in starting a food business is to learn about the regulations governing the making and selling of food and drink. The food business is one of the most closely regulated you can enter. Everyone, from restaurateurs to sidewalk vendors, needs some sort of license. To learn what is required you should first contact:

1. The Food and Drug Administration, Office of Consumer Affairs, HFE-88, 5600 Fishers Lane, Rockville, Maryland

20857, (301)443–3170. Explain the business you are entering and ask for pertinent information.
2. Your local health department. They will guide you through city and state licensing and food selling regulations. Be forewarned that unwritten rules and unscheduled inspections are integral to setting up your business.

In addition to health inspections and licensing, food service and food preparation businesses are subject to the fire department's regulations, local zoning codes, and special occupancy agencies. So check and double-check to find out what you can and can't do before you start cooking.

Restaurants

Of all the food businesses, this is probably the most difficult to run at a profit. There are numerous trade books on the market for the beginning restaurateur, and they are filled with markup formulas, percentage margins, equipment information, licensing information, kitchen planning, and food technology. But no book in the world will serve you as well as experience. Most successful restaurateurs have come up through the ranks. Time spent as a waitress, manager, chef, or assistant will give you the invaluable insider's education you will need when organizing your own establishment.

However, the average new restaurateur seems guided mainly by intuition and blind enthusiasm. The psychological pull of restaurant ownership remains one of the overwhelming drawing cards of the business. It's only after the fact, when she finds herself slaving sixteen hours a day, seven days a week, for a self-imposed nominal salary, watching her investment stagger under the weight of unforeseen expenses, that the small restaurateur begins to study up on industry guidelines.

The National Restaurant Association offers these rules of thumb and averages:

Capitalization: never go in undercapitalized. Plan that it will take from two to five years to make a profit. Budget for it.
Location: as in any retail business, go for a high-traffic location. Ideally, try to lease an existing restaurant facility requiring only interior decoration rather than total refurbishing.

311

Size: your profits are directly related to your seating capacity and rate of turnover. To estimate gross sales, multiply number of seats by the average meal-check figure. Multiply this by turnover (number of times you expect each seat to be occupied each day). Then multiply that figure by the number of days that you will be open each year.

Profits: your profit should be 20 percent of your gross sales. Operational costs break down as follows: 33 percent for payroll; 33 percent for food and beverages; 12 to 15 percent for overhead.

Pricing: In low-rent restaurants, the markup standard is four times the price of food costs. In high-rent operations, it is five times the price of food or anything above that the market will bear.

Liquor: food margins are slim between profit and loss, therefore most restaurant owners lean heavily on wine, beer, and/ or full liquor service, for profits. This can mean 20 percent of the gross. The markup for wine starts at double the wholesale price; mixed-drink markup varies but can go as high as 500 percent over the cost of the bottle.

Of course, numbers mean nothing if your establishment doesn't catch on. Customers will probably flock to your door— the first week or month—but the eating public is a notoriously fickle lot. You must always work for new customers. Publicity, restaurant reviews, catering, private parties, giveaway dinners, complimentary wine to newcomers, gimmicks such as summer picnic baskets or a Sunday morning jogger's special, and advertising all are part of the restaurant owner's busy, exhausting day.

Take-out

Trends show that dining out has lost some of its appeal in recent years. "Foodies" are staying home more and more, but their need for good food has fostered another trend: take-out. We're not talking pizza and Chinese exclusively anymore. All restaurants seem to be getting into this $10 billion a year act. Home delivery from exclusive restaurants is a fast-growing part of the business. Restaurateurs consider these sales more profitable than meals eaten in the restaurant because there is less overhead. Take-out has spawned other businesses, which seem to be thriving. A delivery service in Washington, D.C., Take Out Taxi, has its own telephone dispatchers who order through a large range of restaurants. In New York, a best-selling publication called *We Deliver* lists all the restaurants that will send over hot meals.

Catering

Caterers come in all sizes, from those who do parties for hundreds to those who specialize in one dish. It is a labor-intensive business, and you must find people you can rely on to work with you. Catering is not only a food business, it is equally a service business. Most caterers must work on budgeting, hiring service staff, ordering rentals, overseeing installations of decoration, ordering liquor—in short, managing the whole of an event. As with any events business in which there is a climactic moment, the caterer must have a cool head under fire. Murphy's Law should be her motto: whatever can go wrong, you can bet, will go wrong, in the party planning and catering business. Accept it and plan accordingly.

The catering business needn't be seasonal. The June wedding is giving way to year-round accounts handling corporate lunches, for example. In more and more areas, the planning, cooking, and serving of meals, like everything these days, is being left to the experts. Think creatively when you're looking for customers. Corporate dining rooms, institutions, associations, home deliveries, as well as party givers are fertile markets for the caterer.

Catering prices can be based on these formulas:

Mark up the food and drink costs and quote on a per person basis (for example, a cocktail party for one hundred might be quoted at $15 per person, including liquor and hors d'oeuvres).

Charge for time and talent at an hourly rate, adding the cost of food and expenses.

Charge a percentage, usually 20 to 25 percent, of the overall budget for an entire event (including food, liquor, rentals, staffing, and other costs).

Laws vary from state to state as to whether you can prepare food for commercial consumption in your own home facilities or not. Check with the local board of health.

313

Gift Baskets and "Care" Packages

Gift baskets are one of the hottest new business ideas around. In just the past two years gift basket services have blossomed into part-time and full-time businesses. While they are not limited to food exclusively, food and drink often play a big part in the wares of the basket. Making gift baskets means combining an attractive wicker basket, or any other creative container, with goodies usually pertaining to a theme. For example, a Kentucky Derby basket might have country ham and beaten biscuits, a bottle of vintage bourbon, fresh mint in a silver-plated julep cup, a racing cap, and long-stemmed roses. A New Year's Eve basket could feature champagne, caviar, crystal flutes, a feather boa, silver balloons, and bags of confetti.

Gift baskets are limited only by your imagination, the number of baskets you can produce in a day, and the budget of the buyer. They present an ideal home business requiring just a few thousand dollars set-up. Overhead would be an inventory of baskets, decorative accessories, a shrink-wrap machine, a slick brochure or catalog, a telephone, and basic office equipment. Clients for the baskets come from all sources, but women and corporations seem to buy heaviest. Other specialty markets include: college students, campers, and senior citizens.

Care packages, too, make a lucrative business. Parents of children away at camp and in college are avid subscribers to the care package service. Again, care packages aren't always food, but the most popular ones seem to be. A woman in Atlanta bakes birthday cakes for nearby Georgia Tech students. She gets the names and home addresses of the students, writes to the parents including an order form, and, if hired, delivers a cake on the appointed day.

For both these businesses, acquiring a mailing list for a targeted market is essential. Understanding shipping costs and packaging is equally important.

Wholesaling

The dream of wholesaling is to market a product, such as your great-grandma's secret salad dressing, with such success that a big manufacturer and distributor comes begging at your door, check in hand, to make you as rich as Sara Lee.

Producing wholesale foods combines strict food regulations with manufacturing and wholesaling basics (see chapter 22). The product must be prepared under approved conditions, and it must maintain its stability as it goes from manufacturer to wholesaler to shelf to consumer. Research your market; subscribe to trade journals; study what other independent food manufacturers have done.

For further information:

American Woman's Economic Development Corporation (AWED), 60 East Forty-second Street, Suite 405, New York, N.Y. 10165, (212)692–9100. Seminars and workshops offered in specific food businesses, i.e., Advanced Skills in Operating a Food Business, Food Opportunities for a Small Business, and others. Write or call for more information.

National Restaurant Association, 150 North Michigan Avenue, Chicago, Illinois 60611. Write for trade publications on all types and areas of management in the restaurant business. See also: *The Encyclopedia of Associations* (Gale Research) where over 25,000 national and international organizations are listed. Food related associations have to do with import/export, distribution, fancy foods, wine and beverage, health, etc.

How To Turn Your Passion for Food Into Profit, by Elayne J. Keenan and Jeanne A. Voltz (Rawson, Wade).

Profitable Restaurant Management, by Kenneth I. Solomon and Norman Katz (Prentice-Hall).

NICK AND TONI'S

If you want to see celebrities in the Hamptons, try to book a table at Nick and Toni's. With two small dining rooms, a tiny bar and one of the most innovative kitchens outside New York City, this stylish and informal restaurant has become well established in the space of just two short years. The young owners, Toni Ross and Jeff (Nick) Salaway, are husband and wife.

Here's Toni on running a restaurant.

It's strange to say, but good food is really just a small part of what makes a restaurant successful. More than anything you've got to

315

really love the business. The risks are substantial, the hours are awful, and the pace is nerve-wracking, but there is also a wonderful, glamorous mystique to it. And a kind of drama, too. The entire day is spent in frantic preparation and then, every night at six o'clock the lights are dimmed, the candles are lit and when the first customers arrive—it's show time. For the rest of the night that's all you care about. It's an intensely people-oriented business. You have to like people—like meeting them and talking to them.

For most of our customers, I think, there's a kind of anticipation about going out to eat that verges on genuine excitement. Food is an important part of their lives—they really care about it and they have every right to expect that coming here will be a good experience in every way. In any case that's what we expect for them. I hate for anyone to walk out of here disappointed, and for the most part I think our customers sense that we really are trying to do our best, even when we occasionally mess up. In spite of all that, you do have to expect a certain number of people who are difficult. The thing we try very hard to remember is that those few people are going to be difficult no matter where they are. It simply doesn't pay to take it personally when a customer gives you a hard time.

Jeff and I met in Europe. He was a sculptor and I was a painter. We both enjoyed eating and cooking and I must say we did a lot of both in the course of an absolutely idyllic year in Italy. But when we got back to New York, we knew that being fine artists wasn't going to support us. At that time a New York restaurant called Jams was helping to define what's come to be known as the "new American cooking" and it was an extremely popular place. Jeff started there as a waiter and quickly became the manager. I was interested in knowing more about *pâtisserie* and Jams had an opening for an assistant pastry chef. We made pastries for Jams and for two other restaurants as well. I can tell you it was a very intensive kind of education. Anyone who wants to start a restaurant should work in one first.

When Jeff and I decided we wanted to open our own restaurant, the choice of the town was easy. East Hampton is a summer resort for New Yorkers. I suppose that means it's more sophisticated and the crowds more demanding than they might be in other places. I had been coming here on weekends for years to visit my family and it always seemed very comfortable to me, so we never gave much thought to anywhere else. As for the specific location, when you're looking for restaurant space it's always best if possible to start with a building that has already been used as a restaurant. That way at the very least you can expect that there will be some kind of professional kitchen, and perhaps some rudimentary parking facilities. This place qualified in those two regards, I suppose, but just barely. Though it had been built as a private residence, it had been converted into a restaurant of sorts about twenty years ago—a Mom and Pop pizza place called Ma Bergman's. Ma's pizza was fabulous, but the physical place wasn't exactly what I'd originally had in mind. It was out on the edge of town, away from East Hampton's beautiful Main Street business district (so any chance of a lunch trade would be doomed in advance) and it shared a block with a supermarket, a dry cleaners, and a family-style Italian restaurant.

I must admit I had my doubts, but we went ahead and bought the building, gutted it, and then really got to work. I designed the interior of the restaurant, working about the building's idiosyncrasies, which were plentiful. I tried to keep it clean and light and spare, not only to make the place attractive and comfortable for our customers, but for Jeff and me and the staff as well. After all, we spend more time here than we do at home. So we took some of the paintings and sculpture from our house—the pieces we loved best, in fact, and put them in the restaurant. That included a pair of stone dogs, which now flank the archway between the two dining rooms. Our customers love the "Nick and Toni dogs" and they have become a part of our logo and part of our image generally. We even dress them up for the holidays and work them into all of the graphics in our mailings.

The restaurant business is highly regulated almost everywhere, and East Hampton is no exception. The town had to approve almost everything: where the bathrooms were going, the exterior design, where the refrigerator was placed, the location of the ice machine. Every aspect of the design, in fact, had to be approved in advance, and then inspectors came to ensure that we had complied with the design. The health inspector comes too, once a month and always unannounced. The first time she came, we had just received a huge delivery of fresh produce, which was sitting in crates waiting to be unpacked. I was on the floor next to the crates with a razor blade and ammonia scraping up old paint off the floor and suddenly a pair of feet I didn't know were standing next to me. I looked up and she said, "Hi, I'm the health inspector."

Then there were other problems: construction delays, equipment delays, personnel delays—it was virtually impossible to know with any kind of accuracy when we'd be able to open. At some point in the summer we sent out a postcard to everyone we knew. It was a picture of Jeff behind a beautifully laid table in the midst of all this horrible construction debris. On the back was a photo of me with the caption, "Jeff says we'll be opening any day now."

By the time we finally did open, it was the middle of August, the height of the season. We had two practice runs—one for all the people who had worked for us getting the place ready, and one for our family and friends. Our first night open to the public we were almost too exhausted to be nervous. We just opened the doors without any fanfare (not even so much as a press release for the local paper), and, to our surprise, in walked fifty people. To make matters worse, the first one in the door was none other than Craig Claiborne, the well-known writer and food critic for the *New York Times*. I thought, oh my god, we're sunk.

As things turned out there were no major disasters that night and we weren't sunk at all. In fact, a tremendous amount of press attention followed. We were reviewed well in the *New York Times*, as well as in the local papers and magazines, and that just about eliminated the need for advertising the first year. When a popular reviewer says "this is my favorite place . . ." as one did about us, it can bring in more customers than any ad campaign you could dream up. We seat fifty-two and that's a very manageable size. But in the summer we now average 150 dinners a night, seven nights a week (and Sunday brunch, too). Frankly, we couldn't handle much more than that, and we're still new, so reviewers are still coming to check us out.

Nevertheless, we do know that at some point, like any restaurant that's going to last, we're going to need to go after publicity more aggressively to keep our year-round business up. And, of course, out here everyone has to work hard for off-season business. We run ads in the local papers, we publish our holiday menus, and we've started doing more special events here like weddings and private parties. We also do gift baskets at Christmas filled with our own pastas and breads, condiments and sauces.

There's no question that there is a very high rate of failure in the restaurant business. There are probably a hundred reasons for that, but the most common one, I think, is that people tend to vastly underestimate how much money it takes to start up and run a restaurant. Most people come into the business undercapitalized and you simply can't do that. If anything you need to be *over*capitalized. It's probably going to take two or three years to show a profit and you must have the resources to give the business at least that much time. Payroll, for instance, is a major expense that's pathetically easy to underestimate, especially in a seasonal area. And then there are always the unforeseen equipment breakdowns. We thought we could save money in the kitchen by buying some of the equipment used—the dough mixer, espresso machine, refrigeration. But too late, we found out that when older machines break down, parts are often unavailable. We ended up buying almost everything all over again—new this time. You can say to yourself over and over again (as we did) that you're ready for the unexpected, but inevitably you're not.

I must say that working with someone you live with isn't always easy. We're here together all day and evening, too, and then we go home together. The only possible solution is to keep the division of labor as strict as possible. Jeff manages the floor, the staff, and all day-to-day business. I handle all special events (i.e., private parties), all aspects of design (from menus to interiors), and all matters relating to promotion and publicity. I also am the hostess, greeting people and seating them.

Needless to say, our chef, Gail Arnold, is a crucial part of the restaurant. She and her staff do all the cooking but she and Jeff create the menus together. We serve primarily Italian/Mediterranean food (though not exclusively), trying always to be innovative. All our pastas, breads, and pastries are made on the premises.

As for the rest of the staff, we brought out a few excellent people from the restaurant in New York. They form the core of the year-round staff, and in season we take on extra help—usually college students. We look for people, not too young, with at least a bit of experience, and some intelligence. We expect them to take an interest in the food so they can talk about it knowledge-ably with the customers. We are completely computerized, which not only makes things more efficient but allows us to control our inventory and to ensure that the customer's check accurately reflects what he or she has been served.

In general, the more organized we've become, the fewer people we need. For most of the first year, Jeff and I worked from ten in the morning until one in the morning. Now, with things running more smoothly we have more free time to focus on future plans for the restaurant—perhaps even opening up a new place.

PASTA BY VALENTE

Americans seem to crave pasta. In the eighties the nation consumed upwards of four billion pounds of this basic Italian staple, and there is no end in sight.

For Fran Valente and her daughter Mary Ann, this is good news indeed. In their well-organized, crowded two-room manufacturing plant in Charlottesville, Virginia, they've been making pasta for eight years. Two huge industrial pasta-making machines dominate the space. Packages of rainbow-colored pasta—carrot, tomato-basil, spinach, beet, tomato, red pepper, garlic-parsley, and lemon—hang drying on wooden racks waiting to be packaged in one-pound bags. Distributors deliver to independent grocers and restaurants in three states. And the business keeps growing.

Making pasta was a hobby of mine. My family loved it and so did our friends. One Saturday morning back in 1982, I took a batch down to the farmer's market to see if there might be a market for the product. I did that for about six weeks and found the same people were coming back for it again and again, along with new customers each weekend. I decided there was a market out there.

I converted my sewing room and my husband's office in the basement into a kitchen. And then I bought my first commercial pasta machine. At that point I actively went out and started soliciting business from local grocers and restaurants.

My husband did the initial financing of the business. And he has lent a tremendous amount of moral support and elbow grease, too. For instance, he built our first drying boxes. It's

320

important for a woman going into business to have her husband and family behind her. Otherwise, it's not going to work. A new business takes an enormous amount of your time. It can hurt a marriage if the support isn't there. Make sure your husband is very understanding unless you want to get rid of him. If you want a divorce, then starting a business is a good way to get it.

I called the Department of Agriculture to find out what rules and regulations I had to follow. They came and looked my place over and told me what changes I would have to make to pass inspection. I think so many problems are created when people don't understand what has to be done legally. You can get into a lot of trouble if you don't find out ahead of time.

In the beginning, Mary Ann and I did all the sales promotion for the business. We sold locally and to independent grocers in the region, expanding as they expanded. One of the independent grocers I worked with in the Tidewater area expanded from three stores to ten. Then we got three of the local Safeway stores to stock our product. But they did a reorganization and bumped out all the independent entrepreneurs. They told us they would only buy through a distributor. It was very upsetting to us but we finally got them to give us the names of two distributors. It was a blessing in disguise. The distributor we went with takes our product all over Maryland as well as Virginia and has picked up new accounts for us as well.

We look for expansion all the time. The Maryland distributor is taking us into Pennsylvania and we're getting ready for that. The trick in expansion is you've got to be in a position where you can handle the increase in business. If you're not in that position it can ruin everything.

In 1987 the business got too big for the house. We needed industrial equipment instead of commercial equipment. There are distinct differences. The commercial machines are fine for restaurants or small retail stores. But if you want to put out great quantities you need something more powerful. I had a lead on some used machines, but to buy used equipment you need immediate cash. It also means you have to go pick it up. So I called Toresani, Inc. in New York, the same company that had made the used equipment, and we bought new from them. As far as I'm concerned it's the Cadillac of pasta equipment.

We do three kinds of flat pasta: fettucine, linguine, and tagliarini, and we also do angel hair, very fine pasta. We don't do spaghetti, because in order to do that you have to pass it through a round die, and the flavor is not as good as when you roll it flat. We make about two thousand pounds of pasta a week. When I started I probably did a hundred pounds.

We don't place ads. It's all promotion. We go into stores and do tastings. We go to trade shows, and we go to wine festivals and do the same thing. I designed our first label myself. Later we hired a woman designer to elaborate on the original logo and add color.

My advice for women who think they want to start a business is, you really have to decide if you want to put in the effort it's going to require. You have to be extremely self-motivated. And you have to have common sense. Be practical. Don't hold on to a lot of dreams about how much fun it's going to be. You will enjoy your work, but you're not going to have a lot of fun. It's 5 percent creative and 95 percent hard work. Running a business is definitely not for someone who's looking for a little something to fill their time. We now have the business to a point where we don't have to work weekends unless it's an emergency. For years there were nights when we would be working until midnight, go to bed, and then be back to it around seven in the morning. I don't think we could have done it if we hadn't had each other.

When we walk in that door we stop being mother and daughter and we're Fran and Mary Ann. Mary Ann runs production. She's developed all the recipes. She tells me what to do—puree carrots, clean equipment, whatever needs doing. I'm the president of the corporation. I manage the business. We're equals with different divisions of labor.

What I enjoy most about my work is the fact that the business keeps changing. It took us four years to make a profit and then we turned around and invested in new equipment, which put us behind the eight ball again. But you can't stand still. You have to keep growing and changing. We keep adding new pastas to the product line, and now we're beginning to make marinara sauce. We developed a recipe and took it to a cannery. They tested it and sent it back to us. When we thought it was right we gave it our approval. It's our recipe but their machinery and bottling process. We, of course, will do all the distribution.

A new business will take an amazing amount of time if you're serious about making money out of it. First you have to make it go, then after you do all of that, you hope you can start making money. You have to juggle your time constantly. In the beginning I did all the accounting, did the ledger and the payroll. My husband did the tax returns. But it got to be too much and we hired an accountant. The problem is when you try to do it all you spread yourself too thin. I was falling behind on my forms, and it costs money in penalties to fall behind. So you end up spinning your wheels. You get to a point where you say "I can't take all this pressure" and then you try to find areas to relieve yourself of it. And the ones you can get rid of easily, you do that.

Also, you have to look at your personal life and weigh whether a business and its demands will suit you. If you have small children, you have to realize that you can't just put the business on hold to take care of them. And you can't put the children on hold while you take care of the business. There are days when an employee doesn't show up and you have to be ready to do their job as well as your own, whether it's scrubbing the floor or taking out trash or packing crates. If your driver doesn't show up, you have to drive the truck to make the deliveries on time.

No one can run this company better than Mary Ann or me. It's a pipe dream to think you're going to be able to hire people to manage your business. The company is you. No one knows more about it than you do. It would be very difficult for us to bring in an outsider and have that person project the image and values and standards we've created. Last year I took my first vacation since I started the business. I went to Europe for three weeks and had a lovely time. But I couldn't have done it unless I knew Mary Ann was here running the business. I'm fortunate in my daughter and my partner.

THE BAREFOOT CONTESSA

Ina Garten is the brains and energy behind this elegant food emporium located in what was the old post office in East Hampton, New York. Her store, a feast of sights and smells, combines the aura of an old-world marketplace with the excitement of today's food and design.

The Barefoot Contessa specializes in prepared foods as well as quality produce, fresh herbs, exotic ice creams,

> **fresh-baked breads and pastries, imported goods, cheese, cured meats, and smoked fish. In the summer the grill is fired up, and barbecued ribs and chicken join the fare.**

Shopping for food should be fun. So often you buy something and when you get home, you don't remember the experience. I think shopping should be an experience. I find people come into my store just because they want to see what we're doing.

I worked in Washington, D.C., in the government, and I was bored out of my mind. For amusement I entertained and cooked. I began to think that maybe I should be doing more about what I enjoyed. It was 1978, and specialty food businesses were at the beginning of their popularity. One day I was reading the "business opportunities" section of the *New York Times* and there was an ad for a specialty food shop in Westhampton, on Long Island. I decided I wanted to take a look at it, so my husband and I drove from Washington in the middle of winter to a town I had never been to before, which was dead empty in the off season. There, on Main Street, was this little store, four hundred square feet, with one cook who did all the cooking and two people who worked behind the counter. I just loved it. I made the owner an offer on the business, a low offer, thinking she would come back with another price and we'd negotiate it, and in that time I'd be able to think about what I was getting into. The next day she called and accepted my offer. And I thought, Oh my god! What nightmare have I started?

In retrospect, I think buying an existing business is the best way for someone who has no business background to get into business, because you've got a machine that's already moving and you simply become a part of it. The hardest thing about starting a business is knowing whether your idea will translate— whether people will want it. Especially if you're starting with no background, you can set up a great store in the wrong location; or you can set up the wrong idea in a great location. There are so many variables in business, and it's very hard to know what works. So to buy an ongoing business with potential seems to me a safer way to get started.

I was able to finance part of the original purchase of the business with personal funds. The rest was seller financed. It's impossible to interest a bank, unless you have enormous collateral, to finance a business just starting up, so I didn't even try. Later,

324

when I expanded the business, I had a proven track record and I was able to negotiate a loan with the bank.

Essentially I bought a business that had been going for a year, that had trained the chef, proven recipes, suppliers, equipment, a good reputation, and a clientele. Most important, the business was making a profit.

At the time, it was an extraordinary store. But it was very simple. It sold six salads, smoked salmon, and a selection of unusual cheeses. Part of my deal with the owner was that she stay one month to train me in the business. I didn't know about imported cheeses, I had no idea how to tell whether a brie was ripe, I certainly didn't know how to slice smoked salmon, and I had never had employees working under me. But I found out that once you've learned the details, you get a handle on it quickly. She was a good teacher. She knew when to step in and when to let me figure things out.

At first I ran it exactly the way she had run it—the same recipes, the same systems—but I knew right away there were things I wanted to change. For example, to save money she drove herself to her supplier and carted everything back in her station wagon. The supplier was two hours away. So she would be on the road at three in the morning to the supplier, return to the shop, and work until midnight that night. She was putting in a twenty-hour day. I knew there had to be a better way. I found new suppliers, and though I paid more to have it delivered I figured I couldn't afford not to.

It just takes the slightest amount of digging to find reliable distributors. When I see a product I like, I pick up the phone and call them and find out who distributes for them. Usually it's a specialty food supplier with 150 other items in their catalog. It's pretty easy.

I stayed in that space for three years, but I was unhappy renting and wanted to look for a space that was mine. The ideal space came on the market across the street but it was quite a bit bigger—four thousand square feet. So I bought the building and retained half the space for myself, renting the rest of the two thousand square feet to other specialty food vendors. It became a big open market of my prepared foods and their cookies, homemade pastas, ice cream, breads, and a lot of other specialties.

New products and new displays are the most stimulating aspect of the business for me. The word *accessible* is critical to me in merchandising food. Food should be displayed so that it is very easy to get to. After all, we're not talking about museum pieces. If a product isn't selling I study it. The price may be right, the quality right. I might then try it in a new space or light it differently, or put it next to another, complementary product, or offer samples, and pretty soon it'll walk off the shelf. I like figuring out how I can get more people interested in a product. I remember when blue corn chips first came on the market. People said, "Blue food! Who's going to eat that!" But I thought they were great, so I bought sixteen cases and made a huge pile of the bags, with a bowl of samples and salsa next to the display. They were gone instantly.

I look at the successful displays in the store and decide what it was that made the product sell—was it lighting, was it the size of the display, the colors, the location? I watch the details. One time the chef came out of the kitchen with a pot of pasta sauce and set it on the front counter while he cleared space behind the case where we usually kept the sauce. In that short time two quarts of the sauce sold. So I moved the sauce to that new space permanently.

Listen to your customers. I'm in the store talking to my customers all the time. I ask them what they came in to buy, and I find out what they ended up buying. I tell people if they can't find something to let me know. It may be a product a lot of people want and I don't know about it. One time a man came into the store and asked for a snack, something like breadsticks, he could take back to his office. I thought breadsticks alone weren't very exciting, so I put together a package of about eight different snacks—pretzels, cheese straws, breadsticks, flatbreads and so on—and put them right next to the register. It's now one of the hottest-selling items in the store. We can't bag them fast enough in the summer. You get ideas from everywhere. And if you can get everyone who comes into your store to buy one more thing, to spend a few more dollars, that can add up to a huge amount of business.

The hardest part of running this business is getting good people. I'm balancing a service business with the selling of a product. How the customer feels about the product has a lot to do with how they feel about the people who sold it to them. The key thing I look for in hiring is happy people. You can always teach someone about cheese and baked goods, but you can't teach someone to be happy. I choose people I'd want to have dinner with. I hired one person over the phone. I had never set eyes on her before, but I enjoyed talking to her so much and liked hearing what her activities were that I found myself asking her to come work with us.

I train all the people who work here in every aspect of the food we sell so that they can work every post. Each person has their specialty, but I don't want a customer coming in for cheese and then wanting smoked salmon and being sent to someone else who may or may not be busy. Again, we're selling a service just as much as we're selling a product.

I work closely with the kitchen staff. Basically we have a core of recipes and then, when I have a new idea, I talk it over with the chef and he develops it. We do all our own cooking on the premises, which gives us control over quality and flavor. So many prepared foods look good but don't have much taste.

I opened another store in East Hampton because the space was great and I couldn't turn it down. For a while I ran the two stores and had over a hundred employees. It was a nightmare. The two towns are forty-five minutes from each other on a good day. In the summer, forget it. You can be on the highway for two hours. One day I was in my car trying to get from one location to the other and I realized I couldn't do this anymore. I was cutting the quality of both stores by spreading myself so thin. Some of the summer employees didn't even know who I was! So I decided to concentrate on East Hampton and sold the Westhampton business.

I like the size of the store as it is now. I hire about forty people for the summer season and fifteen in the winter. I like retail. I like East Hampton. I've had a lot of requests to do stores in other locations or to get involved in other new ventures, but I've walked away from all of them because I like what I do here.

My best promotion for the store is my location. Don't ever spend less for location. It doesn't matter what it costs as long as it's the best. In the end, I make it up every day by the additional number of people who just happen in to buy something as incidental as a brownie. I don't advertise beyond publishing my holiday menus in the local papers. But I spend money on my shopping bags. Rather than try to get someone in the next town out of their bed, into their car, to drive to The Barefoot Contessa, I try to get everyone who is on the street into my store. It's easier.

You could spend thousands of dollars for radio advertising and you don't know how effective it is. But when you walk around this town in the summer and everyone has big bags with "The Barefoot Contessa" across them, it sends a powerful message.

The Barefoot Contessa is named for the film, and I think it's a perfect name for the business. It's both elegant and earthy, which is exactly what this store is all about. Barefoot for the beach in one of the most elegant resorts in the world.

HOUSE ON THE QUARRY BED AND BREAKFAST

Pat Richards runs her bed and breakfast in Saugerties, New York. The house is situated beside the late sculptor Harvey Fite's environmental outdoor sculpture *Opus 40*, which adds an extra attraction for the guests. But, like all bed and breakfasts, location is the main thing, and because the house is near the tourist mecca of Woodstock and the skiing area of Hunter Mountain, Richards has a thriving year-round business.

My mother-in-law started the business in the mid-eighties by opening up several rooms to friends and friends of friends. But she kept it low-key and didn't want total strangers staying in her house. When she passed away in 1987 we inherited the house and moved in with my son. After a while, I decided to continue with the bed and breakfast—people were calling occasionally for rooms—but decided to turn it into a more ongoing business.

I rent out two double bedrooms (with baths) for $75 per night, plus tax, and charge the same rates year-round, regardless of whether it's a weekday or weekend. I serve a full breakfast, as opposed to a Continental breakfast. When the guests come into the dining room for breakfast I have fruit, juice, muffins or croissants, and coffee or tea ready for them. While they eat that, I cook the rest of the breakfast, which is an omelet, waffles, or french toast. Everyone seems to praise this menu, so I don't bother with varying it. I don't give them a choice. I serve what I want, but I always tell them beforehand. Occasionally someone will say they don't want broccoli in their omelet, or will suddenly remember to mention that they are allergic to milk, but most people have no problem with the menu. A lot of bed-and-breakfast people put menus in the guests' rooms, with a check-off list of choices, but I think that's too much like a hotel or hospital. And I've never had anyone not eat what I serve. I also give them all they want to eat. If they want a second omelet, or to share a second waffle, fine with me.

There is no kitchen health inspection required for bed and breakfasts. But if you rent out more than five rooms, then you are legally considered an inn, at least in New York State, and then the inspectors come and you have to follow all of their guidelines.

I'm very flexible when it comes to the guests. They can come and go as they please. Some bed and breakfasts establish a nightly curfew or insist that the guests eat by eight A.M. and depart by ten. I always ask them what time they would like breakfast, but if they oversleep, it's okay. And I've found that 90 percent of them want breakfast at nine o'clock. Older people tend to want to eat around seven-thirty or eight. One couple had breakfast at noon, but they were on their honeymoon.

During the day most people don't hang around. They are off sight-seeing or skiing. But if it rains and they suddenly show up, I offer them coffee or tea and cookies, and they are always grateful. By law, I cannot serve alcoholic beverages. But I'm willing to provide ice and glasses if they want to bring in a bottle of wine to sip by the fire.

Checkout time is also flexible. My published time is two o'clock, but there's never a problem. Most people are here to visit the area, not stay here. Generally they are packed up and gone by eleven.

When people make their reservations they never remember to mention any allergies. I tell them we have two dogs and a cat, but the animals are never allowed in the guestrooms, and seldom in the living room. I do not allow smoking in the bedrooms, and I find that generally they won't smoke anywhere else either. Occasionally you have the ardent smoker who does smoke in the bedroom or wants to smoke at the table. If there are other guests, I always check with them first. It's mostly the older people who have been smoking for years who resent all the new restrictions that have been imposed on smokers. But 95 percent of the guests are agreeable because they know they are staying in a home. A few treat it as a hotel, and every so often someone will call at one in the morning for a last-minute reservation.

As far as running your home as a business, for the most part it's not restrictive. In the beginning I was nervous about inviting friends over for dinner when we had guests, but now I've relaxed. As long as we're quiet and not disturbing their peace they don't mind. Guests who come to a bed and breakfast are aware that they are staying in a home and not an inn. And if they aren't, they should be.

My son doesn't resent having strangers in the house, but I've sort of paid him off. I give him 10 percent when the room next to his is occupied and he's forced to be quiet. I also bought him earphones for his television and his stereo, so he doesn't disturb the guests. The only other inconvenience to our lives is that when we have guests we have to keep the watchdog tied up if we want to go out.

I try to be helpful to the guests. We have printed material on things to do in the area, and I suggest restaurants or—if we're booked—other bed and breakfasts. I buy small bars of soap for the showers, and change them after each guest. The board of health recommends that you use liquid soap at the sinks, which I do. I change the towels every day, even if the same guests are keeping the room for two nights. I'm not stingy with towels. I give each person two sets of towels per day, especially in the summer when it's hot.

Many bed and breakfasts in this area require a two-night stay, but I don't, except for holiday weekends. But most people come for two nights anyway, and we've had people stay for a week on many occasions, especially families with children. Some bed and breakfasts don't allow children, but when you're opening up your house you can establish your own rules.

I belong to the National Bed and Breakfast Association, and pay yearly dues to be listed with them. They provide an official plaque, which I keep by the front door. I am also a member of the Ulster County Traditional Bed and Breakfast Association, and pay dues. Traditional, by the way, means a full breakfast, not toast and coffee. This association runs joint ads with the Hudson Valley Maritime Museum. We are trying to set up inspections of the bed and breakfasts that are members, because if you're full and want to recommend someone else, you want to make sure you know what you're recommending. There are some people running bed and breakfasts who should not be running them.

The houses aren't clean. They don't serve full breakfasts. Sometimes their plumbing doesn't even work.

I also belong to the Woodstock Chamber of Commerce. They charge $75 annual dues, and $150 for an ad in their guide, but it's worth it. I also advertise in the *Hudson Valley Guide,* which is $50 quarterly and is handed out free. I advertise in *Ulster Magazine,* which is also given away to tourists, and I belong to the Ulster County Chamber of Commerce. I also advertise in a local alternative Yellow Pages, and that's brought in a lot of business and is so much cheaper than the regular Yellow Pages.

As far as expenses, other than soap, food, and advertising, I have a young woman who comes in and cleans the house and guest rooms one day a week, and more often if we're really busy. But I change the sheets after the guests leave, and I change and launder the towels myself.

As for printed information, besides the ads, I have business cards, a rate card with the checkout time, and House on the Quarry stationery. I have a resale tax number. For insurance, I carry all the regular insurance on my house, and liability umbrella in case someone should trip on a rug or slip on a step. Insurance can be high, depending on where you live and who insures you. We pay about $1,300 per year but I know people who pay lots more.

When people call to book reservations I require a check for one full night in advance. If they don't show up they do not get a refund. If they call to cancel at least two weeks in advance and I can fill the room, I will give a full refund. If it's an off time and I can't rebook the room, then I will refund half of their deposit. When guests call you must find out what time they will be arriving. If not, you can sit around all day waiting.

Over the years I've had only two bounced checks, and in both cases when I've called them they've apologized and sent a new check and covered the bank's service fee. We've had no theft from the house itself, but once a couple found my checkbook and forged a check for $1,500. I went to the bank and then to the police, and after several weeks we got the money back. I didn't press charges. As for no-shows, we have very few.

As I said, most people know that bed and breakfasts are homey affairs and treat you as a host. We've met a lot of interesting and congenial people who much prefer the coziness to a hotel.

Carol Thayer, known to her customers as The Sandwich Lady, offers a traveling lunch counter to the greater Washington, D.C., area.

She started as a one-woman operation in 1985, offering fresh sandwiches, homemade soups, salads, and brownies on a daily basis to people who did not want to leave their offices for lunch or wait for a phoned-in delivery. Today, as president of a thriving enterprise, she and her partner, Mya Marcus, employ seventeen Sandwich Ladies and Men, a head cook, and two sandwich makers. Their trademark red aprons and baskets of goodies travel mapped-out routes to office complexes in the Maryland and Virginia suburbs of Washington. In 1989, she grossed over $400,000.

Before I started The Sandwich Lady, I had inherited some money and I sank $125,000 into a hot tub retail store. I lost the money in that business venture but I learned a lot of things about myself. Most of all, I learned you shouldn't be in a business if you're not crazy about the product. It made me feel bad to ask someone to pay $5,000 for something as frivolous and silly as a hot tub.

After four years I got out. I found myself unemployed, divorced, with two teenage children to support. I didn't know what to do next, but since I loved to cook I thought, "Gee, I wish I could make money doing this." I didn't know anything about the preparing and selling of commercial food, but I knew how to cook and I thought I knew what people wanted to eat.

At first I tried to sell sandwiches as a street vendor, but after one day I had made ten dollars and had forty submarine sandwiches left over. It dawned on me that people on the street were on their way somewhere and didn't need lunch, but people back in the office, too busy to go out, did. The next day, I went into a complex of medical buildings, went from office to office and asked, "How would you like for me to come by every day with homemade sandwiches for lunch?" To my amazement, they all thought it was a great idea. So that got me off and running.

At first I did everything myself. I made the sales calls, shopped, made the sandwiches, sold them, kept the books, and ran everything from my kitchen at home. My day started at 3:00 A.M. and didn't end until after 9:00 P.M. The only time I had to talk to my kids was when we were all making sandwiches. As for a social life—forget it.

I started hiring Sandwich Ladies to travel the routes with the lunch baskets, but I was desperate to get out of my house. I needed a proper space where I could really begin to develop the concept. I called a caterer in the area and asked if I could rent space in his kitchen. He was wonderful. He only charged me $100 a week. Then, a year later I came across a commercial kitchen of a failed pizza maker. He was behind in the rent and needed cash quickly, so I rented his space and bought all his equipment. Only I didn't have the money either, so I took on a partner because I needed to expand and I needed the money. Mya worked for me and I knew she was great, and I knew what she could do for the business. Still and all it was difficult to share "my baby." It has nothing to do with Mya, but if I'd had the choice I would have gone into business better capitalized.

The partnership works well because we have different areas of expertise. Mya is great with details. She picks up the ball and runs with it. I'm the dreamer—the idea person with the big picture of where the company is going.

The way my business works is first I target buildings that don't have a food service in-house. We don't go into buildings if there is a deli that is servicing the building. But we go in if there is a fancy restaurant or only vending machines. We go from office to office, usually asking to speak to the office manager. I introduce myself and explain the service we offer. I tell them, we'll come every single day with a variety of wonderful freshly made foods. The advantage to the customer is that they don't have to order before hand and wait for it, they don't have to buy, there is no obligation, no contract. As long as they're happy, and we make some sales, they can count on us to be there every day. People liked that approach. We never send a Sandwich Lady or Man anywhere that hasn't been presold. I look for complexes of office buildings, because you have to get enough volume so that the Sandwich people can make money. You want to pack in as much business as you can in a small area, and it usually takes anywhere from a week to two weeks to get the route set up and a salesperson assigned to it.

Our people can sell food only between 10 A.M. and 1 P.M. After that, people get too hungry and go off and eat elsewhere. We estimate about ten minutes per office and we prearrange where we will sell the food and how we're going to be announced. Most offices these days have a kitchen area, so that's where we set up the baskets and usually it's the receptionist who announces we're there. We arrive rain or shine, heat or snow. In fact, bad weather is great for business. We vary our menu often but always offer a selection of regular and submarine sandwiches, salads, frozen soups, and pasta main dishes. Almost all offices have a microwave oven. We also sell potato chips and soft drinks and brownies.

I pay my salespeople on commission. Each receives a small car allowance and a percentage of the daily gross—20 percent of the first $100, 25 percent of the next $50, and 30 percent of anything over $150. The average worker makes about $90 a day for four hours of work. I employ retired people, writers, actors, students, and housewives. Employee turnover is high, which is one of the hassles of this kind of business. I would say it's the most difficult problem to solve—it's a part-time job and people go in and out of part-time work.

By now, of course, we're good at estimating the number of meals to send out on each route, but in the beginning it was pure guesswork. Unsold food is donated to a shelter for homeless people. We figure 10 percent of the people per office will buy. At first it will be 20 percent, because it's new and everybody wants to try it out, but then the novelty wears off.

All the food is packed in coolers. We keep the coolers stacked up in the walk-in freezer so that they start out very cold. Everything is packed in sealed bags or containers and then ice. We keep thermometers in each cooler so that the salespeople can make sure the temperature stays cold. On hot days, each Sandwich Lady or Man knows they have to stop somewhere on their route for more ice, so this is built into the delivery schedule. When they get to a stop, they load a selection of foods into smaller carrying baskets or rolling carts.

So far, we've never had a complaint about the freshness of the food, and we're doing fine about health department regulations. Unless you have a problem, they come only twice a year and inspect the central kitchen. But regulations and inspections vary from state to state, so you have to be very in tune to your area. In Maryland, the health department requires that food business owners take a sanitation course to learn how to handle food, and both my head cook and I have taken the course. A big part of our training program for our sales force is teaching them how to handle the food.

Each Sandwich Lady and Man is checked out on a sheet and checked in at the end of the day so we can tally the commissions. But we rely on them to tell us what sells quickly and what sells last, so we can alter the menus. They know their routes best.

It took me almost three years to start making a profit in sandwiches. The only way to make money in this business is by volume. Start-up costs are directly related to the number of things you can sell a day. There are women who do this on their own. But they work harder than you might think, cooking, baking, making sandwiches, and then delivering them—and all for about $150 profit a week. So you won't make money doing this alone or on a small scale. You have to get the routes up. For a volume business you will need a central kitchen and all the equipment it takes—freezers, coolers, and packaging materials. You will need a cook and however many helpers it takes to prepare the food for the volume you're selling and get it ready for the salespeople. And, of course, you need money to live on while you're building the business.

Last year we were featured in *Family Circle* magazine because the wife of a man on my route was a free-lance writer. It was great. I could never buy that kind of advertising. Now, when we make sales calls that article is invaluable in selling our service. So many people wrote me or called, interested in starting a similar business, that I finally wrote a manual, which I sell for $40.* I even looked into franchising, but I don't think that is the route for me. I don't want the complication.

I want to keep the company local. I want to develop the routes so that it's making a million on this side of the Potomac, and then develop Virginia so that it's making a million over there, and develop what I can in the catering business until I have a $3 million or $4 million business. That sounds good to me. If someone wants to hire me as a consultant, I'll do that for a fee, but no strings attached. I don't want the hassles of thinking big. I don't want that craziness in my life. I've got it going and it's working, but I don't want it to get out of hand. The whole thing about growth is maintaining control. If you can't do that, or afford the sophisticated systems with which you keep control,

*Write Carol Thayer, The Sandwich Lady, 4980 D. Wyaconda Road, Rockville, Maryland 20852.

then I can't see doing it. Someday I'll sell the business and move on.

I think one of the most important things people who want to get into business should know is that there's a whole lot more to it than a good idea. The government likes to say that small business is the backbone of this country, but they seem to make it more and more difficult to stay in business. Regulations, insurance requirements, corporate taxes, licensing—all of these things keep you swamped. I have a bookkeeper who does monthly accounting and, of course, an accountant who prepares my taxes and advises me, but I do the payroll and the bills. I think it's very important for the owner of a company to have her finger on the company. It's your money, and it shouldn't be left for other people to manage.

But even with the paperwork, I love being in business. I love being my own boss. There's nothing like it. It can mean plenty of sleepless nights, but there's freedom to make your own decisions, to test who you are, how much pluck you have, how much honesty and integrity you have. If I can't offer somebody an honest product for a fair price, it's not worth it.

You've got to believe in what you're doing and then you've got to stick to it. There are times when you say, "Please just let me die right now in this bed, let the world go away, I don't want to do this anymore." But you get yourself out of bed and you concentrate on what you're trying to achieve, and if you really believe it will work, it will.

It's hard work but it's fun. I say to people who work for me, I want to make some money and I want you to make some money, but let's have fun too. Life is too short not to.

·21·

Direct-Mail Marketing

*Business has only two basic functions—marketing and
innovation.* —Peter Drucker

The mail-order industry is booming. Last year 88 million Americans shopped by catalog, buying everything from aged steaks, ripe fruit, Christmas trees, toys, and computer supplies to ancient icons, paintings by leading artists, jewelry, pet supplies, outerwear, evening wear, and underwear—in short, virtually everything you can buy in stores, and some things you can't. This phenomenal growth has prompted the Direct Marketing Association (DMA) to label our times "the catalog age." The reason? They cite the increase in two-career families, less time available to shop, the convenience of being able to see an enormous array of products from the comfort of home, the prevalence of uninformed salespeople in retail stores, and the availability of credit cards and 800 numbers. They estimate 12.4 billion catalogs were mailed last year.

All that growth and opportunity entices unknown numbers of new as well as established businesses to plunge into the mail-order field each year.

The queen of mail order is Lillian Vernon, who practically invented the specialty mail-order business in 1951. As a young housewife, she invested $2,000 of her wedding money in a supply of shoulder bags and belts, which she would personalize for her customers, said the $500 ad in *Seventeen* magazine, for free. That ad drew $32,000 worth of orders and so began a business that last year grossed $126 million in sales. Lillian Vernon Katz is the only woman founder and CEO of a corporation listed on the American Stock Exchange.

Donna Jeanloz, cofounder of The Renovator's Supply Company, is another mail-order success. The company is the premier mail-order supplier of home renovation artifacts and supplies. Over the course of renovating two old farmhouses Donna and her husband, Claude Jeanloz, had mastered search strategies for old or authentic parts and fixtures they wanted. The looking and traveling, however, was very time-consuming. They thought other renovators would welcome their resources. Using the *Old Home Journal*'s mailing list and a straightforward catalog printed in black and white, they sent out an initial mailing of 30,000. Orders came in, about five per day. They shipped from their garage. To build customers, they advertised the catalog in popular magazines. Business grew steadily. Soon they were sending out full-color catalogs to over 100,000 people.

As the business began to expand with overflowing orders the Jeanlozes began to organize manufacturing to specification. The business diversified. They started a magazine called *Victorian Homes*. They opened two retail stores. They began buying other people's catalog businesses, branching out into specialized products for left-handed people, and products for children.

Pleasant Rowland's is another landmark mail-marketing success story. Her background as a noted educator and author of children's reading and language arts materials, coupled with a chance visit to colonial Williamsburg, inspired in her a concept that became The American Girls Collection. She wanted to bring American history alive for young girls today by creating a play environment that would give them a sense of their heritage. She wanted to create quality products, wonderful books and exciting learning tools, unlike the mass-marketed, overly sophisticated and glitzy toys she saw around her.

The result was a catalog of books, dolls, doll clothes and accessories, games, crafts, and clothing for girls—all replicas of real items played with and used by little girls in various historical periods, from Revolutionary to modern times. Unlike many direct-mail merchandisers who build their catalogs over a number of years, The American Girls Collection was launched in its entirety. It was a considerable manufacturing and publishing commitment but, convinced about the worth of her idea, Ms. Rowland knew she could make it work.

To date, over two million books about the fictional characters featured in the collection have been sold. Through bookstore sales, the company builds its mail-order market via a reader response card placed at the back of each book. Ms. Rowland also writes a newsletter comparing and contrasting the lives of American girls then and now, which is sent in bulk and free to schools, as another way of reaching her potential market. One of the unique elements of her success is in the award-winning catalog. It is written to be read by an eight-year-old girl and is a valuable reading experience in and of itself.

The success stories only make it *look easy*. Easy? No. What is less documented is how many would-be catalog merchants fail. As with any business, there are certain fundamentals and you have to get them right. You must know about test mailings, product acquisition, mailing list rentals, list brokers, response rates, printing options, fulfillment, inventory control, and postal regulations.

Direct marketing experts agree that success in mail order rests on these factors:

Knowledge of the business. Read everything you can get your hands on.* Attend seminars and workshops that may be offered through local business colleges. Check with national business associations (NAWBO, AWED, and the Direct Marketing Association) for specific training information. A background in merchandising, advertising, graphics, design, photography, or direct sales will go a long way in helping you position your business.

Financing. Direct marketing advisers estimate a small mail-order house will cost a minimum of $200,000 to start. The cost of printing, mailing, and *good* list rentals is high. And that's before figuring in costs of inventory, taking orders, and shipping products. For a single product, placing direct-response ads in magazines intended for the target market will require less outlay, but advertising must be ongoing and your ad professionally laid out.

Inventory control. You will need to estimate sales and have in stock sufficient inventory. If you're going to dropship your inventory (e.g., arrange for the manufacturer or distributor to send items to customers as orders come in), know that suppliers often respond slowly, make mistakes, or simply

*See "Outrageous Fortune," by Frances Huffman, *Entrepreneurial Woman,* July/August 1990, for profiles of four successful female mail-order entrepreneurs.

don't have the item in stock just when you need it most. Know your supplier. Be prepared for weak links in the chain.

Targeted market. Begin by going after narrow and easily identifiable markets—e.g., pet owners, gardeners, parents of small children, subscribers to specialty magazines, etc. Study other mail-order ads in publications that interest you. Look at back issues. If someone advertises consistently over a long period of time, you can bet the ad is pulling for them.

Visual layout. Everything in your catalog or ad, right down to paper stock and style of photography, will depend on your target market analysis. Experts advise that a photograph will sell far more products than a drawing. Study the catalogs and ads of others. Adapt your style from the proven success formulas.

Mailing lists. It's important that the list broker has worked with the kind of product your mail-order business is selling. Find someone who will spend time with you. A good list is worth every penny it may cost you.

Customer service. Telephone orders should be taken by friendly, intelligent people. The item requested should be mailed as quickly as possible. Environmentally safe packing materials should ensure that products arrive intact (popcorn is an excellent choice). Shipping delays should be clearly communicated to the customer.

All in all, the mail-order business is one of methodical organization, strict attention to detail, and slow building. It can be enormously successful but only after persistence and effort. It is a complex business, even if you've got only one product. The competition is fierce. The investment is risky. Don't be discouraged—just go in with your eyes open.

For more information:

Direct Marketing Association (DMA), 11 West Forty-second Street, New York, N.Y. 10036, (212)768–7277. Provides information on all aspects of direct marketing from list brokers to computer service bureaus to producers of direct-mail advertising. Publishes a direct-mail/marketing manual and sponsors three-day seminars in basic and advanced techniques of direct-mail marketing.

National Mail Order Association (NMOA), 5818 Venice Boulevard, Los Angeles, California, 90019. Provides information on product sources, ideas, techniques, and services of value to direct-mail marketers. Reviews books, mailing lists, and general data. Publishes *Mail Order Digest.*

Getting Into the Mail Order Business and *How To Start and Operate a Mail Order Business,* 4th edition, by Julian L. Simon (McGraw-Hill).

THE FAITH MOUNTAIN COMPANY

Rappahannock County, Virginia, is rural America at its best. Not far from the foot of the Skyline Drive, the tiny town of Sperryville (population 250) is headquarters for The Faith Mountain Company, which Cheri Faith Woodard started as a country store in 1977. It took $11,000 to renovate the front half of her eighteenth-century house into a shop and $3,000 to stock the first inventory. The shop featured antiques, dried flowers and herbs, local carved and sewn crafts, unique wooden furniture and tabletop objects. Cheri, her husband, Martin, and their son lived in the back of the house.

With Washington, D.C., an hour and a half away and hundreds of people touring the Blue Ridge Mountains in the summer, this home-based cottage industry was profitable in season but it seemed the hard work ought to turn a bigger profit year-round. Then, when a major interstate routed people away from Sperryville in a more direct route to the National Park, Cheri and her husband decided to try expanding their business through catalog sales.

We started in mail order as rank beginners. I strongly advise people to go to seminars, to hire consultants, to get the best professional advice they can up front. It is a very, very intricate business and it takes a lot of know-how to make it successful. However, not everyone can do it that way and we were no exception. We produced our first catalog in black and white for $1,000 on a duplicating machine and sent it to a customer list made up from the people who had already been in the store. It was simply illustrated with line drawings, with many items under $20, and it featured the dried flower arrangements that are our hallmark. We

341

thought customers who had already shopped in the store would respond more than the usual 2% "law of averages" in the mail order business. We were wrong.

It wasn't until we hired a consultant that we got on the right track. A good direct-mail consultant can tell you, first of all, whether or not you have a viable idea for a mail order business. He or she can also explain the time and investment involved. Knowing these two factors is very important because once you get started in it and you've made inroads, it's difficult to know when to stop. That was what we came up against. We'd say, "we've gone this far, we've got to keep going."

We struggled with it for three years before we decided we needed professional advice. Our consultant was a man who was just leaving his position as the director of the Smithsonian Catalog. First of all, he affirmed that our business had a chance in mail order. Then, he helped us analyze the mail order business, analyze our own sales, and advised us on the kind of mailing list we were looking for and the broker who could provide such a list. Anyone looking for a consultant should look at the trade journals, *Catalog Age* and *Direct Marketing* magazine, or call the Direct Marketing Association in New York.

The trouble with mail order is that it looks easy. It's not. You've got to know postal regulations, legalities, be able to evaluate mailing lists, and create dynamic visual presentations. It's a *very* expensive proposition. Depending on how much you know coming into the business, it takes anywhere from $500,000 to a million dollars to get fully started. You need inventory, warehousing, staff, computer systems, and lists, plus operating capital. You also need money for the mistakes you're going to make.

It took four years to build up to a full-color catalog. We started out with one thousand catalogs and now we mail four million a year. We mail twelve times a year, and some people get the catalog twice depending on who they are and what kind of buyer they are. Our catalog is full color and is thirty-two pages long. We sell household and decorative accessories, women's apparel, jewelry, crafts, and dried flower arrangements. We send out customer surveys on a regular basis to find out who our buyers are. The surveys indicate that our best customers are women from thirty-five to fifty-five and older, with income levels of $45,000 and up.

Everything we mail order we stock in the store, if possible. I feel that the Faith Mountain store itself is crucial to our image. It says to the customer, "I am here, I'm not just a P.O. Box, come visit us, we stand behind our products." That has an impact.

You have to like retail to like mail order. Merchandising by mail is still merchandising and even though you're not dealing with your customer face-to-face, customer service, customer relations, and image are just as important to us as they are to a retailer. One of the beauties of mail order is that you can run your operation from anywhere. You don't have to be in a city, you don't have to pay high rents. You get to live where you want, have the lifestyle you want—and still have a business.

The unique benefit in shopping by mail is convenience. We emphasize customer service, so customers will be less inclined to go to the mall and will want to keep shopping with us. We can deliver quickly on an in-stock item; we offer free UPS pick up should the customer not like the product and want to return it. We spend *our* money to bring it back to us. Not many businesses do that and we've found that a powerful selling tool.

The better catalogs go beyond convenience in that they're also fun to read. You can get real enjoyment, ideas, and helpful hints from reading them. You can sit with twelve catalogs and within an hour review an enormous array of merchandise without the fatigue of shopping. There is no pressure to buy. Personally, I find shopping in stores tiring. Much of the time you can't find a clerk, and when you do, often they know nothing about the product. For every product we sell, a full page of information is keyed into the computer. It would be very hard to go to a store and find a clerk with that kind of knowledge.

The frustration that shoppers feel in the retail stores is contributing to the growing popularity of shopping by mail. Mail order used to be a low end business and you were lucky if you were satisfied with the product. In the last ten years, the big catalog houses such as L.L. Bean and Lands' End have established the respectability of mail order.

However, not everything is in our favor. We have problems that don't affect the storefront retailer at all. For example, every time the postal rates go up, it's a critical issue. The post office is, in effect, like our landlord. Yes, because location is not critical we save on high rent—we have a ten thousand square foot warehouse and office facility—but we need a sophisticated computer system, as well as top-notch telephone operators. You can hire outside companies to do this for you but we prefer to keep it all in-house. To me, the staffing of the telephone lines is very important. This is the personality of the business. We have our own training program for our operators. I look for pleasant people who don't easily get upset and who speak clearly, with correct grammar. Overall we employ thirty-five people, which makes us one of the two biggest employers in Sperryville.

The thrill of the business for me is selecting the merchandise, and when I pick something that sells well, it's exciting. Like any good retailer we're constantly probing and questioning and analyzing why things are selling, why they're not, and changing the product line. All mail-order companies have to do that to survive.

I'm doing a time study right now to see exactly how much time I devote to each aspect of the business. We buy at over sixty-five shows a year and see hundreds of crafts people who come to us with goods. I handle all personnel issues, including hiring and training staff. I meet with department heads on a weekly basis and within each department we schedule meetings to resolve issues or plan new directions. We have a general staff meeting once a year to announce benefits and talk about the business. I handle the day-to-day operations and do all the fashion buying. I spend about 20 percent of my time buying.

My husband, Martin, has been full-time in the business with me for five years, and is the catalog director. Although the catalog is put together here—the choice of products, the layout, etc.—he is often on the road overseeing the photography, which is done in our studio in Alexandria, Virginia, and the press runs, which are in Pennsylvania.

My husband is a problem solver and also quite a risk taker. I'm more conservative. I feel we epitomize the entrepreneurial couple because we balance each other. It's fun for us; it's a shared interest. If I weren't married to someone I was in business with, it would create problems because the dedication and time it takes to get a business launched and operating in the black is enormous. Even when we try to program time away, in reality, everything we do relates to the business. It's our life.

Mail order is a stimulating business and, as I said before, with knowledge and investment you can succeed in a big way, but it takes time to bootstrap. After five years, we have reached four million in sales. Another company could do that immediately if they had the resources. The bigger you are, the quicker you can benefit from the economies of scale, which is what you need to succeed in mail order.

I've never taken business courses until now. I don't necessarily recommend that you have a strong business background to succeed, but it helps. On the other hand, I often wonder if I would have gotten into this business had I known what it was all about. Sometimes you can defeat yourself by knowing too much.

As I see it, mail order has some rough years ahead. Congress wants to pass a ruling that will force mail-order companies to charge out-of-state buyers a sales tax. Our industry is fighting it, but the states feel they are losing a big portion of revenue when goods are sold beyond state lines. The 30 percent postal increase coming in 1991 is going to have a big impact on our business. That scares me. It means coming up with that much more business just to maintain the status quo. Many houses will fold and for those of us who stay in business, life will get tougher and more competitive. We may have to cut back on printing costs, for example, and find other ways to appeal to our buyer. But we plan to be smarter. We plan to survive.

PORTFOLIO—THE ULTIMATE CATALOG

Wilma deZanger started her business on a five-hundred-year-old idea. It was a Dutch *poffertjes* pan for making puffy little pancakes. She arranged to have the pans (which she adapted for modern ovens) manufactured at a foundry near her home in Sugar Loaf, New York. Then she ran the smallest ad sold in *House and Garden* magazine.

Today, Portfolio's "Ultimate Catalog" specializes in unusual items imported from all over the world. The products are unique—she carries art objects, antique jewelry collections, decorative household accessories, gourmet foods, and cookwares. Her business practices are as elegant as her products, and special attention is given to gift wrapping, card enclosures, and prompt mailing.

I feel that anyone who thinks about going into mail-order should first do a great deal of research into what it's all about. The process of building a mail-order business is slow, demanding, and quite risky. As in any retail business, it takes up-front money to get started. Inventory investment, advertising, packaging, and mailing charges run high. Timing is important because ads in major magazines must be placed months in advance, and knowing what will sell, and where the best advertising outlets are, takes experience.

I was a photo stylist before starting Portfolio and was aware of products, how to present them visually, trends in merchandise, and the various magazines and their readership. I have an innate sense of what will sell, and my background gave me the marketing confidence in how to go about reaching the right audience.

The *poffertjes* pan was, and continues to be, a best-seller, but because I was manufacturing it myself, I took a prototype around to kitchenware buyers in major New York department stores to test their reactions before investing in my initial run of five thousand pieces. I took orders from the buyers, so before I went into mail order, I had strong wholesale outlets.

Products for mail order are marked up 100 percent over the costs of materials, advertising, packaging, overhead, and shipping. At first I ran the business from my house, as we had a large, open work space. You need room for storage, shipping containers, and work tables. And of course, you need office space for the paperwork operations of the business. Organization and excellent record keeping are a must.

I incorporated the business from the start and also carry a lot of product liability insurance. When dealing with the public, especially in food or cooking wares, there are many unknowns. Some people live to sue, so insurance is important for protection.

It is now a law that any mail-order item must be sent to the buyer within three weeks; otherwise, the seller must return the money or notify the person of any delays. To avoid that, you must have enough products on hand before you receive any orders.

The paperwork in this business is tremendous. Each item must be inventoried from the manufacturing or wholesaling end, then recorded as to when it was shipped, how it was shipped, and how much it has been insured for. Each advertisement we run is also coded, so when orders start coming in, I can tell which publication, and which issue, are producing the most business. I also record which part of the country orders come in from. All this becomes vital information in planning future advertising.

Basically, there are two ways to go in mail order. One is with ads in magazines; the other is with a catalog mailed directly to potential customers. There are few cases where it makes sense for beginners to start out with direct mail. It just isn't practical until you can spread that high cost per person over a large number of products by offering a whole product line, rather than just one or two items.

Finding the best publications for ads depends on what you're selling. You'll want to study the various publications and pick the ones that have readers whose interests or income levels will make them better-than-average prospects for your product. Also, look for publications that carry a noticeably large number of mail-order ads. Obviously, these magazines do well for people in mail order.

My first ads were small, with a photograph of the product. A photograph is always the best way to sell products, although sketches can sell fashion items. Expect to run an ad at least three times in a magazine before you can rate its pulling power.

Because the pans sold well, I began building my inventory in cookwares and gourmet foods. After a year I was able to put together my first catalog. A catalog means you have to inventory many items. Portfolio's catalog is very well done, with excellent photographs, printed on good paper in full color. There is a real art to putting together a catalog, and again, my background as a stylist was invaluable. I know how a product should be photographed and how to lay it on the page in an eye-catching way.

With an expanded line, you must get into concrete projections of sales and work out commitments with wholesale vendors. They must guarantee you a fixed price for a certain amount of time. Otherwise, the price may go up after you've run your ads or sent your catalog, cutting into your profit margin. I have the added problem of the import market and fluctuating dollar values in various countries. It's a constant juggling act. You have to pay a lot of attention to details.

My first mailing list was made up from my previous customers—people who had ordered the *poffertjes* pan. You can also rent lists from professional brokers. Here, as in magazine ads, the aim is to get a selected audience: names and addresses of people whose special interest or income levels are tied in with the type of products you deal in.*

*An extensive listing of mailing list brokers can be found in *Direct Mail List Rates and Data,* published by Standard Rate and Data Service, Inc., 5201 Old Orchard

Another major area of concern is the various ways of mailing. We have a large inventory of boxes and many ways to package goods. Ideally, a mail-order product should be easy to box and unbreakable, but I specialize in such unusual items I must invest in packaging materials that are often costly.

We ship via United Parcel Service whenever possible because its service is far superior to the United States Postal Service. But I do all my direct mail through the post office. When I started, our local post office was about to go out of business because the town is so small. Now I am their primary source of income.

The prevailing myth about mail order is that you can start a business from your kitchen table and turn it overnight into a million-dollar enterprise. People rush into mail order, and it's no wonder that at least 75 percent of mail-order businesses fail. On the other hand, every successful catalog house I know of was started on a small scale, like mine, with one or two items, so it certainly can be done. My point is that you must understand the business before you lay out large sums and then find yourself stuck with inventory that won't sell. You have to learn all the aspects—advertising copy and layout, rates, methods for shipping, postal regulations, systems of control, and bookkeeping. On top of this you must have a product not commonly found in regular retail stores, one that will appeal to a good number of people. There's a special merchandising knack. Unfortunately, even if you've laid a sound base, some things that should sell simply don't. There is a psychology in mail order, just as there is a psychology in retail display.

It's not an easy or fast way to make money, but when it clicks, it can be very profitable. It's fun for me since my products are unique and extensions of my own taste. This makes my business a very personal one, despite the fact that I never see my customers. Many write me long, chatty letters and feel, I think, a kinship with me since my products are so special.

Road, Skokie, Illinois 60077. The directory should be available in most larger libraries.

·22·

Manufacturing
and Wholesaling

*Don't tell me how hard you work, tell me how much you
get done.*   —James Ling

New products come on the market all the time, and behind
them are designers, inventors, and everyday dreamers who have
turned their inspirations into today's best-selling items. Getting
an idea out of your dreams and onto the shelf takes a bit of doing,
but if you are willing to invest time and energy in taking the idea
forward, it can be done.

As in any business, you must establish the marketability of a
product. There must be a need before you manufacture or wholesale. Need does not always mean necessity. Need can be based on
luxury, originality, price, and novelty. Test-market your idea.
Make a prototype and show it to your friends and potential buyers. From their reactions, ask yourself:

What are the qualities of the product that will attract the buyer?
Does it fill a gap or a void?
Is it quality or quantity that's selling?
Is the price right for the product?

Establishing your market will lead you to distribution ideas. Distribution is the key to profits. List the ideal outlets for your
product, and figure out how these outlets are supplied. It may be
as simple as going to the buyers directly and showing them your
samples. Or you may see that placing ads in trade publications
is your best route. You may want to hire sales representatives to

develop larger territories. You might set up a booth at a trade show, contract with mail-order houses, or climb on board with a sophisticated distributor who can network your product nationally, even internationally.

Pricing is everything at this end of the business. In production, you must think not only of your profits but consider the retailer's final selling price as well. Your price must cover all production and marketing costs—raw materials, equipment, overhead, labor, and sales—as well as your profit. After determining these costs, you must figure the final price to the retail buyer. Is it in line with the quality of the product? The rule of thumb is: 20 percent to the manufacturer, 40 percent to the wholesaler, 100 percent to the retailer. If the gadget you've invented costs $5 to produce, and you sell it for $6 to the wholesaler who in turn sells it to the retailer for $8.40, can the retailer sell it to the customer for $16.80?

The simple fact behind wholesaling and manufacturing is anything can be profitable so long as there's a market for it and the price is right. To produce and sell a profitable product, you must understand the many steps it will take to get that product to the general public.

Production

Manufacturing

The Yellow Pages will be your bible. Here are listings for raw material, labor, and packaging. Most libraries carry the Yellow Pages for large cities. Or you can get the Yellow Pages for any city in the country by calling the business office of your telephone company. Most certainly, the New York City Yellow Pages as a source guide is invaluable. New York is a treasure trove of wholesalers and districts large and small, selling almost anything imagined under the sun.

Shop around. Find the best deal you can. The woman making boxes from her garage may suit your needs and budget better than a large manufacturer. Ask other people who they deal with. It's the best way of finding reliable suppliers.

Another important source guide is *Thomas' Register of American Manufacturers*. It is an enormous catalog listing manufacturers and dealers all over the United States. It will tell you what products are produced by which company, and it lists industrial design houses, suppliers, manufactured parts, and addresses.

Timing is important in manufacturing. Production should be closely timed to distribution and sales. It's a common mistake to think that you can manufacture to order—that you can take around a sample, write up orders, and then with guaranteed sales in hand, head back to the factory where your orders will be made up.

Manufacturing means committing yourself to a run of goods, even if you're making them yourself. It's a calculated risk, but like anything in business, risk is the only route to profits. In manufacturing, risk can take on impressive stature, because you may end up with a whole warehouse full of ingenious gadgets only to find that no one but you thinks they will revolutionize the world.

Wholesaling

Here you eliminate one risk, because you can deal in samples. The product is made. It already exists. You buy a product or sample line from the manufacturer and take it to the retail buyers. Your concern is finding the buyers and presenting the line in an appealing way. This can mean opening new markets, or jumping ahead of the competition with service, delivery, and a better price.

Often, however, the wholesaler will commission the manufacturer to make a special run of goods. In this case, the wholesaler is committed to that run.

Marketing Your Wares

In reaching buyers, timing is key. For example, it is futile to attempt to sell Christmas gift items, decorations cards, etc. to stores after October 1. Stores do all their ordering by early fall and won't, or can't (having run over their budgets) buy anything else, no matter how spectacular your product. Trade show and fashion buyers are usually buying six months in advance of a season; for mail-order houses, it's one year.

Seasonal articles and ads must be submitted to monthly magazines at least three months in advance of publication date; to weeklies, two to three weeks ahead. Greeting cards and gift wrap designs often must be submitted one year in advance.

Buyers differ. Having targeted your ideal outlets, it's a matter of finding out by trial how best to approach the buyers.

Cold Calling.

Many retail store buyers are easier to see if you simply drop in on them without an appointment. Buyers are by nature harried. If you try to make an appointment, they will be busy from now until the next millenium. But if you're there in the store, with your samples in hand, it takes only a minute for them to see what you're selling.

Advance Calling

Expect rejection, but keep trying. If you think a distributor or store buyer can use your products, you must persist. What they don't like in April, they might in September, especially if you've added something new to the line or can assure them that Oprah Winfrey will be wearing it on her next show. In sales, you need tenacity. You won't always get an order the first or second time out. But if you keep it up you can get the buyer feeling a little guilty—and a little guilt goes a long way.

Sales Representatives

Sales reps provide a way for small wholesale manufacturers to keep costs down yet still have someone working to bring in more business. A sales representative usually handles the lines of several manufacturers in a specified territory, on commission (and sometimes including expenses). These salespeople generally stick to products of the same nature (books, accessories, decorative arts, etc.) on an exclusive basis for that area. Or, you might consider hiring two reps, one to sell to specialty shops, another to solicit the big chain or department stores.

To find a good sales rep, ask people in your field, or place (and check) ads in trade journals. You can also learn from these sources what percentage of commission is standard for your line of products.*

Look for a rep with a track record, and check all references.

*To locate a sales representative in your field, contact the Merchandise Marts located in Atlanta, Chicago, San Francisco, Dallas (World Trade Center), and Los Angeles (Pacific Design Center), subscribe to trade journals geared to your business for ad listings, or check your Yellow Pages under "manufacturer's agents and representatives."

Make sure she understands your business and your philosophy as well as her duties and responsibilities. Remember, to your company's buyers and consumers the salesperson doesn't just *represent* your company, she *is* your company.

Sign a contract with your representative covering your agreement of territory, commission, and payment terms. You should stay in close touch with your rep, keeping her up-to-date on new developments, new products, competition, etc. In return, she can report on the state of your market in the field and send back advice on new directions or design ideas based on customer reaction and competition. If your product isn't selling, it's either the product's fault or the representative's. Find out which.

When orders come in, send out confirmation notices to customers before filling and shipping the orders placed by your rep. This avoids any mixups and keeps you from getting burned should your representative be misrepresenting you.

Trade Shows

For the small wholesaler and manufacturer, trade shows can be an excellent way to gain broad exposure to potential buyers. Almost every industry features a trade show—e.g., The Boutique Show, The Giftwares Show, The Fancy Foods Show, The Toy Show, The International Home Furnishings Show, The Health and Fitness Show, and hundreds of others.

The large trade shows are held in the major cities (New York, Atlanta, Houston, Chicago, Los Angeles), but small regional trade shows are held in cities of every size around the country. Local convention centers, auditoriums, even high school gyms are likely staging grounds for small exhibitors to come together and display their wares.

Make sure it's worth your while to exhibit in a trade show. The large shows cost money—on average, $2,000 to $3,000 for minimal space—and that's only the beginning. You must be prepared to go in with a professional-looking display, printed information, and perhaps even giveaways or other promotional materials. Travel expenses, staffing, shipping, bonus tips, installations (such as electrical wiring and telephones) are other costs. Of course, it is pointless to display at a large trade show if your production or inventory can't meet large orders.

All trade shows are listed in *Directory of Conventions,* published by *Successful Meetings* magazine, 633 Third Avenue, New York,

New York 10017. Local convention centers and state bureaus of conventions will have regional and local schedules.

Before displaying at a large trade show or a fair, you should attend the show. You will want to talk to the organizers to find out costs and other information (space, attendance, advertising, and other promotional services). Many of the large national shows have two-year to five-year waiting lists, and the organizers will demand that you exhibit in regional shows before gaining entrance to the national.

You will most definitely want to talk to other exhibitors to find out how many exhibit each year and what kind of business they generate from the show. And you will want to see what you're up against as far as your competition. The large centers can house thousands of exhibitors.

Mail-Order Houses

Getting your product or line in a mail-order catalog is a wholesale manufacturer's dream. Here is a buyer who will order in quantity and promote your product to an enormous audience. You contact mail-order buyers the same way you would store buyers. Call them, explain your product, explain why it would suit their particular catalog, send them a sample. Some mail-order houses will not buy outright but want to "drop ship." This means displaying your item in their catalog, taking orders, sending you the order, and having you ship to the customer. This has its advantages; the names they send become the basis for a mailing list for future products you may develop.

All in all, getting a product from your fantasy to the shelf is not really so awesome and mysterious, but it takes energy, persistence, and imagination. If your product is worthy, be assured, there *is* a market for it. You just have to be prepared to study the market, learn its methodology, price well, and devise a step-by-step distribution plan.

For more information:

Thomas' Register of American Manufacturers (11 volumes). New York: Thomas Publishing Co. (Consult reference section of the library.)

Manufacturer's News, Inc., 3 Huron Street, Chicago, Illinois

60611. Publishes directories of manufacturers for nearly every state.

Directory of Conventions. Successful Meetings magazine, 633 Third Avenue, New York, N.Y. 10017. Lists exhibitions all over the country of interest to manufacturers and wholesalers (i.e., gift, toy, home furnishings, etc.).

Design International, 3748 Twenty-second Street, San Francisco, California 94114, (415)647–4700. Provides a forum for creative exchange of ideas and information among members of different design fields.

Invention Marketing Institute, 345 West Cypress Street, Glendale, California 91201, (818)246–6540. Brings together inventors and manufacturers for mutual benefit.

Inventors Club of America, P.O. Box 450261, Atlanta, Georgia 30345, (404)938–5089. Helps inventors in all phases of their work: patenting, development, manufacturing, marketing. Sponsors training programs and provides a computer data base.

FRENCH RAGS

French Rags has seen it all. In twelve years, the business of handloomed sweaters and scarves has gone from "rags" to riches to financial rags to recovery. Owner/ founder Brenda French is an attractive, articulate Englishwoman operating her manufacturing, wholesaling, retailing business in Los Angeles, with a retail store about to open in Santa Fe, New Mexico.

Divorced and with a child to raise, she started French Rags on $3,000 in a spare room. It eventually grew into a huge factory with an annual gross income of $8 million. Then disaster struck and the wolves were at the door.

But French Rags and Brenda French are here to tell an inspiring story of survival and flexibility.

I started my business because I needed money. My husband and I had separated, and I had no alimony and no child support for me or my nine-year-old son. So it was need—pure necessity— that motivated me. It's actually a good way to start a business, because you have to succeed: you've nothing to fall back on. I had

$3,000 in the bank, period. So that money had to work for me.

I had a strong background in fashion and design. I had worked in merchandising. I had done European collections. But I didn't want a job working for someone else, because I didn't want a latchkey child. I was English, living in California, and I had no family to fall back on. The only way I could support myself and my child was to have my own business. I was prepared to work fifteen hours a day—but my own fifteen hours, not someone else's.

Since I had been a knitwear designer, the easiest thing for me to do was to go into knitwear. How to begin? I went out and bought a knitting machine. The first thing was to learn how to use it so I could control my own production. That may have been the most difficult thing about starting my business, but once I had learned how to knit I started making scarves.

I was lucky. Scarves were big in 1978. I started wearing them, figuring if they were any good, people would say something. I went to visit a friend and I had six scarves on, tied all over the place, and my friend said, "What is that rag around your neck?" And I said, "It's not a rag, it's a French rag." I knew immediately that was the name of my business. I registered it the next day.

I had plenty of friends who were in the business, so I made up a bunch of sample scarves, put them in a large basket, and sent them out with a friend who was a sales rep on her way to do a market in San Francisco. She came back with $15,000 worth of orders and I was in business.

I did everything myself. I couldn't get a loan. I had no credit; I had been married sixteen years and nothing was in my name. And so I knitted the scarves. I dyed them. I shipped them. When I got paid I invested in more yarn. I sold out of my house. I sold wholesale. I sold to anyone who wanted them. Every ten dollars was like gold.

I couldn't afford to buy yarn in colors, because in order to get colors you have to have it dyed. The minimum amount they'll dye is twenty-five pounds of yarn per lot. I was buying less than twenty-five pounds total! So I bought white yarn, went to Woolworth's and bought Rit dye, and dyed it in my sink. I dried the yarn over a wooden rack on my patio in the sun.

Pretty soon I discovered that by using cotton and a lurex and then striping it and then dyeing it I got a great multicolored stripe. That was a big hit and I did well that first year. I grossed over $100,000 out of my spare room. I knew I could do much more but I needed help. I found a Korean woman who had a knitting shop with a network of women she contracted out to. I asked her if she could make my scarves, and she said "Are you kidding? Of course we can make these. These are nothing!" That's when I stopped knitting. I delivered the white yarn to them weekly, and brought back the scarves and dyed them, and dried them and ironed them and folded them and shipped them.

Then I discovered rayon. I saw a scarf I liked and bought it. Twelve years ago rayon was an ugly word, but I loved the feel of it and I tracked it down to a manufacturer of heavy rayon curtains, who thought I was crazy to want to make scarves out of it. But he sold me some and I went home and dyed it. It was beautiful. Rayon takes dye like silk. Buyers were ecstatic. They loved the scarves but said their customers wanted it in sweaters as well. I knew many of the inventory pitfalls of trying to do a number of sizes from my years in design. I thought, "If I can make only one sweater, it's got to be a universal shape. What is a universal shape? What is it *everyone* can wear?" Well . . . it's a sweatshirt. I knitted a rayon sweatshirt, one size fits all, in white rayon and then dyed it. Let me tell you, hand-dyeing rayon is a job! It's heavy when wet and takes a long time to dry. I needed equipment. I needed to get out of my apartment. I needed to expand. I needed credit.

I went to a local bank and took a big basket of scarves with me. I said, "This is what I make," and by the time I had finished, the loan manager was dazzled. He had scarves all over the bank, and the girls were coming over and saying "Oh, I want one," which was what I was hoping for. He lent me $5,000 without any credit reference. I went out and rented a small factory space, bought two more knitting machines and more yarn. I grew by demand. If customers asked for short-sleeved sweaters, I made them. If they asked for stripes, I made them.

As I expanded things got more complicated. I got a showroom in New York. In a four-year period I went from a 1,000-square-foot factory to 3,000 to 7,000, until in 1986 I was in a 25,000-square-foot factory with three hundred employees. I was billing eight million dollars a year. I had eight showrooms all over the country. And I was flying high.

Then things started to go wrong. It came from all sides. The knitting business in general started to suffer in Europe and America. At the point when the industry itself was in a malaise, I discovered I was totally overextended. My business was factored.* It's the only way you can do business unless you have tremendous backing. But factoring, unless you're careful, gets to be very leveraged. About three years ago I realized the factor really owned us. I was scared. I didn't know what was going to happen. I had a production manager who ran the factory. He was in charge of the flow and the money; I was in charge of design and merchandising and sales. My business was so big and suddenly, there I was with three hundred employees and a break-even point of $500,000 a month. I had to bring in $500,000 just to get by—overhead, salaries, yarn, shipping. In the garment center today, you have to do five markets a year. That's one every ten weeks. That's a lot for one designer to do alone. To do that *and* run a business is just about impossible; you do one or the other. Plus, clients like Bonwit Teller and Neiman Marcus all wanted you to do a personal appearance, which involved traveling. My son was fifteen by that time. I had a housekeeper and a nice house. On the surface I had all the material comforts, but underneath the business was going afoul. Things were crazed.

And so I brought in a man who was an expert at streamlining companies. And for the next year we reduced the size of the business, cutting overhead, cutting employees, reducing the size of the operation. Then one day I went on a business trip, and when I came back I found out the factor had decided they didn't want me as a customer anymore. They looked at my account getting smaller and were afraid I would turn belly up, so they closed my account. They froze my cash flow. This is something they can do—freeze your account until the stores pay them. Meanwhile, the man I had hired had split—simply disappeared. I came back to forty employees standing around with bounced paychecks. There was no money in the bank.

I could have gone to pieces, but I didn't. I took it day by day, which is really the only thing you can do. I can't begin to tell you the mess I uncovered. I had leases on equipment, a Xerox machine, pay telephones, snack machines—you name it. You know what? You can't get out of a lease. You ask the company to take

*Factoring is a method of commercial lending. The bank (or factoring company) buys receivables outright and assumes the credit risks and takes on collection responsibilities. The factor charges a percentage of the collected money. The cost to the business owner may be quite high but it assures a steady cash flow.

it back and they say, "No. You have a lease. We don't want it back. We want the money." My insurance company got wind of my problems and garnisheed my bank account. My lawyer and my accountant came in and told me to dump the business, to sell the inventory, the yarn, and the machines. I said, "If I do, what will happen?" And they got the figures together and it turned out that I was personally liable for the debt of the company. I hadn't realized that if you sign a contract "Brenda French, President," then you've signed it corporately, but if you sign plain "Brenda French," then you, personally, have guaranteed whatever you're signing. All my contracts were signed "Brenda French." If I went out of business I would still be in debt to the tune of $400,000. I would be wiped out. I would have to sell my house. It would be like starting over again. I said, "No. There's got to be another way." And there was. I owned inventory, I owned a lot of yarn, and I had some very loyal employees who stuck with me.

I went to buyers at department stores and told them if they wanted my stuff, they'd have to pay for it COD. They don't like that. They said, "But we've got wonderful credit." And I said, "It's not about your credit, honey, it's about mine." The stores that had been buying from me for years, that had built-in customers for my designs, agreed to my terms. But I needed other outlets.

I decided to open a retail store. All along I had sold direct from a little store in back of the factory, which I opened only on Saturdays. I never sold my leftovers, damaged goods, or returns to discount houses, because my clients wouldn't have liked that. But I did sell to private customers, and I had over 2,000 names in my computer of people who bought from me retail. The factory was in a nice area. I opened the store with $70,000 worth of my inventory. I moved into a large front area in the factory complete with the worn-out linoleum, bare walls, metal shelves, and fluorescent lighting. I brought the industrial carpeting down from upstairs. I installed mirrors—the $4.99 kind from Woolworth's. There were no frills. I sent a note to everyone on my list, put an ad in the local paper, and opened the door.

It was a smash. Women loved shopping in a factory. They loved being able to see in the back where things were being made. If they asked for alterations, I was able to do them immediately and for very little money.

It turned into something I never expected. I'm having more

fun meeting my customers and cutting through the egos of buyers and merchandising managers. The women who come in my store love life, love color, love clothes, and hate stores. They are delighted to come to the factory and to meet me. I now design and knit directly for my customers, which is the way it should be. I listen to my customers and I find it's the most rewarding thing I have ever done. I think of my store as a gallery of knitwear and of myself as a designer of knitted textiles.

What have I learned from all of this?

Listen to your public. In the old days the customer was always right, but it's been a long time since the big stores have felt that way. The customer is very hip now. That's why mail order has taken so much away from the department stores.

Be flexible. You're never locked in. Flexibility is essential to a business owner.

You can't rely on anybody. You really can't. Check up on everyone and everything. Learn to read your balance sheet properly. Don't let anyone sign checks but you. Don't *ever* give your power away.

Don't expect the experts to take responsibility for your decisions. Advice is only advice. You can take it or not. Don't do anything if it doesn't make sense to you and you don't understand it. Ask questions.

Know that you have to fire people who are not producing for you. It has nothing to do with personal feeling and friendships, it has to do with the job. I have a handpicked team of dedicated people, but I watch them like a hawk. If someone takes a two-hour lunch I want to know why. I think it's my right. I'm paying them, after all.

If you owe money, never walk away from it. I told my creditors I was available to them six days a week, that I would call them regularly to let them know what was happening. They gradually backed off and gave me some breathing space. Often, I could only send ten dollars a week to some of them, but it showed I was there, reorganizing and rebuilding.

There is really no mystery to business. It's all common sense. You have to take in more than you spend; you have to make sure that the money is wisely spent; and you've got to be available. The best advice I ever heard was from a successful businesswoman who, when asked "how did you do it?" replied, "I continued." It's so true. The people who succeed in life are the people who continue. It's easy to give up, very easy. But the rewards come if you persevere.

MARY DONALD FLOOR CLOTHS

For most of her professional life, artist and designer Mary Donald painted wall murals by commission until one day a client in Rhode Island exclaimed she wished she could transport the artwork to her house in Greenwich. That set the wheels in motion for a cottage industry of portable decorative art that, six years later, sells nationwide in catalogs, department stores, and gift shops.

The "cottage" is in Devon, Pennsylvania. As many as twenty-five artists work to order from their own studios. The final product line is shown at major trade shows throughout the country.

I started in my basement with fifty dollars and a roll of canvas. I began by painting floor cloths, which are canvas floor coverings painted in the folk art tradition. I would design and paint a few of them, and then I would sell them to generate enough money to buy more canvas. Eventually I took the work to a gallery, and they loved it and gave me a show. The show sold out. I made enough money from that to know I had a business.

Through a friend who was in a similar kind of business, I found a sales representative who agreed to show my floor cloths in her booth at the New York Gift Show. Reps take fifteen percent of anything they sell. She didn't sell many, but through that exposure I was accepted by two mail-order catalogs. One was very well known and I was sure I was going to be an instant hit nationwide. I sold a disappointing ten pieces and never heard from them again. The other, smaller catalog ordered and reordered at such a fast pace and did so much publicity on the floor cloths that I had to hire someone to come in and work with me. I couldn't keep up with production. I advertised for artists in the local newspapers and got a great response. One artist would bring in two or three more. I hired on a subcontract agreement basis.

I quickly realized that I needed a breadth of design and that I was incapable of designing a certain aspect this market needed.

So, from the start, the artists I hire are free to come up with their own designs. I direct the artists—I say, "These are the colors you should use," I encourage them to move in certain directions. I channel certain kinds of design work to artists who have the hand for it. But I encourage their own freedom and creativity, because if they're just painting assembly-line painting, they burn out. I try to nurture their creative side.

Artists are a very difficult work force. They're quixotic. They have no sense of time, and when you're dealing with production and time-sensitive orders, it can cause serious problems. And the labor cost is high—about 45 percent of my cost. But the alternative is to go overseas, and then you lose all quality control. The artists work to order. You can't pressure artists. They fall apart. I would say production is my greatest problem.

The business grew quickly, and when I started exhibiting at trade shows, I felt I needed to develop more of a line. For one thing, hanging floor cloths or placing them on the floor of a ten-by-ten-foot cubicle was visually very flat and two-dimensional. I started adding accessories to liven things up, and from that developed a painted, decorative accessories line.

My clients are mail-order houses, department stores, interior designers, and gift boutiques. Initially I did the New York and Chicago gift shows. I now find that because of my price point, which is high for the gift market, the coastal markets serve me best—Atlanta, New York, Los Angeles, and Dallas. I gave up Chicago because the Midwest is very price sensitive. Now, I'm moving into the home furnishings market in addition to the gift market.

In the course of six years my business has gone from floor cloths to a full line of painted furniture and decorative accessories. Furniture now makes up the bulk of our sales, with the top of the line wholesaling for $2,000. In the gift market we were the first people to introduce painted furniture. Now we're swamped with competition. You're always up against the competition.

Trade shows are where we sell. They are exhausting and they are expensive, but they do generate business. There are all sizes of markets to exhibit in, and often you will have to go to a regional market, like Knoxville, Seattle, Kansas City, before you can get space in the national shows. For instance, the Atlanta show can take anywhere from four to seven years to get into.

First you write to the organizers of the show, and tell them the size booth you will need and explain your product line. When you contract for your space you pay your money six months in advance. I lease a space that is generally anywhere from $11 to $14 a square foot for four days. That adds up to about $3,000 per show. Two months before the show you receive your show book, which lists subcontractors. These are the people you can hire to do your electrical work, installations, drayage, table and furniture rentals, rugs, caterers—whatever you might need.

You've got to imagine a convention hall that is a huge, enclosed stretch of raw space—a cement floor, walls, and a roof. Then, imagine it with fifty rows of these little ten-by-ten-foot cubicles divided by gray draperies held up on poles. At the Javits Center in New York there are twelve miles of exhibitors for any one show, so you've got to come in there and shine. You have to create a visual stimulant through one means or another. There are trade show rules that say you can't have naked ladies in the aisles because, believe me, people would do it if they could. They'll do anything to attract the buyer. So, the cost of the space is only the beginning. We contract for the electrical hookup, which is $150. Each spotlight is also $150.

Now you have a booth with lights but you don't have anything in it. We ship our goods in exhibit crates via common carrier, which costs $250 each way for each crate. The crates get as far as the door to the hall, but you have to pay the foreman to bring them to your booth and to bring them back to you after the show is over. At the beginning and end of a show there are a thousand people who need their crates, and so you pass a lot of money under the table.

You get to the show a few days before the opening to set up. I'm a small exhibitor and it takes me two days with three people helping me. The show hours are 9:00 to 6:30. You're on your feet the entire time. Hopefully, you're writing orders, but there are times when you're not. You still have to project energy. You can't sit down, you can't read or relax with a cup of coffee. If you do, the buyers pass you by. By the third day you reach a zombie stage. But you can't let down. If you've spent $5,000 to be there, you want to write orders.

The business has grown 160 percent since its inception. But if I want to survive, I'll have to shrink it. It seems to be a pattern for small businesses. You start small, and if you're fortunate your business grows to middle size. At this stage you have an enormous amount of paperwork, a high volume of business dealings, and you have to hire people to help you manage the business. You borrow money. Then, you either take the quantum leap into a very large sized business, or you backtrack. I see this time and again. My choice has been always to grow. Our volume has doubled every year except for last year, when it tripled. But our costs have skyrocketed and our profit margin is less. I don't see that as an appropriate place to be.

I've been going to the Wharton Business School, working with a marketing team. They've just come up with a marketing strategy and from it, I've learned a lot about my business and the directions I can go in. A lot of it looks good on paper. But it's not that easy. For example, since production is my problem, they've suggested I tell my subcontractors that they have ten late days a year and after that they're fired. But that's impossible with the kind of work force I'm dealing with. Pressure artists and they're out the door. They're in the field they're in because they didn't fit into that kind of program someplace else.

I see a very different kind of business five years down the road. The purpose of my business is to produce art that functions. To that end, I see my artists coming more into their own talent through this business, creating pieces of furnishings and accessories that are far more artistic in nature than decorative. It's a risk, because you narrow your market to a more eccentric buyer. But I'm a risk taker. I wouldn't have gotten into business if I wasn't.

One of the biggest problems for me personally, and for the business, is I don't have time for developing new products. I'm too busy putting out fires. For me, a smaller, more contained business with a higher level of artistic achievement is the answer.

I feel good as an entrepreneur. I know I couldn't survive in the corporate world. It's dogmatic, political, and there's no freedom. Being in business for yourself means you have to work twice as hard. You've always got to be regenerating your own energy, coming up with new ideas and new designs. Accomplishment isn't enough. I think of myself as successful, but I mostly think of things I could be doing better.

STUBER/STONE INC.

If you saw Woody Allen's 1989 movie, *Crimes and Misdemeanors*, you saw the fruits of Suzi Stone's labors. Her

> **lamps were featured in one of the sets. Elsewhere, stores on the cutting edge of design display the work of Stuber/ Stone.**
>
> **Stuber/Stone designs and manufactures contemporary home furnishings—lamps, clocks, candlesticks, and other objects. Gary Stuber is the artist and designer, while Suzi is the marketing and promotion brains of the partnership.**

A lot of people must get into business exactly as I did. I was looking for something I couldn't find. In this case it was lighting for my apartment, and someone told me about a very creative artist who was making lamps. I went to his studio and loved what I saw. At the time he was selling to a few stores, but he couldn't keep up with the demand. He needed someone to infuse money into the business and help him in sales and promotion. Artists don't like to do that sort of thing. I like marketing and promoting and selling. So we were a perfect match.

I had been in the wholesale/manufacturing business before I moved to New York. I was an art history major in college, with no background in business and no inclination that way, or so I thought. My first venture into business came simply from needing a product that didn't exist. In the mid-seventies I lived in Cincinnati and taught yoga classes. Everyone came to class with sleeping bags or grungy old mats, including myself. I wanted to have an exercise mat that had a removable machine-washable cover, that was an easy-to-carry, compact, lightweight roll. It was a simple, basic idea that no one had thought of.

So I designed a prototype mat and before I knew it I was in production. I sold thousands of them through mail order. It was incredible. I had the right idea at the right time, because two things were beginning to happen big all over the country—the health/exercise boom and mail order.

Mail order was key. I called the buyers of the big mail-order houses and department stores and told them what I had, told them I thought it would be great in their catalog, and asked if I could send them a sample. I also called editors of magazines. Editors are always looking for new products, and if you have something new and different and worthwhile, they'll give you editorial space. The mats were shown in *Esquire* and *Vogue.* I sold through Horchow, Nieman Marcus, and Bloomingdale's. Then,

I got the idea to customize the mats with screened logos. I sold them to clients like the QEII and Elizabeth Arden.

Manufacturing is a tough business. You have to understand production cycles and how deal with raw materials. I borrowed some money and at first I owned the manufacturing. I ultimately subcontracted all my manufacturing to the foam manufacturer who, in turn, dealt with the mills.

When I moved to New York I really wasn't thinking of going into another business until I saw Gary's lamps and decorative objects. It seemed we could have a successful venture by pooling our talents. We had a color brochure made up, with photographs of the work and a brief description of the company and the process Gary worked in. Then, I canvased the city for stores where I thought the lamps could be sold. Fortunately, New York City is very receptive to new work, and there are hundreds of outlets. We targeted stores that sold exciting, modern design, and then I called the buyer and asked to send a brochure or stop in and show samples.

The buyers in New York were enthusiastic, so I began contacting stores in California and Santa Fe and Chicago—any place I got leads. I sent magazine editors our brochure. Although many buyers were enthusiastic, there was also a lot of rejection, but you have to be prepared for it. And, ultimately, it doesn't matter, because if only one person gets interested, you're launched. We've been featured in *House Beautiful, Brides* magazine, the *New York Times;* and the *New Yorker* gave us a mention in "On the Avenue." Our best exposure was in *Interiors* magazine, because they use card response. This means they insert a card in the magazine that the readers send back if they want more information on an item. We got a huge response from that.

One of the ways we make ourselves visible is by entering trade shows. This offers great exposure, but you have to be careful to display in the right show for your product. The First International Contemporary Furniture Fair was held here in New York last year and buyers came from all over the country. We had a display there and it was quite successful for us. People who never in a million years would have known about our products saw our line there.

Prior to that we had been in a show called Accent on Design, which is a juried show and you have to be approved to take part in it. However, it is part of the Gift Show, and the primary buyer at the show is a giftwares buyer. We're not a gift item, we're home furnishings. So while we did pick up some accounts, those weren't really our customers. It costs several thousand dollars just to have the right to display, and then you have the additional cost of creating or renting a display booth as well as all the printed information you need to be effective. For a small company a trade show entails a big outlay of time and money, so you must make sure you're in the right one for your product.

It's also important to place your products in the right stores. We don't want our lamps, for example, in stores that discount. Because our studio and factory is in Brooklyn, I send buyers who want to see our work to stores where our works are displayed—for example, Zona in Soho, Lee's on both the upper East and West Sides, and Elements in Chicago. These stores show the work to its best advantage. Design editors and film and advertising stylists also go to stores like these looking for ideas. That's how our lamps got into the Woody Allen film. We were also featured in the *Chicago Tribune* magazine section because the editor saw us in Elements.

Our retail range on lamps is from $200 to $800. We're not for the budget minded. On the other hand, by designer standards, we're not expensive. Gary oversees the manufacturing. We manufacture to order and we fill our orders in four to six weeks, which is very good in this business.

I think perseverance is the best word to describe what it's like being in business. To be a good entrepreneur you have to *like* to make things happen. You have to have the energy to carry something forward, because believe me, if you don't do it no one else is going to do it for you. You can't just want the end result, the profits. You have to thrive on all the effort it takes to make something happen. There's a lot of rejection. A lot of disappointment. Things don't go your way all the time. You can't lose your energy to that. You have to be willing to try a lot of different things and know that most of them are not going to work.

I like the idea of being on my own, I like the risk, I like to make things happen. It's not easy, but it's exciting. No one can tell you what it's like, really. You have to get in there and find things out for yourself.

And now, a word from the competition. Suzanna Rivera had never designed a belt, nor was she interested in fashion when she started manufacturing. She went into business as a competitor. She took a known seller with a classic design and offered the retail buyer the same kind of product but with finer workmanship, a larger selection of colors, and a more personalized service.

Belts Unlimited was launched on sheer chutzpah. Rivera needed an income to support her writing career and she needed it fast. That classic belt is still part of her product line but in the ten years she has been in business she has expanded into jewelry, hair ornaments, and other fashion accessories. She runs the business from a large studio loft in Los Angeles.

When I first got into this business I had just gotten a divorce and very much wanted to be on my own, but my funds were alarmingly low. I needed an income quickly but one that would leave time for what I really wanted to do, which was write. The idea that clicked was making belts. There was nothing at all original in my thinking. A belt I really liked had been on the market for years. It was a classic, like Pappagallo shoes, and it was sold in all the exclusive department stores and upscale suburban specialty shops.

The belt is a leather strip cut to one length that can be attached to different buckles (sold separately). They're interchangeable, so you can coordinate different-colored belt strips with different outfits.

My first sales call was to a store in Beverly Hills. I had done my homework and knew where to get my supplies and what my markup should be, but I had never made even one of the belts, nor had I bought any materials. I just went to the store with a color chart and asked to see the accessories buyer. I thought that if I was lucky, she might order fifty or so belts. In addition to the standard order forms I had bought at a stationer, my only other investment had been a pair of good scissors. I thought for fifty belts I could cut them myself. I had no idea what would happen, but I figured I had nothing to lose by trying.

Well, I sat with the buyer for about three hours while she ordered over $4,000 worth of belts. I calmly pretended I was well established in the business and in a wild moment promised them one-week delivery. All the time I knew I didn't have one ounce of raw material or the wherewithal to cut all those belts in one week. Each belt has six cuts; using the scissors, I would have had to make six thousand cuts!

The order was taken on a Saturday. They were due the following Friday. On Monday morning, I put in an order for the leather in the colors I needed and a cutting machine, which cost me $400—not a bad investment, considering the first sale paid well over that cost. Tuesday I bought boxes and tissue paper for wrapping and stenciled Belts Unlimited on my forms. Both the leather, which comes from the supplier in rolls, and the cutting machine were ready on Wednesday. I sat up all Wednesday night and Thursday cutting belts. They were ready and packed for delivery by Friday. It was a frantic week, but definitely a spectacular way to get the business started.

Simply put, my business was competitive. The only actual innovation I added was to have the supplier make me a multicolored strip; I was the only manufacturer with that in its line. It also helped buyers to notice me, because the basic design had been on the market at that point for nine years and I was the first to offer something new. My competitor was a large manufacturer whose main interest was in handbags. They offered twenty colors; I offered over a hundred. I gave immediate delivery, which the competition couldn't do because they were so big. My price was a little cheaper, but not much. Because of my low overhead, I could undercut the competition and still make the same profit. My quality was better, too, because I did the cutting myself. So by offering better delivery, better selection, and better quality as well as price, I was able to beat the competition.

Personality has a lot to do with making the sale, too. But selling comes easily to me and I knew I had something the buyers wanted. Although I had a flier made up, I found it was much easier to drive to the stores that stocked this item and introduce myself to the buyer. Since they were already buying the belt from another source, I put a lot of fun and pizzazz into my selling approach. I traveled with my Siberian husky so that people would definitely remember me.

I found out quickly it was better to just walk in and present my wares to the buyer rather than make an appointment ahead of time. Buyers are the most frenetic people I have ever run into.

If you call for an appointment maybe they can see you in three weeks, and maybe not. But if you just walk in, and if the buyer is there, she'll see you. Again, I wasn't pushing a new idea, I was merely offering them better colors and service. I concentrated on the parent stores of companies that had shops all over the country: Lilly Pulitzer had twenty-four stores and I got the order for all twenty-four. Pappagallo had a hundred stores, and I got their order. I used these names when I went to new stores as further incentive for the buyer to order from me.

Pretty soon I had built up a pretty impressive buyers list. I kept my eyes open for new ideas—again, nothing risky or faddish but proven sellers that I could wholesale. I expanded the line into jewelry and hair accessories—headbands, decorative combs, buckles, and other accessories. My emphasis has always been in the quality of my products and service. My relationships with the buyers are solid. They like dealing with me and they give me ideas and a lot of information about competitors.

I'm still pretty much a one-woman operation. I have an accountant and I hire people part time to help with shipping. I have an answering service and a computer. You have to be efficient in this kind of business and very dependable. When an order comes in, I get it right out. I keep a card on all my customers with a history of my dealings with them—the date I contacted them, the order, billing dates, money received or not received, the name of the buyer, whether or not we're on a first name basis—anything that's relevant to the transaction. When a buyer calls me, I can go right to this information and know exactly where we stand. I try to keep it fresh and friendly and very personal—something the big companies just can't offer.

My strongest advice to someone who has never been in business before is to start small. Give yourself some time to develop and grow in your business without a big overhead staring you in the face every month. Work within your profit and don't let a good month fool you into thinking every month is going to be better. And be prepared to deliver the service you promise; just one slipup can lose a good customer forever.

THE AMERICAN NATURAL BEVERAGE COMPANY

Having to compete with the likes of Coke and Pepsi could crush many an entrepreneur's spirit. But that didn't stop

Sophia Collier from introducing her all-natural Soho Soda in 1978. She was just twenty-one years old and admits she didn't know anything about the soda industry or about business.

Some 250 million cans and bottles of her sparkling soda later, she sold her business to Seagram Co. for an effervescent $15 million. Today she is an "angel," investing her time, expertise, and money in fledgling businesses.

Her interview highlights the beginnings of Soho Soda.

The food business was always attractive to me. Soda is, of course, a nonessential food, but it's a fun product, and Americans are soda drinkers. And I thought they might as well be drinking something that wasn't bad for them. Soho is a light, fruity, bubbly, all-natural drink, sweetened with fructose. A ten-ounce bottle of Soho has less sugar in it than an apple.

Soho came about not so much because I had suddenly invented a new drink, but because of my basic interest in how things are made. I had tried making beer at home and had an idea of how flavors are put together.

I like finding a need and creating the organization that produces a final result to fill the need. I think one of the real satisfactions of being in manufacturing is having to do the whole thing: to create something out of raw materials and then to channel it down the right road to its final market.

When you start to deal with any industry, you should know how to talk shop. For us, the profession was the beverage industry, which includes the bottlers, the flavor companies, the soft-drink distributors, and the supermarkets. I had to know as much as or more than the people I was going to be dealing with, so first I subscribed to all the beverage industry trade magazines. It was a fantastic way for me to learn everything I could, from names and resources for suppliers and dealers right down to the history of carbonated drinks.

My father had a friend who owned a beverage plant and arranged for me to spend a day there, talking to the foremen and the managers, learning exactly how a soft drink is made, bottled, and distributed. I think it was an important moment; it made everything seem as though it could be done. There was no longer any mystery involved.

Which is not to say that it's simple. Getting any invention, design, or formula to a final, salable form can be very complex. There are a million details in manufacturing a product. Add those to the million more details of distribution and promotion, and you can see that you've got to be pretty interested in the entire process if you want your business to succeed.

The first step is to get the idea into a manufacturing system. I talked to a flavor chemist, who gave me a lot of advice on how to keep flavors stable. To maintain a stable environment inside a bottle of soda, you have to understand microbiology. Our raw materials came from many sources. These ingredients had to be put together and then mass-produced. Mass production can very often alter the original flavor, just as it can alter an original drawing or model construction.

We had to get our formula inside a bottle, get the bottle from the plant to the store, from the store to the buyer, perhaps to a refrigerator, and then from the refrigerator to final consumption. All this had to be accomplished without losing the quality of taste, color, carbonation, and clearness.

I sent for the Federal Food and Drug Administration's Code of Federal Regulations. There are FDA guidelines for making any food product. The most important restriction is that you can use only ingredients on the GRAS (Generally Recognized as Safe) list. Working with these lists, I came up with a flavor concept, which I then took to a flavor extract company.

Once there, I explained my concept verbally, and on speculation their chemists came up with an interpretation of my concept. Once we settled on a flavor, the company made it up for us in a concentrated form.

A bottling plant was my next concern. I needed to investigate various water purification systems since I was not adding preservatives. The length of the shelf life would depend on the degree of the purification. This was particularly important to supermarket sales.

By now, money was a factor. In manufacturing, 95 percent of the people you deal with are on a cash-only basis. Initially, I was able to raise $20,000 through my own savings and a loan from a friend. Once we had gone into production I was able to raise more through investors and the bank. Money is easier to raise once you've gone into production and can show the investor both a product and the ongoing nature of the business.

The original run was sixteen thousand bottles of soda, the amount one gallon of the concentrate would make. It was a matter of delivering the concentrate, the fructose, the labels, the bottles, and the formula to the bottler. They put it all in a vat, and pretty soon the product came out bottled, labeled, and capped.

I had hired a graphics designer to design the logo on a royalty basis rather than a flat fee. I tried to work out various options with people to save on the initial outlay of money. I finally found a bottler who would give us a fifteen-day credit, which is important because I gave a ten-day credit to the distributor. Without credit from the bottlers, the cash flow would freeze.

And so I had product. The next step was to distribute it. Along about then, I took on a partner, Connie Best, and together we found we had to distribute the soda ourselves. Distributors won't take on a product unless they think the product will sell. This meant we had to go to small retail stores and shops in Manhattan. We felt that positioning Soho in health-food stores and specialty shops would create an identification for the product and lend integrity to it.

We ran ads in the health-food trade papers to promote interest. We also got some publicity—writeups in "Best Bets" in *New York* magazine, in *Enterprising Women,* and in newspapers around town. Once we had established customers for the product, we approached the big supermarket chains. There we had to get listed in their authorization book before any store manager could buy our product. This can take months, because the authorization committees meet sporadically. We had to make a presentation to them describing how the product would be delivered, its shelf life, and what kind of promotion we were doing. Price is important, too. We priced Soho at slightly more than regular sodas, but less than other natural drinks.

We did not advertise on a national scale as we were not yet prepared to distribute nationally. When we sold the company, our two best markets were the East Coast and the mountain states. Our main sales effort went into point-of-sale. This included in-store promotions, free samples, display, posters, stickers, and a booklet with each six-pack explaining the product.

In any selling situation you have to expect negative responses. Then plan to go back and back again, until the buyer says yes. Each time you reapproach a sale, you must have something new to say about the line. Perhaps it's being sold through a major distributor or competitive outlet; perhaps you have recent publicity, new packaging, or whatever. The point is that any inch of progress gives you a new sales tactic.

On the administrative side the business was kept as simple as possible. We had single-entry books, operated from my apartment, and did not patent the product. Our protection came through secrecy rather than law. The flavor company had no idea what happened after it gave us the concentrate, and the bottler knew only the combinations of concentrate to water to fructose. No one but us knew how Soho was put together. We carried a $300,000 product insurance policy.

My advice to anyone going into manufacturing is not to limit yourself by trying to do everything by the book. Any field is wide open for innovative thinking. And listen to people; get their advice.

· Part IV ·

Business Reading and Informational Sources

Bibliography

The following is a listing of books, periodicals, directories, as well as business associations, government agencies, and other resources useful for both entrepreneurs in general and women in particular.

Libraries offer extensive resource materials including reference volumes, classified directories, and periodicals, many of which would be impossible to find elsewhere and too costly to buy. Check out your local public library, as well as nearby private, college, and university libraries, which you can join for a membership fee.

An indispensable source guide for new entrepreneurs, and a good starting point, is the *Small Business Sourcebook,* edited by Charity Anne Dorgan, from Gale Research, Inc. In it, 163 specific small businesses are profiled, as well as small businesses in general. For each business you will find listed sixteen different kinds of information sources, including start-up information, associations, reference works, supply sources, statistical sources, trade periodicals, trade shows and conventions, consultants, franchises, and computer resources. Additionally, it lists federal and state government resources, educational institutions, venture capital firms and incubators pertinent to various small business enterprises.

Within each industry, there are periodicals and associations that, when subscribed to or joined, can provide you with specific information on your business. It is important that you plug into the networks available to you. The more you know and the more aware you are of the business climate at large, the better off you and your business will be.

Business, Self-Help, and Management Books for Women

Auerbach, Sylvia. *A Woman's Book of Money: A Guide to Financial Independence.* New York: Dolphin Books/Doubleday & Co.

Barnett, Frank, and Sharon Barnett. *Working Together: Entrepreneurial Couples.* Berkeley, Calif.: Ten Speed Press.

Bird, Caroline. *Enterprising Women.* New York: W. W. Norton & Co.

Collins, Nancy W., Susan K. Gilbert, and Susan H. Nycum. *Women Leading: Making Tough Choices on the Fast Track.* Lexington, Mass.: Greene.

Harragan, Betty Lehan. *Games Mother Never Taught You: Corporate Gamesmanship for Women.* New York: Rawson Associates.

Helgesen, Sally. *The Female Advantage: Women's Ways of Leadership.* New York: Doubleday & Co.

Hennig, Margaret, and Anne Jardim. *The Managerial Woman.* New York: Doubleday & Co. (Paperback: New York: Pocket Books.)

Hilton, Terri. *Small Business Ideas for Women—And How to Get Started.* New York: Pilot Books. (Pilot publishes a number of small business booklets, including *A Woman's Guide to Her Own Franchised Business; Starting a Business after Fifty; A Franchising Guide for Blacks; How to Buy a Small Business; How to Make Money Selling at Flea Markets and Antique Fairs; How to Turn Your Ideas into Dollars; Directory of State and Federal Funds for Business Development,* and many more. Write to Pilot Books, 347 Fifth Avenue, New York, N.Y. 10016, for a current list of titles.)

Hisrich, Robert D., and Candida G. Brush. *The Woman Entrepreneur: Starting, Financing, and Managing a Successful New Business.* Lexington, Mass.: Lexington Books.

Hughes, Marija Matich. *The Sexual Barrier.* Washington, D.C.: Hughes Press. (Has a complete bibliography on women and work-related subjects.)

Hyatt, Carole. *The Woman's Selling Game: How to Sell Yourself . . . and Anything Else.* New York: M. Evans.

Jennings, Diane. *Self-Made Women: Twelve of America's Leading Entrepreneurial Women Talk about Success, Self-image, and the Superwoman.* Dallas, Tex.: Taylor Publishing Co.

Jessup, Claudia, and Genie Chipps. *Supergirls: The Autobiography of an Outrageous Business.* New York: Harper & Row.

Kundsin, Ruth B. *Women and Success: The Anatomy of Achievement.* New York: William Morrow.

Leslie, Mary, and David D. Seltz. *New Businesses Women Can Start and*

Successfully Operate: The Woman's Guide to Financial Independence. Rockville Centre, N.Y.: Farnsworth Publishing.

Lynch, Edith M. *The Woman's Guide to Management.* New York: Cornerstone Library.

Nelson, Paula. *The Joy of Money.* New York: Bantam Books.

Nierenberg, Juliet, and Irene S. Ross. *Women and the Art of Negotiating.* New York: Simon & Schuster.

Paulsen, Kathryn, and Ryan A. Kuhn. *Woman's Almanac.* New York: J. B. Lippincott Co. (Includes a special section on owning a business.)

Rogers, Mary, and Nancy Joyce. *Women and Money.* New York: McGraw-Hill.

Scollard, Jeannette R. *Risk to Win: A Woman's Guide to Success.* New York: Macmillan.

Stern, Ava. *The Self-Made Woman—and the Challenge of Free Enterprise.* New York: Doubleday & Co. (Includes in-depth interviews with women entrepreneurs.)

Stone, Janet, and Jane Bachner. *Speaking Up: A Book for Every Woman Who Talks.* New York: McGraw-Hill. (How to improve your verbal impact on the telephone, in speeches, in selling yourself.)

Taylor, Russel R. *Exceptional Entrepreneurial Women: Strategies for Success.* New York: Praeger.

Tepper, Terri P., and Nona Dawe Tepper. *The New Entrepreneurs: Women Working from Home.* New York: Universe Books.

Uris, Dorothy. *A Woman's Voice: A Handbook for Successful Private and Public Speaking.* New York: Stein & Day.

Van Hulsteyn, Peggy. *Mind Your Own Business: A Guide for Successful Women.* Santa Fe, N. Mex.: Bentley Press.

———. *What Every Woman Needs to Know to Get Ahead.* New York: Dodd, Mead.

Weiser, Marjorie P. K., and Jean S. Arbeiter. *Womanlists.* New York: Atheneum.

Welch, Mary Scott. *Networking: The Great New Way for Women to Get Ahead.* New York: Harcourt, Brace, Jovanovich.

Wisely, Rae, and Gladys Sanders. *The Independent Woman: How to Start and Succeed in Your Own Business.* Los Angeles: J. P. Tarcher.

General Titles on Starting, Financing, and Managing a Business

Allen, L.L. *Starting and Succeeding in Your Own Small Business.* New York: Grosset & Dunlap.

Baumback, Clifford M., Kenneth Lawyer, and Pearce C. Kelley. *How to Organize and Operate a Small Business.* Englewood Cliffs, N.J.: Prentice-Hall. (Includes extensive bibliography.)

Bittel, Lester R., and John Newstrom. *What Every Supervisor Should Know.* 6th ed. New York: McGraw-Hill.

Breen, George, and A. B. Blankenship. *Do-It-Yourself Marketing Research.* 3d ed. New York: McGraw-Hill.

Brightly, D. S., et al. *Complete Guide to Financial Management for Small and Medium-Sized Companies.* Englewood Cliffs, N.J.: Prentice-Hall.

Bunn, Verne A. *Buying and Selling a Small Business.* Salem, N.H.: Ayer Co.

Business Week's Guide to the Best Business Schools. New York: McGraw-Hill.

Cook, James R. *The Start-up Entrepreneur: How You Can Succeed in Building Your Own Company into a Major Enterprise Starting from Scratch.* New York: Harper & Row Perennial Library.

Crosby, Philip B. *Leading: The Art of Becoming an Executive.* New York: McGraw-Hill.

Davidow, William H., and Bro Uttal. *Total Customer Service: The Ultimate Weapon.* New York: Harper & Row.

Davidson, Jeffrey P. *Avoiding the Pitfalls of Starting Your Own Business.* New York: Walker & Co.

———. *Marketing on a Shoestring: Low-Cost Tips for Marketing Your Products or Services.* New York: John Wiley & Sons.

Dyer, Mary Lee. *Practical Bookkeeping for the Small Business.* Chicago: Henry Regnery Co.

Fortune Book Club. (A concise review of the best business books, operated by Book of the Month Club, Inc., P.O. Box 8805, Camp Hill, Pa. 17011–8805.)

Fritz, Roger. *Nobody Gets Rich Working for Somebody Else: An Entrepreneur's Guide.* New York: Dodd, Mead & Co.

Hammer, Marian Behan. *The Complete Handbook of How to Start and Run a Money-Making Business in Your Home.* Englewood Cliffs, N.J.: Prentice-Hall.

Hancock, William A. *The Small Business Legal Advisor.* New York: McGraw-Hill Paperbacks.

Hawken, Paul. *The Companion Volume to Growing a Business: The 17-Part P.B.S. Series.* New York: Fireside Books, Simon & Schuster.

Holtz, Herman R. *The Secrets of Practical Marketing for Small Business.* Englewood Cliffs, N.J.: Prentice-Hall.

———. *Choosing and Using a Consultant: A Manager's Guide to Consulting Services.* New York: John Wiley & Sons.

———. *How to Start Your Own Small Business.* 4 vols. New York: Drake Publishers. (In-depth information on many types of enterprises.)

Kamoroff, Bernard. *Small-Time Operator: How to Start Your Own Small Business, Keep Your Books, Pay Your Taxes, and Stay out of Trouble!* Laytonville, Calif.: Bell Springs Publishing.

Kenley, Joan. *Voice Power: A Break-through Method to Enhance Your Speaking Voice.* New York: Henry Holt & Co.

Lane, Marc J. *Legal Handbook for Small Business.* New York: Amacom.

J. K. Lasser Tax Institute. *How to Run a Small Business.* 6th ed. New York: McGraw-Hill.

Lesko, Matthew. *Government Giveaways for Entrepreneurs.* Bethesda, Maryland: Information USA, Inc.

Lowry, Albert J. *How to Become Financially Successful by Owning Your Own Business.* New York: Simon & Schuster.

McCormack, Mark H. *What They Don't Teach You at Harvard Business School.* New York: Bantam.

———. *What They Still Don't Teach You at Harvard Business School.* New York: Bantam.

McVicker, Mary Freech. *Small Business Matters.* Radnor, Pa.: Chilton Book Co.

Melberg, Aaron S., and Henry Shain. *How to Do Your Own Bankruptcy.* New York: McGraw-Hill.

Penzias, Arno. *Ideas and Information: Managing in a High-Tech World.* New York: W. W. Norton & Co.

Peterson, C.D. *How to Leave Your Job and Buy a Business of Your Own.* New York: McGraw-Hill.

———. *How to Sell Your Business: For More Money, in Less Time, with Fewer Problems.* New York: McGraw-Hill.

Raab, Steven S., with Gregory Matusky. *Blueprint for Franchising a Business.* New York: John Wiley & Sons.

Raiffa, Howard. *The Art and Science of Negotiation.* Cambridge, Mass.: Harvard University Press.

Ray, Michael, and Rochelle Myers. *Creativity in Business.* New York: Doubleday & Co.

Rich, Stanley R., and David E. Gumpert. *Business Plans That Win Money: Lessons from the M.I.T. Enterprise Forum.* New York: Harper & Row.

Rubin, Richard L., and Philip Goldberg. *The Small Business Guide to Borrowing Money.* New York: McGraw-Hill.

Shames, Laurence. *The Hunger for More: Searching for Values in an Age of Greed.* New York: Times Books.

Siegel, Connie McClung. *How to Advertise and Promote Your Small Business.* New York: John Wiley & Sons.

Silver, A. David. *Business Bible for Survival: What to Do When Your Company Falls on Hard Times.* New York: Prima Publishing.

———. *The Entrepreneurial Life: How to Go for It and Get It.* New York: John Wiley & Sons.

———. *The Radical New Road to Wealth: How to Raise Venture Capital for a New Business.* 3d revised ed. New York: International Wealth.

———. *Successful Entrepreneurship.* Guilford, Conn.: J. Norton. (Book and cassettes.)

———. *Up Front Money: The Entrepreneurs.* New York: John Wiley & Sons.

381

————. *Venture Capital: The Complete Guide for Investors.* New York: John Wiley & Sons.

————. *Who's Who in Venture Capital.* New York: John Wiley & Sons.

Silvester, James L. *How to Start, Finance, and Operate Your Own Business.* Revised ed. New York: Lyle Stuart.

Stevens, Mark. *36 Small Business Mistakes—and How to Avoid Them.* New York: Reward Books.

Taylor, Charlotte. *The Entrepreneurial Workbook.* New York: Plume, New American Library.

Taylor, John R. *How to Start and Succeed in a Business of Your Own.* Reston, Va.: Reston Publishing.

Van Horne, James C. *Financial Management and Policy.* 7th ed. Englewood Cliffs, N.J.: Prentice-Hall.

How-to Books for Specific Businesses

Alcorn, Pat B. *Success and Survival in the Family-Owned Business.* New York: McGraw-Hill.

Allen, Randy L. *Bottom Line in Retailing: The Touche Ross Guide to Retail Management.* Radnor, Pa.: Chilton Book Co.

Anderson, C. B., and G. R. Smith, eds. *A Manual on Bookselling: How to Open and Run Your Own Bookstore.* New York: Harmony Books/Crown.

Baker & Taylor's U.S. Government Publications Service. *Basic Guide to Exporting.* Somerville, N.J.: Baker & Taylor.

Clark, Leta W. *How to Make Money with Your Crafts.* New York: William Morrow.

————. *How to Open Your Own Shop or Gallery.* New York: St. Martin's Press.

Gibson, Mary Bass. *The Family Circle Book of Careers at Home.* New York: Cowles.

Gross, Sidney, and Phyllis B. Steckler. *How to Run a Paperback Bookshop.* New York: R. R. Bowker & Co.

Henderson, Bill. *The Art of Literary Publishing.* Wainscott, N.Y.: The Pushcart Press.

————. *The Publish-It-Yourself Handbook.* Wainscott, N.Y.: The Pushcart Press.

Holtz, Herman R. *The Complete Work-at-Home Companion.* New York: Prima Publishing.

————. *The Consultant's Guide to Winning Clients.* New York: John Wiley & Sons.

————. *How to Succeed as an Independent Consultant.* New York: John Wiley & Sons.

Holz, Loretta. *How to Sell Your Arts and Crafts.* New York: Scribner's.

Jones, Stacy V. *The Inventor's Patent Handbook.* New York: Dial Press.

Keenan, Elayne J., and Jeanne A. Voltz. *How to Turn a Passion for Food into Profit.* New York: Rawson, Wade.

Paige, Richard E. *Complete Guide to Making Money with Your Ideas and Inventions.* Englewood Cliffs, N.J.: Prentice-Hall.

Petteruto, Ray. *How to Open and Operate a Restaurant.* New York: Van Nostrand Reinhold Co.

Shaffer, Harold, and Herbert Greenwald. *Independent Retailing.* Englewood Cliffs, N.J.: Prentice-Hall.

Simon, Julian L. *Getting into the Mail Order Business.* New York: McGraw-Hill Paperbacks.

————. *How to Start and Operate a Mail Order Business.* 4th ed. New York: McGraw-Hill.

Solomon, Kenneth I., and Norman Katz. *Profitable Restaurant Management.* Englewood Cliffs, N.J.: Prentice-Hall.

White, Richard M., Jr. *The Entrepreneur's Manual: Business Start-ups, Spin-offs, and Innovative Management.* Radnor, Pa.: Chilton Book Co. (Special emphasis on manufacturing, retail sales and services, industrial services, franchises.)

Directories

Bacon's Newspaper Directory.
Bacon's Publicity Checker.
Baker & Taylor's U.S. Government Publications Service. (Includes 700 popular government publications under headings such as: Business and industry, Careers, Computers, Economics, etc. They also provide a data base of 25,000 standing order titles, representing publications from over 14,000 publishers. Order catalogs: [800]526–3825; or write Baker & Taylor, 50 Kirby Avenue, Somerville, N.J. 08876.)
Business Publication Rates and Data. (Found in the reference section of your library, it lists all industry periodicals by type of business.)
Consumer Information Catalog. Washington, D.C.: General Services Administration. (A catalog of selected federal publications of consumer interest including: doing business with the federal government; directory of business development publications; and many publications on starting and managing a business.)
Directory of Conventions. Successful Meetings Magazine, 633 Third Avenue, New York, N.Y. 10017. (A nationwide listing of conventions and trade shows.)
Manufacturer's News, Inc. 3 Huron Street, Chicago, Ill. 60611. (Publishes directories of manufacturers for nearly every state.)
National Trade and Professional Associations of the U.S. and Canada. Washington, D.C.: Columbia Books. (See your library reference section.)
Small Business Sourcebook. Edited by Charity Anne Dorgon. Gale Research,

Inc., Book Tower, Detroit, Mich. 48226. (Order from: 1212 New York Avenue NW, Suite 330, Washington, D.C. 20005. An indispensable source guide for the entrepreneur who wants to know where to go for information and help on specific types of business.)

Standard Periodical Directory. New York: Oxbridge Directories, Inc. (See your library reference section. Lists more than 63,000 U.S. and Canadian periodicals.)

Thomas' Register of American Manufacturers, 11 vols. New York: Thomas Publishing Co. (Consult reference section of the library.)

Trade Directories of the World. Queens, N.Y.: Corner Publications, Inc. (A directory of industry trade directories, e.g., the gift/tableware industry, the coffee/tea industry, the fancy foods industry, the toy industry, etc.)

Periodicals

Currently, most women's magazines run articles on business ideas, professional women, and female entrepreneurs. For back articles of specific interest, consult your librarian and *The Reader's Guide to Periodical Literature:* look under "Women Entrepreneurs" and other business-related topics.

Listed below are periodicals of specific interest. Subscription rates are not included because they change often.

American Journal of Small Business, official journal of the U.S. Association for Small Business and Entrepreneurship, University of Baltimore, 1420 North Charles Street, Baltimore, Maryland 21201.

Barron's National Business & Financial Weekly, Dow Jones & Co., Inc., 200 Burnett Road, Chicopee, Massachusetts 01020.

Best's Review (formerly: *Best's Insurance News*), A. M. Best & Co., Inc., Ambest Road, Oldwick, New Jersey 08858.

Business & Professional Ethics Journal, Center for Applied Philosophy, University of Florida, Gainesville, Florida 32611.

Business & Society Review, Management Reports, Inc., 101 West Union Wharf, Boston, Massachusetts 02109.

Business Horizons, Graduate School of Business, Indiana University, Bloomington, Indiana 47405.

Business Month (formerly: *Dun's Business Month; Dun's Review*), Business Month Corp., 488 Madison Avenue, New York, New York 10022.

Business Week, McGraw-Hill, Inc., 1221 Avenue of the Americas, New York, New York 10020.

Columbia Journal of World Business (formerly: *Journal of World Business*), Columbia Business School, Columbia University, 315 Uris Hall, New York, New York 10027.

Communications News, Edgell Communications, 7500 Old Oak Boulevard, Cleveland, Ohio 44130.

D&B Reports: the Dun & Bradstreet Magazine for Small Business Management, Dun & Bradstreet Credit Services, 1 Diamond Hill Road, Murray Hill, New Jersey 07974–0027.

Entrepreneur Magazine, and *Entrepreneurial Woman,* Entrepreneur Inc., 2392 Morse Avenue, P.O. Box 19787, Irvine, California 92714–9787. (*Entrepreneur* publishes *The Be-Your-Own-Boss Catalog* yearly. It lists well over 200 different types of businesses for which they provide business guides. Each guide costs around $60 and contains an average of 200 pages of information you will need to start and operate that particular business. The Entrepreneur Institute also offers various software programs that provide financial analysis for various businesses. To order the catalog, call [800]421–2300; in California, [800]352–7449.

Entreprenurial Woman also offers guides to 167 new business opportunities for women. Some guides include their own financial software disks and/or video cassettes. To order, see phone numbers listed above.)

Executive Female, National Association for Female Executives, Inc., P.O. Box 1902, Marion, Ohio 43306–1902.

Family Business, Family Business Publishing Co., 38 Mahaiwe Street, Great Barrington, Massachusetts 01230.

Forbes, 60 Fifth Avenue, New York, New York 10011.

Fortune, Time, Inc., Time & Life Building, Rockefeller Center, New York, New York 10020–1393.

Harvard Business Review, Graduate School of Business, Harvard University, Boston, Massachusetts 02163.

In Business: The Magazine for Environmental Entrepreneuring, P.O. Box 351, Emmaus, Pennsylvania 18049–9979. (Full of information on how to succeed as an eco-entrepreneur.)

Inc.: The Magazine for Growing Companies, Inc. Publishing Corp., 38 Commercial Wharf, Boston, Massachusetts 02110. (*Inc.* also offers numerous videos on business, including "Women in Business," "How to Really Start Your Own Business," "Secrets of Successful Marketing," "Real Selling," etc. In addition they publish numerous books and special reports on all aspects of starting and marketing a business, including *How to Really Create a Successful Business Plan.* For information and a list of prices, call [800]327–0018.)

Investing for a Better World, Franklin's insight, 711 Atlantic Avenue, Boston, Massachusetts 02111.

Journal of Marketing and *Marketing News,* American Marketing Association, 250 South Wacker Drive, Chicago, Illinois 60606–5819.

Manhattan, inc.: The Business of New York, Manhattan Magazine, Inc., 420 Lexington Avenue, New York, New York 10170.

Michigan Woman: The Magazine for Influential Women, TMW, Inc. P.O. Box 1171, Birmingham, Michigan 48012.

Money, Time, Inc., Rockefeller Center, New York, New York 10020–1393.

Ms. magazine, Fairfax Publishers, Ltd., One Times Square, New York, New York 10036.

National Business Woman, National Federation of Business and Professional Women's Clubs, Inc., 2012 Massachusetts Avenue NW, Washington, D.C. 20036.

Savvy: For the Successful Woman, Family Media, Inc., P.O. Box 6048, Palm Coast, Florida 32037–6048.

Small Business Reporter, Bank of America, Department 3631, P.O. Box 37000, San Francisco, California 94137. (Write for comprehensive list of back issues available, on a variety of subjects including "Steps to Starting a Business" and "Guide to Tax Reform.")

Small Business Reports, Small Business Reports, Inc., P.O. Box 53140, Boulder, Colorado 80321–3140.

Success: The Magazine for Today's Entrepreneurial Mind, Success Magazine Company, P.O. Box 3038, Harlan, Iowa 51537–3038.

Venture: For Entrepreneurial Business Owners and Investors, Venture Magazine, Inc., 521 Fifth Avenue, New York, New York 10175–0028.

Working Woman, Working Woman, P.O. Box 10132, Des Moines, Iowa 50340, or 342 Madison Avenue, New York, New York 10173. (Includes a regular monthly section, "Enterprise," for entrepreneurial women.)

Business Associations, Organizations, and Networks

The following associations, many of which are specifically for women entrepreneurs, will provide additional source material, business workshops and seminars, or educational programs. Check your area for local organizations and network groups, and be aware that banks, your regional Small Business Administration, local universities, and so forth, periodically sponsor seminars for women in business. See also *Entrepreneurial Woman* magazine's column, "Network News," which adds and/or updates networking associations in each issue.

American Business Women's Association (ABWA), National Headquarters, 9100 Ward Parkway, P.O. Box 8728, Kansas City, Missouri 64114–0728, (816)361–6621. (ABWA holds educational seminars that deal with issues surrounding small business at their regional and national meetings. There are 2,100 chapters around the country. The annual national dues of the nonprofit organization are $25, and membership includes a subscription to ABWA's *Women in Business.*)

American Craft Council, National Headquarters, 40 West Fifty-third Street, New York, New York 10019, (212)869–9422 (for membership information). ACC Library is located at 45 West Forty-fifth Street, New York, New York 10036, (212)869–9422. (Founded in 1943, this nonprofit organization offers myriad services for craftspeople on a yearly membership basis. Membership includes subscription to its publication *American Craft,* which lists crafts shows and fairs around the country, and unlimited free admission to exhibitions at the American Craft Museum in New York City and ACC Craftfairs across the country. There is also an extensive American Craft Council Library in New York and an Artist Registry of approximately two thousand craftspeople working in all media. Write for membership information and a catalog of their available publications, slides, films, and videos.)

American Society of Women Accountants, 35 East Wacker Drive, Chicago, Illinois 60601, (312)726–9030.

American Woman's Economic Development Corporation (AWED), 60 East Forty-second Street, Suite 405, New York, New York 10165, (212)692–9100. (The country's leading nonprofit organization providing entrepreneurial women with a wide range of management training and business counseling. Also sponsors an annual conference for women interested in starting their own businesses or making their businesses grow.)

Association of American Universities, One Dupont Circle NW, Washington, D.C. 20036, (202)466–5030.

Association of Black Women Entrepreneurs, c/o Corita Communications, P.O. Box 49368, Los Angeles, California 90049, (213)559–2375. (For membership information: contact Dolores Ratcliffe, president and founder.)

Association of Small Business Development Centers, 1050 Seventeenth Street NW, Suite 810, Washington, D.C. 20036, (202)887–5599. (Small Business Development Centers [SBDCs] are located in all states, plus the District of Columbia, Puerto Rico, and the Virgin Islands. These centers serve small business owners and prospective entrepreneurs, providing training and free consulting. They provide small businesses with access to the expertise of professional firms, banks, chambers of commerce, trade associations, university faculty, economic development organizations, and community and technical colleges. In addition, SBDCs offer special emphasis programs in international trade, research and development funding, business law, procurement, rural and community development, etc. For example, the Pennsylvania SBDC [a unit of the Sol C. Snider Entrepreneurial Center at the Wharton School of Business of the University of Pennsylvania, 444 Vance Hall, 3733 Spruce Street, Philadelphia, Pennsylvania 19104-6374] offers 250 training seminars a year on topics that range from starting a business to marketing a high-tech firm. In Pennsylvania, about 38 percent of the seven thousand businesspersons who receive consulting assistance annually are women. The Pennsylvania SBDC helped develop the prototype for the Women in Business Conferences that the Small Business Administration sponsored in the mid-eighties, and published *For Women! Managing Your Business* as part of that effort.)

Bureau of the Census, Washington, D.C. 20233. (Write the director for a listing of for-sale booklets on business demographics.)

Business and Professional Women's Foundation, 2012 Massachusetts Avenue NW, Washington, D.C. 20036. (Write for information and available pamphlets.)

Canadian Association of Women Executives and Entrepreneurs, c/o Eden Cohn, 25 Garnack Avenue, Toronto, Ontario, Canada M4K1M1; (416)778–6145. (Write for information on dues and meetings.)

Catalyst, 64 Main Street, Montpelier, Vermont 05602, (802)223–7943. (This nonprofit organization provides resources and networking for those interested in starting their own businesses—especially businesses aligned with personal values and the natural systems and limitations of the earth. Catalyst provides a forum whereby entrepreneurs can reach socially conscious investors. They provide resource information for entrepreneurs, and publish the book *Economics as if the earth really mattered: A CATALYST Guide to Socially Conscious Investing,* by Susan Meeker-Lowry [$9.95]. Write for a list of back issues of their *Catalyst* magazine, covering topics of interest for the socially conscious entrepreneur.)

The Center for Family Business, 5862 Mayfield Road, P.O. Box 24268, Cleveland, Ohio 44124, (216)442–0800.

Center for Women Policy Studies, 2000 P Street NW, Suite 508, Washington, D.C. 20036, (202)872–1770. (Founded in 1972, the Center was the first national policy institute focused on issues of women's rights. CWPS was key in the passage of the Equal Credit Opportunity Act, and produced the landmark study, "Harrassment and Discrimination of Women in Employment." Write for information and a list of their publications.)

Chamber of Commerce of the U.S., 1615 H Street NW, Washington, D.C. 20062, (202)659–6000. (Publishes *Sources of State Information* and *Small Business: Building America's Future,* and many other pamphlets and directories. Write for list of publications and programs geared to small business.)

Coalition of Women in National and International Business, 1900 L Street NW, Washington, D.C. 20036.

Co-op America, 2100 M Street NW, Suite 310, Washington, D.C. 20063, (202)872–5307, (800)424–2667. (Since 1982, Co-op America has been a nonprofit, member-controlled, worker-managed association linking socially responsible businesses and consumers in a national network, creating a new alternative marketplace. It allows consumers to align their buying habits with their values. It enables businesses, coops, and nonprofits that put people ahead of profits to expand the market for their goods and services. Although their focus is primarily individual consumers, they have over four hundred socially responsible business members. All members receive many benefits, including financial planning assistance, a wide range of support services, and their publication, *Building Economic Alternatives.* Write for membership information and a catalog.)

Council of Better Business Bureaus, Inc., National Headquarters, 4200 Wilson Boulevard, Suite 800, Arlington, Virginia 22203-1804, (703)-276–0100. (Both the Council of BBB and your local BBB can provide information about a company before you do business with it, and can help you resolve a complaint against a specific company. The BBB fosters ethical advertising and selling practices, alerts consumers to bad business and advertising practices, and provides speakers for business organizations, among other things. For more information, consult your local area BBB, or call Dianne Skeltis Ward, Director of Public Affairs, at the number listed above.)

The Entrepreneurship Institute, 3592 Corporate Drive, Suite 112, Columbus, Ohio 43231–4988, (614)895–1153. (An international, nonprofit networking and educational organization designed to assist and encourage entrepreneurship. Founded in 1976, the Institute's primary mission is to provide unlimited opportunities for entrepreneurs to create and grow with their companies—"learning to do business while doing business." TEI provides two-day business forums across the country, local networking chapters, and local institutes in many cities/areas. In addition, TEI library offers taped presentations by America's most successful entrepreneurs, on numerous business subjects. Write or call for more information.)

Federal Trade Commission (FTC), Room 238, Washington, D.C. 20580, (202)326–2000 (for information) or (202)326–2395 (library). (Write for listing of publications. Free publications are available from the FTC's Division of Legal and Public Records, at the address above. For-sale booklets are available from the Superintendent of Documents, U.S. Government Printing Office, Washington, D.C. 20402.)

Federation of Organizations for Professional Women, 2001 S Street NW, Suite 540, Washington, D.C. 20009, (202)328–1415. (FOWP provides entrepreneurs with referral information. Founded in 1972, FOWP is a federation of organizations devoted to equal opportunities for women. Their bimonthly newsletter, *Alert,* notifies business owners about legislative matters that might affect them professionally. FOWP is also a network group and hosts receptions honoring women of achievement in the arts, sciences, media, and other professions. They sponsor career development seminars and publish the *Women's Yellow Book,* a national directory of women's organizations. Write or call for more information and a list of FOWP publications.)

House of Representatives Committee on Small Business, Room 2361,

Rayburn House Office Building, Washington, D.C. 20515, (202)225–5821.

Institute for Women's Policy Research, 1400 Twentieth Street NW, Suite 104, Washington, D.C. 20036, (202)785–5100. (IWPR publishes numerous periodicals for women, on work and family issues, employment equity issues, child care, etc. Their *Research News Reporter* is a bimonthly information service for members. Write for membership information and list of available publications.)

International Association of Business Communicators, One Hallidie Plaza, Suite 600, San Francisco, California 94102, (415)433–3400. (IABC offers services and programs for both newcomers and seasoned veterans in the field of communications—public affairs, marketing, customer relations, community relations, employee communication, etc. IABC has local chapters across the country; membership dues vary according to chapter. They also sponsor chapter, district, and international seminars, workshops, and conferences, as well as publish the magazine *Communication World* and communication-related books.)

International Franchise Association, World Headquarters, 1350 New York Avenue NW, Suite 900, Washington, D.C. 20005. (Among its many services, the IFA sponsors more than sixty educational seminars and forums throughout the year on various topics such as franchise start-ups, franchise relations, training and operations, legal compliance and disclosure, marketing, and public relations. They publish a special report on minorities, including women, in franchising, as well as myriad publications for people interested in buying a franchise and companies interested in franchising. IFA is the world's leading source of information about franchising. For a list of publications and prices, phone [800]543–1038.)

Minority Business Development Agency (MBDA) of the U.S. Department of Commerce, Fourteenth and Constitution Avenue NW, Room 6723, Washington, D.C. 20230, (202)377–8275; regional offices also in Atlanta, Chicago, Dallas, New York City, and San Francisco. (MBDA is the only federal agency created specifically to foster the establishment and growth of minority-owned businesses in America. MBDA provides funding for a network of approximately a hundred Minority Business Development Centers located across the country. These centers provide minority entrepreneurs with management and technical assistance services to start, expand, or manage a business. MBDA also helps federal, state, and local government agencies—as well as major corporations—to increase their purchases from minority-owned firms. Those eligible for MBDA assistance include: Blacks, Puerto Ricans, Spanish-speaking Americans, American Indians, Eskimos, Aleuts, Asian Pacific Americans, Asian Indians, and Hasidic Jews.)

National Association for Female Executives, Inc., 127 West Twenty-fourth Street, New York, New York 10011, (212)645–0770. (NAFE has close to 200,000 members across the country, with NAFE networks in most large cities, offering contacts, opportunities, information, advice, and moral support for female executives and entrepreneurs. NAFE's magazine, *Executive Female,* offers regular advice for entrepreneurs. Membership includes access to NAFE's venture capital program, loans-by-mail, and their career options test—a free test that uncovers one's business potential and pinpoints one's greatest strengths—as well as many business publications and backlist articles of special interest to the female entrepreneur, such as "Business Plan Basics: How to write a plan that will raise funds and keep your company on course," by Judith C. Anderson.)

National Association of Bank Women, 500 North Michigan Avenue, Chicago, Illinois 60611, (312)661–1700.

National Association of Black Women Attorneys, 3711 Macomb Street NW, Washington, D.C. 20016, (202)966–9693.

National Association of Black Women Entrepreneurs (NABWE), c/o Mary French Hubbard, P.O. Box 1375, Detroit, Michigan 48231, (313)341–7400. (Founded in 1978, NABWE has over 5,000 members. Write for membership information, a schedule of meetings in your area, and the dates of their annual conference.)

National Association of Insurance Women, 1847 East Fifteenth Street, Tulsa, Oklahoma 74104, (918)744–5195.

National Association of Small Business Investment Companies (NASBIC), 1156 Fifteenth Street NW, Suite 1101, Washington, D.C. 20005, (202)833–8230. (NASBIC is the national trade association that represents the overwhelming majority of small business investment companies [SBICs]. Members have access to a monthly newsletter, meetings and other forums, and an extensive list of publications, surveys, and studies. Their book *Venture Capital—Where to Find It* is available for $5, postage included.)

National Association of Women Business Owners, Capital Area Chapter, 1507 D Street SE, Washington, D.C. 20003, (202)955–5790. (Holds regular meetings with speakers, publishes a newsletter providing pertinent information for women entrepreneurs on such topics as obtaining federal contracts and developing businesses for the international marketplace.)

National Association of Women Business Owners (NAWBO), National Chapter, 600 South Federal Street, Suite 400, Chicago, Illinois 60605, (312)922–0465. (Offers women entrepreneurs management and technical assistance, and works in partnership with major corporations on programs and issues of mutual benefit and to increase contracting opportunities for women business owners. Has thirty-six chapters across the country, and at-large memberships are available for women business owners located where no NAWBO chapter exists. Founded in 1974, NAWBO is the official U.S. member of Les Femmes Chefs d'Entreprises Mondiales [F.C.E.M.], the World Association of Women Entrepreneurs. In regular chapter meetings and seminars NAWBO members develop business and leadership skills. Membership dues vary according to chapter.)

National Business Incubation Association (NBIA), One President Street, Athens, Ohio 45701, (614)593–4331. (Established in 1985, NBIA is committed to providing members with the resources needed to be successful in the growing incubator field, and offers information, ideas, news alerts, contacts, referrals, research, and information resources. NBIA also sponsors annual conferences and national training institutes, as well as books and tapes on the subject. *The NBIA National Directory of Incubators in the United States and Canada* is available only to members. For membership information, contact Dinah Adkins, Executive Director.)

National Council of Career Women, 3222 N Street, NW, Washington, D.C. 20007, (202)333–8578.

National Entrepreneurship Foundation, P.O. Box 5521, Bloomington, Indiana 47407-5521, (812)339–5700. (NEF, affiliated with Indiana University, offers both undergraduate and graduate courses in entrepreneurship. Through its Center for Entrepreneurship and Innovation it offers programs for CEOs of mid-size companies and conducts research in entrepreneurship; it also sponsors the National Entrepreneurship Academies program for aspiring entrepreneurs.)

National Federation of Business & Professional Women's Clubs, 2012 Massachusetts Avenue NW, Washington, D.C. 20036, (202)293–1100. (BPW is a professional network for career women, and also a nonprofit research and educational organization. It was established in 1956 to promote full participation, equity, and economic self-sufficiency for America's working women. The international federation, made up of more than 250,000 women from sixty countries, is working to improve the lives of women worldwide. There is also the BPW/USA Political Action Committee, which assists candidates for federal office who support the goals of BPW—equal opportunity in the workplace and in education and training. They publish the magazine *National Business Woman.* Write for membership information: BPW has both active members and members-at-large.)

National Federation of Independent Businesses, 600 Maryland Avenue SW, Suite 700, Washington, D.C. 20024, (202)554–9000. Requests for membership information should be sent to NFIB, 150 West Twentieth Avenue, San Mateo, California 94403, (415)341–7441. (NFIB is the largest small business advocacy organization in the nation, with more than 560,000 members, who are owners of small independent businesses. Although they do not run any programs specifically designed for women entrepreneurs, they do provide women with a packet of publications put out by other groups, particularly the Small Business Administration's Office of Women Business Ownership.)

National Retail Merchants Association, 100 West Thirty-first Street, New York, New York 10001, (212)244–8780. (Write to the Book Order Department for their catalog of books, films, and periodicals.)

National Small Business United, 1155 Fifteenth Street NW, Suite 710, Washington, D.C. 20005, (202)293–8830. (Founded in 1937, NSBU is the oldest trade association in America and today represents more than 50,000 small businesspeople. NSBU's main objective, as a nonprofit, nonpartisan association, is to fight for an economic environment that allows small businesses to operate at a profit. NBSU represents its members before Congress, at the White House, and in every facet of government. Members, besides receiving discounts on many services and publications, also receive the monthly newspaper, *Small Business USA,* political bulletins called *Action Alerts,* and other publications. NBSU represents small business interests in legislative concerns such as mandated benefits, minimum wage, SBA loans, international trade, capital gains, etc. They make it possible for business owners to come to Washington to be heard by legislators and talk with elected officials about areas of specific concern.)

National Organization of Women, National Headquarters, 1000 Sixteenth Street NW, Suite 700, Washington, D.C. 20005–5705, (202)-331–0066. (Publishes a newspaper and action alert bulletins on major issues of concern to women, available to members. Write for membership information.)

Office of Minority Business Enterprise (OMBE), Department of Commerce, Washington, D.C. 20230, (202)377–2000. (It funds several hundred business development offices; write for a list. Currently available only to minority women.)

Renaissance Business Associates, Inc. (RBA), 4817 North County Road 29, Loveland, Colorado 80538–9515, (303)679–4305; or 595 Bay Street, Suite 1203, Toronto, Ontario, Canada, M5G 2C6 (416)581–1131. (RBA's primary purpose is to provide a context and a gathering place/network for people from all walks of business, including entrepreneurs, who are interested in using the business setting for their expression of excellence and integrity. RBA members have access to local meetings as well as consulting services and seminars. Among their myriad programs is Breakthrough to You, professional/personal development for women in business. Seminar topics include: professional self-presentation, beyond time management, facilitator training programs, and telephone skills. They publish a journal, *Business Dynamics,* as well as the booklets *The Business of Integrity* and *The Renais-*

sance in Business [$2 each, postpaid]. For membership information and the name of the local activities director in your area, contact T. Elaine Gagné, Executive Director.)

Senate Small Business Committee, Minority Staff, 424 Russell Building, Washington, D.C. 20510.

Small Business Administration, Office of Women's Business Ownership, 1441 L Street NW, Suite 414, Washington, D.C. 20416, (202)653–8000. (The SBA's Office of Women's Business Ownership provides information for female entrepreneurs, including an extensive list of free and for-sale booklets on all aspects of starting and running a business. In addition, all local SBA offices have a women's advocate. The SBA's newest mentoring program, the Women's Network for Entrepreneurial Training, was started in 1988 because, by the year 2000, women will account for 50 percent of the nation's new start-up businesses. Other SBA programs that provide free counseling for entrepreneurs and prospective entrepreneurs include SCORE [Service Corps of Retired Executives], ACE [Active Corps of Executives], SBDCs [Small Business Development Centers], and SBIs [Small Business Institutes]. In addition, they sponsor the Answer Desk [800–368–5855 or 202–653–7562] to provide information on start-ups, financing, SBA services, local assistance, and business data. The SBA also helps finance small business loans.)

U.S. Department of Agriculture, Office of Information, Washington, D.C. 20250, (202)447–8732. (Write for list of services and publications; some handcrafts fall under its aegis.)

U.S. Department of Commerce, Washington, D.C. 20230. For the address of the district office nearest you, write to the District Office, U.S. Department of Commerce, Room 1406, Mid-Continental Plaza Building, 55 East Monroe Street, Chicago, Illinois 60603, or call their hotline: (800)424–5197. (A selected publications catalog, which aids business, franchises, and industry, is available from any of the district offices around the country. The Economic Development Administration of the Department of Commerce [EDA] has research and development centers in a number of major cities to provide technical assistance to small business owners. It also helps in finding capital and developing loan packages, and it works with universities to provide free assistance in setting up businesses. For the EDA Office nearest you, call the hotline number above.)

Venture Capital Network, Inc., P.O. Box 882, Durham, New Hampshire 03824–9964. (VCN, founded in 1984, is a not-for-profit corporation managed by the Center for Venture Research at the University of New Hampshire. VCN provides high net worth individuals with a convenient, confidential mechanism for examining opportunities to invest in entrepreneurial ventures. It provides entrepreneurs requiring from

$50,000 to $1 million of equity-type financing with a cost-effective process for reaching wealthy individuals interested in investing in early-stage or high-growth private companies. VCN charges a fee for each profile submitted, but receives no additional fees, commissions, or other remuneration related to the eventual outcome of any entrepreneur/investor negotiations.)

Women Going Places, 900 Winderly Place, Suite 232, Maitland, Florida 32751 (407)660–0999, (800)869–7955. (This organization is for networking on local, national, and international levels, and sponsors travel groups and conferences. Contact Jennifer Jenkins for membership information.)

Women in Franchising, 175 North Harbor Drive, Suite 405, Chicago, Illinois 60601, (800)222–4943. (This is a national membership association for women interested or involved in franchising and marketing. Contact Pamela Smith for information.)

Women in Management, P.O. Box 691, Stamford, Connecticut 06904, (203)329–0854. (Founded in 1979 for women in the tri-state area, WIM members are both corporate managers and entrepreneurs, in all fields of business. WIM provides forums for learning and exchange.)

Women's Action Alliance, Inc., 370 Lexington Avenue, Suite 603, New York, New York 10017, (212)532–8330. (Founded in 1971, the Alliance is a national organization committed to furthering the goal of full equality for all women. They provide educational programs and services that assist women and women's organizations in accomplishing their goals. Write for a catalog of available books and pamphlets.)

The Women's Bureau, U.S. Department of Labor, 200 Constitution Avenue NW, Washington, D.C. 20210, (202)523–8913 (programs and technical assistance), (202)523–6667 (policy analysis and information), and (202)523–6611 (general information). (Write for current catalog of pamphlets, including *Women Business Owners, Black Women Business Owners, Hispanic Women Business Owners, Asian American Women Business Owners,* and *American Indian Women Business Owners.*)

Women's Business Development Center, 230 North Michigan, Suite 1800, Chicago, Illinois 60601, (312)853–3477. (Founded by codirectors Carol Dougal and Hedy Ratner in 1986, WBDC fosters the economic empowerment of women through business ownership. It was cited in 1988 by the U.S. Department of Commerce as one of the most effective and comprehensive technical assistance programs for women in the United States. The major services of WBDC are entrepreneurial training and consulting in management, marketing, strategic planning, recordkeeping and other accounting/financial services, and business plan help. A nonprofit women's business resource center; its counseling services are free.)

Women's Economic Round Table, 866 United Nations Plaza, New York,

New York 10017, (212)759–4360. (Founded in 1978, the Women's Economic Round Table is a non-partisan, nonprofit, educational organization providing numerous services, activities, and programs to its members and the public. Besides being a network, WERT "provides a channel through which the nation's economic policy leaders are accessible to members, and through them, to the American people." It also educates members in ways to maintain and use their economic power to influence economic policymakers. Members are from fifty professions and reside in the U.S. and abroad.)

Women's Equity Action League, 1250 I Street NW, Washington, D.C. 20005, (202)898–1588.

Women's International Resource Exchange, 475 Riverside Drive, Room 570, New York, New York 10115, (212)870–2783. (WIRE is a nonprofit women's collective, which, since 1979, has been committed to reprinting and distributing information on and analyses of the problems, struggles, and achievements of women in the Third World. Write for their catalog of publications, which are printed in Spanish as well as English.)

Women's Referral Service, 13601 Ventura Boulevard, Suite 374, Sherman Oaks, California 91423, (818)995–6646. (Founded in 1977, WRS is a free telephone referral service and business networking organization for women in Southern California. WRS's Entrepreneur Division provides regular networking meetings and a forum for its members to make important contacts vital to the continued success of their businesses. It publishes a newsletter and an annual membership directory. In addition, there is an Executive Division. Write for more information and a membership application form.)

Women's Work Force Network of Wider Opportunities for Women (WOW), and National Commission On Working Women, 1325 G Street NW, Lower Level, Washington, D.C. 20005, (202)638–3143. (WOW is a business information exchange to provide leadership development opportunities, facilitate technical assistance, and coordinate public policy advocacy. Write for membership fees and additional information.)

Women's World Banking, 8 West Fortieth Street, 10th Floor, New York, New York 10018, (212)768–8513. (WWB is a nonprofit organization established in 1979 to promote entrepreneurship among women, particularly those who have not had access to formal financial institutions. WWB is an international organization founded to establish a global network of women leaders in banking, finance, and business, and to encourage women's confidence and trust in themselves as capable, professional businesspersons. WWB makes loans available to women who own and manage at least 50 percent of their own enterprises. For more information, contact Ms. Michaela Walsh, President.)

Index

American Association of Responsible Business, 46n
American Booksellers Convention, 269
American Girls Collection, 338
American Health, 220
American Natural Beverage Company, 370–74
American Society of Women Accountants, 107n
American Stock Exchange, 337
American Woman's Economic Development Corporation (AWED), 5, 27, 64, 251, 260, 286, 315, 339
Amortization, 231
Annual expenses, 119
Answering machines, 78–79
Apparel business, 355–61
credit in, 145
Application forms, 205–6
Arnold, Gail, 319
Art galleries, 272–75
Ashley, Laura, 177
Assets
intangible, 51, 52
tangible, 50–52
Association for Women in Computing, 79n
AT&T, 77, 78, 80n
Audits, tax, 232–33
Automobile insurance, 128

Bacon's Publicity Checker, 167n
Balance sheet, 118
Banaszewski, John, 240n
Bankruptcy, 103–4
Banks, 139–46
business accounts, 142–45
expansion financing by, 238
loans from, 16–20
service businesses and, 305
services, 141–42
Barefoot Contessa, The, 323–28
Bartering, 113–14

Battle, Anne, 290–95
Bed and breakfast, 328–31
BellSouth, 78
Belts Unlimited, 368–70
Berkley Macintosh Users' Group (BMUG), Inc., 80
Best, Connie, 373
Best's Insurance Reports, 128
Better Business Bureau, 57, 193
Billboard Publication, 181
Billing, 193–94
Blanket bonds, 138
Blue sky laws, 96
Bonding, 127, 137–38
Bookkeeping, 114–19
methods, 116–17
for service businesses, 309
Book stores, 267–71
Borman, Nancy, 9
Boston Computer Society, 80n
Bottom Line in Retailing: The Touche Ross Guide to Retail Management (Allen), 256
Boutique building, 261–67
Brainstorming, 182
Brain Trust, The, 297
Break-even point, 109
Brenner, Carol, 271
Brochures, 161
Brokaw, Meredith, 256–61
Burglary insurance, 129
Business cards, 83–84
Business conferences, finding prospects at, 181
Business development centers, 67–68
Business Ethics magazine, 46n
Business idea, 38, 43–45
defining, 45
marketing of, 38–39
quality of, 45
Business incubators, 26, 67–68
Business interruption insurance, 130
Business lunches, 188